HBR'S
10
MUST
READS

On
Managing Yourself

HBR'S
10
MUST
READS

On
Managing
Yourself

HARVARD BUSINESS REVIEW PRESS
Boston, Massachusetts

The web addresses referenced in this book were live and correct at the time of the book's publication but may be subject to change.

Library of Congress Cataloging-in-Publication Data

HBR's 10 must reads on managing yourself.
    p. cm.
    Includes index.
    ISBN 978-1-63369-447-7
    1. Management.   I. Harvard business review. II. Title: HBR's ten must reads on managing yourself. III. Title: Harvard business review's 10 must reads on managing yourself.
    HD31.H3946 2010

ISBN: 9781633694477
eISBN: 9781422172032

Contents

On
Managing Yourself

How Will You Measure Your Life?

by Clayton M. Christensen

BEFORE I PUBLISHED *The Innovator's Dilemma,* I got a call from Andrew Grove, then the chairman of Intel. He had read one of my early papers about disruptive technology, and he asked if I could talk to his direct reports and explain my research and what it implied for Intel. Excited, I flew to Silicon Valley and showed up at the appointed time, only to have Grove say, "Look, stuff has happened. We have only 10 minutes for you. Tell us what your model of disruption means for Intel." I said that I couldn't—that I needed a full 30 minutes to explain the model, because only with it as context would any comments about Intel make sense. Ten minutes into my explanation, Grove interrupted: "Look, I've got your model. Just tell us what it means for Intel."

I insisted that I needed 10 more minutes to describe how the process of disruption had worked its way through a very different industry, steel, so that he and his team could understand how disruption worked. I told the story of how Nucor and other steel minimills had begun by attacking the lowest end of the market—steel reinforcing bars, or rebar—and later moved up toward the high end, undercutting the traditional steel mills.

When I finished the minimill story, Grove said, "OK, I get it. What it means for Intel is ...," and then went on to articulate what would become the company's strategy for going to the bottom of the market to launch the Celeron processor.

I've thought about that a million times since. If I had been suckered into telling Andy Grove what he should think about the microprocessor business, I'd have been killed. But instead of telling him what to think, I taught him how to think—and then he reached what I felt was the correct decision on his own.

That experience had a profound influence on me. When people ask what I think they should do, I rarely answer their question directly. Instead, I run the question aloud through one of my models. I'll describe how the process in the model worked its way through an industry quite different from their own. And then, more often than not, they'll say, "OK, I get it." And they'll answer their own question more insightfully than I could have.

My class at HBS is structured to help my students understand what good management theory is and how it is built. To that backbone I attach different models or theories that help students think about the various dimensions of a general manager's job in stimulating innovation and growth. In each session we look at one company through the lenses of those theories—using them to explain how the company got into its situation and to examine what managerial actions will yield the needed results.

On the last day of class, I ask my students to turn those theoretical lenses on themselves, to find cogent answers to three questions: First, how can I be sure that I'll be happy in my career? Second, how can I be sure that my relationships with my spouse and my family become an enduring source of happiness? Third, how can I be sure I'll stay out of jail? Though the last question sounds lighthearted, it's not. Two of the 32 people in my Rhodes scholar class spent time in jail. Jeff Skilling of Enron fame was a classmate of mine at HBS. These were good guys—but something in their lives sent them off in the wrong direction.

Idea in Brief

Harvard Business School's Christensen teaches aspiring MBAs how to apply management and innovation theories to build stronger companies. But he also believes that these models can help people lead better lives. In this article, he explains how, exploring questions everyone needs to ask. How can I be happy in my career? How can I be sure that my relationship with my family is an enduring source of happiness? And how can I live my life with integrity? The answer to the first question comes from Frederick Herzberg's assertion that the most powerful motivator isn't money; it's the opportunity to learn, grow in responsibilities, contribute, and be recognized. That's why management, if practiced well, can be the noblest of occupations; no others offer as many ways to help people find those opportunities. It isn't about buying, selling, and

investing in companies, as many think. The principles of resource allocation can help people attain happiness at home. If not managed masterfully, what emerges from a firm's resource allocation process can be very different from the strategy management intended to follow. That's true in life too: If you're not guided by a clear sense of purpose, you're likely to fritter away your time and energy on obtaining the most tangible, short-term signs of achievement, not what's really important to you. And just as a focus on marginal costs can cause bad corporate decisions, it can lead people astray. The marginal cost of doing something wrong "just this once" always seems alluringly low. You don't see the end result to which that path leads. The key is to define what you stand for and draw the line in a safe place.

As the students discuss the answers to these questions, I open my own life to them as a case study of sorts, to illustrate how they can use the theories from our course to guide their life decisions.

One of the theories that gives great insight on the first question—how to be sure we find happiness in our careers—is from Frederick Herzberg, who asserts that the powerful motivator in our lives isn't money; it's the opportunity to learn, grow in responsibilities, contribute to others, and be recognized for achievements. I tell the students about a vision of sorts I had while I was running the company I founded before becoming an academic. In my mind's eye I saw one of my managers leave for work one morning with a relatively strong

3

level of self-esteem. Then I pictured her driving home to her family 10 hours later, feeling unappreciated, frustrated, underutilized, and demeaned. I imagined how profoundly her lowered self-esteem affected the way she interacted with her children. The vision in my mind then fast-forwarded to another day, when she drove home with greater self-esteem—feeling that she had learned a lot, been recognized for achieving valuable things, and played a significant role in the success of some important initiatives. I then imagined how positively that affected her as a spouse and a parent. My conclusion: Management is the most noble of professions if it's practiced well. No other occupation offers as many ways to help others learn and grow, take responsibility and be recognized for achievement, and contribute to the success of a team. More and more MBA students come to school thinking that a career in business means buying, selling, and investing in companies. That's unfortunate. Doing deals doesn't yield the deep rewards that come from building up people.

I want students to leave my classroom knowing that.

Create a Strategy for Your Life

A theory that is helpful in answering the second question—How can I ensure that my relationship with my family proves to be an enduring source of happiness?—concerns how strategy is defined and implemented. Its primary insight is that a company's strategy is determined by the types of initiatives that management invests in. If a company's resource allocation process is not managed masterfully, what emerges from it can be very different from what management intended. Because companies' decision-making systems are designed to steer investments to initiatives that offer the most tangible and immediate returns, companies shortchange investments in initiatives that are crucial to their long-term strategies.

Over the years I've watched the fates of my HBS classmates from 1979 unfold; I've seen more and more of them come to reunions unhappy, divorced, and alienated from their children. I can guarantee you that not a single one of them graduated with the deliberate strategy of getting divorced and raising children who would become estranged from them. And yet a shocking number of them implemented that strategy. The reason? They didn't keep the purpose of their lives front and center as they decided how to spend their time, talents, and energy.

It's quite startling that a significant fraction of the 900 students that HBS draws each year from the world's best have given little thought to the purpose of their lives. I tell the students that HBS might be one of their last chances to reflect deeply on that question. If they think that they'll have more time and energy to reflect later, they're nuts, because life only gets more demanding: You take on a mortgage; you're working 70 hours a week; you have a spouse and children.

For me, having a clear purpose in my life has been essential. But it was something I had to think long and hard about before I understood it. When I was a Rhodes scholar, I was in a very demanding academic program, trying to cram an extra year's worth of work into my time at Oxford. I decided to spend an hour every night reading, thinking, and praying about why God put me on this earth. That was a very challenging commitment to keep, because every hour I spent doing that, I wasn't studying applied econometrics. I was conflicted about whether I could really afford to take that time away from my studies, but I stuck with it—and ultimately figured out the purpose of my life.

Had I instead spent that hour each day learning the latest techniques for mastering the problems of autocorrelation in regression analysis, I would have badly misspent my life. I apply the tools of econometrics a few times a year, but I apply my knowledge of the purpose of my life every day. It's the single most useful thing I've ever learned. I promise my students that if they take the time to figure out their life purpose, they'll look back on it as the most important thing they discovered at HBS. If they don't figure it out, they will just sail off without a rudder and get buffeted in the very rough seas of life. Clarity about their purpose will trump knowledge of activity-based costing, balanced scorecards, core competence, disruptive innovation, the four Ps, and the five forces.

My purpose grew out of my religious faith, but faith isn't the only thing that gives people direction. For example, one of my former

The Class of 2010

"I CAME TO BUSINESS SCHOOL knowing exactly what I wanted to do—and I'm leaving choosing the exact opposite. I've worked in the private sector all my life, because everyone always told me that's where smart people are. But I've decided to try government and see if I can find more meaning there.

"I used to think that industry was very safe. The recession has shown us that nothing is safe."

Ruhana Hafiz, Harvard Business School, Class of 2010
Her Plans: To join the FBI as a special adviser (a management track position)

"You could see a shift happening at HBS. Money used to be number one in the job search. When you make a ton of money, you want more of it. Ironic thing. You start to forget what the drivers of happiness are and what things are really important. A lot of people on campus see money differently now. They think, 'What's the minimum I need to have, and what else drives my life?' instead of 'What's the place where I can get the maximum of both?'"

Patrick Chun, Harvard Business School, Class of 2010
His Plans: To join Bain Capital

"The financial crisis helped me realize that you have to do what you really love in life. My current vision of success is based on the impact I can have, the

---

students decided that his purpose was to bring honesty and economic prosperity to his country and to raise children who were as capably committed to this cause, and to each other, as he was. His purpose is focused on family and others—as mine is.

The choice and successful pursuit of a profession is but one tool for achieving your purpose. But without a purpose, life can become hollow.

Allocate Your Resources

Your decisions about allocating your personal time, energy, and talent ultimately shape your life's strategy.

I have a bunch of "businesses" that compete for these resources: I'm trying to have a rewarding relationship with my wife, raise great kids, contribute to my community, succeed in my career, contribute

experiences I can gain, and the happiness I can find personally, much more so than the pursuit of money or prestige. My main motivations are (1) to be with my family and people I care about; (2) to do something fun, exciting, and impactful; and (3) to pursue a long-term career in entrepreneurship, where I can build companies that change the way the world works."

Matt Salzberg, Harvard Business School, Class of 2010
His Plans: To work for Bessemer Venture Partners

"Because I'm returning to McKinsey, it probably seems like not all that much has changed for me. But while I was at HBS, I decided to do the dual degree at the Kennedy School. With the elections in 2008 and the economy looking shaky, it seemed more compelling for me to get a better understanding of the public and nonprofit sectors. In a way, that drove my return to McKinsey, where I'll have the ability to explore private, public, and nonprofit sectors.

"The recession has made us step back and take stock of how lucky we are. The crisis to us is 'Are we going to have a job by April?' Crisis to a lot of people is 'Are we going to stay in our home?'"

John Coleman, Harvard Business School, Class of 2010
His Plans: To return to McKinsey & Company

to my church, and so on. And I have exactly the same problem that a corporation does. I have a limited amount of time and energy and talent. How much do I devote to each of these pursuits?

Allocation choices can make your life turn out to be very different from what you intended. Sometimes that's good: Opportunities that you never planned for emerge. But if you misinvest your resources, the outcome can be bad. As I think about my former classmates who inadvertently invested for lives of hollow unhappiness, I can't help believing that their troubles relate right back to a short-term perspective.

When people who have a high need for achievement—and that includes all Harvard Business School graduates—have an extra half hour of time or an extra ounce of energy, they'll unconsciously allocate it to activities that yield the most tangible accomplishments. And our careers provide the most concrete evidence that we're moving forward. You ship a product, finish a design, complete a presentation, close a sale, teach a class, publish a paper, get paid, get promoted. In contrast, investing time and energy in your relationship with your spouse and children typically doesn't offer that same immediate sense of achievement. Kids misbehave every day. It's really not until 20 years down the road that you can put your hands on your hips and say, "I raised a good son or a good daughter." You can neglect your relationship with your spouse, and on a day-to-day basis, it doesn't seem as if things are deteriorating. People who are driven to excel have this unconscious propensity to underinvest in their families and overinvest in their careers—even though intimate and loving relationships with their families are the most powerful and enduring source of happiness.

If you study the root causes of business disasters, over and over you'll find this predisposition toward endeavors that offer immediate gratification. If you look at personal lives through that lens, you'll see the same stunning and sobering pattern: people allocating fewer and fewer resources to the things they would have once said mattered most.

Create a Culture

There's an important model in our class called the Tools of Cooperation, which basically says that being a visionary manager isn't all it's cracked up to be. It's one thing to see into the foggy future with acuity and chart the course corrections that the company must make. But it's quite another to persuade employees who might not see the changes ahead to line up and work cooperatively to take the company in that new direction. Knowing what tools to wield to elicit the needed cooperation is a critical managerial skill.

The theory arrays these tools along two dimensions—the extent to which members of the organization agree on what they want from their participation in the enterprise, and the extent to which they agree on what actions will produce the desired results. When there is little agreement on both axes, you have to use "power tools"—coercion, threats, punishment, and so on—to secure cooperation.

Many companies start in this quadrant, which is why the founding executive team must play such an assertive role in defining what must be done and how. If employees' ways of working together to address those tasks succeed over and over, consensus begins to form. MIT's Edgar Schein has described this process as the mechanism by which a culture is built. Ultimately, people don't even think about whether their way of doing things yields success. They embrace priorities and follow procedures by instinct and assumption rather than by explicit decision—which means that they've created a culture. Culture, in compelling but unspoken ways, dictates the proven, acceptable methods by which members of the group address recurrent problems. And culture defines the priority given to different types of problems. It can be a powerful management tool.

In using this model to address the question, How can I be sure that my family becomes an enduring source of happiness?, my students quickly see that the simplest tools that parents can wield to elicit cooperation from children are power tools. But there comes a point during the teen years when power tools no longer work. At that point parents start wishing that they had begun working with their children at a very young age to build a culture at home in which children instinctively behave respectfully toward one another, obey their parents, and choose the right thing to do. Families have cultures, just as companies do. Those cultures can be built consciously or evolve inadvertently.

If you want your kids to have strong self-esteem and confidence that they can solve hard problems, those qualities won't magically materialize in high school. You have to design them into your family's culture—and you have to think about this very early on. Like employees, children build self-esteem by doing things that are hard and learning what works.

Avoid the "Marginal Costs" Mistake

We're taught in finance and economics that in evaluating alternative investments, we should ignore sunk and fixed costs, and instead base decisions on the marginal costs and marginal revenues that each alternative entails. We learn in our course that this doctrine biases companies to leverage what they have put in place to succeed in the past, instead of guiding them to create the capabilities they'll need in the future. If we knew the future would be exactly the same as the past, that approach would be fine. But if the future's different—and it almost always is—then it's the wrong thing to do.

This theory addresses the third question I discuss with my students—how to live a life of integrity (stay out of jail). Unconsciously, we often employ the marginal cost doctrine in our personal lives when we choose between right and wrong. A voice in our head says, "Look, I know that as a general rule, most people shouldn't do this. But in this particular extenuating circumstance, just this once, it's OK." The marginal cost of doing something wrong "just this once" always seems alluringly low. It suckers you in, and you don't ever look at where that path ultimately is headed and at the full costs that the choice entails. Justification for infidelity and dishonesty in all their manifestations lies in the marginal cost economics of "just this once."

I'd like to share a story about how I came to understand the potential damage of "just this once" in my own life. I played on the Oxford University varsity basketball team. We worked our tails off and finished the season undefeated. The guys on the team were the best friends I've ever had in my life. We got to the British equivalent of the NCAA tournament—and made it to the final four. It turned out the championship game was scheduled to be played on a Sunday. I had made a personal commitment to God at age 16 that I would never play ball on Sunday. So I went to the coach and explained my problem. He was incredulous. My teammates were, too, because I was the starting center. Every one of the guys on the team came to me and said, "You've got to play. Can't you break the rule just this one time?"

I'm a deeply religious man, so I went away and prayed about what I should do. I got a very clear feeling that I shouldn't break my commitment—so I didn't play in the championship game.

In many ways that was a small decision—involving one of several thousand Sundays in my life. In theory, surely I could have crossed over the line just that one time and then not done it again. But looking back on it, resisting the temptation whose logic was "In this extenuating circumstance, just this once, it's OK" has proven to be one of the most important decisions of my life. Why? My life has been one unending stream of extenuating circumstances. Had I crossed the line that one time, I would have done it over and over in the years that followed.

The lesson I learned from this is that it's easier to hold to your principles 100% of the time than it is to hold to them 98% of the time. If you give in to "just this once," based on a marginal cost analysis, as some of my former classmates have done, you'll regret where you end up. You've got to define for yourself what you stand for and draw the line in a safe place.

Remember the Importance of Humility

I got this insight when I was asked to teach a class on humility at Harvard College. I asked all the students to describe the most humble person they knew. One characteristic of these humble people stood out: They had a high level of self-esteem. They knew who they were, and they felt good about who they were. We also decided that humility was defined not by self-deprecating behavior or attitudes but by the esteem with which you regard others. Good behavior flows naturally from that kind of humility. For example, you would never steal from someone, because you respect that person too much. You'd never lie to someone, either.

It's crucial to take a sense of humility into the world. By the time you make it to a top graduate school, almost all your learning has come from people who are smarter and more experienced than you: parents, teachers, bosses. But once you've finished at Harvard Business School or any other top academic institution, the vast majority of people you'll interact with on a day-to-day basis may not be smarter than you. And if your attitude is that only smarter people have something to teach you, your learning opportunities will be very limited. But if you have a humble eagerness to learn something from everybody, your learning opportunities will be unlimited.

Generally, you can be humble only if you feel really good about yourself—and you want to help those around you feel really good about themselves, too. When we see people acting in an abusive, arrogant, or demeaning manner toward others, their behavior almost always is a symptom of their lack of self-esteem. They need to put someone else down to feel good about themselves.

Choose the Right Yardstick

This past year I was diagnosed with cancer and faced the possibility that my life would end sooner than I'd planned. Thankfully, it now looks as if I'll be spared. But the experience has given me important insight into my life.

I have a pretty clear idea of how my ideas have generated enormous revenue for companies that have used my research; I know I've had a substantial impact. But as I've confronted this disease, it's been interesting to see how unimportant that impact is to me now. I've concluded that the metric by which God will assess my life isn't dollars but the individual people whose lives I've touched.

I think that's the way it will work for us all. Don't worry about the level of individual prominence you have achieved; worry about the individuals you have helped become better people. This is my final recommendation: Think about the metric by which your life will be judged, and make a resolution to live every day so that in the end, your life will be judged a success.

Originally published in July 2010. Reprint R1007B

Managing Oneself

by Peter F. Drucker

HISTORY'S GREAT ACHIEVERS—a Napoléon, a da Vinci, a Mozart—
have always managed themselves. That, in large measure, is what
makes them great achievers. But they are rare exceptions, so unusual both in their talents and their accomplishments as to be
considered outside the boundaries of ordinary human existence.
Now, most of us, even those of us with modest endowments, will
have to learn to manage ourselves. We will have to learn to develop
ourselves. We will have to place ourselves where we can make the
greatest contribution. And we will have to stay mentally alert and
engaged during a 50-year working life, which means knowing how
and when to change the work we do.

What Are My Strengths?

Most people think they know what they are good at. They are usually wrong. More often, people know what they are not good at—and
even then more people are wrong than right. And yet, a person can
perform only from strength. One cannot build performance on
weaknesses, let alone on something one cannot do at all.

Throughout history, people had little need to know their strengths.
A person was born into a position and a line of work: The peasant's son
would also be a peasant; the artisan's daughter, an artisan's wife; and

so on. But now people have choices. We need to know our strengths in order to know where we belong.

The only way to discover your strengths is through feedback analysis. Whenever you make a key decision or take a key action, write down what you expect will happen. Nine or 12 months later, compare the actual results with your expectations. I have been practicing this method for 15 to 20 years now, and every time I do it, I am surprised. The feedback analysis showed me, for instance—and to my great surprise—that I have an intuitive understanding of technical people, whether they are engineers or accountants or market researchers. It also showed me that I don't really resonate with generalists.

Feedback analysis is by no means new. It was invented sometime in the fourteenth century by an otherwise totally obscure German theologian and picked up quite independently, some 150 years later, by John Calvin and Ignatius of Loyola, each of whom incorporated it into the practice of his followers. In fact, the steadfast focus on performance and results that this habit produces explains why the institutions these two men founded, the Calvinist church and the Jesuit order, came to dominate Europe within 30 years.

Practiced consistently, this simple method will show you within a fairly short period of time, maybe two or three years, where your strengths lie—and this is the most important thing to know. The method will show you what you are doing or failing to do that deprives you of the full benefits of your strengths. It will show you where you are not particularly competent. And finally, it will show you where you have no strengths and cannot perform.

Several implications for action follow from feedback analysis. First and foremost, concentrate on your strengths. Put yourself where your strengths can produce results.

Second, work on improving your strengths. Analysis will rapidly show where you need to improve skills or acquire new ones. It will also show the gaps in your knowledge—and those can usually be filled. Mathematicians are born, but everyone can learn trigonometry.

Third, discover where your intellectual arrogance is causing disabling ignorance and overcome it. Far too many people—especially

Idea in Brief

We live in an age of unprecedented opportunity: If you've got ambition, drive, and smarts, you can rise to the top of your chosen profession—regardless of where you started out. But with opportunity comes responsibility. Companies today aren't managing their knowledge workers' careers. Rather, we must each be our own chief executive officer.

Simply put, it's up to you to carve out your place in the work world and know when to change course. And it's up to you to keep yourself engaged and productive during a work life that may span some 50 years.

To do all of these things well, you'll need to cultivate a deep understanding of yourself. What are your most valuable strengths and most dangerous weaknesses? Equally important, how do you learn and work with others? What are your most deeply held values? And in what type of work environment can you make the greatest contribution?

The implication is clear: Only when you operate from a combination of your strengths and self-knowledge can you achieve true—and lasting— excellence.

people with great expertise in one area—are contemptuous of knowledge in other areas or believe that being bright is a substitute for knowledge. First-rate engineers, for instance, tend to take pride in not knowing anything about people. Human beings, they believe, are much too disorderly for the good engineering mind. Human resources professionals, by contrast, often pride themselves on their ignorance of elementary accounting or of quantitative methods altogether. But taking pride in such ignorance is self-defeating. Go to work on acquiring the skills and knowledge you need to fully realize your strengths.

It is equally essential to remedy your bad habits—the things you do or fail to do that inhibit your effectiveness and performance. Such habits will quickly show up in the feedback. For example, a planner may find that his beautiful plans fail because he does not follow through on them. Like so many brilliant people, he believes that ideas move mountains. But bulldozers move mountains; ideas show where the bulldozers should go to work. This planner will have to learn that the work does not stop when the plan is completed. He

Idea in Practice

To build a life of excellence, begin by asking yourself these questions:

"What are my strengths?"

To accurately identify your strengths, use **feedback analysis**. Every time you make a key decision, write down the outcome you expect. Several months later, compare the actual results with your expected results. Look for patterns in what you're seeing: What results are you skilled at generating? What abilities do you need to enhance in order to get the results you want? What unproductive habits are preventing you from creating the outcomes you desire? In identifying opportunities for improvement, don't waste time cultivating skill areas where you have little competence. Instead, concentrate on—and build on—your strengths.

"How do I work?"

In what ways do you work best? Do you process information most effectively by reading it, or by hearing others discuss it? Do you accomplish the most by working with other people, or by working alone? Do you perform best while making decisions, or while advising others on key matters? Are you in top form when things get stressful, or do you function optimally in a highly predictable environment?

"What are my values?"

What are your ethics? What do you see as your most important responsibilities for living a worthy, ethical life? Do your organization's ethics resonate with your own values? If not, your career will likely be marked by frustration and poor performance.

"Where do I belong?"

Consider your strengths, preferred work style, and values. Based on these qualities, in what kind of work environment would you fit in best? Find the perfect fit, and you'll transform yourself from a merely acceptable employee into a star performer.

"What can I contribute?"

In earlier eras, companies told businesspeople what their contribution should be. Today, you have choices. To decide how you can best enhance your organization's performance, first ask what the situation requires. Based on your strengths, work style, and values, how might you make the greatest contribution to your organization's efforts?

must find people to carry out the plan and explain it to them. He must adapt and change it as he puts it into action. And finally, he must decide when to stop pushing the plan.

At the same time, feedback will also reveal when the problem is a lack of manners. Manners are the lubricating oil of an organization. It is a law of nature that two moving bodies in contact with each other create friction. This is as true for human beings as it is for inanimate objects. Manners—simple things like saying "please" and "thank you" and knowing a person's name or asking after her family—enable two people to work together whether they like each other or not. Bright people, especially bright young people, often do not understand this. If analysis shows that someone's brilliant work fails again and again as soon as cooperation from others is required, it probably indicates a lack of courtesy—that is, a lack of manners.

Comparing your expectations with your results also indicates what not to do. We all have a vast number of areas in which we have no talent or skill and little chance of becoming even mediocre. In those areas a person—and especially a knowledge worker—should not take on work, jobs, and assignments. One should waste as little effort as possible on improving areas of low competence. It takes far more energy and work to improve from incompetence to mediocrity than it takes to improve from first-rate performance to excellence. And yet most people—especially most teachers and most organizations—concentrate on making incompetent performers into mediocre ones. Energy, resources, and time should go instead to making a competent person into a star performer.

How Do I Perform?

Amazingly few people know how they get things done. Indeed, most of us do not even know that different people work and perform differently. Too many people work in ways that are not their ways, and that almost guarantees nonperformance. For knowledge workers, How do I perform? may be an even more important question than What are my strengths?

Like one's strengths, how one performs is unique. It is a matter of personality. Whether personality be a matter of nature or nurture, it surely is formed long before a person goes to work. And *how* a person performs is a given, just as *what* a person is good at or not good at is a given. A person's way of performing can be slightly modified, but it is unlikely to be completely changed—and certainly not easily. Just as people achieve results by doing what they are good at, they also achieve results by working in ways that they best perform. A few common personality traits usually determine how a person performs.

Am I a reader or a listener?

The first thing to know is whether you are a reader or a listener. Far too few people even know that there are readers and listeners and that people are rarely both. Even fewer know which of the two they themselves are. But some examples will show how damaging such ignorance can be.

When Dwight Eisenhower was Supreme Commander of the Allied forces in Europe, he was the darling of the press. His press conferences were famous for their style—General Eisenhower showed total command of whatever question he was asked, and he was able to describe a situation and explain a policy in two or three beautifully polished and elegant sentences. Ten years later, the same journalists who had been his admirers held President Eisenhower in open contempt. He never addressed the questions, they complained, but rambled on endlessly about something else. And they constantly ridiculed him for butchering the King's English in incoherent and ungrammatical answers.

Eisenhower apparently did not know that he was a reader, not a listener. When he was Supreme Commander in Europe, his aides made sure that every question from the press was presented in writing at least half an hour before a conference was to begin. And then Eisenhower was in total command. When he became president, he succeeded two listeners, Franklin D. Roosevelt and Harry Truman. Both men knew themselves to be listeners and both enjoyed free-for-all press conferences. Eisenhower may have felt that he had to do what his two predecessors had done. As a result, he never even heard the questions journalists asked. And Eisenhower is not even an extreme case of a nonlistener.

A few years later, Lyndon Johnson destroyed his presidency, in large measure, by not knowing that he was a listener. His predecessor, John Kennedy, was a reader who had assembled a brilliant group of writers as his assistants, making sure that they wrote to him before discussing their memos in person. Johnson kept these people on his staff—and they kept on writing. He never, apparently, understood one word of what they wrote. Yet as a senator, Johnson had been superb; for parliamentarians have to be, above all, listeners.

Few listeners can be made, or can make themselves, into competent readers—and vice versa. The listener who tries to be a reader will, therefore, suffer the fate of Lyndon Johnson, whereas the reader who tries to be a listener will suffer the fate of Dwight Eisenhower. They will not perform or achieve.

How do I learn?
The second thing to know about how one performs is to know how one learns. Many first-class writers—Winston Churchill is but one example—do poorly in school. They tend to remember their schooling as pure torture. Yet few of their classmates remember it the same way. They may not have enjoyed the school very much, but the worst they suffered was boredom. The explanation is that writers do not, as a rule, learn by listening and reading. They learn by writing. Because schools do not allow them to learn this way, they get poor grades.

Schools everywhere are organized on the assumption that there is only one right way to learn and that it is the same way for everybody. But to be forced to learn the way a school teaches is sheer hell for students who learn differently. Indeed, there are probably half a dozen different ways to learn.

There are people, like Churchill, who learn by writing. Some people learn by taking copious notes. Beethoven, for example, left behind an enormous number of sketchbooks, yet he said he never actually looked at them when he composed. Asked why he kept them, he is reported to have replied, "If I don't write it down immediately, I forget it right away. If I put it into a sketchbook, I never forget it and I never have to look it up again." Some people learn by doing. Others learn by hearing themselves talk.

A chief executive I know who converted a small and mediocre family business into the leading company in its industry was one of those people who learn by talking. He was in the habit of calling his entire senior staff into his office once a week and then talking at them for two or three hours. He would raise policy issues and argue three different positions on each one. He rarely asked his associates for comments or questions; he simply needed an audience to hear himself talk. That's how he learned. And although he is a fairly extreme case, learning through talking is by no means an unusual method. Successful trial lawyers learn the same way, as do many medical diagnosticians (and so do I).

Of all the important pieces of self-knowledge, understanding how you learn is the easiest to acquire. When I ask people, "How do you learn?" most of them know the answer. But when I ask, "Do you act on this knowledge?" few answer yes. And yet, acting on this knowledge is the key to performance; or rather, *not* acting on this knowledge condemns one to nonperformance.

Am I a reader or a listener? and How do I learn? are the first questions to ask. But they are by no means the only ones. To manage yourself effectively, you also have to ask, Do I work well with people, or am I a loner? And if you do work well with people, you then must ask, In what relationship?

Some people work best as subordinates. General George Patton, the great American military hero of World War II, is a prime example. Patton was America's top troop commander. Yet when he was proposed for an independent command, General George Marshall, the U.S. chief of staff—and probably the most successful picker of men in U.S. history—said, "Patton is the best subordinate the American army has ever produced, but he would be the worst commander."

Some people work best as team members. Others work best alone. Some are exceptionally talented as coaches and mentors; others are simply incompetent as mentors.

Another crucial question is, Do I produce results as a decision maker or as an adviser? A great many people perform best as advisers but cannot take the burden and pressure of making the decision. A good many other people, by contrast, need an adviser to force themselves to think; then they can make decisions and act on them with speed, self-confidence, and courage.

This is a reason, by the way, that the number two person in an organization often fails when promoted to the number one position. The top spot requires a decision maker. Strong decision makers often put somebody they trust into the number two spot as their adviser—and in that position the person is outstanding. But in the number one spot, the same person fails. He or she knows what the decision should be but cannot accept the responsibility of actually making it.

Other important questions to ask include, Do I perform well under stress, or do I need a highly structured and predictable environment? Do I work best in a big organization or a small one? Few people work well in all kinds of environments. Again and again, I have seen people who were very successful in large organizations flounder miserably when they moved into smaller ones. And the reverse is equally true.

The conclusion bears repeating: Do not try to change yourself—you are unlikely to succeed. But work hard to improve the way you perform. And try not to take on work you cannot perform or will only perform poorly.

What Are My Values?

To be able to manage yourself, you finally have to ask, What are my values? This is not a question of ethics. With respect to ethics, the rules are the same for everybody, and the test is a simple one. I call it the "mirror test."

In the early years of this century, the most highly respected diplomat of all the great powers was the German ambassador in London. He was clearly destined for great things—to become his country's foreign minister, at least, if not its federal chancellor. Yet in 1906 he abruptly resigned rather than preside over a dinner given by the diplomatic corps for Edward VII. The king was a notorious womanizer and made it clear what kind of dinner he wanted. The ambassador is reported to have said, "I refuse to see a pimp in the mirror in the morning when I shave."

That is the mirror test. Ethics requires that you ask yourself, What kind of person do I want to see in the mirror in the morning? What is ethical behavior in one kind of organization or situation is ethical behavior in another. But ethics is only part of a value system—especially of an organization's value system.

To work in an organization whose value system is unacceptable or incompatible with one's own condemns a person both to frustration and to nonperformance.

Consider the experience of a highly successful human resources executive whose company was acquired by a bigger organization. After the acquisition, she was promoted to do the kind of work she did best, which included selecting people for important positions. The executive deeply believed that a company should hire people for such positions from the outside only after exhausting all the inside possibilities. But her new company believed in first looking outside "to bring in fresh blood." There is something to be said for both approaches—in my experience, the proper one is to do some of both. They are, however, fundamentally incompatible—not as policies but as values. They bespeak different views of the relationship between organizations and people; different views of the responsibility of an organization to its people and their development; and different views of a person's most important contribution to an enterprise. After several years of frustration, the executive quit—at considerable financial loss. Her values and the values of the organization simply were not compatible.

Similarly, whether a pharmaceutical company tries to obtain results by making constant, small improvements or by achieving occasional, highly expensive, and risky "breakthroughs" is not primarily an economic question. The results of either strategy may be pretty much the same. At bottom, there is a conflict between a value system that sees the company's contribution in terms of helping physicians do better what they already do and a value system that is oriented toward making scientific discoveries.

Whether a business should be run for short-term results or with a focus on the long term is likewise a question of values. Financial analysts believe that businesses can be run for both simultaneously. Successful businesspeople know better. To be sure, every company has to produce short-term results. But in any conflict between short-term results and long-term growth, each company will determine its own priority. This is not primarily a disagreement about economics. It is fundamentally a value conflict regarding the function of a business and the responsibility of management.

Value conflicts are not limited to business organizations. One of the fastest-growing pastoral churches in the United States measures success by the number of new parishioners. Its leadership believes that what matters is how many newcomers join the congregation. The Good Lord will then minister to their spiritual needs or at least to the needs of a sufficient percentage. Another pastoral, evangelical church believes that what matters is people's spiritual growth. The church eases out newcomers who join but do not enter into its spiritual life.

Again, this is not a matter of numbers. At first glance, it appears that the second church grows more slowly. But it retains a far larger proportion of newcomers than the first one does. Its growth, in other words, is more solid. This is also not a theological problem, or only secondarily so. It is a problem about values. In a public debate, one pastor argued, "Unless you first come to church, you will never find the gate to the Kingdom of Heaven."

"No," answered the other. "Until you first look for the gate to the Kingdom of Heaven, you don't belong in church."

Organizations, like people, have values. To be effective in an organization, a person's values must be compatible with the organization's values. They do not need to be the same, but they must be close enough to coexist. Otherwise, the person will not only be frustrated but also will not produce results.

A person's strengths and the way that person performs rarely conflict; the two are complementary. But there is sometimes a conflict between a person's values and his or her strengths. What one does well—even very well and successfully—may not fit with one's value system. In that case, the work may not appear to be worth devoting one's life to (or even a substantial portion thereof).

If I may, allow me to interject a personal note. Many years ago, I too had to decide between my values and what I was doing successfully. I was doing very well as a young investment banker in London in the mid-1930s, and the work clearly fit my strengths. Yet I did not see myself making a contribution as an asset manager. People, I realized, were what I valued, and I saw no point in being the richest man in the cemetery. I had no money and no other job prospects. Despite the continuing Depression, I quit—and it was the right thing to do. Values, in other words, are and should be the ultimate test.

Where Do I Belong?

A small number of people know very early where they belong. Mathematicians, musicians, and cooks, for instance, are usually mathematicians, musicians, and cooks by the time they are four or five years old. Physicians usually decide on their careers in their teens, if not earlier. But most people, especially highly gifted people, do not really know where they belong until they are well past their mid-twenties. By that time, however, they should know the answers to the three questions: What are my strengths? How do I perform? and, What are my values? And then they can and should decide where they belong.

Or rather, they should be able to decide where they do *not* belong. The person who has learned that he or she does not perform well in a big organization should have learned to say no to a position in one. The person who has learned that he or she is not a decision maker should have learned to say no to a decision-making assignment. A General Patton (who probably never learned this himself) should have learned to say no to an independent command.

Equally important, knowing the answer to these questions enables a person to say to an opportunity, an offer, or an assignment, "Yes, I will do that. But this is the way I should be doing it. This is the way it should be structured. This is the way the relationships should be. These are the kind of results you should expect from me, and in this time frame, because this is who I am."

Successful careers are not planned. They develop when people are prepared for opportunities because they know their strengths, their method of work, and their values. Knowing where one belongs can transform an ordinary person—hardworking and competent but otherwise mediocre—into an outstanding performer.

What Should I Contribute?

Throughout history, the great majority of people never had to ask the question, What should I contribute? They were told what to contribute, and their tasks were dictated either by the work itself—as it was for the peasant or artisan—or by a master or a mistress—as it was for domestic servants. And until very recently, it was taken for granted that most people were subordinates who did as they were told. Even in the 1950s and 1960s, the new knowledge workers (the so-called organization men) looked to their company's personnel department to plan their careers.

Then in the late 1960s, no one wanted to be told what to do any longer. Young men and women began to ask, What do *I* want to do? And what they heard was that the way to contribute was to "do your own thing." But this solution was as wrong as the organization men's had been. Very few of the people who believed that doing one's own thing would lead to contribution, self-fulfillment, and success achieved any of the three.

But still, there is no return to the old answer of doing what you are told or assigned to do. Knowledge workers in particular have to learn to ask a question that has not been asked before: What *should* my contribution be? To answer it, they must address three distinct elements: What does the situation require? Given my strengths, my way of performing, and my values, how can I make the greatest contribution to what needs to be done? And finally, What results have to be achieved to make a difference?

Consider the experience of a newly appointed hospital administrator. The hospital was big and prestigious, but it had been coasting on its reputation for 30 years. The new administrator decided that his contribution should be to establish a standard of excellence in one important area within two years. He chose to focus on the emergency room, which was big, visible, and sloppy. He decided that every patient who came into the ER had to be seen by a qualified nurse within 60 seconds. Within 12 months, the hospital's emergency room had become a model for all hospitals in the United States, and within another two years, the whole hospital had been transformed.

As this example suggests, it is rarely possible—or even particularly fruitful—to look too far ahead. A plan can usually cover no more than 18 months and still be reasonably clear and specific. So the question in most cases should be, Where and how can I achieve results that will make a difference within the next year and a half? The answer must balance several things. First, the results should be hard to achieve—they should require "stretching," to use the current buzzword. But also, they should be within reach. To aim at results that cannot be achieved—or that can be only under the most unlikely circumstances—is not being ambitious; it is being foolish. Second, the results should be meaningful. They should make a difference. Finally, results should be visible and, if at all possible, measurable. From this will come a course of action: what to do, where and how to start, and what goals and deadlines to set.

Responsibility for Relationships

Very few people work by themselves and achieve results by themselves—a few great artists, a few great scientists, a few great athletes. Most people work with others and are effective with other people. That is true whether they are members of an organization or independently employed. Managing yourself requires taking responsibility for relationships. This has two parts.

The first is to accept the fact that other people are as much individuals as you yourself are. They perversely insist on behaving like human beings. This means that they too have their strengths; they too have their ways of getting things done; they too have their values. To be effective, therefore, you have to know the strengths, the performance modes, and the values of your coworkers.

That sounds obvious, but few people pay attention to it. Typical is the person who was trained to write reports in his or her first assignment because that boss was a reader. Even if the next boss is a listener, the person goes on writing reports that, invariably, produce no results. Invariably the boss will think the employee is stupid, incompetent, and lazy, and he or she will fail. But that could have been avoided if the employee had only looked at the new boss and analyzed how *this* boss performs.

Bosses are neither a title on the organization chart nor a "function." They are individuals and are entitled to do their work in the way they do it best. It is incumbent on the people who work with them to observe them, to find out how they work, and to adapt themselves to what makes their bosses most effective. This, in fact, is the secret of "managing" the boss.

The same holds true for all your coworkers. Each works his or her way, not your way. And each is entitled to work in his or her way. What matters is whether they perform and what their values are. As for how they perform—each is likely to do it differently. The first secret of effectiveness is to understand the people you work with and depend on so that you can make use of their strengths, their ways of working, and their values. Working relationships are as much based on the people as they are on the work.

The second part of relationship responsibility is taking responsibility for communication. Whenever I, or any other consultant, start to work with an organization, the first thing I hear about are all the personality conflicts. Most of these arise from the fact that people do not know what other people are doing and how they do their work, or what contribution the other people are concentrating on and what results they expect. And the reason they do not know is that they have not asked and therefore have not been told.

This failure to ask reflects human stupidity less than it reflects human history. Until recently, it was unnecessary to tell any of these things to anybody. In the medieval city, everyone in a district plied the same trade. In the countryside, everyone in a valley planted the same crop as soon as the frost was out of the ground. Even those few people who did things that were not "common" worked alone, so they did not have to tell anyone what they were doing.

Today the great majority of people work with others who have different tasks and responsibilities. The marketing vice president may have come out of sales and know everything about sales, but she knows nothing about the things she has never done—pricing, advertising, packaging, and the like. So the people who do these things must make sure that the marketing vice president understands what they are trying to do, why they are trying to do it, how they are going to do it, and what results to expect.

If the marketing vice president does not understand what these high-grade knowledge specialists are doing, it is primarily their fault, not hers. They have not educated her. Conversely, it is the marketing vice president's responsibility to make sure that all of her coworkers understand how she looks at marketing: what her goals are, how she works, and what she expects of herself and of each one of them.

Even people who understand the importance of taking responsibility for relationships often do not communicate sufficiently with their associates. They are afraid of being thought presumptuous or inquisitive or stupid. They are wrong. Whenever someone goes to his or her associates and says, "This is what I am good at. This is how I work. These are my values. This is the contribution I plan to concentrate on and the results I should be expected to deliver," the response is always, "This is most helpful. But why didn't you tell me earlier?"

And one gets the same reaction—without exception, in my experience—if one continues by asking, "And what do I need to know about your strengths, how you perform, your values, and your proposed contribution?" In fact, knowledge workers should request this of everyone with whom they work, whether as subordinate, superior, colleague, or team member. And again, whenever this is done, the reaction is always, "Thanks for asking me. But why didn't you ask me earlier?"

Organizations are no longer built on force but on trust. The existence of trust between people does not necessarily mean that they like one another. It means that they understand one another. Taking responsibility for relationships is therefore an absolute necessity. It is a duty. Whether one is a member of the organization, a consultant to it, a supplier, or a distributor, one owes that responsibility to all one's coworkers: those whose work one depends on as well as those who depend on one's own work.

The Second Half of Your Life

When work for most people meant manual labor, there was no need to worry about the second half of your life. You simply kept on doing what you had always done. And if you were lucky enough to survive 40 years of hard work in the mill or on the railroad, you were quite happy to spend the rest of your life doing nothing. Today, however, most work is knowledge work, and knowledge workers are not "finished" after 40 years on the job, they are merely bored.

We hear a great deal of talk about the midlife crisis of the executive. It is mostly boredom. At 45, most executives have reached the peak of their business careers, and they know it. After 20 years of doing very much the same kind of work, they are very good at their jobs. But they are not learning or contributing or deriving challenge and satisfaction from the job. And yet they are still likely to face another 20 if not 25 years of work. That is why managing oneself increasingly leads one to begin a second career.

There are three ways to develop a second career. The first is actually to start one. Often this takes nothing more than moving from one kind of organization to another: the divisional controller in a large corporation, for instance, becomes the controller of a medium-sized hospital. But there are also growing numbers of people who move into different lines of work altogether: the business executive or government official who enters the ministry at 45, for instance; or the midlevel manager who leaves corporate life after 20 years to attend law school and become a small-town attorney.

We will see many more second careers undertaken by people who have achieved modest success in their first jobs. Such people have substantial skills, and they know how to work. They need a community—the house is empty with the children gone—and they need income as well. But above all, they need challenge.

The second way to prepare for the second half of your life is to develop a parallel career. Many people who are very successful in their first careers stay in the work they have been doing, either on a full-time or part-time or consulting basis. But in addition, they create a parallel job, usually in a nonprofit organization, that takes another ten hours of work a week. They might take over the administration of their church, for instance, or the presidency of the local Girl Scouts council. They might run the battered women's shelter, work as a children's librarian for the local public library, sit on the school board, and so on.

Finally, there are the social entrepreneurs. These are usually people who have been very successful in their first careers. They love their work, but it no longer challenges them. In many cases they keep on doing what they have been doing all along but spend less and less of their time on it. They also start another activity, usually a nonprofit. My friend Bob Buford, for example, built a very successful television company that he still runs. But he has also founded and built a successful nonprofit organization that works with Protestant churches, and he is building another to teach social entrepreneurs how to manage their own nonprofit ventures while still running their original businesses.

People who manage the second half of their lives may always be a minority. The majority may "retire on the job" and count the years until their actual retirement. But it is this minority, the men and women who see a long working-life expectancy as an opportunity both for themselves and for society, who will become leaders and models.

There is one prerequisite for managing the second half of your life: You must begin long before you enter it. When it first became clear 30 years ago that working-life expectancies were lengthening very fast, many observers (including myself) believed that retired people would increasingly become volunteers for nonprofit institutions. That has not happened. If one does not begin to volunteer before one is 40 or so, one will not volunteer once past 60.

Similarly, all the social entrepreneurs I know began to work in their chosen second enterprise long before they reached their peak in their original business. Consider the example of a successful lawyer, the legal counsel to a large corporation, who has started a venture to establish model schools in his state. He began to do volunteer legal work for the schools when he was around 35. He was elected to the school board at age 40. At age 50, when he had amassed a fortune, he started his own enterprise to build and to run model schools. He is, however, still working nearly full-time as the lead counsel in the company he helped found as a young lawyer.

There is another reason to develop a second major interest, and to develop it early. No one can expect to live very long without experiencing a serious setback in his or her life or work. There is the competent engineer who is passed over for promotion at age 45. There is the competent college professor who realizes at age 42 that she will never get a professorship at a big university, even though she may be fully qualified for it. There are tragedies in one's family life: the breakup of one's marriage or the loss of a child. At such times, a second major interest—not just a hobby—may make all the difference. The engineer, for example, now knows that he has not been very successful in his job. But in his outside activity—as church treasurer, for example—he is a success. One's family may break up, but in that outside activity there is still a community.

In a society in which success has become so terribly important, having options will become increasingly vital. Historically, there was no such thing as "success." The overwhelming majority of people did not expect anything but to stay in their "proper station," as an old English prayer has it. The only mobility was downward mobility.

In a knowledge society, however, we expect everyone to be a success. This is clearly an impossibility. For a great many people, there is at best an absence of failure. Wherever there is success, there has to be failure. And then it is vitally important for the individual, and equally for the individual's family, to have an area in which he or she can contribute, make a difference, and be *somebody*. That means finding a second area—whether in a second career, a parallel career, or a social venture—that offers an opportunity for being a leader, for being respected, for being a success.

The challenges of managing oneself may seem obvious, if not elementary. And the answers may seem self-evident to the point of appearing naïve. But managing oneself requires new and unprecedented things from the individual, and especially from the knowledge worker. In effect, managing oneself demands that each knowledge worker think and behave like a chief executive officer. Further, the shift from manual workers who do as they are told to knowledge workers who have to manage themselves profoundly challenges social structure. Every existing society, even the most individualistic one, takes two things for granted, if only subconsciously: that organizations outlive workers, and that most people stay put.

But today the opposite is true. Knowledge workers outlive organizations, and they are mobile. The need to manage oneself is therefore creating a revolution in human affairs.

Originally published in January 1999. Reprint R0501K

Management Time: Who's Got the Monkey?

by William Oncken, Jr., and Donald L. Wass

WHY IS IT THAT MANAGERS are typically running out of time while their subordinates are typically running out of work? Here we shall explore the meaning of management time as it relates to the inter-action between managers and their bosses, their peers, and their subordinates.

Specifically, we shall deal with three kinds of management time:

Boss-imposed time—used to accomplish those activities that the boss requires and that the manager cannot disregard without direct and swift penalty.

System-imposed time—used to accommodate requests from peers for active support. Neglecting these requests will also result in penalties, though not always as direct or swift.

Self-imposed time—used to do those things that the manager originates or agrees to do. A certain portion of this kind of time, however, will be taken by subordinates and is called *subordinate-imposed time*. The remaining portion will be the manager's own and is called *discretionary time*. Self-imposed time is not subject to penalty since neither the boss nor the system can discipline the manager for not doing what they didn't know he had intended to do in the first place.

To accommodate those demands, managers need to control the timing and the content of what they do. Since what their bosses and the system impose on them are subject to penalty, managers cannot tamper with those requirements. Thus their self-imposed time becomes their major area of concern.

Managers should try to increase the discretionary component of their self-imposed time by minimizing or doing away with the subordinate component. They will then use the added increment to get better control over their boss-imposed and system-imposed activities. Most managers spend much more time dealing with subordinates' problems than they even faintly realize. Hence we shall use the monkey-on-the-back metaphor to examine how subordinate-imposed time comes into being and what the superior can do about it.

Where Is the Monkey?

Let us imagine that a manager is walking down the hall and that he notices one of his subordinates, Jones, coming his way. When the two meet, Jones greets the manager with, "Good morning. By the way, we've got a problem. You see . . . ." As Jones continues, the manager recognizes in this problem the two characteristics common to all the problems his subordinates gratuitously bring to his attention. Namely, the manager knows (a) enough to get involved, but (b) not enough to make the on-the-spot decision expected of him. Eventually, the manager says, "So glad you brought this up. I'm in a rush right now. Meanwhile, let me think about it, and I'll let you know." Then he and Jones part company.

Let us analyze what just happened. Before the two of them met, on whose back was the "monkey"? The subordinate's. After they parted, on whose back was it? The manager's. Subordinate-imposed time begins the moment a monkey successfully leaps from the back of a subordinate to the back of his or her superior and does not end until the monkey is returned to its proper owner for care and feeding. In accepting the monkey, the manager has voluntarily assumed a position subordinate to his subordinate. That is, he has allowed

Idea in Brief

You're racing down the hall. An employee stops you and says, "We've got a problem." You assume you should get involved but can't make an on-the-spot decision. You say, "Let me think about it."

You've just allowed a "monkey" to leap from your subordinate's back to yours. *You're* now working for your *subordinate*. Take on enough monkeys, and you won't have time to handle your *real* job: fulfilling your own boss's mandates and helping peers generate business results.

How to avoid accumulating monkeys? Develop your subordinates' initiative, say Oncken and Wass. For example, when an employee tries to hand you a problem, clarify whether he should: recommend and implement a solution, take action then brief you immediately, or act and report the outcome at a regular update.

When you encourage employees to handle their own monkeys, they acquire new skills—and you liberate time to do your own job.

Jones to make him her subordinate by doing two things a subordinate is generally expected to do for a boss—the manager has accepted a responsibility from his subordinate, and the manager has promised her a progress report.

The subordinate, to make sure the manager does not miss this point, will later stick her head in the manager's office and cheerily query, "How's it coming?" (This is called supervision.)

Or let us imagine in concluding a conference with Johnson, another subordinate, the manager's parting words are, "Fine. Send me a memo on that."

Let us analyze this one. The monkey is now on the subordinate's back because the next move is his, but it is poised for a leap. Watch that monkey. Johnson dutifully writes the requested memo and drops it in his out-basket. Shortly thereafter, the manager plucks it from his in-basket and reads it. Whose move is it now? The manager's. If he does not make that move soon, he will get a follow-up memo from the subordinate. (This is another form of supervision.) The longer the manager delays, the more frustrated the subordinate will become (he'll be spinning his wheels) and the more guilty the

Idea in Practice

How to return monkeys to their proper owners? Oncken, Wass, and Steven Covey (in an afterword to this classic article) offer these suggestions.

Make Appointments to Deal with Monkeys

Avoid discussing any monkey on an ad hoc basis—for example, when you pass a subordinate in the hallway. You won't convey the proper seriousness. Instead, schedule an appointment to discuss the issue.

Specify Level of Initiative

Your employees can exercise five levels of initiative in handling on-the-job problems. From lowest to highest, the levels are:

1. Wait until told what to do.

2. Ask what to do.

3. Recommend an action, then with your approval, implement it.

4. Take independent action but advise you at once.

5. Take independent action and update you through routine procedure.

When an employee brings a problem to you, outlaw use of level 1 or 2. Agree on and assign level 3, 4, or 5 to the monkey. Take no more than 15 minutes to discuss the problem.

Agree on a Status Update

After deciding how to proceed, agree on a time and place when the employee will give you a progress report.

Examine Your Own Motives

Some managers secretly worry that if they encourage subordinates to take more initiative, they'll appear less strong, more vulnerable, and less useful. Instead, cultivate an inward sense of security that frees you to relinquish direct control and support employees' growth.

Develop Employees' Skills

Employees try to hand off monkeys when they lack the desire or ability to handle them. Help employees develop needed problem-solving skills. It's initially more time consuming than tackling problems yourself—but it saves time in the long run.

Foster Trust

Developing employees' initiative requires a trusting relationship between you and your subordinates. If they're afraid of failing, they'll keep bringing their monkeys to you rather than working to solve their own problems. To promote trust, reassure them it's safe to make mistakes.

manager will feel (his backlog of subordinate-imposed time will be mounting).

Or suppose once again that at a meeting with a third subordinate, Smith, the manager agrees to provide all the necessary backing for a public relations proposal he has just asked Smith to develop. The manager's parting words to her are, "Just let me know how I can help."

Now let us analyze this. Again the monkey is initially on the subordinate's back. But for how long? Smith realizes that she cannot let the manager "know" until her proposal has the manager's approval. And from experience, she also realizes that her proposal will likely be sitting in the manager's briefcase for weeks before he eventually gets to it. Who's really got the monkey? Who will be checking up on whom? Wheel spinning and bottlenecking are well on their way again.

A fourth subordinate, Reed, has just been transferred from another part of the company so that he can launch and eventually manage a newly created business venture. The manager has said they should get together soon to hammer out a set of objectives for the new job, adding, "I will draw up an initial draft for discussion with you."

Let us analyze this one, too. The subordinate has the new job (by formal assignment) and the full responsibility (by formal delegation), but the manager has the next move. Until he makes it, he will have the monkey, and the subordinate will be immobilized.

Why does all of this happen? Because in each instance the manager and the subordinate assume at the outset, wittingly or unwittingly, that the matter under consideration is a joint problem. The monkey in each case begins its career astride both their backs. All it has to do is move the wrong leg, and—presto!—the subordinate deftly disappears. The manager is thus left with another acquisition for his menagerie. Of course, monkeys can be trained not to move the wrong leg. But it is easier to prevent them from straddling backs in the first place.

Who Is Working for Whom?

Let us suppose that these same four subordinates are so thoughtful and considerate of their superior's time that they take pains to allow no more than three monkeys to leap from each of their backs to his in any one day. In a five-day week, the manager will have picked up 60 screaming monkeys—far too many to do anything about them individually. So he spends his subordinate-imposed time juggling his "priorities."

Late Friday afternoon, the manager is in his office with the door closed for privacy so he can contemplate the situation, while his subordinates are waiting outside to get their last chance before the weekend to remind him that he will have to "fish or cut bait." Imagine what they are saying to one another about the manager as they wait: "What a bottleneck. He just can't make up his mind. How anyone ever got that high up in our company without being able to make a decision we'll never know."

Worst of all, the reason the manager cannot make any of these "next moves" is that his time is almost entirely eaten up by meeting his own boss-imposed and system-imposed requirements. To control those tasks, he needs discretionary time that is in turn denied him when he is preoccupied with all these monkeys. The manager is caught in a vicious circle. But time is a-wasting (an understatement). The manager calls his secretary on the intercom and instructs her to tell his subordinates that he won't be able to see them until Monday morning. At 7 PM, he drives home, intending with firm resolve to return to the office tomorrow to get caught up over the weekend. He returns bright and early the next day only to see, on the nearest green of the golf course across from his office window, a foursome. Guess who?

That does it. He now knows who is really working for whom. Moreover, he now sees that if he actually accomplishes during this weekend what he came to accomplish, his subordinates' morale will go up so sharply that they will each raise the limit on the number of monkeys they will let jump from their backs to his. In short, he now sees, with the clarity of a revelation on a mountaintop, that the more he gets caught up, the more he will fall behind.

He leaves the office with the speed of a person running away from a plague. His plan? To get caught up on something else he hasn't had time for in years: a weekend with his family. (This is one of the many varieties of discretionary time.)

Sunday night he enjoys ten hours of sweet, untroubled slumber, because he has clear-cut plans for Monday. He is going to get rid of his subordinate-imposed time. In exchange, he will get an equal amount of discretionary time, part of which he will spend with his subordinates to make sure that they learn the difficult but rewarding managerial art called "The Care and Feeding of Monkeys."

The manager will also have plenty of discretionary time left over for getting control of the timing and the content not only of his boss-imposed time but also of his system-imposed time. It may take months, but compared with the way things have been, the rewards will be enormous. His ultimate objective is to manage his time.

Getting Rid of the Monkeys

The manager returns to the office Monday morning just late enough so that his four subordinates have collected outside his office waiting to see him about their monkeys. He calls them in one by one. The purpose of each interview is to take a monkey, place it on the desk between them, and figure out together how the next move might conceivably be the subordinate's. For certain monkeys, that will take some doing. The subordinate's next move may be so elusive that the manager may decide—just for now—merely to let the monkey sleep on the subordinate's back overnight and have him or her return with it at an appointed time the next morning to continue the joint quest for a more substantive move by the subordinate. (Monkeys sleep just as soundly overnight on subordinates' backs as they do on superiors'.)

As each subordinate leaves the office, the manager is rewarded by the sight of a monkey leaving his office on the subordinate's back. For the next 24 hours, the subordinate will not be waiting for the manager; instead, the manager will be waiting for the subordinate.

Later, as if to remind himself that there is no law against his engaging in a constructive exercise in the interim, the manager strolls by the subordinate's office, sticks his head in the door, and cheerily asks, "How's it coming?" (The time consumed in doing this is discretionary for the manager and boss imposed for the subordinate.)

Making Time for Gorillas

by Stephen R. Covey

WHEN BILL ONCKEN WROTE this article in 1974, managers were in a terrible bind. They were desperate for a way to free up their time, but command and control was the status quo. Managers felt they weren't allowed to empower their subordinates to make decisions. Too dangerous. Too risky. That's why Oncken's message—give the monkey back to its rightful owner—involved a critically important paradigm shift. Many managers working today owe him a debt of gratitude.

It is something of an understatement, however, to observe that much has changed since Oncken's radical recommendation. Command and control as a management philosophy is all but dead, and "empowerment" is the word of the day in most organizations trying to thrive in global, intensely competitive markets. But command and control stubbornly remains a common practice. Management thinkers and executives have discovered in the last decade that bosses cannot just give a monkey back to their subordinates and then merrily get on with their own business. Empowering subordinates is hard and complicated work.

The reason: when you give problems back to subordinates to solve themselves, you have to be sure that they have both the desire and the ability to do so. As every executive knows, that isn't always the case. Enter a whole new set of problems. Empowerment often means you have to develop people, which is initially much more time consuming than solving the problem on your own.

Just as important, empowerment can only thrive when the whole organization buys into it—when formal systems and the informal culture support it. Managers need to be rewarded for delegating decisions and developing people. Otherwise, the degree of real empowerment in an organization will vary according to the beliefs and practices of individual managers.

But perhaps the most important lesson about empowerment is that effective delegation—the kind Oncken advocated—depends on a trusting relationship between a manager and his subordinate. Oncken's message may have been ahead of his time, but what he suggested was still a fairly dictatorial solution. He basically told bosses, "Give the problem back!" Today, we know that this approach by itself is too authoritarian. To delegate effectively, executives need to establish a running dialogue with subordinates. They need to establish a partnership. After all, if subordinates are afraid of failing in front of their boss, they'll keep coming back for help rather than truly take initiative.

Oncken's article also doesn't address an aspect of delegation that has greatly interested me during the past two decades—that many managers are actually *eager* to take on their subordinates' monkeys. Nearly all the managers I talk with agree that their people are underutilized in their present jobs. But even some of the most successful, seemingly self-assured executives have talked about how hard it is to give up control to their subordinates.

I've come to attribute that eagerness for control to a common, deep-seated belief that rewards in life are scarce and fragile. Whether they learn it from their family, school, or athletics, many people establish an identity by comparing themselves with others. When they see others gain power, information, money, or recognition, for instance, they experience what the psychologist Abraham Maslow called "a feeling of deficiency"—a sense that something is being taken from them. That makes it hard for them to be genuinely happy about the success of others—even of their loved ones. Oncken implies that managers can easily give back or refuse monkeys, but many managers may subconsciously fear that a subordinate taking the initiative will make them appear a little less strong and a little more vulnerable.

How, then, do managers develop the inward security, the mentality of "abundance," that would enable them to relinquish control and seek the growth and development of those around them? The work I've done with numerous organizations suggests that managers who live with integrity according to a principle-based value system are most likely to sustain an empowering style of leadership.

Given the times in which he wrote, it was no wonder that Oncken's message resonated with managers. But it was reinforced by Oncken's wonderful gift for storytelling. I got to know Oncken on the speaker's circuit in the 1970s, and I was always impressed by how he dramatized his ideas in colorful detail. Like the Dilbert comic strip, Oncken had a tongue-in-cheek style that got to the core of managers' frustrations and made them want to take back control of their time. And the monkey on your back wasn't just a metaphor for Oncken—it was his personal symbol. I saw him several times walking through airports with a stuffed monkey on his shoulder.

I'm not surprised that his article is one of the two best-selling HBR articles ever. Even with all we know about empowerment, its vivid message is even more important and relevant now than it was 25 years ago. Indeed, Oncken's insight is a basis for my own work on time management, in which I have people categorize their activities according to urgency and importance. I've heard from executives again and again that half or more of their time is spent on matters that are urgent but not important. They're trapped in an endless

(continued)

cycle of dealing with other people's monkeys, yet they're reluctant to help those people take their own initiative. As a result, they're often too busy to spend the time they need on the real gorillas in their organization. Oncken's article remains a powerful wake-up call for managers who need to delegate effectively.

Stephen R. Covey is vice chairman of the Franklin Covey Company, a global provider of leadership development and productivity services and products.

When the subordinate (with the monkey on his or her back) and the manager meet at the appointed hour the next day, the manager explains the ground rules in words to this effect:

"At no time while I am helping you with this or any other problem will your problem become my problem. The instant your problem becomes mine, you no longer have a problem. I cannot help a person who hasn't got a problem.

"When this meeting is over, the problem will leave this office exactly the way it came in—on your back. You may ask my help at any appointed time, and we will make a joint determination of what the next move will be and which of us will make it.

"In those rare instances where the next move turns out to be mine, you and I will determine it together. I will not make any move alone."

The manager follows this same line of thought with each subordinate until about 11 AM, when he realizes that he doesn't have to close his door. His monkeys are gone. They will return—but by appointment only. His calendar will assure this.

Transferring the Initiative

What we have been driving at in this monkey-on-the-back analogy is that managers can transfer initiative back to their subordinates and keep it there. We have tried to highlight a truism as obvious as it is subtle: namely, before developing initiative in subordinates, the manager must see to it that they *have* the initiative. Once the manager takes it back, he will no longer have it and he can kiss his discretionary time good-bye. It will all revert to subordinate-imposed time.

Nor can the manager and the subordinate effectively have the same initiative at the same time. The opener, "Boss, we've got a problem," implies this duality and represents, as noted earlier, a monkey astride two backs, which is a very bad way to start a monkey on its career. Let us, therefore, take a few moments to examine what we call "The Anatomy of Managerial Initiative."

There are five degrees of initiative that the manager can exercise in relation to the boss and to the system:

1. wait until told (lowest initiative);

2. ask what to do;

3. recommend, then take resulting action;

4. act, but advise at once;

5. and act on own, then routinely report (highest initiative).

Clearly, the manager should be professional enough not to indulge in initiatives 1 and 2 in relation either to the boss or to the system. A manager who uses initiative 1 has no control over either the timing or the content of boss-imposed or system-imposed time and thereby forfeits any right to complain about what he or she is told to do or when. The manager who uses initiative 2 has control over the timing but not over the content. Initiatives 3, 4, and 5 leave the manager in control of both, with the greatest amount of control being exercised at level 5.

In relation to subordinates, the manager's job is twofold. First, to outlaw the use of initiatives 1 and 2, thus giving subordinates no choice but to learn and master "Completed Staff Work." Second, to see that for each problem leaving his or her office there is an agreed-upon level of initiative assigned to it, in addition to an agreed-upon time and place for the next manager-subordinate conference. The latter should be duly noted on the manager's calendar.

The Care and Feeding of Monkeys

To further clarify our analogy between the monkey on the back and the processes of assigning and controlling, we shall refer briefly to the manager's appointment schedule, which calls for five hard-and-fast rules governing the "Care and Feeding of Monkeys." (Violation of these rules will cost discretionary time.)

Rule 1

Monkeys should be fed or shot. Otherwise, they will starve to death, and the manager will waste valuable time on postmortems or attempted resurrections.

Rule 2

The monkey population should be kept below the maximum number the manager has time to feed. Subordinates will find time to work as many monkeys as he or she finds time to feed, but no more. It shouldn't take more than five to 15 minutes to feed a properly maintained monkey.

Rule 3

Monkeys should be fed by appointment only. The manager should not have to hunt down starving monkeys and feed them on a catch-as-catch-can basis.

Rule 4

Monkeys should be fed face-to-face or by telephone, but never by mail. (Remember—with mail, the next move will be the manager's.) Documentation may add to the feeding process, but it cannot take the place of feeding.

Rule 5

Every monkey should have an assigned next feeding time and degree of initiative. These may be revised at any time by mutual consent but never allowed to become vague or indefinite. Otherwise, the monkey will either starve to death or wind up on the manager's back.

"Get control over the timing and content of what you do" is appropriate advice for managing time. The first order of business is for the manager to enlarge his or her discretionary time by eliminating subordinate-imposed time. The second is for the manager to use a portion of this newfound discretionary time to see to it that each subordinate actually has the initiative and applies it. The third is for the manager to use another portion of the increased discretionary time to get and keep control of the timing and content of both boss-imposed and system-imposed time. All these steps will increase the manager's leverage and enable the value of each hour spent in managing management time to multiply without theoretical limit.

Originally published in November 1999. Reprint 99609

How Resilience Works

by Diane L. Coutu

WHEN I BEGAN MY CAREER IN JOURNALISM—I was a reporter at a national magazine in those days—there was a man I'll call Claus Schmidt. He was in his mid-fifties, and to my impressionable eyes, he was the quintessential newsman: cynical at times, but unrelentingly curious and full of life, and often hilariously funny in a sandpaper-dry kind of way. He churned out hard-hitting cover stories and features with a speed and elegance I could only dream of. It always astounded me that he was never promoted to managing editor.

But people who knew Claus better than I did thought of him not just as a great newsman but as a quintessential survivor, someone who had endured in an environment often hostile to talent. He had lived through at least three major changes in the magazine's leadership, losing most of his best friends and colleagues on the way. At home, two of his children succumbed to incurable illnesses, and a third was killed in a traffic accident. Despite all this—or maybe because of it—he milled around the newsroom day after day, mentoring the cub reporters, talking about the novels he was writing—always looking forward to what the future held for him.

Why do some people suffer real hardships and not falter? Claus Schmidt could have reacted very differently. We've all seen that happen: One person cannot seem to get the confidence back after a layoff; another, persistently depressed, takes a few years off from life after her divorce. The question we would all like answered is, Why? What exactly is that quality of resilience that carries people through life?

It's a question that has fascinated me ever since I first learned of the Holocaust survivors in elementary school. In college, and later in my studies as an affiliate scholar at the Boston Psychoanalytic Society and Institute, I returned to the subject. For the past several months, however, I have looked on it with a new urgency, for it seems to me that the terrorism, war, and recession of recent months have made understanding resilience more important than ever. I have considered both the nature of individual resilience and what makes some organizations as a whole more resilient than others. Why do some people and some companies buckle under pressure? And what makes others bend and ultimately bounce back?

My exploration has taught me much about resilience, although it's a subject none of us will ever understand fully. Indeed, resilience is one of the great puzzles of human nature, like creativity or the religious instinct. But in sifting through psychological research and in reflecting on the many stories of resilience I've heard, I have seen a little more deeply into the hearts and minds of people like Claus Schmidt and, in doing so, looked more deeply into the human psyche as well.

The Buzz About Resilience

Resilience is a hot topic in business these days. Not long ago, I was talking to a senior partner at a respected consulting firm about how to land the very best MBAs—the name of the game in that particular industry. The partner, Daniel Savageau (not his real name), ticked off a long list of qualities his firm sought in its hires: intelligence, ambition, integrity, analytic ability, and so on. "What about resilience?" I asked. "Well, that's very popular right now," he said. "It's the new buzzword. Candidates even tell us they're resilient; they volunteer the information. But frankly, they're just too young to know that about themselves. Resilience is something you realize you have *after* the fact."

Idea in Brief

These are dark days: people are losing jobs, taking pay cuts, suffering foreclosure on their homes. Some of them are snapping—sinking into depression or suffering a permanent loss of confidence.

But others are snapping back; for example, taking advantage of a layoff to build a new career. What carries them through tough times? Resilience.

Resilient people possess three defining characteristics: They coolly accept the harsh realities facing them. They find meaning in terrible times. And they have an uncanny ability to improvise, making do with whatever's at hand.

In deep recessions, resilience becomes more important than ever. Fortunately, you can learn to be resilient.

"But if you could, would you test for it?" I asked. "Does it matter in business?"

Savageau paused. He's a man in his late forties and a success personally and professionally. Yet it hadn't been a smooth ride to the top. He'd started his life as a poor French Canadian in Woonsocket, Rhode Island, and had lost his father at six. He lucked into a football scholarship but was kicked out of Boston University twice for drinking. He turned his life around in his twenties, married, divorced, remarried, and raised five children. Along the way, he made and lost two fortunes before helping to found the consulting firm he now runs. "Yes, it does matter," he said at last. "In fact, it probably matters more than any of the usual things we look for." In the course of reporting this article, I heard the same assertion time and again. As Dean Becker, the president and CEO of Adaptiv Learning Systems, a four-year-old company in King of Prussia, Pennsylvania, that develops and delivers programs about resilience training, puts it: "More than education, more than experience, more than training, a person's level of resilience will determine who succeeds and who fails. That's true in the cancer ward, it's true in the Olympics, and it's true in the boardroom."

Academic research into resilience started about 40 years ago with pioneering studies by Norman Garmezy, now a professor emeritus at the University of Minnesota in Minneapolis. After studying why

Idea in Practice

Resilience can help you survive and recover from even the most brutal experiences. To cultivate resilience, apply these practices.

Face Down Reality

Instead of slipping into denial to cope with hardship, take a sober, down-to-earth view of the reality of your situation. You'll prepare yourself to act in ways that enable you to endure—training yourself to survive before the fact.

> **Example:** Admiral Jim Stockdale survived being held prisoner and tortured by the Vietcong in part by accepting he could be held for a long time. (He was held for eight years.) Those who didn't make it out of the camps kept optimistically assuming they'd be released on shorter timetables—by Christmas, by Easter, by the Fourth of July. "I think they all died of broken hearts," Stockdale said.

Search for Meaning

When hard times strike, resist any impulse to view yourself as a victim and to cry, "Why me?" Rather, devise constructs about your suffering to create meaning for yourself and others. You'll build bridges from your present-day ordeal to a fuller, better future. Those bridges will make the present manageable, by removing the sense that the present is overwhelming.

> **Example:** Austrian psychiatrist and Auschwitz survivor Victor Frankl realized that to survive

many children of schizophrenic parents did not suffer psychological illness as a result of growing up with them, he concluded that a certain quality of resilience played a greater role in mental health than anyone had previously suspected.

Today, theories abound about what makes resilience. Looking at Holocaust victims, Maurice Vanderpol, a former president of the Boston Psychoanalytic Society and Institute, found that many of the healthy survivors of concentration camps had what he calls a "plastic shield." The shield was comprised of several factors, including a sense of humor. Often the humor was black, but nonetheless it provided a critical sense of perspective. Other core characteristics that helped included the ability to form attachments to others and the possession of an inner psychological space that protected the survivors from the intrusions of abusive others. Research about other

the camp, he had to find some purpose. He did so by imagining himself giving a lecture after the war on the psychology of the concentration camp to help outsiders understand what he had been through. By creating concrete goals for himself, he rose above the sufferings of the moment.

Continually Improvise

When disaster hits, be inventive. Make the most of what you have, putting resources to unfamiliar uses and imagining possibilities others don't see.

Example: Mike founded a business with his friend Paul, selling educational materials to schools, businesses, and consulting firms. When a recession hit, they lost many core clients. Paul went through a bitter divorce, suffered a depression, and couldn't work. When Mike offered to buy him out, Paul slapped him with a lawsuit claiming Mike was trying to steal the business.

Mike kept the company going any way he could—going into joint ventures to sell English-language training materials to Russian and Chinese competitors, publishing newsletters for clients, and even writing video scripts for competitors. The lawsuit was eventually settled in his favor, and he had a new and much more solid business than the one he started out with.

groups uncovered different qualities associated with resilience. The Search Institute, a Minneapolis-based nonprofit organization that focuses on resilience and youth, found that the more resilient kids have an uncanny ability to get adults to help them out. Still other research showed that resilient inner-city youth often have talents such as athletic abilities that attract others to them.

Many of the early theories about resilience stressed the role of genetics. Some people are just born resilient, so the arguments went. There's some truth to that, of course, but an increasing body of empirical evidence shows that resilience—whether in children, survivors of concentration camps, or businesses back from the brink—can be learned. For example, George Vaillant, the director of the Study of Adult Development at Harvard Medical School in Boston, observes that within various groups studied during a 60-year period, some people became markedly more resilient over their lifetimes. Other psychologists claim that unresilient people more easily develop resiliency skills than those with head starts.

Most of the resilience theories I encountered in my research make good common sense. But I also observed that almost all the theories overlap in three ways. Resilient people, they posit, possess three characteristics: a staunch acceptance of reality; a deep belief, often buttressed by strongly held values, that life is meaningful; and an uncanny ability to improvise. You can bounce back from hardship with just one or two of these qualities, but you will only be truly resilient with all three. These three characteristics hold true for resilient organizations as well. Let's take a look at each of them in turn.

Facing Down Reality

A common belief about resilience is that it stems from an optimistic nature. That's true but only as long as such optimism doesn't distort your sense of reality. In extremely adverse situations, rose-colored thinking can actually spell disaster. This point was made poignantly to me by management researcher and writer Jim Collins, who happened upon this concept while researching *Good to Great*, his book on how companies transform themselves out of mediocrity. Collins had a hunch (an exactly wrong hunch) that resilient companies were filled with optimistic people. He tried out that idea on Admiral Jim Stockdale, who was held prisoner and tortured by the Vietcong for eight years.

Collins recalls: "I asked Stockdale: 'Who didn't make it out of the camps?' And he said, 'Oh, that's easy. It was the optimists. They were the ones who said we were going to be out by Christmas. And then they said we'd be out by Easter and then out by Fourth of July and out by Thanksgiving, and then it was Christmas again.' Then Stockdale turned to me and said, 'You know, I think they all died of broken hearts.'"

In the business world, Collins found the same unblinking attitude shared by executives at all the most successful companies he studied.

Like Stockdale, resilient people have very sober and down-to-earth views of those parts of reality that matter for survival. That's not to say that optimism doesn't have its place: In turning around a demoralized sales force, for instance, conjuring a sense of possibility can be a very powerful tool. But for bigger challenges, a cool, almost pessimistic, sense of reality is far more important.

Perhaps you're asking yourself, "Do I truly understand—and accept—the reality of my situation? Does my organization?" Those are good questions, particularly because research suggests most people slip into denial as a coping mechanism. Facing reality, really facing it, is grueling work. Indeed, it can be unpleasant and often emotionally wrenching. Consider the following story of organizational resilience, and see what it means to confront reality.

Prior to September 11, 2001, Morgan Stanley, the famous investment bank, was the largest tenant in the World Trade Center. The company had some 2,700 employees working in the south tower on 22 floors between the 43rd and the 74th. On that horrible day, the first plane hit the north tower at 8:46 AM, and Morgan Stanley started evacuating just one minute later, at 8:47 AM. When the second plane crashed into the south tower 15 minutes after that, Morgan Stanley's offices were largely empty. All told, the company lost only seven employees despite receiving an almost direct hit.

Of course, the organization was just plain lucky to be in the second tower. Cantor Fitzgerald, whose offices were hit in the first attack, couldn't have done anything to save its employees. Still, it was Morgan Stanley's hard-nosed realism that enabled the company to benefit from its luck. Soon after the 1993 attack on the World Trade Center, senior management recognized that working in such a symbolic center of U.S. commercial power made the company vulnerable to attention from terrorists and possible attack.

With this grim realization, Morgan Stanley launched a program of preparedness at the micro level. Few companies take their fire drills seriously. Not so Morgan Stanley, whose VP of security for the Individual Investor Group, Rick Rescorla, brought a military discipline to the job. Rescorla, himself a highly resilient, decorated Vietnam vet, made sure that people were fully drilled about what to do in a catastrophe. When disaster struck on September 11, Rescorla was on a bullhorn telling Morgan Stanley employees to stay calm and follow their well-practiced drill, even though some building supervisors were telling occupants that all was well. Sadly, Rescorla himself, whose life story has been widely covered in recent months, was one of the seven who didn't make it out.

"When you're in financial services where so much depends on technology, contingency planning is a major part of your business," says President and COO Robert G. Scott. But Morgan Stanley was prepared for the very toughest reality. It had not just one, but three, recovery sites where employees could congregate and business could take place if work locales were ever disrupted. "Multiple backup sites seemed like an incredible extravagance on September 10," concedes Scott. "But on September 12, they seemed like genius."

Maybe it was genius; it was undoubtedly resilience at work. The fact is, when we truly stare down reality, we prepare ourselves to act in ways that allow us to endure and survive extraordinary hardship. We train ourselves how to survive before the fact.

The Search for Meaning

The ability to see reality is closely linked to the second building block of resilience, the propensity to make meaning of terrible times. We all know people who, under duress, throw up their hands and cry, "How can this be happening to me?" Such people see themselves as victims, and living through hardship carries no lessons for them. But resilient people devise constructs about their suffering to create some sort of meaning for themselves and others.

I have a friend I'll call Jackie Oiseaux who suffered repeated psychoses over a ten-year period due to an undiagnosed bipolar disorder. Today, she holds down a big job in one of the top publishing companies in the country, has a family, and is a prominent member of her church community. When people ask her how she bounced back from her crises, she runs her hands through her hair. "People sometimes say, 'Why me?' But I've always said, 'Why *not* me?' True, I lost many things during my illness," she says, "but I found many more—incredible friends who saw me through the bleakest times and who will give meaning to my life forever."

This dynamic of meaning making is, most researchers agree, the way resilient people build bridges from present-day hardships to a fuller, better constructed future. Those bridges make the present manageable, for lack of a better word, removing the sense that the present is overwhelming. This concept was beautifully articulated by Viktor E. Frankl, an Austrian psychiatrist and an Auschwitz survivor. In the midst of staggering suffering, Frankl invented "meaning therapy," a humanistic therapy technique that helps individuals make the kinds of decisions that will create significance in their lives.

In his book *Man's Search for Meaning*, Frankl described the pivotal moment in the camp when he developed meaning therapy. He was on his way to work one day, worrying whether he should trade his last cigarette for a bowl of soup. He wondered how he was going to work with a new foreman whom he knew to be particularly sadistic. Suddenly, he was disgusted by just how trivial and meaningless his life had become. He realized that to survive, he had to find some purpose. Frankl did so by imagining himself giving a lecture after the war on the psychology of the concentration camp, to help outsiders understand what he had been through. Although he wasn't even sure he would survive, Frankl created some concrete goals for himself. In doing so, he succeeded in rising above the sufferings of the moment. As he put it in his book: "We must never forget that we may also find meaning in life even when confronted with a hopeless situation, when facing a fate that cannot be changed."

Frankl's theory underlies most resilience coaching in business. Indeed, I was struck by how often businesspeople referred to his work. "Resilience training—what we call hardiness—is a way for us to help people construct meaning in their everyday lives," explains Salvatore R. Maddi, a University of California, Irvine psychology professor and the director of the Hardiness Institute in Newport Beach, California. "When people realize the power of resilience training, they often say, 'Doc, is this what psychotherapy is?' But psychotherapy is for people whose lives have fallen apart badly and need repair. We see our work as showing people life skills and attitudes. Maybe

55

those things should be taught at home, maybe they should be taught in schools, but they're not. So we end up doing it in business."

Yet the challenge confronting resilience trainers is often more difficult than we might imagine. Meaning can be elusive, and just because you found it once doesn't mean you'll keep it or find it again. Consider Aleksandr Solzhenitsyn, who survived the war against the Nazis, imprisonment in the gulag, and cancer. Yet when he moved to a farm in peaceful, safe Vermont, he could not cope with the "infantile West." He was unable to discern any real meaning in what he felt to be the destructive and irresponsible freedom of the West. Upset by his critics, he withdrew into his farmhouse, behind a locked fence, seldom to be seen in public. In 1994, a bitter man, Solzhenitsyn moved back to Russia.

Since finding meaning in one's environment is such an important aspect of resilience, it should come as no surprise that the most successful organizations and people possess strong value systems. Strong values infuse an environment with meaning because they offer ways to interpret and shape events. While it's popular these days to ridicule values, it's surely no coincidence that the most resilient organization in the world has been the Catholic Church, which has survived wars, corruption, and schism for more than 2,000 years, thanks largely to its immutable set of values. Businesses that survive also have their creeds, which give them purposes beyond just making money. Strikingly, many companies describe their value systems in religious terms. Pharmaceutical giant Johnson & Johnson, for instance, calls its value system, set out in a document given to every new employee at orientation, the Credo. Parcel company UPS talks constantly about its Noble Purpose.

Value systems at resilient companies change very little over the years and are used as scaffolding in times of trouble. UPS Chairman and CEO Mike Eskew believes that the Noble Purpose helped the company to rally after the agonizing strike in 1997. Says Eskew: "It was a hugely difficult time, like a family feud. Everyone had close friends on both sides of the fence, and it was tough for us to pick sides. But what saved us was our Noble Purpose. Whatever side people were on, they all shared a common set of values. Those values are core to us and never change; they frame most of our important decisions. Our strategy and our mission may change, but our values never do."

The religious connotations of words like "credo," "values," and "noble purpose," however, should not be confused with the actual content of the values. Companies can hold ethically questionable values and still be very resilient. Consider Phillip Morris, which has demonstrated impressive resilience in the face of increasing unpopularity. As Jim Collins points out, Phillip Morris has very strong values, although we might not agree with them—for instance, the value of "adult choice." But there's no doubt that Phillip Morris executives believe strongly in its values, and the strength of their beliefs sets the company apart from most of the other tobacco companies. In this context, it is worth noting that resilience is neither ethically good nor bad. It is merely the skill and the capacity to be robust under conditions of enormous stress and change. As Viktor Frankl wrote: "On the average, only those prisoners could keep alive who, after years of trekking from camp to camp, had lost all scruples in their fight for existence; they were prepared to use every means, honest and otherwise, even brutal . . ., in order to save themselves. We who have come back . . . we know: The best of us did not return."

Values, positive or negative, are actually more important for organizational resilience than having resilient people on the payroll. If resilient employees are all interpreting reality in different ways, their decisions and actions may well conflict, calling into doubt the survival of their organization. And as the weakness of an organization becomes apparent, highly resilient individuals are more likely to jettison the organization than to imperil their own survival.

Ritualized Ingenuity

The third building block of resilience is the ability to make do with whatever is at hand. Psychologists follow the lead of French anthropologist Claude Levi-Strauss in calling this skill bricolage.[1] Intriguingly, the roots of that word are closely tied to the concept of resilience, which literally means "bouncing back." Says Levi-Strauss: "In its old sense, the verb *bricoler* . . . was always used with reference to some extraneous movement: a ball rebounding, a dog straying, or a horse swerving from its direct course to avoid an obstacle."

Bricolage in the modern sense can be defined as a kind of inventiveness, an ability to improvise a solution to a problem without proper or obvious tools or materials. *Bricoleurs* are always tinkering—building radios from household effects or fixing their own cars. They make the most of what they have, putting objects to unfamiliar uses. In the concentration camps, for example, resilient inmates knew to pocket pieces of string or wire whenever they found them. The string or wire might later become useful—to fix a pair of shoes, perhaps, which in freezing conditions might make the difference between life and death.

When situations unravel, bricoleurs muddle through, imagining possibilities where others are confounded. I have two friends, whom I'll call Paul Shields and Mike Andrews, who were roommates throughout their college years. To no one's surprise, when they graduated, they set up a business together, selling educational materials to schools, businesses, and consulting firms. At first, the company was a great success, making both founders paper millionaires. But the recession of the early 1990s hit the company hard, and many core clients fell away. At the same time, Paul experienced a bitter divorce and a depression that made it impossible for him to work. Mike offered to buy Paul out but was instead slapped with a lawsuit claiming that Mike was trying to steal the business. At this point, a less resilient person might have just walked away from the mess. Not Mike. As the case wound through the courts, he kept the company going any way he could—constantly morphing the business until he found a model that worked: going into joint ventures to sell English-language training materials to Russian and Chinese companies. Later, he branched off into publishing newsletters for clients. At one point, he was even writing video scripts for his competitors. Thanks to all this bricolage, by the time the lawsuit was settled in his favor, Mike had an entirely different, and much more solid, business than the one he had started with.

Bricolage can be practiced on a higher level as well. Richard Feynman, winner of the 1965 Nobel Prize in physics, exemplified what I like to think of as intellectual bricolage. Out of pure curiosity,

Feynman made himself an expert on cracking safes, not only looking at the mechanics of safecracking but also cobbling together psychological insights about people who used safes and set the locks. He cracked many of the safes at Los Alamos, for instance, because he guessed that theoretical physicists would not set the locks with random code numbers they might forget but would instead use a sequence with mathematical significance. It turned out that the three safes containing all the secrets to the atomic bomb were set to the same mathematical constant, e, whose first six digits are 2.71828.

Resilient organizations are stuffed with bricoleurs, though not all of them, of course, are Richard Feynmans. Indeed, companies that survive regard improvisation as a core skill. Consider UPS, which empowers its drivers to do whatever it takes to deliver packages on time. Says CEO Eskew: "We tell our employees to get the job done. If that means they need to improvise, they improvise. Otherwise we just couldn't do what we do every day. Just think what can go wrong: a busted traffic light, a flat tire, a bridge washed out. If a snowstorm hits Louisville tonight, a group of people will sit together and discuss how to handle the problem. Nobody tells them to do that. They come together because it's our tradition to do so."

That tradition meant that the company was delivering parcels in southeast Florida just one day after Hurricane Andrew devastated the region in 1992, causing billions of dollars in damage. Many people were living in their cars because their homes had been destroyed, yet UPS drivers and managers sorted packages at a diversion site and made deliveries even to those who were stranded in their cars. It was largely UPS's improvisational skills that enabled it to keep functioning after the catastrophic hit. And the fact that the company continued on gave others a sense of purpose or meaning amid the chaos.

Improvisation of the sort practiced by UPS, however, is a far cry from unbridled creativity. Indeed, much like the military, UPS lives on rules and regulations. As Eskew says: "Drivers always put their keys in the same place. They close the doors the same way. They wear their uniforms the same way. We are a company of precision." He believes that although they may seem stifling, UPS's rules were what allowed the company to bounce back immediately after Hurricane

Andrew, for they enabled people to focus on the one or two fixes they needed to make in order to keep going.

Eskew's opinion is echoed by Karl E. Weick, a professor of organizational behavior at the University of Michigan Business School in Ann Arbor and one of the most respected thinkers on organizational psychology. "There is good evidence that when people are put under pressure, they regress to their most habituated ways of responding," Weick has written. "What we do not expect under life-threatening pressure is creativity." In other words, the rules and regulations that make some companies appear less creative may actually make them more resilient in times of real turbulence.

Claus Schmidt, the newsman I mentioned earlier, died about five years ago, but I'm not sure I could have interviewed him about his own resilience even if he were alive. It would have felt strange, I think, to ask him, "Claus, did you really face down reality? Did you make meaning out of your hardships? Did you improvise your recovery after each professional and personal disaster?" He may not have been able to answer. In my experience, resilient people don't often describe themselves that way. They shrug off their survival stories and very often assign them to luck.

Obviously, luck does have a lot to do with surviving. It was luck that Morgan Stanley was situated in the south tower and could put its preparedness training to work. But being lucky is not the same as being resilient. Resilience is a reflex, a way of facing and understanding the world, that is deeply etched into a person's mind and soul. Resilient people and companies face reality with staunchness, make meaning of hardship instead of crying out in despair, and improvise solutions from thin air. Others do not. This is the nature of resilience, and we will never completely understand it.

Originally published in May 2002. Reprint R0205B

Note

1. See, e.g., Karl E. Weick, "The Collapse of Sense-making in Organizations: The Mann Gulch Disaster," *Administrative Science Quarterly*, December 1993.

Manage Your Energy, Not Your Time

by Tony Schwartz and Catherine McCarthy

STEVE WANNER IS A HIGHLY respected 37-year-old partner at Ernst & Young, married with four young children. When we met him a year ago, he was working 12- to 14-hour days, felt perpetually exhausted, and found it difficult to fully engage with his family in the evenings, which left him feeling guilty and dissatisfied. He slept poorly, made no time to exercise, and seldom ate healthy meals, instead grabbing a bite to eat on the run or while working at his desk.

Wanner's experience is not uncommon. Most of us respond to rising demands in the workplace by putting in longer hours, which inevitably take a toll on us physically, mentally, and emotionally. That leads to declining levels of engagement, increasing levels of distraction, high turnover rates, and soaring medical costs among employees. We at the Energy Project have worked with thousands of leaders and managers in the course of doing consulting and coaching at large organizations during the past five years. With remarkable consistency, these executives tell us they're pushing themselves harder than ever to keep up and increasingly feel they are at a breaking point.

The core problem with working longer hours is that time is a finite resource. Energy is a different story. Defined in physics as the capacity to work, energy comes from four main wellsprings in human beings: the body, emotions, mind, and spirit. In each, energy can be systematically expanded and regularly renewed by establishing specific rituals—behaviors that are intentionally practiced and precisely scheduled, with the goal of making them unconscious and automatic as quickly as possible.

To effectively reenergize their workforces, organizations need to shift their emphasis from getting more out of people to investing more in them, so they are motivated—and able—to bring more of themselves to work every day. To recharge themselves, individuals need to recognize the costs of energy-depleting behaviors and then take responsibility for changing them, regardless of the circumstances they're facing.

The rituals and behaviors Wanner established to better manage his energy transformed his life. He set an earlier bedtime and gave up drinking, which had disrupted his sleep. As a consequence, when he woke up he felt more rested and more motivated to exercise, which he now does almost every morning. In less than two months he lost 15 pounds. After working out he now sits down with his family for breakfast. Wanner still puts in long hours on the job, but he renews himself regularly along the way. He leaves his desk for lunch and usually takes a morning and an afternoon walk outside. When he arrives at home in the evening, he's more relaxed and better able to connect with his wife and children.

Establishing simple rituals like these can lead to striking results across organizations. At Wachovia Bank, we took a group of employees through a pilot energy management program and then measured their performance against that of a control group. The participants outperformed the controls on a series of financial metrics, such as the value of loans they generated. They also reported substantial improvements in their customer relationships, their engagement with work, and their personal satisfaction. In this article, we'll describe the Wachovia study in a little more detail. Then we'll explain what executives and managers can do to increase and regularly renew work capacity—the approach used by the Energy Project, which builds on, deepens, and extends several core concepts developed by Tony's former partner Jim Loehr in his seminal work with athletes.

Idea in Brief

Organizations are demanding ever-higher performance from their workforces. People are trying to comply, but the usual method—putting in longer hours—has backfired. They're getting exhausted, disengaged, and sick. And they're defecting to healthier job environments.

Longer days at the office don't work because time is a limited resource. But personal energy is renewable, say Schwartz and McCarthy. By fostering deceptively simple **rituals** that help employees regularly replenish their energy, organizations build workers' physical, emotional, and mental

resilience. These rituals include taking brief breaks at specific intervals, expressing appreciation to others, reducing interruptions, and spending more time on activities people do best and enjoy most.

Help your employees systematically rejuvenate their personal energy, and the benefits go straight to your bottom line. Take Wachovia Bank: Participants in an energy renewal program produced 13 percentage points greater year-over-year in revenues from loans than a control group did. And they exceeded the control group's gains in revenues from deposits by 20 percentage points.

Linking Capacity and Performance at Wachovia

Most large organizations invest in developing employees' skills, knowledge, and competence. Very few help build and sustain their capacity—their energy—which is typically taken for granted. In fact, greater capacity makes it possible to get more done in less time at a higher level of engagement and with more sustainability. Our experience at Wachovia bore this out.

In early 2006 we took 106 employees at 12 regional banks in southern New Jersey through a curriculum of four modules, each of which focused on specific strategies for strengthening one of the four main dimensions of energy. We delivered it at one-month intervals to groups of approximately 20 to 25, ranging from senior leaders to lower-level managers. We also assigned each attendee a fellow employee as a source of support between sessions. Using Wachovia's own key performance metrics, we evaluated how the participant group performed compared with a group of employees at similar levels at a nearby set of Wachovia banks who did not go through the

Idea in Practice

Schwartz and McCarthy recommend these practices for renewing four dimensions of personal energy.

Physical Energy

- Enhance your sleep by setting an earlier bedtime and reducing alcohol use.

- Reduce stress by engaging in cardiovascular activity at least three times a week and strength training at least once.

- Eat small meals and light snacks every three hours.

- Learn to notice signs of imminent energy flagging, including restlessness, yawning, hunger, and difficulty concentrating.

- Take brief but regular breaks, away from your desk, at 90- to 120-minute intervals throughout the day.

Emotional Energy

- Defuse negative emotions— irritability, impatience, anxiety, insecurity—through deep abdominal breathing.

- Fuel positive emotions in yourself and others by regularly expressing appreciation to others in detailed, specific terms through notes, e-mails, calls, or conversations.

- Look at upsetting situations through new lenses. Adopt a "reverse lens" to ask, "What would the other person in this conflict say, and how might he be right?" Use a "long lens" to ask, "How will I likely view this situation in six months?" Employ a "wide lens" to ask, "How can I grow and learn from this situation?"

Mental Energy

- Reduce interruptions by performing high-concentration tasks away from phones and e-mail.

- Respond to voice mails and e-mails at designated times during the day.

training. To create a credible basis for comparison, we looked at year-over-year percentage changes in performance across several metrics.

On a measure called the "Big 3"—revenues from three kinds of loans—the participants showed a year-over-year increase that was 13 percentage points greater than the control group's in the first three months of our study. On revenues from deposits, the participants exceeded the control group's year-over-year gain by 20 percentage points during that same period. The precise gains varied month by month, but with only a handful of exceptions, the participants

- Every night, identify the most important challenge for the next day. Then make it your first priority when you arrive at work in the morning.

Spiritual Energy

- Identify your "sweet spot" activities—those that give you feelings of effectiveness, effortless absorption, and fulfillment. Find ways to do more of these. One executive who hated doing sales reports delegated them to someone who loved that activity.

- Allocate time and energy to what you consider most important. For example, spend the last 20 minutes of your evening commute relaxing, so you can connect with your family once you're home.

- Live your core values. For instance, if consideration is important to you but you're

perpetually late for meetings, practice intentionally showing up five minutes early for meetings.

How Companies Can Help

To support energy renewal rituals in your firm:

- Build "renewal rooms" where people can go to relax and re-fuel.

- Subsidize gym memberships.

- Encourage managers to gather employees for midday workouts.

- Suggest that people stop checking e-mails during meetings.

continued to significantly outperform the control group for a full year after completing the program. Although other variables undoubtedly influenced these outcomes, the participants' superior performance was notable in its consistency. (See the exhibit "How Energy Renewal Programs Boosted Productivity at Wachovia.")

We also asked participants how the program influenced them personally. Sixty-eight percent reported that it had a positive impact on their relationships with clients and customers. Seventy-one percent said that it had a noticeable or substantial positive impact on their

---

How energy renewal programs boosted productivity at Wachovia

At Wachovia Bank, employees participating in an energy renewal program outperformed a control group of employees, demonstrating significantly greater improvements in year-over-year performance during the first quarter of 2006.

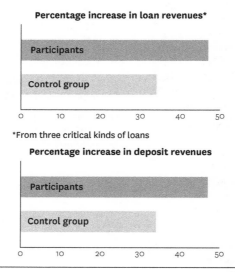

Percentage increase in loan revenues*

*From three critical kinds of loans

Percentage increase in deposit revenues

---

productivity and performance. These findings corroborated a raft of anecdotal evidence we've gathered about the effectiveness of this approach among leaders at other large companies such as Ernst & Young, Sony, Deutsche Bank, Nokia, ING Direct, Ford, and MasterCard.

The Body: Physical Energy

Our program begins by focusing on physical energy. It is scarcely news that inadequate nutrition, exercise, sleep, and rest diminish people's basic energy levels, as well as their ability to manage their emotions and focus their attention. Nonetheless, many executives don't find ways to practice consistently healthy behaviors, given all the other demands in their lives.

Before participants in our program begin to explore ways to increase their physical energy, they take an energy audit, which includes four questions in each energy dimension—body, emotions, mind, and spirit. (See the exhibit "Are You Headed for an Energy Crisis?") On average, participants get eight to ten of those 16 questions "wrong," meaning they're doing things such as skipping breakfast, failing to express appreciation to others, struggling to focus on one thing at a time, or spending too little time on activities that give them a sense of purpose. While most participants aren't surprised to learn these behaviors are counterproductive, having them all listed in one place is often uncomfortable, sobering, and galvanizing. The audit highlights employees' greatest energy deficits. Participants also fill out charts designed to raise their awareness about how their exercise, diet, and sleep practices influence their energy levels.

The next step is to identify rituals for building and renewing physical energy. When Gary Faro, a vice president at Wachovia, began the program, he was significantly overweight, ate poorly, lacked a regular exercise routine, worked long hours, and typically slept no more than five or six hours a night. That is not an unusual profile among the leaders and managers we see. Over the course of the program, Faro began regular cardiovascular and strength training. He started going to bed at a designated time and sleeping longer. He changed his eating habits from two big meals a day ("Where I usually gorged myself," he says) to smaller meals and light snacks every three hours. The aim was to help him stabilize his glucose levels over the course of the day, avoiding peaks and valleys. He lost 50 pounds in the process, and his energy levels soared. "I used to schedule tough projects for the morning, when I knew that I would be more focused," Faro says. "I don't have to do that anymore because I find that I'm just as focused now at 5 PM as I am at 8 AM."

Another key ritual Faro adopted was to take brief but regular breaks at specific intervals throughout the workday—always leaving his desk. The value of such breaks is grounded in our physiology.

Are you headed for an energy crisis?

Please check the statements below that are true for you.

Body

☐ I don't regularly get at least seven to eight hours of sleep, and I often wake up feeling tired.

☐ I frequently skip breakfast, or I settle for something that isn't nutritious.

☐ I don't work out enough (meaning cardiovascular training at least three times a week and strength training at least once a week).

☐ I don't take regular breaks during the day to truly renew and recharge, or I often eat lunch at my desk, if I eat it at all.

Emotions

☐ I frequently find myself feeling irritable, impatient, or anxious at work, especially when work is demanding.

☐ I don't have enough time with my family and loved ones, and when I'm with them, I'm not always really with them.

☐ I have too little time for the activities that I most deeply enjoy.

☐ I don't stop frequently enough to express my appreciation to others or to savor my accomplishments and blessings.

Mind

☐ I have difficulty focusing on one thing at a time, and I am easily distracted during the day, especially by e-mail.

☐ I spend much of my day reacting to immediate crises and demands rather than focusing on activities with longer-term value and high leverage.

☐ I don't take enough time for reflection, strategizing, and creative thinking.

☐ I work in the evenings or on weekends, and I almost never take an e-mail–free vacation.

Spirit

☐ I don't spend enough time at work doing what I do best and enjoy most.

☐ There are significant gaps between what I say is most important to me in my life and how I actually allocate my time and energy.

☐ My decisions at work are more often influenced by external demands than by a strong, clear sense of my own purpose.

☐ I don't invest enough time and energy in making a positive difference to others or to the world.

How is your overall energy?

Total number of statements checked: __

Guide to scores

0–3: Excellent energy management skills
4–6: Reasonable energy management skills

(continued)

7–10: Significant energy management deficits
11–16: A full-fledged energy management crisis

What do you need to work on?

Number of checks in each category:
Body __
Mind __
Emotions __
Spirit __

Guide to category scores

0: Excellent energy management skills
1: Strong energy management skills
2: Significant deficits
3: Poor energy management skills
4: A full-fledged energy crisis

"Ultradian rhythms" refer to 90- to 120-minute cycles during which our bodies slowly move from a high-energy state into a physiological trough. Toward the end of each cycle, the body begins to crave a period of recovery. The signals include physical restlessness, yawning, hunger, and difficulty concentrating, but many of us ignore them and keep working. The consequence is that our energy reservoir—our remaining capacity—burns down as the day wears on.

Intermittent breaks for renewal, we have found, result in higher and more sustainable performance. The length of renewal is less important than the quality. It is possible to get a great deal of recovery in a short time—as little as several minutes—if it involves a ritual that allows you to disengage from work and truly change channels. That could range from getting up to talk to a colleague about something other than work, to listening to music on an iPod, to walking up and down stairs in an office building. While breaks are countercultural in most organizations and counterintuitive for many high achievers, their value is multifaceted.

Matthew Lang is a managing director for Sony in South Africa. He adopted some of the same rituals that Faro did, including a

20-minute walk in the afternoons. Lang's walk not only gives him a mental and emotional breather and some exercise but also has become the time when he gets his best creative ideas. That's because when he walks he is not actively thinking, which allows the dominant left hemisphere of his brain to give way to the right hemisphere with its greater capacity to see the big picture and make imaginative leaps.

The Emotions: Quality of Energy

When people are able to take more control of their emotions, they can improve the quality of their energy, regardless of the external pressures they're facing. To do this, they first must become more aware of how they feel at various points during the workday and of the impact these emotions have on their effectiveness. Most people realize that they tend to perform best when they're feeling positive energy. What they find surprising is that they're not able to perform well or to lead effectively when they're feeling any other way.

Unfortunately, without intermittent recovery, we're not physiologically capable of sustaining highly positive emotions for long periods. Confronted with relentless demands and unexpected challenges, people tend to slip into negative emotions—the fight-or-flight mode—often multiple times in a day. They become irritable and impatient, or anxious and insecure. Such states of mind drain people's energy and cause friction in their relationships. Fight-or-flight emotions also make it impossible to think clearly, logically, and reflectively. When executives learn to recognize what kinds of events trigger their negative emotions, they gain greater capacity to take control of their reactions.

One simple but powerful ritual for defusing negative emotions is what we call "buying time." Deep abdominal breathing is one way to do that. Exhaling slowly for five or six seconds induces relaxation and recovery, and turns off the fight-or-flight response. When we began working with Fujio Nishida, president of Sony Europe, he had a habit of lighting up a cigarette each time something especially stressful occurred—at least two or three times a day. Otherwise, he didn't smoke. We taught him the breathing exercise as an alternative, and it worked immediately: Nishida found he no longer had the desire for a cigarette. It wasn't the smoking that had given him relief from the stress, we concluded, but the relaxation prompted by the deep inhalation and exhalation.

A powerful ritual that fuels positive emotions is expressing appreciation to others, a practice that seems to be as beneficial to the giver as to the receiver. It can take the form of a handwritten note, an e-mail, a call, or a conversation—and the more detailed and specific, the higher the impact. As with all rituals, setting aside a particular time to do it vastly increases the chances of success. Ben Jenkins, vice chairman and president of the General Bank at Wachovia in Charlotte, North Carolina, built his appreciation ritual into time set aside for mentoring. He began scheduling lunches or dinners regularly with people who worked for him. Previously, the only sit-downs he'd had with his direct reports were to hear monthly reports on their numbers or to give them yearly performance reviews. Now, over meals, he makes it a priority to recognize their accomplishments and also to talk with them about their lives and their aspirations rather than their immediate work responsibilities.

Finally, people can cultivate positive emotions by learning to change the stories they tell themselves about the events in their lives. Often, people in conflict cast themselves in the role of victim, blaming others or external circumstances for their problems. Becoming aware of the difference between the facts in a given situation and the way we interpret those facts can be powerful in itself. It's been a revelation for many of the people we work with to discover they have a choice about how to view a given event and to recognize how powerfully the story they tell influences the emotions they feel. We teach them to tell the most hopeful and personally empowering story possible in any given situation, without denying or minimizing the facts.

The most effective way people can change a story is to view it through any of three new lenses, which are all alternatives to seeing the world from the victim perspective. With the *reverse lens*, for example, people ask themselves, "What would the other person in this conflict say and in what ways might that be true?" With the *long lens* they ask, "How will I most likely view this situation in six months?"

With the *wide lens* they ask themselves, "Regardless of the outcome of this issue, how can I grow and learn from it?" Each of these lenses can help people intentionally cultivate more positive emotions.

Nicolas Babin, director of corporate communications for Sony Europe, was the point person for calls from reporters when Sony went through several recalls of its batteries in 2006. Over time he found his work increasingly exhausting and dispiriting. After practicing the lens exercises, he began finding ways to tell himself a more positive and empowering story about his role. "I realized," he explains, "that this was an opportunity for me to build stronger relationships with journalists by being accessible to them and to increase Sony's credibility by being straightforward and honest."

The Mind: Focus of Energy

Many executives view multitasking as a necessity in the face of all the demands they juggle, but it actually undermines productivity. Distractions are costly: A temporary shift in attention from one task to another—stopping to answer an e-mail or take a phone call, for instance—increases the amount of time necessary to finish the primary task by as much as 25%, a phenomenon known as "switching time." It's far more efficient to fully focus for 90 to 120 minutes, take a true break, and then fully focus on the next activity. We refer to these work periods as "ultradian sprints."

Once people see how much they struggle to concentrate, they can create rituals to reduce the relentless interruptions that technology has introduced in their lives. We start out with an exercise that forces them to face the impact of daily distractions. They attempt to complete a complex task and are regularly interrupted—an experience that, people report, ends up feeling much like everyday life.

Dan Cluna, a vice president at Wachovia, designed two rituals to better focus his attention. The first one is to leave his desk and go into a conference room, away from phones and e-mail, whenever he has a task that requires concentration. He now finishes reports in a third of the time they used to require. Cluna built his second ritual around meetings at branches with the financial specialists who report to him. Previously, he would answer his phone whenever it rang during these meetings. As a consequence, the meetings he scheduled for an hour often stretched to two, and he rarely gave anyone his full attention. Now Cluna lets his phone go to voice mail, so that he can focus completely on the person in front of him. He now answers the accumulated voice-mail messages when he has downtime between meetings.

E&Y's hard-charging Wanner used to answer e-mail constantly throughout the day—whenever he heard a "ping." Then he created a ritual of checking his e-mail just twice a day—at 10:15 AM and 2:30 PM. Whereas previously he couldn't keep up with all his messages, he discovered he could clear his in-box each time he opened it— the reward of fully focusing his attention on e-mail for 45 minutes at a time. Wanner has also reset the expectations of all the people he regularly communicates with by e-mail. "I've told them if it's an emergency and they need an instant response, they can call me and I'll always pick up," he says. Nine months later he has yet to receive such a call.

Michael Henke, a senior manager at E&Y, sat his team down at the start of the busy season last winter and told them that at certain points during the day he was going to turn off his Sametime (an in-house instant-message system). The result, he said, was that he would be less available to them for questions. Like Wanner, he told his team to call him if any emergency arose, but they rarely did. He also encouraged the group to take regular breaks throughout the day and to eat more regularly. They finished the busy season under budget and more profitable than other teams that hadn't followed the energy renewal program. "We got the same amount of work done in less time," says Henke. "It made for a win-win."

Another way to mobilize mental energy is to focus systematically on activities that have the most long-term leverage. Unless people intentionally schedule time for more challenging work, they tend not to get to it at all or rush through it at the last minute. Perhaps the most effective focus ritual the executives we work with have adopted is to identify each night the most important challenge for the next day and make it their very first priority when they arrive in the morning. Jean Luc Duquesne, a vice president for Sony Europe in

Paris, used to answer his e-mail as soon as he got to the office, just as many people do. He now tries to concentrate the first hour of every day on the most important topic. He finds that he often emerges at 10 AM feeling as if he's already had a productive day.

The Human Spirit: Energy of Meaning and Purpose

People tap into the energy of the human spirit when their everyday work and activities are consistent with what they value most and with what gives them a sense of meaning and purpose. If the work they're doing really matters to them, they typically feel more positive energy, focus better, and demonstrate greater perseverance. Regrettably, the high demands and fast pace of corporate life don't leave much time to pay attention to these issues, and many people don't even recognize meaning and purpose as potential sources of energy. Indeed, if we tried to begin our program by focusing on the human spirit, it would likely have minimal impact. Only when participants have experienced the value of the rituals they establish in the other dimensions do they start to see that being attentive to their own deeper needs dramatically influences their effectiveness and satisfaction at work.

For E&Y partner Jonathan Anspacher, simply having the opportunity to ask himself a series of questions about what really mattered to him was both illuminating and energizing. "I think it's important to be a little introspective and say, 'What do you want to be remembered for?'" he told us. "You don't want to be remembered as the crazy partner who worked these long hours and had his people be miserable. When my kids call me and ask, 'Can you come to my band concert?' I want to say, 'Yes, I'll be there and I'll be in the front row.' I don't want to be the father that comes in and sits in the back and is on his Blackberry and has to step out to take a phone call."

To access the energy of the human spirit, people need to clarify priorities and establish accompanying rituals in three categories: doing what they do best and enjoy most at work; consciously allocating time and energy to the areas of their lives—work, family, health, service to others—they deem most important; and living their core values in their daily behaviors.

When you're attempting to discover what you do best and what you enjoy most, it's important to realize that these two things aren't necessarily mutually inclusive. You may get lots of positive feedback about something you're very good at but not truly enjoy it. Conversely, you can love doing something but have no gift for it, so that achieving success requires much more energy than it makes sense to invest.

To help program participants discover their areas of strength, we ask them to recall at least two work experiences in the past several months during which they found themselves in their "sweet spot"— feeling effective, effortlessly absorbed, inspired, and fulfilled. Then we have them deconstruct those experiences to understand precisely what energized them so positively and what specific talents they were drawing on. If leading strategy feels like a sweet spot, for example, is it being in charge that's most invigorating or participating in a creative endeavor? Or is it using a skill that comes to you easily and so feels good to exercise? Finally, we have people establish a ritual that will encourage them to do more of exactly that kind of activity at work.

A senior leader we worked with realized that one of the activities he least liked was reading and summarizing detailed sales reports, whereas one of his favorites was brainstorming new strategies. The leader found a direct report who loved immersing himself in numbers and delegated the sales report task to him—happily settling for brief oral summaries from him each day. The leader also began scheduling a free-form 90-minute strategy session every other week with the most creative people in his group.

In the second category, devoting time and energy to what's important to you, there is often a similar divide between what people say is important and what they actually do. Rituals can help close this gap. When Jean Luc Duquesne, the Sony Europe vice president, thought hard about his personal priorities, he realized that spending time with his family was what mattered most to him, but it often got squeezed out of his day. So he instituted a ritual in which he switches off for at least three hours every evening when he gets home, so he can focus on his family. "I'm still not an expert on

PlayStation," he told us, "but according to my youngest son, I'm learning and I'm a good student." Steve Wanner, who used to talk on the cell phone all the way to his front door on his commute home, has chosen a specific spot 20 minutes from his house where he ends whatever call he's on and puts away the phone. He spends the rest of his commute relaxing so that when he does arrive home, he's less preoccupied with work and more available to his wife and children.

The third category, practicing your core values in your everyday behavior, is a challenge for many as well. Most people are living at such a furious pace that they rarely stop to ask themselves what they stand for and who they want to be. As a consequence, they let external demands dictate their actions.

We don't suggest that people explicitly define their values, because the results are usually too predictable. Instead, we seek to uncover them, in part by asking questions that are inadvertently revealing, such as, "What are the qualities that you find most off-putting when you see them in others?" By describing what they can't stand, people unintentionally divulge what they stand for. If you are very offended by stinginess, for example, generosity is probably one of your key values. If you are especially put off by rudeness in others, it's likely that consideration is a high value for you. As in the other categories, establishing rituals can help bridge the gap between the values you aspire to and how you currently behave. If you discover that consideration is a key value, but you are perpetually late for meetings, the ritual might be to end the meetings you run five minutes earlier than usual and intentionally show up five minutes early for the meeting that follows.

Addressing these three categories helps people go a long way toward achieving a greater sense of alignment, satisfaction, and well-being in their lives on and off the job. Those feelings are a source of positive energy in their own right and reinforce people's desire to persist at rituals in other energy dimensions as well.

This new way of working takes hold only to the degree that organizations support their people in adopting new behaviors. We have learned, sometimes painfully, that not all executives and companies are prepared to embrace the notion that personal renewal for employ-ees will lead to better and more sustainable performance. To suc-ceed, renewal efforts need solid support and commitment from senior management, beginning with the key decision maker.

At Wachovia, Susanne Svizeny, the president of the region in which we conducted our study, was the primary cheerleader for the program. She embraced the principles in her own life and made a series of personal changes, including a visible commitment to building more regular renewal rituals into her work life. Next, she took it upon herself to foster the excitement and commitment of her leadership team. Finally, she regularly reached out by e-mail to all participants in the project to encourage them in their rituals and seek their feedback. It was clear to everyone that she took the work seriously. Her enthusiasm was infectious, and the results spoke for themselves.

At Sony Europe, several hundred leaders have embraced the prin-ciples of energy management. Over the next year, more than 2,000 of their direct reports will go through the energy renewal program. From Fujio Nishida on down, it has become increasingly culturally acceptable at Sony to take intermittent breaks, work out at midday, answer e-mail only at designated times, and even ask colleagues who seem irritable or impatient what stories they're telling themselves.

Organizational support also entails shifts in policies, practices, and cultural messages. A number of firms we worked with have built "renewal rooms" where people can regularly go to relax and refuel. Others offer subsidized gym memberships. In some cases, leaders themselves gather groups of employees for midday workouts. One company instituted a no-meeting zone between 8 and 9 AM to ensure that people had at least one hour absolutely free of meetings. At several companies, including Sony, senior leaders collectively agreed to stop checking e-mail during meetings as a way to make the meet-ings more focused and efficient.

One factor that can get in the way of success is a crisis mentality. The optimal candidates for energy renewal programs are organizations that are feeling enough pain to be eager for new solutions but not so much that they're completely overwhelmed. At one organization

77

where we had the active support of the CEO, the company was under intense pressure to grow rapidly, and the senior team couldn't tear themselves away from their focus on immediate survival—even though taking time out for renewal might have allowed them to be more productive at a more sustainable level.

By contrast, the group at Ernst & Young successfully went through the process at the height of tax season. With the permission of their leaders, they practiced defusing negative emotions by breathing or telling themselves different stories, and alternated highly focused periods of work with renewal breaks. Most people in the group reported that this busy season was the least stressful they'd ever experienced.

The implicit contract between organizations and their employees today is that each will try to get as much from the other as they can, as quickly as possible, and then move on without looking back. We believe that is mutually self-defeating. Both individuals and the organizations they work for end up depleted rather than enriched. Employees feel increasingly beleaguered and burned out. Organizations are forced to settle for employees who are less than fully engaged and to constantly hire and train new people to replace those who choose to leave. We envision a new and explicit contract that benefits all parties: Organizations invest in their people across all dimensions of their lives to help them build and sustain their value. Individuals respond by bringing all their multidimensional energy wholeheartedly to work every day. Both grow in value as a result.

Originally published in October 2007. Reprint R0710B

Overloaded Circuits

by Edward M. Hallowell

DAVID DRUMS HIS FINGERS on his desk as he scans the e-mail on his computer screen. At the same time, he's talking on the phone to an executive halfway around the world. His knee bounces up and down like a jackhammer. He intermittently bites his lip and reaches for his constant companion, the coffee cup. He's so deeply involved in multitasking that he has forgotten the appointment his Outlook calendar reminded him of 15 minutes ago.

Jane, a senior vice president, and Mike, her CEO, have adjoining offices so they can communicate quickly, yet communication never seems to happen. "Whenever I go into Mike's office, his phone lights up, my cell phone goes off, someone knocks on the door, he suddenly turns to his screen and writes an e-mail, or he tells me about a new issue he wants me to address," Jane complains. "We're working flat out just to stay afloat, and we're not getting anything important accomplished. It's driving me crazy."

David, Jane, and Mike aren't crazy, but they're certainly crazed. Their experience is becoming the norm for overworked managers who suffer—like many of your colleagues, and possibly like you—from a very real but unrecognized neurological phenomenon that I call attention deficit trait, or ADT. Caused by brain overload, ADT is now epidemic in organizations. The core symptoms are distractibility, inner frenzy, and impatience. People with ADT have difficulty staying organized, setting priorities, and managing time. These symptoms can undermine the work of an otherwise gifted executive. If

David, Jane, Mike, and the millions like them understood themselves in neurological terms, they could actively manage their lives instead of reacting to problems as they happen.

As a psychiatrist who has diagnosed and treated thousands of people over the past 25 years for a medical condition called attention deficit disorder, or ADD (now known clinically as attention-deficit/hyperactivity disorder), I have observed firsthand how a rapidly growing segment of the adult population is developing this new, related condition. The number of people with ADT coming into my clinical practice has mushroomed by a factor of ten in the past decade. Unfortunately, most of the remedies for chronic overload proposed by time-management consultants and executive coaches do not address the underlying causes of ADT.

Unlike ADD, a neurological disorder that has a genetic component and can be aggravated by environmental and physical factors, ADT springs entirely from the environment. Like the traffic jam, ADT is an artifact of modern life. It is brought on by the demands on our time and attention that have exploded over the past two decades. As our minds fill with noise—feckless synaptic events signifying nothing—the brain gradually loses its capacity to attend fully and thoroughly to anything.

The symptoms of ADT come upon a person gradually. The sufferer doesn't experience a single crisis but rather a series of minor emergencies while he or she tries harder and harder to keep up. Shouldering a responsibility to "suck it up" and not complain as the workload increases, executives with ADT do whatever they can to handle a load they simply cannot manage as well as they'd like. The ADT sufferer therefore feels a constant low level of panic and guilt. Facing a tidal wave of tasks, the executive becomes increasingly hurried, curt, peremptory, and unfocused, while pretending that everything is fine.

To control ADT, we first have to recognize it. And control it we must, if we as individuals and organizational leaders are to be effective. In the following pages, I'll offer an analysis of the origins of ADT and provide some suggestions that may help you manage it.

Idea in Brief

Frenzied executives who fidget through meetings, miss appointments, and jab at the elevator's "door close" button aren't crazy—just crazed. They're suffering from a newly recognized neurological phenomenon called **attention deficit trait (ADT)**. Marked by distractibility, inner frenzy, and impatience, ADT prevents managers from clarifying priorities, making smart decisions, and managing their time. This insidious condition turns otherwise talented performers into harried underachievers. And it's reaching epidemic proportions.

ADT isn't an illness or character defect. It's our brains' natural response to exploding demands on our time and attention. As data increasingly floods our brains, we lose our ability to solve problems and handle the unknown. Creativity shrivels; mistakes multiply. Some sufferers eventually melt down.

How to control ADT's ravaging impact on performance? *Foster positive emotions* by connecting face-to-face with people you like throughout the day. *Take physical care of your brain* by getting enough sleep, eating healthfully, and exercising regularly. *Organize for ADT*, designating part of each day for thinking and planning, and setting up your office to foster mental functioning (for example, keeping part of your desk clear at all times).

These strategies may seem like no-brainers. But they'll help you vanquish the ADT demon before it can strike.

Attention Deficit Cousins

To understand the nature and treatment of ADT, it's useful to know something of its cousin, ADD.

Usually seen as a learning disability in children, ADD also afflicts about 5% of the adult population. Researchers using MRI scans have found that people with ADD suffer a slightly diminished volume in four specific brain regions that have various functions such as modulating emotion (especially anger and frustration) and assisting in learning. One of the regions, made up of the frontal and prefrontal lobes, generates thoughts, makes decisions, sets priorities, and organizes activities. While the medications used to treat ADD don't change

Idea in Practice

How You Can Combat ADT

Promote positive emotions.
Negative emotions—especially fear—can hamper productive brain functioning. To promote positive feelings, especially during highly stressful times, interact directly with someone you like at least every four to six hours. In environments where people are in physical contact with people they trust, brain functioning hums. By connecting comfortably with colleagues, you'll help your brain's "executive" center (responsible for decision making, planning, and information prioritizing) perform at its best.

Take physical care of your brain.
Ample sleep, a good diet, and exercise are critical for staving off ADT. You're getting enough sleep if you can awake without an alarm clock. You're eating well if you're avoiding sugar and white flour and consuming more fruits, whole grains, vegetables, and protein instead. You're exercising enough if you're taking a brisk walk or going up and down a flight of stairs a few times a day.

Organize for ADT. Instead of getting sucked into the vortices of e-mail or voice mail first thing in the morning, attend to a critical task. With paperwork, apply the OHIO ("Only handle it once") rule: Whenever you touch a document,

act on it, file it, or throw it away. Do crucial work during times of the day when you perform at your best. Use whatever small strategies help you function well mentally—whether it's listening to music or walking around while working, or doodling during meetings. And before you leave for the day, list three to five priority items you'll need to address tomorrow.

What Your Company Can Do. In firms that ignore ADT symptoms, employees underachieve, create clutter, and cut corners. Careless mistakes, illness, and turnover increase, as people squander their brainpower. To counteract ADT and harness employees' brainpower, invest in amenities that foster a positive, productive atmosphere.

> *Example:* Major software company SAS Institute creates a warm, connected, and relaxed work environment by offering employees perks such as a seven-hour workday that ends at 5:00; large on-site gym and day-care facility; and cafeteria that provides baby seats and high chairs so parents can eat lunch with their children. The payoff? Employees return the favors with high productivity. And SAS's turnover never exceeds 5%—saving the company millions on recruiting, training, and severance.

the anatomy of the brain, they alter brain chemistry, which in turn improves function in each of the four regions and so dramatically bolsters the performance of ADD sufferers.

ADD confers both disadvantages and advantages. The negative characteristics include a tendency to procrastinate and miss deadlines. People with ADD struggle with disorganization and tardiness; they can be forgetful and drift away mentally in the middle of a conversation or while reading. Their performance can be inconsistent: brilliant one moment and unsatisfactory the next. ADD sufferers also tend to demonstrate impatience and lose focus unless, oddly enough, they are under stress or handling multiple inputs. (This is because stress leads to the production of adrenaline, which is chemically similar to the medications we use to treat ADD.) Finally, people with ADD sometimes also self-medicate with excessive alcohol or other substances.

On the positive side, those with ADD usually possess rare talents and gifts. Those gifts often go unnoticed or undeveloped, however, because of the problems caused by the condition's negative symptoms. ADD sufferers can be remarkably creative and original. They are unusually persistent under certain circumstances and often possess an entrepreneurial flair. They display ingenuity and encourage that trait in others. They tend to improvise well under pressure. Because they have the ability to field multiple inputs simultaneously, they can be strong leaders during times of change. They also tend to rebound quickly after setbacks and bring fresh energy to the company every day.

Executives with ADD typically achieve inconsistent results. Sometimes they fail miserably because they're disorganized and make mistakes. At other times, they perform brilliantly, offering original ideas and strategies that lead to performance at the highest level.

David Neeleman, the CEO of JetBlue Airways, has ADD. School was torture; unable to focus, he hated to study and procrastinated endlessly. "I felt like I should be out doing things, moving things along, but here I was, stuck studying statistics, which I knew had no application to my life," Neeleman told me. "I knew I had to have an education, but at the first opportunity to start a business, I just blew out of college." He climbed quickly in the corporate world, making use of his strengths—original thinking, high energy, an ability to draw out the best in people—and getting help with organization and time management.

Like most people with ADD, Neeleman could sometimes offend with his blunt words, but his ideas were good enough to change the airline industry. For example, he invented the electronic ticket. "When I proposed that idea, people laughed at me, saying no one would go to the airport without a paper ticket," he says. "Now everyone does, and it has saved the industry millions of dollars." It seems fitting that someone with ADD would invent a way around having to remember to bring a paper ticket. Neeleman believes ADD is one of the keys to his success. Far from regretting having it, he celebrates it. But he understands that he must manage his ADD carefully.

Attention deficit trait is characterized by ADD's negative symptoms. Rather than being rooted in genetics, however, ADT is purely a response to the hyperkinetic environment in which we live. Indeed, modern culture all but requires many of us to develop ADT. Never in history has the human brain been asked to track so many data points. Everywhere, people rely on their cell phones, e-mail, and digital assistants in the race to gather and transmit data, plans, and ideas faster and faster. One could argue that the chief value of the modern era is speed, which the novelist Milan Kundera described as "the form of ecstasy that technology has bestowed upon modern man." Addicted to speed, we demand it even when we can't possibly go faster. James Gleick wryly noted in *Faster: The Acceleration of Just About Everything* that the "close door" button in elevators is often the one with the paint worn off. As the human brain struggles to keep up, it falters and then falls into the world of ADT.

This Is Your Brain

While brain scans cannot display anatomical differences between people with "normal" brains and people suffering from ADT, studies have shown that as the human brain is asked to process dizzying amounts of data, its ability to solve problems flexibly and creatively declines and the number of mistakes increases. To find out why, let's go on a brief neurological journey.

Blessed with the largest cortex in all of nature, owners of this trillion-celled organ today put singular pressure on the frontal and prefrontal lobes, which I'll refer to in this article as simply the frontal lobes. This region governs what is called, aptly enough, executive functioning (EF). EF guides decision making and planning; the organization and prioritization of information and ideas; time management; and various other sophisticated, uniquely human, managerial tasks. As long as our frontal lobes remain in charge, everything is fine.

Beneath the frontal lobes lie the parts of the brain devoted to survival. These deep centers govern basic functions like sleep, hunger, sexual desire, breathing, and heart rate, as well as crudely positive and negative emotions. When you are doing well and operating at peak level, the deep centers send up messages of excitement, satisfaction, and joy. They pump up your motivation, help you maintain attention, and don't interfere with working memory, the number of data points you can keep track of at once. But when you are confronted with the sixth decision after the fifth interruption in the midst of a search for the ninth missing piece of information on the day that the third deal has collapsed and the 12th impossible request has blipped unbidden across your computer screen, your brain begins to panic, reacting just as if that sixth decision were a bloodthirsty, man-eating tiger.

As a specialist in learning disabilities, I have found that the most dangerous disability is not any formally diagnosable condition like dyslexia or ADD. It is fear. Fear shifts us into survival mode and thus prevents fluid learning and nuanced understanding. Certainly, if a real tiger is about to attack you, survival is the mode you want to be in. But if you're trying to deal intelligently with a subtle task, survival mode is highly unpleasant and counterproductive.

When the frontal lobes approach capacity and we begin to fear that we can't keep up, the relationship between the higher and lower regions of the brain takes an ominous turn. Thousands of years of evolution have taught the higher brain not to ignore the lower brain's distress signals. In survival mode, the deep areas of the brain assume control and begin to direct the higher regions. As a result, the whole brain gets caught in a neurological catch-22. The deep regions interpret the messages of overload they receive from the frontal lobes in the same way they interpret everything: primitively. They furiously fire signals of fear, anxiety, impatience, irritability, anger, or panic. These alarm signals shanghai the attention of the frontal lobes, forcing them to forfeit much of their power. Because survival signals are irresistible, the frontal lobes get stuck sending messages back to the deep centers saying, "Message received. Trying to work on it but without success." These messages further perturb the deep centers, which send even more powerful messages of distress back up to the frontal lobes.

Meanwhile, in response to what's going on in the brain, the rest of the body—particularly the endocrine, respiratory, cardiovascular, musculoskeletal, and peripheral nervous systems—has shifted into crisis mode and changed its baseline physiology from peace and quiet to red alert. The brain and body are locked in a reverberating circuit while the frontal lobes lose their sophistication, as if vinegar were added to wine. In this state, EF reverts to simpleminded black-and-white thinking; perspective and shades of gray disappear. Intelligence dims. In a futile attempt to do more than is possible, the brain paradoxically reduces its ability to think clearly.

This neurological event occurs when a manager is desperately trying to deal with more input than he possibly can. In survival mode, the manager makes impulsive judgments, angrily rushing to bring closure to whatever matter is at hand. He feels compelled to get the problem under control immediately, to extinguish the perceived danger lest it destroy him. He is robbed of his flexibility, his sense of humor, his ability to deal with the unknown. He forgets the big picture and the goals and values he stands for. He loses his creativity and his ability to change plans. He desperately wants to kill the metaphorical tiger. At these moments he is prone to melting down, to throwing a tantrum, to blaming others, and to sabotaging himself. Or he may go in the opposite direction, falling into denial and total avoidance of the problems attacking him, only to be devoured. This is ADT at its worst.

Though ADT does not always reach such extreme proportions, it does wreak havoc among harried workers. Because no two brains are alike, some people deal with the condition better than others. Regardless of how well executives appear to function, however, no one has total control over his or her executive functioning.

Managing ADT

Unfortunately, top management has so far viewed the symptoms of ADT through the distorting lens of morality or character. Employees who seem unable to keep up the pace are seen as deficient or weak. Consider the case of an executive who came to see me when he was completely overloaded. I suggested he talk the situation over with his superior and ask for help. When my client did so, he was told that if he couldn't handle the work, he ought to think about resigning. Even though his performance assessments were stellar and he'd earned praise for being one of the most creative people in the organization, he was allowed to leave. Because the firm sought to preserve the myth that no straw would ever break its people's backs, it could not tolerate the manager's stating that his back was breaking. After he went out on his own, he flourished.

How can we control the rampaging effects of ADT, both in ourselves and in our organizations? While ADD often requires medication, the treatment of ADT certainly does not. ADT can be controlled only by creatively engineering one's environment and one's emotional and physical health. I have found that the following preventive measures go a long way toward helping executives control their symptoms of ADT.

Promote positive emotions
The most important step in controlling ADT is not to buy a superturbocharged BlackBerry and fill it up with to-dos but rather to create an environment in which the brain can function at its best. This

means building a positive, fear-free emotional atmosphere, because emotion is the on/off switch for executive functioning.

There are neurological reasons why ADT occurs less in environments where people are in physical contact and where they trust and respect one another. When you comfortably connect with a colleague, even if you are dealing with an overwhelming problem, the deep centers of the brain send messages through the pleasure center to the area that assigns resources to the frontal lobes. Even when you're under extreme stress, this sense of human connection causes executive functioning to hum.

By contrast, people who work in physical isolation are more likely to suffer from ADT, for the more isolated we are, the more stressed we become. I witnessed a dramatic example of the danger of a disconnected environment and the healing power of a connected one when I consulted for one of the world's foremost university chemistry departments. In the department's formerly hard-driven culture, ADT was rampant, exacerbated by an ethic that forbade anyone to ask for help or even state that anything was wrong. People did not trust one another; they worked on projects alone, which led to more mistrust. Most people were in emotional pain, but implicit in the department's culture was the notion that great pain led to great gain.

In the late 1990s, one of the department's most gifted graduate students killed himself. His suicide note explicitly blamed the university for pushing him past his limit. The department's culture was literally lethal.

Instead of trying to sweep the tragedy under the rug, the chair of the department and his successor acted boldly and creatively. They immediately changed the structure of the supervisory system so that each graduate student and postdoc was assigned three supervisors, rather than a single one with a death grip on the trainee's career. The department set up informal biweekly buffets that allowed people to connect. (Even the most reclusive chemist came out of hiding for food, one of life's great connectors.) The department heads went as far as changing the architecture of the department's main building, taking down walls and adding common areas and an espresso bar complete with a grand piano. They provided lectures and written information to all students about the danger signs of mental wear and tear and offered confidential procedures for students who needed help. These steps, along with regular meetings that included senior faculty and university administrators, led to a more humane, productive culture in which the students and faculty felt fully engaged. The department's performance remained first-rate, and creative research blossomed.

The bottom line is this: Fostering connections and reducing fear promote brainpower. When you make time at least every four to six hours for a "human moment," a face-to-face exchange with a person you like, you are giving your brain what it needs.

Take physical care of your brain

Sleep, a good diet, and exercise are critical for staving off ADT. Though this sounds like a no-brainer, too many of us abuse our brains by neglecting obvious principles of care.

You may try to cope with ADT by sleeping less, in the vain hope that you can get more done. This is the opposite of what you need to do, for ADT sets in when you don't get enough sleep. There is ample documentation to suggest that sleep deprivation engenders a host of problems, from impaired decision making and reduced creativity to reckless behavior and paranoia. We vary in how much sleep we require; a good rule of thumb is that you're getting enough sleep if you can wake up without an alarm clock.

Diet also plays a crucial role in brain health. Many hardworking people habitually inhale carbohydrates, which cause blood glucose levels to yo-yo. This leads to a vicious cycle: Rapid fluctuations in insulin levels further increase the craving for carbohydrates. The brain, which relies on glucose for energy, is left either glutted or gasping, neither of which makes for optimal cognitive functioning.

The brain does much better if the blood glucose level can be held relatively stable. To do this, avoid simple carbohydrates containing sugar and white flour (pastries, white bread, and pasta, for example). Rely on the complex carbohydrates found in fruits, whole grains, and vegetables. Protein is important: Instead of starting your day with coffee and a Danish, try tea and an egg or a piece of smoked salmon on wheat toast. Take a multivitamin every day as well as supplementary omega-3 fatty acids, an excellent source of which is fish oil. The omega-3s and the E and B complex contained in multivitamins promote healthy brain function and may even stave off Alzheimer's disease and inflammatory ills (which can be the starting point for major killers like heart disease, stroke, diabetes, and cancer). Moderate your intake of alcohol, too, because too much kills brain cells and accelerates the development of memory loss and even dementia. As you change your diet to promote optimal brain function and good general health, your body will also shed excess pounds.

If you think you can't afford the time to exercise, think again. Sitting at a desk for hours on end decreases mental acuity, not only because of reduced blood flow to the brain but for other biochemical reasons as well. Physical exercise induces the body to produce an array of chemicals that the brain loves, including endorphins, serotonin, dopamine, epinephrine, and norepinephrine, as well as two recently discovered compounds, brain-derived neurotrophic factor (BDNF) and nerve growth factor (NGF). Both BDNF and NGF promote cell health and development in the brain, stave off the ravages of aging and stress, and keep the brain in tip-top condition. Nothing stimulates the production of BDNF and NGF as robustly as physical exercise, which explains why those who exercise regularly talk about the letdown and sluggishness they experience if they miss their exercise for a few days. You will more than compensate for the time you invest on the treadmill with improved productivity and efficiency. To fend off the symptoms of ADT while you're at work, get up from your desk and go up and down a flight of stairs a few times or walk briskly down a hallway. These quick, simple efforts will push your brain's reset button.

Organize for ADT

It's important to develop tactics for getting organized, but not in the sense of empty New Year's resolutions. Rather, your goal is to order your work in a way that suits you, so that disorganization does not keep you from reaching your goals.

First, devise strategies to help your frontal lobes stay in control. These might include breaking down large tasks into smaller ones and keeping a section of your work space or desk clear at all times. (You do not need to have a neat office, just a neat section of your office.) Similarly, you might try keeping a portion of your day free of appointments, e-mail, and other distractions so that you have time to think and plan. Because e-mail is a wonderful way to procrastinate and set yourself up for ADT at the same time, you might consider holding specific "e-mail hours," since it isn't necessary to reply to every e-mail right away.

When you start your day, don't allow yourself to get sucked into vortices of e-mail or voice mail or into attending to minor tasks that eat up your time but don't pack a punch. Attend to a critical task instead. Before you leave for the day, make a list of no more than five priority items that will require your attention tomorrow. Short lists force you to prioritize and complete your tasks. Additionally, keep torrents of documents at bay. One of my patients, an executive with ADD, uses the OHIO rule: Only handle it once. If he touches a document, he acts on it, files it, or throws it away. "I don't put it in a pile," he says. "Piles are like weeds. If you let them grow, they take over everything."

Pay attention to the times of day when you feel that you perform at your best; do your most important work then and save the rote work for other times. Set up your office in a way that helps mental functioning. If you focus better with music, have music (if need be, use earphones). If you think best on your feet, work standing up or walk around frequently. If doodling or drumming your fingers helps, figure out a way to do so without bothering anyone, or get a fidget toy to bring to meetings. These small strategies sound mundane, but they address the ADT devil that resides in distracting details.

Protect your frontal lobes

To stay out of survival mode and keep your lower brain from usurping control, slow down. Take the time you need to comprehend what is going on, to listen, to ask questions, and to digest what's been said so that you don't get confused and send your brain into panic. Empower an assistant to ride herd on you; insist that he or she tell you to stop e-mailing, get off the telephone, or leave the office.

Control Your ADT

In General

- Get adequate sleep.

- Watch what you eat. Avoid simple, sugary carbohydrates, moderate your intake of alcohol, add protein, stick to complex carbohydrates (vegetables, whole grains, fruit).

- Exercise at least 30 minutes at least every other day.

- Take a daily multivitamin and an omega-3 fatty acid supplement.

At Work

- Do all you can to create a trusting, connected work environment.

- Have a friendly, face-to-face talk with a person you like every four to six hours.

- Break large tasks into smaller ones.

- Keep a section of your work space or desk clear at all times.

- Each day, reserve some "think time" that's free from appointments, e-mail, and phone calls.

- Set aside e-mail until you've completed at least one or two more important tasks.

If you do begin to feel overwhelmed, try the following mind-clearing tricks. Do an easy rote task, such as resetting the calendar on your watch or writing a memo on a neutral topic. If you feel anxious about beginning a project, pull out a sheet of paper or fire up your word processor and write a paragraph about something unrelated to the project (a description of your house, your car, your shoes—anything you know well). You can also tackle the easiest part of the task; for example, write just the title of a memo about it. Open a dictionary and read a few definitions, or spend five minutes doing a crossword puzzle. Each of these little tasks quiets your lower brain by tricking it into shutting off alarmist messages and puts your frontal lobes back in full control.

- Before you leave work each day, create a short list of three to five items you will attend to the next day.

- Try to act on, file, or toss every document you touch.

- Don't let papers accumulate.

- Pay attention to the times of day when you feel that you are at your best; do your most important work then, and save the rote work for other times.

- Do whatever you need to do to work in a more focused way: Add background music, walk around, and so on.

- Ask a colleague or an assistant to help you stop talking on the telephone, e-mailing, or working too late.

When You Feel Overwhelmed

- Slow down.

- Do an easy rote task: Reset your watch, write a note about a neutral topic (such as a description of your house), read a few dictionary definitions, do a short crossword puzzle.

- Move around: Go up and down a flight of stairs or walk briskly.

- Ask for help, delegate a task, or brainstorm with a colleague. In short, do not worry alone.

Finally, be ready for the next attack of ADT by posting the sidebar "Control Your ADT" near your desk where you can see it. Knowing that you are prepared diminishes the likelihood of an attack, because you're not susceptible to panic.

What Leaders Can Do

All too often, companies induce and exacerbate ADT in their employees by demanding fast thinking rather than deep thinking. Firms also ask employees to work on multiple overlapping projects and initiatives, resulting in second-rate thinking. Worse, companies that ask their employees to do too much at once tend to reward those who say yes to overload while punishing those who choose to focus and say no.

Moreover, organizations make the mistake of forcing their employees to do more and more with less and less by eliminating support staff. Such companies end up losing money in the long run, for the more time a manager has to spend being his own administrative assistant and the less he is able to delegate, the less effective he will be in doing the important work of moving the organization forward. Additionally, firms that ignore the symptoms of ADT in their employees suffer its ill effects: Employees underachieve, create clutter, cut corners, make careless mistakes, and squander their brainpower. As demands continue to increase, a toxic, high-pressure environment leads to high rates of employee illness and turnover.

To counteract ADT and harness employee brainpower, firms should invest in amenities that contribute to a positive atmosphere. One company that has done an excellent job in this regard is SAS Institute, a major software company in North Carolina. The company famously offers its employees a long list of perks: a 36,000-square-foot, on-site gym; a seven-hour workday that ends at 5 PM; the largest on-site day care facility in North Carolina; a cafeteria that provides baby seats and high chairs so parents can eat lunch with their children; unlimited sick days; and much more. The atmosphere at SAS is warm, connected, and relaxed. The effect on the bottom line is profoundly positive; turnover is never higher than 5%. The company saves the millions other software companies spend on recruiting, training, and severance (estimated to be at least 1.5 times salary in the software industry). Employees return the favors with high productivity. The forces of ADT that shred other organizations never gain momentum at SAS.

Leaders can also help prevent ADT by matching employees' skills to tasks. When managers assign goals that stretch people too far or ask workers to focus on what they're not good at rather than what they do well, stress rises. By contrast, managers who understand the dangers of ADT can find ways of keeping themselves and their organizations on track. JetBlue's David Neeleman, for example, has shamelessly and publicly identified what he is not good at and found ways to deal with his shortcomings, either by delegating or by empowering his assistant to direct him. Neeleman also models this behavior for everyone else in the organization. His openness about the challenges of his ADD gives others permission to speak about their own attention deficit difficulties and to garner the support they need. He also encourages his managers to match people with tasks that fit their cognitive and emotional styles, knowing that no one style is best. Neeleman believes that helping people work to their strengths is not just a mark of sophisticated management; it's also an excellent way to boost worker productivity and morale.

ADT is a very real threat to all of us. If we do not manage it, it manages us. But an understanding of ADT and its ravages allows us to apply practical methods to improve our work and our lives. In the end, the most critical step an enlightened leader can take to address the problem of ADT is to name it. Bringing ADT out of the closet and describing its symptoms removes the stigma and eliminates the moral condemnation companies have for so long mistakenly leveled at overburdened employees. By giving people permission to ask for help and remaining vigilant for signs of stress, organizations will go a long way toward fostering more productive, well-balanced, and intelligent work environments.

Originally published in January 2005. Reprint R0501E

Be a Better Leader, Have a Richer Life

by Stewart D. Friedman

IN MY RESEARCH AND COACHING WORK over the past two decades, I have met many people who feel unfulfilled, overwhelmed, or stagnant because they are forsaking performance in one or more aspects of their lives. They aren't bringing their leadership abilities to bear in all of life's domains—work, home, community, and self (mind, body, and spirit). Of course, there will always be some tension among the different roles we play. But, contrary to the common wisdom, there's no reason to assume that it's a zero-sum game. It makes more sense to pursue excellent performance as a leader in all four domains—achieving what I call "four-way wins"—not trading off one for another but finding mutual value among them.

This is the main idea in a program called Total Leadership that I teach at the Wharton School and at companies and workshops around the world. "Total" because it's about the whole person and "Leadership" because it's about creating sustainable change to benefit not just you but the most important people around you.

Scoring four-way wins starts by taking a clear view of what you want from and can contribute to each domain of your life, now and in the future, with thoughtful consideration of the people who matter most to you and the expectations you have for one another. This is followed by systematically designing and implementing carefully crafted experiments—doing something new for a short period to see how it affects all four domains. If an experiment doesn't work out, you stop or adjust, and little is lost. If it does work out, it's a small win; over time these add up so that your overall efforts are focused increasingly on what and who matter most. Either way, you learn more about how to lead in all parts of your life.

This process doesn't require inordinate risk. On the contrary, it works because it entails realistic expectations, short-term changes that are in your control, and the explicit support of those around you. Take, for instance, Kenneth Chen, a manager I met at a workshop in 2005. (All names in this article are pseudonyms.) His professional goal was to become CEO, but he had other goals as well, which on the face of it might have appeared conflicting. He had recently moved to Philadelphia and wanted to get more involved with his community. He also wished to strengthen bonds with his family. To further all of these goals, he decided to join a city-based community board, which would not only allow him to hone his leadership skills (in support of his professional goal) but also have benefits in the family domain. It would give him more in common with his sister, a teacher who gave back to the community every day, and he hoped his fiancée would participate as well, enabling them to do something together for the greater good. He would feel more spiritually alive and this, in turn, would increase his self-confidence at work.

Now, about three years later, he reports that he is not only on a community board with his fiancée but also on the formal succession track for CEO. He's a better leader in all aspects of his life because he is acting in ways that are more consistent with his values. He is creatively enhancing his performance in all domains of his life and leading others to improve their performance by encouraging them to better integrate the different parts of their lives, too.

Kenneth is not alone. Workshop participants assess themselves at the beginning and the end of the program, and they consistently report improvements in their effectiveness, as well as a greater sense of harmony among the once-competing domains of their lives. In a study over a four-month period of more than 300 business professionals

Idea in Brief

Life's a zero-sum game, right? The more you strive to win in one dimension (e.g., your work), the more the other three dimensions (your self, your home, and your community) must lose. Not according to Friedman. You don't have to make trade-offs among life's domains. Nor should you: trading off can leave you feeling exhausted, unfulfilled, or isolated. And it hurts the people you care about most.

To excel in all dimensions of life, use Friedman's **Total Leadership** process. First, articulate who and what matters most in your life.

Then experiment with small changes that enhance your satisfaction and performance in *all four domains*. For example, exercising three mornings a week gives you more energy for work and improves your self-esteem and health, which makes you a better parent and friend.

Friedman's research suggests that people who focus on the concept of Total Leadership have a 20%–39% increase in satisfaction in all life domains, and a 9% improvement in job performance—even while working shorter weeks.

(whose average age was about 35), their *satisfaction* increased by an average of 20% in their work lives, 28% in their home lives, and 31% in their community lives. Perhaps most significant, their satisfaction in the domain of the self—their physical and emotional health and their intellectual and spiritual growth—increased by 39%. But they also reported that their *performance* improved: at work (by 9%), at home (15%), in the community (12%), and personally (25%). Paradoxically, these gains were made even as participants spent less time on work and more on other aspects of their lives. They're working smarter—and they're more focused, passionate, and committed to what they're doing.

While hundreds of leaders at all levels go through this program every year, you don't need a workshop to identify worthwhile experiments. The process is pretty straightforward, though not simple. In the sections that follow, I will give you an overview of the process and take you through the basics of designing and implementing experiments to produce four-way wins.

Idea in Practice

Total Leadership helps you mitigate a range of problems that stem from making trade-offs among the different dimensions of your life:

- Feeling **unfulfilled** because you're not doing what you love

- Feeling **inauthentic** because you're not acting according to your values

- Feeling **disconnected** from people who matter to you

- Feeling **exhausted** by trying to keep up with it all

To tackle such problems using Total Leadership, take these steps.

1. Reflect

For each of the four domains of your life—work, home, community, and self, reflect on how important each is to you, how much time and energy you devote to each, and how satisfied you are in each. Are there discrepancies between what is important to you and how you spend your time and energy? What is your overall life satisfaction?

2. Brainstorm Possibilities

Based on the insights you've achieved during your four-way reflection, brainstorm a long list of small experiments that may help you move closer to greater satisfaction in all four domains. These are new ways of doing things that would carry minimal risk and let you see results quickly. For example:

- Turning off cell phones during family dinners could help you sharpen your focus on the people who matter most to you.

- Exercising several times a week could give you more energy.

- Joining a club with coworkers could help you forge closer friendships with them.

- Preparing for the week ahead on Sunday evenings could help you sleep better and go into the new week refreshed.

3. Choose Experiments

Narrow the list of experiments you've brainstormed to the three most promising. They should:

The Total Leadership Process

The Total Leadership concept rests on three principles:

- Be real: Act with authenticity by clarifying what's important.

- Be whole: Act with integrity by respecting the whole person.

- Improve your satisfaction and performance in all four dimensions of your life.
- Have effects viewed as positive by the people who matter to you in every dimension of your life.
- Be the most costly—in regret and missed opportunities—if you *don't* do them.

- Position you to practice skills you most want to develop and do more of what you *want* to be doing.

4. Measure Progress

Develop a scorecard for each experiment you've chosen. For example:

Experiment: Exercise three mornings a week with spouse.

Life dimension	Experiment's goals	How I will measure success	Implementation steps
Work	Improved alertness and productivity	No caffeine to get through the day; more productive sales calls	• Get doctor's feedback on exercise plan. • Join gym. • Set alarm earlier on exercise days. • Tell coworkers, family, and friends about my plan, how I need their help, and how it will benefit them.
Home	Increased closeness with spouse	Fewer arguments with spouse	
Community	Greater strength to participate in athletic fundraising events with friends	Three 10K fundraising walks completed by end of year	
Self	Improved self-esteem	Greater confidence	

- Be innovative: Act with creativity by experimenting with how things get done.

You begin the process by thinking, writing, and talking with peer coaches to identify your core values, your leadership vision, and the current alignment of your actions and values—clarifying what's important. Peer coaching is enormously valuable, at this stage and throughout, because an outside perspective provides a sounding board for your ideas, challenges you, gives you a fresh way to see the possibilities for innovation, and helps hold you accountable to your commitments.

You then identify the most important people—"key stakeholders"—in all domains and the performance expectations you have of one another. Then you talk with them: If you're like most participants, you'll be surprised to find that what, and how much, your key stakeholders actually need from you is different from, and less than, what you thought beforehand.

These insights create opportunities for you to focus your attention more intelligently, spurring innovative action. Now, with a firmer grounding in what's most important, and a more complete picture of your inner circle, you begin to see new ways of making life better, not just for you but for the people around you.

The next step is to design experiments and then try them out during a controlled period of time. The best experiments are changes that your stakeholders wish for as much as, if not more than, you do.

Designing Experiments

To pursue a four-way win means to produce a change intended to fulfill multiple goals that benefit each and every domain of your life. In the domain of work, typical goals for an experiment can be captured under these broad headings: taking advantage of new opportunities for increasing productivity, reducing hidden costs, and improving the work environment. Goals for home and community tend to revolve around improving relationships and contributing more to society. For the self, it's usually about improving health and finding greater meaning in life.

As you think through the goals for your experiment, keep in mind the interests and opinions of your key stakeholders and anyone else who might be affected by the changes you are envisioning. In exploring the idea of joining a community board, for instance, Kenneth Chen sought advice from his boss, who had served on many boards, and also from the company's charitable director and the vice president of talent. In this way, he got their support. His employers could see how his participation on a board would benefit the company by developing Kenneth's leadership skills and his social network.

Some experiments benefit only a single domain directly while having indirect benefits in the others. For example, setting aside three mornings a week to exercise improves your health directly but may indirectly give you more energy for your work and raise your self-esteem, which in turn might make you a better father and friend. Other activities—such as running a half-marathon with your kids to raise funds for a charity sponsored by your company—occur in, and directly benefit, all four domains simultaneously. Whether the benefits are direct or indirect, achieving a four-way win is the goal. That's what makes the changes sustainable: Everyone benefits. The expected gains need not accrue until sometime in the future, so keep in mind that some benefits may not be obvious—far-off career advancements, for instance, or a contact who might ultimately offer valuable connections.

Identify possibilities

Open your mind to what's possible and try to think of as many potential experiments as you can, describing in a sentence or two what you would do in each. This is a time to let your imagination run free. Don't worry about all the potential obstacles at this point.

At first blush, conceiving of experiments that produce benefits for all the different realms may seem a formidable task. After all, if it were easy, people wouldn't be feeling so much tension between work and the rest of their lives. But I've found that most people realize it's not that hard once they approach the challenge systematically. And, like a puzzle, it can be fun, especially if you keep in mind that experiments must fit your particular circumstances. Experiments can and do take myriad forms. But having sifted through hundreds of experiment designs, my research team and I have found that they tend to fall into nine general types. Use the nine categories described in the exhibit "How Can I Design an Experiment to Improve All Domains of My Life?" to organize your thinking.

How can I design an experiment to improve all domains of my life?

Our research has revealed that most successful experiments combine components of nine general categories. Thinking about possibilities in this way will make it easier for you to conceive of the small changes you can make that will mutually benefit your work, your home, your community, and yourself. Most experiments are a hybrid of some combination of these categories.

Tracking and Reflecting

Keeping a record of activities, thoughts, and feelings (and perhaps distributing it to friends, family, and coworkers) to assess progress on personal and professional goals, thereby increasing self-awareness and maintaining priorities.

Examples

- Record visits to the gym along with changes in energy levels
- Track the times of day when you feel most engaged or most lethargic

Planning and Organizing

Taking actions designed to better use time and prepare and plan for the future.

Examples

- Use a PDA for all activities, not just work
- Share your schedule with someone else
- Prepare for the week on Sunday evening

Rejuvenating and Restoring

Attending to body, mind, and spirit so that the tasks of daily living and working are undertaken with renewed power, focus, and commitment.

Examples

- Quit unhealthy physical habits (smoking, drinking)
- Make time for reading a novel
- Engage in activities that improve emotional and spiritual health (yoga, meditation, etc.)

Appreciating and Caring

Having fun with people (typically, by doing things with coworkers outside work), caring for others, and appreciating relationships as a way of bonding at a basic human level to respect the whole person, which increases trust.

Examples

- Join a book group or health club with coworkers
- Help your son complete his homework
- Devote one day a month to community service

Focusing and Concentrating

Being physically present, psychologically present, or both when needed to pay attention to stakeholders who matter most. Sometimes this means saying no to opportunities or obligations. Includes attempts to show more respect to important people encountered in different domains and the need to be accessible to them.

Examples

- Turn off digital communication devices at a set time
- Set aside a specific time to focus on one thing or person
- Review e-mail at preset times during the day

Revealing and Engaging

Sharing more of yourself with others—and listening—so they can better support your values and the steps you want to take toward your leadership vision. By enhancing communication about different aspects of life, you demonstrate respect for the whole person.

Examples

- Have weekly conversations about religion with spouse
- Describe your vision to others
- Mentor a new employee

Time Shifting and "Re-Placing"

Working remotely or during different hours to increase flexibility and thus better fit in community, family, and personal activities while increasing efficiency; questioning traditional assumptions and trying new ways to get things done.

Examples

- Work from home
- Take music lessons during your lunch hour
- Do work during your commute

Delegating and Developing

Reallocating tasks in ways that increase trust, free up time, and develop skills in yourself and others; working smarter by reducing or eliminating low-priority activities.

(continued)

Examples

- Hire a personal assistant
- Have a subordinate take on some of your responsibilities

Exploring and Venturing

Taking steps toward a new job, career, or other activity that better aligns your work, home, community, and self with your core values and aspirations.

Examples

- Take on new roles at work, such as a cross-functional assignment
- Try a new coaching style
- Join the board of your child's day care center

One category of experiment involves changes in where and when work gets done. One workshop participant, a sales director for a global cement producer, tried working online from his local public library one day a week to free himself from his very long commute. This was a break from a company culture that didn't traditionally support employees working remotely, but the change benefited everyone. He had more time for outside interests, and he was more engaged and productive at work.

Another category has to do with regular self-reflection. As an example, you might keep a record of your activities, thoughts, and feelings over the course of a month to see how various actions influence your performance and quality of life. Still another category focuses on planning and organizing your time—such as trying out a new technology that coordinates commitments at work with those in the other domains.

Conversations about work and the rest of life tend to emphasize segmentation: How do I shut out the office when I am with my family? How can I eliminate distractions and concentrate purely on work? But, in some cases, it might be better to make boundaries between domains more permeable, not thicker. The very technologies that make it hard for us to maintain healthy boundaries among domains also enable us to blend them in ways—unfathomable even a decade ago—that can render us more productive and more ful-filled. These tools give us choices. The challenge we all face is learn-ing how to use them wisely, and smart experiments give you an opportunity to increase your skill in doing so. The main point is to identify possibilities that will work well in your unique situation.

All effective experiments require that you question traditional as-sumptions about how things get done, as the sales director did. It's easier to feel free to do this, and to take innovative action, when you know that your goal is to improve performance in all domains and that you'll be gathering data about the impact of your experiment to determine if indeed it is working—for your key stakeholders and for you.

Whatever type you choose, the most useful experiments feel like something of a stretch: not too easy, not too daunting. It might be something quite mundane for someone else, but that doesn't matter. What's critical is that *you* see it as a moderately difficult challenge.

Choose a few, get started, and adapt

Coming up with possibilities is an exercise in unbounded imagina-tion. But when it comes time to take action, it's not practical to try out more than three experiments at once. Typically, two turn out to be relatively successful and one goes haywire, so you will earn some small wins, and learn something useful about leadership, without biting off more than you can chew. Now the priority is to narrow the list to the three most-promising candidates by reviewing which will:

- Give you the best overall return on your investment

- Be the most costly in regret and missed opportunities if you don't do it

- Allow you to practice the leadership skills you most want to develop

- Be the most fun by involving more of what you want to be doing

- Move you furthest toward your vision of how you want to lead your life

Once you choose and begin to move down the road with your experiment, however, be prepared to adapt to the unforeseen. Don't become too wedded to the details of any one experiment's plan, because you will at some point be surprised and need to adjust. An executive I'll call Lim, for example, chose as one experiment to run the Chicago Marathon. He had been feeling out of shape, which in turn diminished his energy and focus both at work and at home. His wife, Joanne, was pregnant with their first child and initially supported the plan because she believed that the focus required by the training and the physical outlet it provided would make Lim a better father. The family also had a strong tradition of athleticism, and Joanne herself was an accomplished athlete. Lim was training with his boss and other colleagues, and all agreed that it would be a healthy endeavor that would improve professional communication (as they thought there would be plenty of time to bond during training).

But as her delivery date approached, Joanne became apprehensive, which she expressed to Lim as concern that he might get injured. Her real concern, though, was that he was spending so much time on an activity that might drain his energy at a point when the family needed him most. One adjustment that Lim made to reassure Joanne of his commitment to their family was to initiate another experiment in which he took the steps needed to allow him to work at home on Thursday afternoons. He had to set up some new technologies and agree to send a monthly memo to his boss summarizing what he was accomplishing on those afternoons. He also bought a baby sling, which would allow him to keep his new son with him while at home.

In the end, not only were Joanne and their baby on hand to cheer Lim on while he ran the marathon, but she ended up joining him for the second half of the race to give him a boost when she saw his energy flagging. His business unit's numbers improved during the period when he was training and working at home. So did the unit's morale—people began to see the company as more flexible, and they were encouraged to be more creative in how they got their own work done—and word got around. Executives throughout the firm began to come up with their own ideas for ways to pay more attention to other sides of their employees' lives and so build a stronger sense of community at work.

The investment in a well-designed experiment almost always pays off because you learn how to lead in new and creative ways in all parts of your life. And if your experiments turn out well—as they usually, but not always, do—it will benefit everyone: you, your business, your family, and your community.

Measuring Progress

The only way to fail with an experiment is to fail to learn from it, and this makes useful metrics essential. No doubt it's better to achieve the results you are after than to fall short, but hitting targets does not in itself advance you toward becoming the leader you want to be. Failed experiments give you, and those around you, information that helps create better ones in the future.

The exhibit "How Do I Know If My Experiment Is Working?" shows how Kenneth Chen measured his progress. He used this simple chart to spell out the intended benefits of his experiment in each of the four domains and how he would assess whether he had realized these benefits. To set up your own scorecard, use a separate sheet for each experiment; at the top of the page, write a brief description of it. Then record your goals for each domain in the first column. In the middle column, describe your results metrics: how you will measure whether the goals for each domain have been achieved. In the third column, describe your action metrics—the plan for the steps you will take to implement your experiment. As you begin to implement your plan, you may find that your initial indicators are too broad or too vague, so refine your scorecard as you go along to make it more useful for you. The main point is to have practical ways of measuring your outcomes and your progress toward them, and the approach you take only needs to work for you and your stakeholders.

Workshop participants have used all kinds of metrics: cost savings from reduced travel, number of e-mail misunderstandings averted, degree of satisfaction with family time, hours spent volunteering at a

How do I know if my experiment is working?

Using this tool, an executive I'll call Kenneth Chen systematically set out in detail his various goals, the metrics he would use to measure his progress, and the steps he would take in conducting an experiment that would further those goals—joining the board of a nonprofit organization. Kenneth's work sheet is merely an example: Every person's experiments, goals, and metrics are unique.

A Sample Scorecard

	EXPERIMENT'S GOALS	HOW I WILL MEASURE SUCCESS	IMPLEMENTATION STEPS
Work	▲ To fulfill the expectation that executives will give back to the local community	▲ Collect business cards from everyone I meet on the board and during board meetings, and keep track of the number of professionals I meet	☐ Meet with my manager, who has sat on many boards and can provide support and advice
	▲ To establish networks with other officers in my company and other professionals in the area	▲ After each meeting, regularly record the leadership skills of those I would like to emulate	☐ Meet with the director of my company's foundation to determine my real interests and to help assess what relationship our firm has with various community organizations
	▲ To learn leadership skills from other board members and from the organization I join		☐ Discuss my course of action with my fiancée and see whether joining a board interests her
Home	▲ To join a board that can involve my fiancée, Celine	▲ See whether Celine gets involved in the board	☐ Sign up to attend the December 15 overview session of the Business on Board program
	▲ To have something to discuss with my sister (a special-education instructor)	▲ Record the number of conversations my sister and I have about community service for the next three months and see whether they have brought us closer	☐ Assess different opportunities within the community and then reach out to organizations I'm interested in

Community

▲ To provide my leadership skills to a nonprofit organization

▲ To get more involved in giving back to the community

▲ Record what I learn about each nonprofit organization I research

▲ Record the number of times I attend board meetings

☐ Apply for membership to a community board

Self

▲ To feel good about contributing to others' welfare

▲ To see others grow as a result of my efforts

▲ To become more compassionate

▲ Assess how I feel about myself in a daily journal

▲ Assess the effect I have on others in terms of potential number of people affected

▲ Ask for feedback from others about whether I've become more compassionate

teen center, and so on. Metrics may be objective or subjective, qualitative or quantitative, reported by you or by others, and frequently or intermittently observed. When it comes to frequency, for instance, it helps to consider how long you'll be able to remember what you did. For example, if you were to go on a diet to get healthier, increase energy, and enhance key relationships, food intake would be an important metric. But would you be able to remember what you ate two days ago?

Small Wins for Big Change

Experiments shouldn't be massive, all-encompassing shifts in the way you live. Highly ambitious designs usually fail because they're too much to handle. The best experiments let you try something new while minimizing the inevitable risks associated with change. When the stakes are smaller, it's easier to overcome the fear of failure that inhibits innovation. You start to see results, and others take note, which both inspires you to go further and builds support from your key stakeholders.

Another benefit of the small-wins approach to experiments is that it opens doors that would otherwise be closed. You can say to people invested in the decision, "Let's just try this. If it doesn't work, we'll go back to the old way or try something different." By framing an experiment as a trial, you reduce resistance because people are more likely to try something new if they know it's not permanent and if they have control over deciding whether the experiment is working according to *their* performance expectations.

But "small" is a relative term—what might look like a small step for you could seem like a giant leap to me, and vice versa. So don't get hung up on the word. What's more, this isn't about the scope or importance of the changes you eventually make. Large-scale change is grounded in small steps toward a big idea. So while the steps in an experiment might be small, the goals are not. Ismail, a successful 50-year-old entrepreneur and CEO of an engineering services company, described the goal for his first experiment this way: "Restructure my company and my role in it." There's nothing small about that. He felt he was missing a sense of purpose.

Ismail designed practical steps that would allow him to move toward his large goal over time. His first experiments were small and achievable. He introduced a new method that both his colleagues and his wife could use to communicate with him. He began to hold sacrosanct time for his family and his church. As he looked for ways to free up more time, he initiated delegation experiments that had the effect of flattening his organization's structure. These small wins crossed over several domains, and eventually he did indeed transform his company and his own role in it. When I spoke with him 18 months after he'd started, he acknowledged that he'd had a hard time coping with the loss of control over tactical business matters, but he described his experiments as "a testament to the idea of winning the small battles and letting the war be won as a result." He and his leadership team both felt more confident about the firm's new organizational structure.

People try the Total Leadership program for a variety of reasons. Some feel unfulfilled because they're not doing what they love. Some don't feel genuine because they're not acting according to their values. Others feel disconnected, isolated from people who matter to them. They crave stronger relationships, built on trust, and yearn for enriched social networks. Still others are just in a rut. They want to tap into their creative energy but don't know how (and sometimes lack the courage) to do so. They feel out of control and unable to fit in all that's important to them.

My hunch is that there are more four-way wins available to you than you'd think. They are there for the taking. You have to know how to look for them and then find the support and zeal to pursue them. By providing a blueprint for how you can be real, be whole, and be innovative as a leader in all parts of your life, this program helps you perform better according to the standards of the most important people in your life; feel better in all the domains of your life;

and foster greater harmony among the domains by increasing the resources available to you to fit all the parts of your life together. No matter what your career stage or current position, you can be a better leader and have a richer life—if you are ready and willing to rise to the challenge.

Originally published in April 2008. Reprint R0804H

Reclaim Your Job

by Sumantra Ghoshal and Heike Bruch

ASK MOST MANAGERS WHAT GETS in the way of success at work, and you hear the familiar litany of complaints: Not enough time. Shrinking resources. Lack of opportunity. When you look more closely, you begin to see that these are, for the most part, excuses. What gets in the way of managers' success is something much more personal—a deep uncertainty about acting according to their own best judgment. Rather than doing what they really need to do to advance the company's fortunes—and their own careers—they spin their wheels doing what they presume everyone else wants them to do.

Over the past five years, we have studied hundreds of managers as they have gone about their daily work in a variety of settings, including a global airline and a large U.S. oil company. As we demonstrated in "Beware the Busy Manager" (HBR February 2002), fully 90% of the managers we observed wasted their time and frittered away their productivity, despite having well-defined projects, goals, and the knowledge necessary to get their jobs done. Such managers remain trapped in inefficiency because they simply assume that they do not have enough personal discretion or control. The ability to seize initiative is the most essential quality of any truly successful manager.

In most instances, the demands that managers accept as givens are actually discretionary in nature. We have repeatedly confronted in our research a curious but pervasive reality of corporate life: Most managers complain about having too little freedom in their jobs, while their bosses complain about managers' failure to grasp opportunities. The truly effective managers we've observed are purposeful, trust in their own judgment, and adopt long-term, big-picture views to fulfill personal goals that tally with those of the organization as a whole. They break out of their perceived boxes, take control of their jobs, and become more productive by learning to do the following:

Manage demands

Most managers feel overwhelmed by demands. They assume that the business will come to a crashing halt without them and so allow real or imagined day-to-day work demands to subsume their own judgment. Effective managers proactively control their tasks and the expectations of their major stakeholders, which allows them to meet strategic goals rather than fight fires.

Generate resources

By following what they believe are strict orders from the top, many typical managers tend to concentrate on working within budget and resource constraints—thereby developing a boxed-in, "can't do" mind-set. By contrast, effective managers develop inventive strategies for circumventing real or imagined limitations. They map out ways around constraints by developing and acting on long-term strategies, making trade-offs, and occasionally breaking rules to achieve their goals.

Recognize and exploit alternatives

Average managers don't have enough perspective on the company's overall business strategy to present an alternative view. Effective managers, by contrast, develop and use deep expertise about an individual area that dovetails with the company's strategy. This tactic allows them to come up with a variety of innovative approaches to a given situation.[1]

In short, truly effective managers don't operate in the context of individual tasks or jobs but in the much broader context of their organizations and careers. That approach sounds simple enough, but it is sometimes hard to act on because some organizational cultures that

Idea in Brief

90% of managers waste time and fritter away their productivity by grappling with an endless list of demands from others. Why? We assume—wrongly—that those demands are *requirements,* and that we lack personal discretion or control over our jobs. The consequence? We remain trapped in inefficiency.

But we can escape this trap—if we learn how to grasp opportunities, trust our own judgment, and methodically fulfill personal goals that tally with our organizations' objectives. The keys? Set priorities— then stick to them, focusing on

efforts that support those priorities. Overcome resource constraints by attacking goals strategically, demonstrating success at every step. And develop a range of alternatives to exploit when plan A fails.

We all want to make a difference in our organizations, as well as build satisfying careers. By understanding how we inhibit ourselves and taking purposeful, strategic action, we can seize control of our jobs—rather than letting our jobs control us. The payoff? Impressive results for our companies and rewarding work lives for us.

tout "empowerment" actually discourage volition among their managers. Young, high-tech companies, for example, sometimes hold their managers hostage to frenzy, thus inhibiting the reflective and persistent pursuit of long-term goals. Other cultures—particularly those of old and established corporations with command-and-control hierarchies—can encourage people to go along with the status quo, regardless of the level of organizational dysfunction. In both kinds of environments, managers tend to fall into a reactive state of mind, assuming that any initiative they show will be either ignored or discouraged.

In most cases, however, it is not the environment that inhibits managers from taking purposeful action. Rather, it is managers themselves. We have found that managers can learn to act on their own potential and make a difference. Here's how.

Dealing with Demands

Almost everyone complains about not having enough time to deal with all the demands on them, but, in reality, a highly fragmented

Idea in Practice

To reclaim your job and better support your company's priorities, apply three strategies.

Prioritize Demands

To achieve personal and organizational goals quickly, *slow down* and focus your time and attention.

> *Example:* McKinsey associate principal Jessica Spungin took on too many projects that had little connection to her skills and interests. Result? Her project teams rated her second from the bottom among her peers.
>
> Realizing her desire to be indispensable sprang from lack of confidence, Spungin took steps to manage demands. She clarified her goal: to become a partner. Then she set long-term priorities supporting that goal. She began managing her own development; for example, choosing assignments that

most interested her. And she started orchestrating her time, meeting only with people who really needed her and working on long-term projects during months when she traveled less.

> Her reward? She scored second from the top in her peer group—and was named a McKinsey partner.

Liberate Resources

To relax resource constraints and win the backing you want, attack your goals strategically. Be patient. The process can take years.

> *Example:* As the new head of HR development at airline Lufthansa, Thomas Sattelberger dreamed of launching Germany's first corporate business school. Knowing he needed several years to establish his credibility, he first overhauled inefficient HR processes. He then developed

day is also a very lazy day. It can seem easier to fight fires than to set priorities and stick to them. The truth is that managers who carefully set boundaries and priorities achieve far more than busy ones do.

To beat the busy habit, managers must overcome the psychological desire to be indispensable. Because their work is interactive and interdependent, most managers thrive on their sense of importance to others. When they are not worrying about meeting their superiors' (or their clients') expectations, they fret about their direct reports, often falling victim to the popular fallacy that good bosses

initiatives supporting the school, raising money for these projects by presenting compelling facts and arguments to his counterparts and CEO.

After four years of methodical work on Sattelberger's part, Lufthansa's CEO and board understood how his programs fit together. When he wrote a memo to directors requesting creation of the school before Daimler-Benz could beat Lufthansa to the punch, the board promptly approved the request.

Exploit Alternatives

Use your expertise to anticipate—and circumvent—possible obstacles to your goals. You'll expand the scope of opportunity for your company *and* yourself.

> *Example:* Dan Andersson, a manager at oil refiner Conoco-Phillips, was part of a team exploring Conoco's entrance into the Finnish market. Conoco decided to store petrol in tanks in Finland that Shell had abandoned. But Andersson developed contingency plans. Plan B, for instance, involved building a new facility.
>
> His efforts paid off. When research revealed the abandoned tanks were unsuitable for petrol storage, Andersson activated Plan B. Though the new-facility target site was contaminated, Andersson discovered that Shell was responsible for cleaning the site. Once cleanup ended, Conoco built the tanks.
>
> Conoco became the most efficient operator of automated self-service filling stations in Finland. Andersson now heads Conoco's retail development in Europe.

always make themselves available. At first, managers—particularly novices—seem to thrive on all this clamoring for their time; the busier they are, the more valuable they feel. Inevitably, however, things start to slip. Eventually, many managers simply burn out and fail, not only because they find little time to pursue their own agendas but also because, in trying to please everyone, they typically end up pleasing no one.

Jessica Spungin found herself caught in this trap when she was promoted to associate principal in McKinsey's London office. As an AP, a consultant is expected to take on more responsibilities of the partnership group, juggle multiple projects, serve as a team leader, and play an active role in office life. Spungin dove in to all these tasks headfirst. While she was handling two major client projects, she was asked to jointly lead recruitment for U.K. universities and business schools, participate in an internal research initiative, serve as a senior coach for six business analysts, run an office party for 750 people, get involved in internal training, and help out on a new project for a health care company.

In her first round of feedback from the three project teams she oversaw, she was rated second from the bottom among her peers. Spungin realized that her desire to be indispensable sprang from a lack of confidence. "I never said no to people in case they thought I couldn't cope. I never said no to a client who wanted me to be present at a meeting," she told us. "I did what I thought was expected—regardless of what I was good at, what was important, or what I could physically do."

The first step in Spungin's transformation from a busy to an effective manager was to develop a vision of what she really wanted to achieve at McKinsey: to be named a partner. In developing a clear mental picture of herself in that role, she traded in her habit of thinking in short time spans of three to six months to thinking in strategic time spans of one to five years.

This longer-term planning allowed Spungin to develop a set of long-term goals and priorities. Soon, she took control of her own development. For example, it became clear to Spungin that corporate banking—which her colleagues believed to be her area of expertise based on her past experience—did not hold any real interest for her, even though she had accepted one banking project after another. Instead, she decided to shift her focus to the organizational practice, something she really enjoyed. (McKinsey, like many companies, allows its consultants significant flexibility in terms of choosing assignments, but most managers do not avail themselves of this opportunity.) By claiming a personal agenda and integrating short-, medium-, and long-term responsibilities into her broader master plan, Spungin felt much more motivated and excited about her work than she had when she was merely responding to everyday demands.

Finally, Spungin took charge of her time. She realized that trying to be accessible to everyone made her inaccessible to those who really needed her. She began prioritizing the time she spent with clients and team members. With her personal assistant's help, she streamlined her work. Previously, her assistant would schedule meetings in an ad hoc manner. Now, Spungin drove the calendar, so she could make the calls about which meetings she needed to attend. She began to recognize patterns of work intensity according to the time of year; for example, she travelled less in the fall, so Spungin set aside half a day each week to work on her long-term projects then. In the end, Spungin realized the irony of effective management: To quickly achieve the goals that mattered, she had to slow down and take control. To her surprise, the people who reported to her, as well as her supervisors and clients, responded well to her saying no.

Spungin was better able to respond to and shape the demands she chose to meet once she stopped trying to please everyone. She became more proactive—presenting her own goals and ideas to influence what others expected of her. By focusing on the most important demands, she exceeded expectations. One year after having been rated second from the bottom in her peer group, she scored second from the top. In June 2003, Spungin was named a McKinsey partner.

Developing Resources

In addition to lack of time, many managers complain about a shortage of people, money, and equipment, and a surplus of rules and regulations. They struggle with limited resources. While some feel frustrated and keep beating their heads against a wall to no avail, others just give up. Managers who develop a long-term strategy and attack their goals slowly, steadily, and strategically, on the other hand, can eventually win the backing they want.

Thomas Sattelberger faced all kinds of impossible constraints in 1994 when he left Daimler-Benz to join Lufthansa as the head of corporate management and human resources development. At the time, Lufthansa was in the middle of a strategic cost-savings program that required every unit to reduce its total expenditures by 4% each year for the next five years. Employees generally interpreted the cost-cutting directive to mean that investing in anything other than what was necessary to keep the lights on was verboten. Additionally, Lufthansa's HR processes were a mess; responses to routine requests often took months, and contracts frequently contained typographical errors. These kinds of operational problems had existed in the department for years.

For most managers in Sattelberger's position, the goals would have been simple: Get the HR department to a functional level without increasing costs, make sure it doesn't backslide, and collect a paycheck. But Sattelberger had much higher aspirations. He had come to Lufthansa with the dream of building Germany's most progressive corporate human resources organization, which would help transform the formerly state-operated company into a world-class airline. Specifically, he envisioned starting Germany's first corporate university, the Lufthansa School of Business, which would extend far beyond traditional approaches to training and development. The university would tighten the links between strategy and organizational and individual development. Its curricula, including master's and nondegree management programs, would be designed, run, and evaluated by academics and leaders from global companies, so Lufthansa's managers would learn from the best.

In pursuing his dream, Sattelberger chose a methodical, clever, and patient mode of attack. First, he created an imaginary blueprint depicting his university as a kind of leadership development temple. The architectural conceit—the temple being built brick by brick and pillar by pillar—helped Sattelberger develop a long-term, strategic implementation plan. Cleaning up basic HR processes, he reasoned, was analogous to laying the foundation. With that accomplished, he would erect a series of development programs, each acting as a pillar that would hold up the "roof" of Lufthansa's overall corporate strategy. Seeing his plan as a blueprint also helped Sattelberger separate the "must-haves" from the "nice-to-haves" and the "can-live-withouts," which enabled him to focus on only the most vital and achievable elements.

Sattelberger understood that he had to be flexible and that building his temple would demand years of methodical work. He never spoke about his vision as a whole because its overall cost would have frightened most of the stakeholders. Instead, he secured their commitment for individual projects and programs and implemented the initiatives sequentially.

Step two was to lay the foundation that he had imagined. Over the course of two years, Sattelberger reorganized HR processes so that requests were met in a timely matter and operations made more efficient. Given the dismal state of Lufthansa's HR systems, no one anticipated that Sattelberger could possibly meet, much less exceed, expectations. He showed them wrong.

Capitalizing on his new credibility, he next set to work on step three: building the individual pillars. One project, Explorer 21, was a comprehensive development initiative in which managers would learn from one another. A separate program, ProTeam, was designed for management trainees. And another large-scale program focused on emulating best practices from companies such as General Electric, Citibank, Deutsche Bank, Daimler-Benz, and SAS.

The spending cap was a significant hurdle. Sattelberger had persuaded top management to allow him to rent out some training rooms to other companies to raise money for these projects, but he needed more. He understood that there was a limit to how far and how fast he could push: If he pressed too hard, a backlash would ensue. So in petitioning for funds, Sattelberger made sure he was better prepared than his counterparts with arguments and facts. When the controller failed to give him the green light, he made his case directly to Jürgen Weber, the CEO. Weber agreed in principle that the corporate university project was worthwhile, although the conversation was not an easy one. "For God's sake, do it," he ended up telling Sattelberger, "but do it right and stick to your budget."

Weber and the board eventually began to see how Sattelberger's development programs fit together. Then, in March 1998—when he learned that Daimler-Benz was about to beat Lufthansa to the punch with a corporate university of its own—Sattelberger made his final move. Determined not to let Daimler prevail, he wrote a memo requesting the creation of the Lufthansa School of Business to the board of directors. It approved the request without a moment's hesitation or debate, and Lufthansa opened Europe's first corporate university the following month.

The whole process took time, something purposeful managers, as we have shown previously, claim for themselves. Sattelberger coped with many setbacks and accepted significant delays and even cancellations of different aspects of his initiative. He delayed his plans for the corporate university for the first two years so he could focus solely on putting HR in order. Then, slowly and progressively, he worked to relax resource constraints. Although he started with much less than he expected, he never allowed his resolve to wither. Lufthansa has never measured the precise payback from its school of business, but the subjective judgment of top management is that the return has been much higher than the investment.

Exploiting Alternatives

When it comes to making decisions or pursuing initiatives, managers also fall victim to the trap of unexplored choices. Specifically, they either do not recognize that they have choices or do not take advantage of those they know they have. Because managers ignore their freedom to act, they surrender their options. Purposeful initiators, by contrast, hone their personal expertise, which confers confidence, a wide perspective of a particular arena, and greater credibility. These managers develop the ability to see, grasp, and fight for opportunities as they arise.

Dan Andersson was a midlevel manager who worked for the oil-refining company ConocoPhillips in Stockholm. As a native of Finland, he brought to Conoco a precious managerial commodity: deep knowledge of the Finnish market. This knowledge enabled him to convey information about specific regional conditions to senior managers, who did not speak the language or understand Finland's business issues. Because he had been mentored by the managing director of Conoco's Nordic operations, Andersson quickly grasped how the managerial invisibles—informal rules and norms, decision-making processes, interpersonal relationships, and social dynamics— influenced the reception of new ideas. He intuitively sensed the right way to present a proposal and the extent to which he could push at a particular point of time.

Andersson was assigned to a team charged with exploring Conoco's possible entrance into the Finnish market, which involved breaking a 50-year monopoly in the region. The first task was to set up storage facilities in Finland, an estimated $1 million project that would allow Conoco to import its own petrol. After several months of intense searching, the team eventually found an existing tank terminal, located in the city of Turku, that Shell had abandoned decades previously. Built in the 1920s, the old tanks appeared to be clean and usable. The Conoco team thought the solution had been found. In the back of his mind, however, Andersson was already at work on contingency plans. Plan B was to build a new facility, plan C was to create a joint venture with a competitor, and plan D was to find an investor for the tanks.

After months of negotiation, Turku's officials approved Conoco's lease of the old tanks. Then came the fateful phone call from Conoco's laboratory: There was too much carbon in the steel; the tanks were unsuitable for storing petrol. Without its own storage facility, Conoco could not enter the Finnish market. There was no other facility in the country that Conoco could buy. Abandoning the project seemed the only choice. Everyone on the team gave up except Andersson, who proposed putting plan B into action.

With the support of the local authorities, he persuaded the Conoco senior team to visit Finland for face-to-face discussions about the possibility of Conoco building its own tanks at the site. Once Andersson's boss saw the land and sensed the opportunity, he grew enthusiastic about a ground-up approach. As it happened, however, the land was contaminated; cleanup would have cost tens of millions of euros. Still, Andersson persisted. Working with city officials, he discovered the original contracts clearly showed that Shell was responsible for the cleanup of the land. Once the cleanup was complete, Conoco began work on the new tanks. When the first Conoco ship arrived at the harbor, three years after the project had begun, city representatives, hundreds of spectators, Finnish television crews, and Conoco's top management were present to celebrate. Today, Conoco is the most efficient operator of automated self-service filling stations in Finland.

As a manager, Andersson's allegiance was not merely to a job but to accomplishing, one way or another, the strategic goals of his company. By scanning the environment for possible obstacles and searching for ways around them, he was able to expand his company's, and his own, scope of opportunity. Today, he is responsible for ConocoPhillips' retail development in Europe.

A bias for action is not a special gift of a few. Most managers can develop this capacity. Spungin's story demonstrates how focusing on a clear, long-term goal widened her horizon. Sattelberger and Andersson countered limitations with plans of their own and showed their companies what was possible.

In our studies of managers, we have found that the difference between those who take the initiative and those who do not becomes particularly evident during phases of major change, when managerial work becomes relatively chaotic and unstructured. Managers who fret about conforming to the explicit or imagined expectations of others respond to lack of structure by becoming disoriented and paralyzed. Effective managers, by contrast, seize the opportunity to extend the scope of their jobs, expand their choices, and pursue ambitious goals.

Once managers command their agendas and sense their own freedom of choice, they come to relish their roles. They begin to search for situations that go beyond their scope and enjoy seizing opportunities as they arise. Above all, effective managers with a bias for action aren't managed by their jobs; rather, the reverse is true.

Originally published in March 2004. Reprint R0403B

Note

1. The framework of demands, constraints, and choices as a way to think about managerial jobs was first suggested by Rosemary Stewart in her book *Managers and Their Jobs* (Macmillan, 1967). See also Rosemary Stewart, *Choices for the Manager* (Prentice Hall, 1982).

Moments of Greatness

Entering the Fundamental State of Leadership.
by Robert E. Quinn

AS LEADERS, SOMETIMES we're truly "on," and sometimes we're not. Why is that? What separates the episodes of excellence from those of mere competence? In striving to tip the balance toward excellence, we try to identify great leaders' qualities and behaviors so we can develop them ourselves. Nearly all corporate training programs and books on leadership are grounded in the assumption that we should study the behaviors of those who have been successful and teach people to emulate them.

But my colleagues and I have found that when leaders do their best work, they don't copy anyone. Instead, they draw on their own fundamental values and capabilities—operating in a frame of mind that is true to them yet, paradoxically, not their normal state of being. I call it the *fundamental state of leadership*. It's the way we lead when we encounter a crisis and finally choose to move forward. Think back to a time when you faced a significant life challenge: a promotion opportunity, the risk of professional failure, a serious illness, a divorce, the death of a loved one, or any other major jolt. Most likely, if you made decisions not to meet others' expectations but to suit what you instinctively understood to be right—in other words, if you were at your very best—you rose to the task because you were being tested.

Is it possible to enter the fundamental state of leadership without crisis? In my work coaching business executives, I've found that if we ask ourselves—and honestly answer—just four questions, we can make the shift at any time. It's a temporary state. Fatigue and external resistance pull us out of it. But each time we reach it, we return to our everyday selves a bit more capable, and we usually elevate the performance of the people around us as well. Over time, we all can become more effective leaders by deliberately choosing to enter the fundamental state of leadership rather than waiting for crisis to force us there.

Defining the Fundamental State

Even those who are widely admired for their seemingly easy and natural leadership skills—presidents, prime ministers, CEOs—do not usually function in the fundamental state of leadership. Most of the time, they are in their normal state—a healthy and even necessary condition under many circumstances, but not one that's conducive to coping with crisis. In the normal state, people tend to stay within their comfort zones and allow external forces to direct their behaviors and decisions. They lose moral influence and often rely on rational argument and the exercise of authority to bring about change. Others comply with what these leaders ask, out of fear, but the result is usually unimaginative and incremental—and largely reproduces what already exists.

To elevate the performance of others, we must elevate ourselves into the fundamental state of leadership. Getting there requires a shift along four dimensions. (See the exhibit "There's Normal, and There's Fundamental.")

First, we move from being comfort centered to being results centered. The former feels safe but eventually leads to a sense of languishing and meaninglessness. In his book *The Path of Least Resistance,* Robert Fritz carefully explains how asking a single question can move us from the normal, reactive state to a much more generative condition. That question is this: What result do I want to

Idea in Brief

Like all leaders, sometimes you're "on," and sometimes you're not. How to tip the scale toward excellence and away from mere competence? Don't rely on imitating other leaders or poring over leadership manuals. Instead, enter the **fundamental state of leadership**: the way you lead when a crisis forces you to tap into your deepest values and instincts. In this state, you instinctively know what to do: You rise to the occasion and perform at your best.

Fortunately, you don't need a crisis to shift into the fundamental state of leadership. You can do so any time (before a crucial conversation, during a key meeting) by asking four questions:

- **"Am I results centered?"** Have you articulated the result you want to create?

- **"Am I internally directed?"** Are you willing to challenge others' expectations?

- **"Am I other focused?"** Have you put your organization's needs above your own?

- **"Am I externally open?"** Do you recognize signals suggesting the need for change?

No one can operate at the top of their game 24/7. But each time you enter the fundamental state of leadership, you make it easier to return to that state again. And you inspire others around you to higher levels of excellence.

create? Giving an honest answer pushes us off nature's path of least resistance. It leads us from problem solving to purpose finding.

Second, we move from being externally directed to being more internally directed. That means that we stop merely complying with others' expectations and conforming to the current culture. To become more internally directed is to clarify our core values and increase our integrity, confidence, and authenticity. As we become more confident and more authentic, we behave differently. Others must make sense of our new behavior. Some will be attracted to it, and some will be offended by it. That's not prohibitive, though: When we are true to our values, we are willing to initiate such conflict.

Third, we become less self-focused and more focused on others. We put the needs of the organization as a whole above our own. Few among us would admit that personal needs trump the collective

Idea in Practice

To enter the fundamental state of leadership, apply these steps:

1. **Recognize you've already been there.** You've faced great challenges before and, in surmounting them, you entered the fundamental state. By recalling these moments' lessons, you release positive emotions and see new possibilities for your current situation.

2. **Analyze your current state.** Compare your normal performance with what you've done at your very best. You'll fuel a desire to elevate what you're doing now and instill confidence that you can reenter the fundamental state.

3. **Ask the four questions shown in the following chart.**

BY ASKING . . .	YOU SHIFT FROM . . .	TO . . .
Am I results centered?	Remaining in your comfort zone and solving familiar problems	Moving toward possibilities that don't yet exist
Am I internally directed?	Complying with others' expectations and conforming to existing conditions	Clarifying your core values, acting with authenticity and confidence, and willingly initiating productive conflict
Am I other focused?	Allowing pursuit of your own self-interest to shape your relationships	Committing to the collective good in your organization—even at personal cost

good, but the impulse to control relationships in a way that feeds our own interests is natural and normal. That said, self-focus over time leads to feelings of isolation. When we put the collective good first, others reward us with their trust and respect. We form tighter, more sensitive bonds. Empathy increases, and cohesion follows. We create an enriched sense of community, and that helps us transcend the conflicts that are a necessary element in high-performing organizations.

Am I externally open?	Controlling your environment, making incremental changes, and relying on established routines	Learning from your environment, acknowledging the need for major change, and departing from routines

Example: John Jones, a successful change leader, had turned around two struggling divisions in his corporation. Promised the presidency of the largest division when the incumbent retired, he was told meanwhile to bide his time overseeing a dying division's "funeral." He determined to turn the division around. After nine months, though, he'd seen little improvement. Employees weren't engaged.

To enter the fundamental state, John asked:

- **"Am I results oriented?"** He suddenly envisioned a new strategy for his struggling division, along with a plan (including staff reassignments) for implementing it. With a clear, compelling strategy in mind, his energy soared.

- **"Am I internally directed?"** He realized that his focus on the promised plum job had prevented him from doing the hard work needed to motivate his division's people to give more.

- **"Am I other focused?"** He decided to turn down the presidency in favor of rescuing his failing division—a course truer to his leadership values. He thus traded personal security for a greater good.

- **"Am I externally open?"** He stopped deceiving himself into thinking he'd done all he could for his failing division and realized he had the capacity to improve things.

Fourth, we become more open to outside signals or stimuli, including those that require us to do things we are not comfortable doing. In the normal state, we pay attention to signals that we know to be relevant. If they suggest incremental adjustments, we respond. If, however, they call for more dramatic changes, we may adopt a posture of defensiveness and denial; this mode of self-protection and self-deception separates us from the ever-changing external world. We live according to an outdated, less valid, image of what is

There's normal, and there's fundamental

Under everyday circumstances, leaders can remain in their normal state of being and do what they need to do. But some challenges require a heightened perspective—what can be called the fundamental state of leadership. Here's how the two states differ.

In the normal state, I am ...	In the fundamental state, I am ...
COMFORT CENTERED	**RESULTS CENTERED**
I stick with what I know.	I venture beyond familiar territory to pursue ambitious new outcomes.
EXTERNALLY DIRECTED	**INTERNALLY DIRECTED**
I comply with others' wishes in an effort to keep the peace.	I behave according to my values.
SELF-FOCUSED	**OTHER FOCUSED**
I place my interests above those of the group.	I put the collective good first.
INTERNALLY CLOSED	**EXTERNALLY OPEN**
I block out external stimuli in order to stay on task and avoid risk.	I learn from my environment and recognize when there's a need for change.

real. But in the fundamental state of leadership, we are more aware of what is unfolding, and we generate new images all the time. We are adaptive, credible, and unique. In this externally open state, no two people are alike.

These four qualities—being results centered, internally directed, other focused, and externally open—are at the heart of positive human influence, which is generative and attractive. A person without these four characteristics can also be highly influential, but his or her influence tends to be predicated on some form of control or force, which does not usually give rise to committed followers. By entering the fundamental state of leadership, we increase the likelihood of attracting others to an elevated level of community, a high-performance state that may continue even when we are not present.

Preparing for the Fundamental State

Because people usually do not leave their comfort zones unless forced, many find it helpful to follow a process when they choose to enter the fundamental state of leadership. I teach a technique to executives and use it in my own work. It simply involves asking four awareness-raising questions designed to help us transcend our natural denial mechanisms. When people become aware of their hypocrisies, they are more likely to change. Those who are new to the "fundamental state" concept, however, need to take two preliminary steps before they can understand and employ it.

Step 1: Recognize that you have previously entered the fundamental state of leadership

Every reader of this publication has reached, at one time or another, the fundamental state of leadership. We've all faced a great personal or professional challenge and spent time in the dark night of the soul. In successfully working through such episodes, we inevitably enter the fundamental state of leadership.

When I introduce people to this concept, I ask them to identify two demanding experiences from their past and ponder what happened in terms of intention, integrity, trust, and adaptability. At first, they resist the exercise because I am asking them to revisit times of great personal pain. But as they recount their experiences, they begin to see that they are also returning to moments of greatness. Our painful experiences often bring out our best selves. Recalling the lessons of such moments releases positive emotions and makes it easier to see what's possible in the present. In this exercise, I ask people to consider their behavior during these episodes in relation to the characteristics of the fundamental state of leadership. (See the exhibit "You've Already Been There" for analyses of two actual episodes.)

Sometimes I also ask workshop participants to share their stories with one another. Naturally, they are reluctant to talk about such dark moments. To help people open up, I share my own moments of great challenge, the ones I would normally keep to myself. By exhibiting

You've already been there

Two participants in a leadership workshop at the University of Michigan's Ross School of Business used this self-assessment tool to figure out how they've transcended their greatest life challenges by entering the fundamental state of leadership. You can use the same approach in analyzing how you've conquered your most significant challenges.

	PARTICIPANT A	PARTICIPANT B
The pivotal crisis:	I was thrust into a job that was crucial to the organization but greatly exceeded my capabilities. I had to get people to do things they did not want to do.	I was driving myself hard at work, and things kept getting worse at home. Finally my wife told me she wanted a divorce.
How did you become more results centered?	I kept trying to escape doing what was required, but I could not stand the guilt. I finally decided I had to change. I envisioned what success might look like, and I committed to making whatever changes were necessary.	I felt I'd lost everything: family, wealth, and stature. I withdrew from relationships. I started drinking heavily. I finally sought professional help for my sorrow and, with guidance, clarified my values and made choices about my future.
How did you become more internally directed?	I stopped worrying so much about how other people would evaluate and judge me. I was starting to operate from my own values. I felt more self-empowered than ever and realized how fear driven I had been.	I engaged in a lot of self-reflection and journal writing. It became clear that I was not defined by marriage, wealth, or stature. I was more than that. I began to focus on how I could make a difference for other people. I got more involved in my community.
How did you become more focused on others?	I realized how much I needed people, and I became more concerned about them. I was better able to hear what they were saying. I talked not just from my head but also from my heart. My colleagues responded. Today, I am still close to those people.	As I started to grow and feel more self-confident, I became better at relating. At work, I now ask more of people than I ever did before, but I also give them far more support. I care about them, and they can tell.
How did you becom more externally open?	I experimented with new approaches. They often did not work, but they kept the brainstorming in motion. I paid attention to every kind of feedback. I was hungry to get it right. There was a lot of discovery. Each step forward was exhilarating.	I began to feel stronger. I was less intimidated when people gave me negative feedback. I think it was because I was less afraid of changing and growing.

vulnerability, I'm able to win the group's trust and embolden other people to exercise the same courage. I recently ran a workshop with a cynical group of executives. After I broke the testimonial ice, one of the participants told us of a time when he had accepted a new job that required him to relocate his family. Just before he was to start, his new boss called in a panic, asking him to cut his vacation short and begin work immediately. The entire New England engineering team had quit; clients in the region had no support whatsoever. The executive started his job early, and his family had to navigate the move without his help. He described the next few months as "the worst and best experience" of his life.

Another executive shared that he'd found out he had cancer the same week he was promoted and relocated to Paris, not knowing how to speak French. His voice cracked as he recalled these stressful events. But then he told us about the good that came out of them— how he conquered both the disease and the job while also becoming a more authentic and influential leader.

Others came forward with their own stories, and I saw a great change in the group. The initial resistance and cynicism began to disappear, and participants started exploring the fundamental state of leadership in a serious way. They saw the power in the concept and recognized that hiding behind their pride or reputation would only get in the way of future progress. In recounting their experiences, they came to realize that they had become more purposive, authentic, compassionate, and responsive.

Step 2: Analyze your current state
When we're in the fundamental state, we take on various positive characteristics, such as clarity of vision, self-empowerment, empathy, and creative thinking. (See the exhibit "Are You in the Fundamental State of Leadership?" for a checklist organized along the four dimensions.) Most of us would like to say we display these characteristics at all times, but we really do so only sporadically.

Comparing our normal performance with what we have done at our very best often creates a desire to elevate what we are doing now. Knowing we've operated at a higher level in the past instills

Are you in the fundamental state of leadership?

Think of a time when you reached the fundamental state of leadership—that is, when you were at your best as a leader—and use this checklist to identify the qualities you displayed. Then check off the items that describe your behavior today. Compare the past and present. If there's a significant difference, what changes do you need to make to get back to the fundamental state?

At my best I was ...	Today I am ...	
		RESULTS CENTERED
____	____	Knowing what result I'd like to create
____	____	Holding high standards
____	____	Initiating actions
____	____	Challenging people
____	____	Disrupting the status quo
____	____	Capturing people's attention
____	____	Feeling a sense of shared purpose
____	____	Engaging in urgent conversations
		INTERNALLY DIRECTED
____	____	Operating from my core values
____	____	Finding motivation from within
____	____	Feeling self-empowered
____	____	Leading courageously
____	____	Bringing hidden conflicts to the surface
____	____	Expressing what I really believe
____	____	Feeling a sense of shared reality
____	____	Engaging in authentic conversations
		OTHER FOCUSED
____	____	Sacrificing personal interests for the common good
____	____	Seeing the potential in everyone
____	____	Trusting others and fostering interdependence
____	____	Empathizing with people's needs
____	____	Expressing concern
____	____	Supporting people
____	____	Feeling a sense of shared identity
____	____	Engaging in participative conversations

		EXTERNALLY OPEN
——	——	Moving forward into uncertainty
——	——	Inviting feedback
——	——	Paying deep attention to what's unfolding
——	——	Learning exponentially
——	——	Watching for new opportunities
——	——	Growing continually
——	——	Feeling a sense of shared contribution
——	——	Engaging in creative conversations

confidence that we can do so again; it quells our fear of stepping into unknown and risky territory.

Asking Four Transformative Questions

Of course, understanding the fundamental state of leadership and recognizing its power are not the same as being there. Entering that state is where the real work comes in. To get started, we can ask ourselves four questions that correspond with the four qualities of the fundamental state.

To show how each of these qualities affects our behavior while we're in the fundamental state of leadership, I'll draw on stories from two executives. One is a company president; we'll call him John Jones. The other, Robert Yamamoto, is the executive director of the Los Angeles Junior Chamber of Commerce. Both once struggled with major challenges that changed the way they thought about their jobs and their lives.

I met John in an executive course I was teaching. He was a successful change leader who had turned around two companies in his corporation. Yet he was frustrated. He had been promised he'd become president of the largest company in the corporation as soon as the current president retired, which would happen in the near future. In the meantime, he had been told to bide his time with a company that everyone considered dead. His assignment was simply to oversee the funeral, yet he took it as a personal challenge to turn the company around. After he had been there nine months, however, there was little improvement, and the people were still not very engaged.

As for Robert, he had been getting what he considered to be acceptable (if not exceptional) results in his company. So when the new board president asked him to prepare a letter of resignation, Robert was stunned. He underwent a period of anguished introspection, during which he began to distrust others and question his own management skills and leadership ability. Concerned for his family and his future, he started to seek another job and wrote the requested letter.

As you will see, however, even though things looked grim for both Robert and John, they were on the threshold of positive change.

Am I results centered?

Most of the time, we are comfort centered. We try to continue doing what we know how to do. We may think we are pursuing new outcomes, but if achieving them means leaving our comfort zones, we subtly—even unconsciously—find ways to avoid doing so. We typically advocate ambitious outcomes while designing our work for maximum administrative convenience, which allows us to avoid conflict but frequently ends up reproducing what already exists. Often, others collude with us to act out this deception. Being comfort centered is hypocritical, self-deceptive, and normal.

Clarifying the result we want to create requires us to reorganize our lives. Instead of moving away from a problem, we move toward a possibility that does not yet exist. We become more proactive, intentional, optimistic, invested, and persistent. We also tend to become more energized, and our impact on others becomes energizing.

Consider what happened with John. When I first spoke with him, he sketched out his strategy with little enthusiasm. Sensing that lack of passion, I asked him a question designed to test his commitment to the end he claimed he wanted to obtain:

> What if you told your people the truth? Suppose you told them that nobody really expects you to succeed, that you were assigned to be a caretaker for 18 months, and that you

have been promised a plum job once your assignment is through. And then you tell them that you have chosen instead to give up that plum job and bet your career on the people present. Then, from your newly acquired stance of optimism for the company's prospects, you issue some challenges beyond your employees' normal capacity.

To my surprise, John responded that he was beginning to think along similar lines. He grabbed a napkin and rapidly sketched out a new strategy along with a plan for carrying it out, including reassignments for his staff. It was clear and compelling, and he was suddenly full of energy.

What happened here? John was the president of his company and therefore had authority. And he'd turned around two other companies—evidence that he had the knowledge and competencies of a change leader. Yet he was *failing* as a change leader. That's because he had slipped into his comfort zone. He was going through the motions, doing what had worked elsewhere. He was imitating a great leader—in this case, John himself. But imitation is not the way to enter the fundamental state of leadership. If I had accused John of not being committed to a real vision, he would have been incensed. He would have argued heatedly in denial of the truth. All I had to do, though, was nudge him in the right direction. As soon as he envisioned the result he wanted to create and committed himself to it, a new strategy emerged and he was reenergized.

Then there was Robert, who went to what he assumed would be his last board meeting and found that he had more support than he'd been led to believe. Shockingly, at the end of the meeting, he still had his job. Even so, this fortuitous turn brought on further soul-searching. Robert started to pay more attention to what he was doing; he began to see his tendency to be tactical and to gravitate toward routine tasks. He concluded that he was managing, not leading. He was playing a role and abdicating leadership to the board president—not because that person had the knowledge and vision to lead but because the position came with the statutory right to lead.

"I suddenly decided to really lead my organization," Robert said. "It was as if a new person emerged. The decision was not about me. I needed to do it for the good of the organization."

In deciding to "really lead," Robert started identifying the strategic outcomes he wanted to create. As he did this, he found himself leaving his zone of comfort—behaving in new ways and generating new outcomes.

Am I internally directed?

In the normal state, we comply with social pressures in order to avoid conflict and remain connected with our coworkers. However, we end up feeling *less* connected because conflict avoidance results in political compromise. We begin to lose our uniqueness and our sense of integrity. The agenda gradually shifts from creating an external result to preserving political peace. As this problem intensifies, we begin to lose hope and energy.

This loss was readily apparent in the case of John. He was his corporation's shining star. But since he was at least partially focused on the future reward—the plum job—he was not fully focused on doing the hard work he needed to do at the moment. So he didn't ask enough of the people he was leading. To get more from them, John needed to be more internally directed.

Am I other focused?

It's hard to admit, but most of us, most of the time, put our own needs above those of the whole. Indeed, it is healthy to do so; it's a survival mechanism. But when the pursuit of our own interests controls our relationships, we erode others' trust in us. Although people may comply with our wishes, they no longer derive energy from their relationships with us. Over time we drive away the very social support we seek.

To become more focused on others is to commit to the collective good in relationships, groups, or organizations, even if it means incurring personal costs. When John made the shift into the fundamental state of leadership, he committed to an uncertain future for himself. He had been promised a coveted job. All he had to do was wait a few months. Still, he was unhappy, so he chose to turn down the opportunity in favor of a course that was truer to his leadership values. When he shifted gears, he sacrificed his personal security in favor of a greater good.

Remember Robert's words: "The decision was not about me. I needed to do it for the good of the organization." After entering the fundamental state of leadership, he proposed a new strategic direction to the board's president and said that if the board didn't like it, he would walk away with no regrets. He knew that the strategy would benefit the organization, regardless of how it would affect him personally. Robert put the good of the organization first. When a leader does this, people notice, and the leader gains respect and trust. Group members, in turn, become more likely to put the collective good first. When they do, tasks that previously seemed impossible become doable.

Am I externally open?

Being closed to external stimuli has the benefit of keeping us on task, but it also allows us to ignore signals that suggest a need for change. Such signals would force us to cede control and face risk, so denying them is self-protective, but it is also self-deceptive. John convinced himself he'd done all he could for his failing company when, deep down, he knew that he had the capacity to improve things. Robert was self-deceptive, too, until crisis and renewed opportunity caused him to open up and explore the fact that he was playing a role accorded him but not using his knowledge and emotional capacity to transcend that role and truly lead his people.

Asking ourselves whether we're externally open shifts our focus from controlling our environment to learning from it and helps us recognize the need for change. Two things happen as a result. First, we are forced to improvise in response to previously unrecognized cues—that is, to depart from established routines. And second, because trial-and-error survival requires an accurate picture of the results we're creating, we actively and genuinely seek honest feedback. Since people trust us more when we're in this state, they tend to offer more accurate feedback, understanding that we are likely to learn from the message rather than kill the messenger.

A cycle of learning and empowerment is created, allowing us to see things that people normally cannot see and to formulate transformational strategies.

Applying the Fundamental Principles

Just as I teach others about the fundamental state of leadership, I also try to apply the concept in my own life. I was a team leader on a project for the University of Michigan's Executive Education Center. Usually, the center runs weeklong courses that bring in 30 to 40 executives. It was proposed that we develop a new product, an integrated week of perspectives on leadership. C. K. Prahalad would begin with a strategic perspective, then Noel Tichy, Dave Ulrich, Karl Weick, and I would follow with our own presentations. The objective was to fill a 400-seat auditorium. Since each presenter had a reasonably large following in some domain of the executive world, we were confident we could fill the seats, so we scheduled the program for the month of July, when our facilities were typically underutilized.

In the early months of planning and organizing, everything went perfectly. A marketing consultant had said we could expect to secure half our enrollment three weeks prior to the event. When that time rolled around, slightly less than half of the target audience had signed up, so we thought all was well. But then a different consultant indicated that for our kind of event we would get few additional enrollments during the last three weeks. This stunning prediction meant that attendance would be half of what we expected and we would be lucky to break even.

As the team leader, I could envision the fallout. Our faculty members, accustomed to drawing a full house, would be offended by a half-empty room; the dean would want to know what went wrong; and the center's staff would probably point to the team leader as the problem. That night I spent several hours pacing the floor. I was filled with dread and shame. Finally I told myself that this kind of behavior was useless. I went to my desk and wrote down the four questions. As I considered them, I concluded that I was comfort centered, externally directed, self-focused, and internally closed.

So I asked myself, "What result do I want to create?" I wrote that I wanted the center to learn how to offer a new, world-class product that would be in demand over time. With that clarification came a freeing insight: Because this was our first offering of the product, turning a large profit was not essential. That would be nice, of course, but we'd be happy to learn how to do such an event properly, break even, and lay the groundwork for making a profit in the future.

I then asked myself, "How can I become other focused?" At that moment, I was totally self-focused—I was worried about my reputation—and my first inclination was to be angry with the staff. But in shifting my focus to what they might be thinking that night, I realized they were most likely worried that I'd come to work in the morning ready to assign blame. Suddenly, I saw a need to both challenge and support them.

Finally, I thought about how I could become externally open. It would mean moving forward and learning something new, even if that made me uncomfortable. I needed to engage in an exploratory dialogue rather than preside as the expert in charge.

I immediately began making a list of marketing strategies, though I expected many of them would prove foolish since I knew nothing about marketing. The next day, I brought the staff together—and they, naturally, were guarded. I asked them what result we wanted to create. What happened next is a good example of how contagious the fundamental state of leadership can be.

We talked about strategies for increasing attendance, and after a while, I told the staff that I had some silly marketing ideas and was embarrassed to share them but was willing to do anything to help. They laughed at many of my naive thoughts about how to increase publicity and create pricing incentives. Yet my proposals also sparked serious discussion, and the group began to brainstorm its way into a collective strategy. Because I was externally open, there was space and time for everyone to lead. People came up with better ways of approaching media outlets and creating incentives. In that meeting, the group developed a shared sense of purpose, reality, identity, and contribution. They left feeling reasonable optimism and went forward as a committed team.

In the end, we did not get 400 participants, but we filled more than enough seats to have a successful event. We more than broke even, and we developed the skills we needed to run such an event better in the future. The program was a success because something transformational occurred among the staff. Yet the transformation did not originate in the meeting. It began the night before, when I asked myself the four questions and moved from the normal, reactive state to the fundamental state of leadership. And my entry into the fundamental state encouraged the staff to enter as well.

While the fundamental state proves useful in times of crisis, it can also help us cope with more mundane challenges. If I am going to have an important conversation, attend a key meeting, participate in a significant event, or teach a class, part of my preparation is to try to reach the fundamental state of leadership. Whether I am working with an individual, a group, or an organization, I ask the same four questions. They often lead to high-performance outcomes, and the repetition of high-performance outcomes can eventually create a high-performance culture.

Inspiring Others to High Performance

When we enter the fundamental state of leadership, we immediately have new thoughts and engage in new behaviors. We can't remain in this state forever. It can last for hours, days, or sometimes months, but eventually we come back to our normal frame of mind. While the fundamental state is temporary, each time we are in it we learn more about people and our environment and increase the probability that we will be able to return to it. Moreover, we inspire those around us to higher levels of performance.

To this day, Robert marvels at the contrast between his organization's past and present. His transformation into a leader with positive energy and a willingness and ability to tackle challenges in new ways helped shape the L.A. Junior Chamber of Commerce into a high-functioning and creative enterprise. When I last spoke to Robert, here's what he had to say:

> I have a critical mass of individuals on both the staff and the board who are willing to look at our challenges in a new way and work on solutions together. At our meetings, new energy is present. What previously seemed unimaginable now seems to happen with ease.

Any CEO would be delighted to be able to say these things. But the truth is, it's not a typical situation. When Robert shifted into the fundamental state of leadership, his group (which started off in a normal state) came to life, infused with his renewed energy and vision. Even after he'd left the fundamental state, the group sustained a higher level of performance. It continues to flourish, without significant staff changes or restructuring.

All this didn't happen because Robert read a book or an article about the best practices of some great leader. It did not happen because he was imitating someone else. It happened because he was jolted out of his comfort zone and was forced to enter the fundamental state of leadership. He was driven to clarify the result he wanted to create, to act courageously from his core values, to surrender his self-interest to the collective good, and to open himself up to learning in real time. From Robert, and others like him, we can learn the value of challenging ourselves in this way—a painful process but one with great potential to make a positive impact on our own lives and on the people around us.

Originally published in July 2005. Reprint R0507F

What to Ask the Person in the Mirror

by Robert S. Kaplan

IF YOU'RE LIKE MOST successful leaders, you were, in the early stages of your career, given plenty of guidance and support. You were closely monitored, coached, and mentored. But as you moved up the ladder, the sources of honest and useful feedback became fewer, and after a certain point, you were pretty much on your own. Now, your boss—if you have one—is no longer giving much consideration to your day-to-day actions. By the time any mistakes come to light, it's probably too late to fix them—or your boss's perceptions of you. And by the time your management missteps negatively affect your business results, it's usually too late to make corrections that will get you back on course.

No matter how talented and successful you are, you will make mistakes. You will develop bad habits. The world will change subtly, without your even noticing, and behaviors that once worked will be rendered ineffective. Over a 22-year career at Goldman Sachs, I had the opportunity to run various businesses and to work with or coach numerous business leaders. I chaired the firm's senior leadership training efforts and cochaired its partnership committee, which focused on reviews, promotions, and development of managing directors. Through this experience and subsequent interviews with a large number of executives in a broad range of industries, I have observed that even outstanding leaders invariably struggle through stretches of their careers where they get off track for some period of time.

It's hard to see it when you're in the midst of it; changes in the environment, competitors, or even personal circumstances can quietly guide you off your game. I have learned that a key characteristic of highly successful leaders is not that they figure out how to always stay on course, but that they develop techniques to help them recognize a deteriorating situation and get back on track as quickly as possible. In my experience, the best way to do that is to step back regularly, say, every three to six months (and certainly whenever things feel as though they aren't going well), and honestly ask yourself some questions about how you're doing and what you may need to do differently. As simple as this process sounds, people are often shocked by their own answers to basic management and leadership questions.

One manager in a large financial services company who had been passed over for promotion told me he was quite surprised by his year-end performance review, which highlighted several management issues that had not been previously brought to his attention. His boss read several comments from the review that faulted him for poor communication, failure to effectively articulate a strategy for the business, and a tendency to isolate himself from his team. He believed that the review was unfair. After 15 years at the company, he began to feel confused and misunderstood and wondered whether he still had a future there. He decided to seek feedback directly from five of his key contributors and longtime collaborators. In one-on-one meetings, he asked them for blunt feedback and advice. He was shocked to hear that they were highly critical of several of his recent actions, were confused about the direction he wanted to take the business, and felt he no longer valued their input. Their feedback helped him see that he had been so immersed in the day-to-day business that he had failed to step back and think about what he was doing. This was a serious wake-up call. He immediately took steps to change his behavior and address these issues. His review the following year was dramatically better, he was finally promoted, and his business's performance improved. The manager was lucky to have received this feedback in time to get his career back on track, although he regretted that he had waited for a negative review to ask

Idea in Brief

If you're like most managers, the higher you go up the corporate ladder, the harder it is to get candid feedback on your performance. And without crucial input from bosses and colleagues, you can make mistakes that irreparably damage your organization—and your reputation.

How can you figure out how you're *really* doing and avoid business disasters? Kaplan recommends looking to *yourself* for answers. Regularly ask yourself questions like these: "Am I communicating a vision for my business to my employees?" "Am I spending my time in ways that enable me to achieve my priorities?" "Do I give people timely and direct feedback they can act on?" "How do I behave under pressure?"

It's far more important to ask the *right* questions than to have all the answers. By applying this process, you tackle the leadership challenges that inevitably arise during the course of your career—and craft new plans for staying on your game.

basic questions about his leadership activities. He promised himself he would not make that mistake again.

In this article, I outline seven types of questions that leaders should ask themselves on some periodic basis. I am not suggesting that there is a "right" answer to any of them or that they all will resonate with a given executive at any point in time. I am suggesting that successful executives can regularly improve their performance and preempt serious business problems by stepping back and taking the time to ask themselves certain key questions.

Vision and Priorities

It's surprising how often business leaders fail to ask themselves: *How frequently do I communicate a vision and priorities for my business? Would my employees, if asked, be able to articulate the vision and priorities?* Many leaders have, on paper, a wealth of leadership talents: interpersonal, strategic, and analytic skills; a knack for team building; and certainly the ability to develop a vision. Unfortunately, in the press of day-to-day activities, they often don't adequately communicate the vision to the organization, and in particular, they

Idea in Practice

Kaplan suggests periodically asking yourself questions related to seven leadership challenges.

To address this leadership challenge . . .	Ask . . .	Because . . .
Vision and priorities	How often do I communicate a vision and key priorities to achieve that vision?	Employees want to know where the business is going and what they need to focus on in order to help drive the business. As the world changes, they want to know how the vision and priorities might change.
Managing time	Does the way I spend my time match my key priorities?	Tracking your use of time can reveal startling—even horrifying—disconnects between your top priorities and your actions. Such disconnects send confusing messages to employees about your true priorities.
Feedback	Do I give people timely and direct feedback they can act on?	Employees want truthful, direct, and timely feedback. Retention and productivity improve when employees trust you to raise issues promptly and honestly.

don't convey it in a way that helps their people understand what they are supposed to be doing to drive the business. It is very difficult to lead people if they don't have a firm grasp of where they're heading and what's expected of them.

This was the problem at a large *Fortune* 200 company that had decided to invest in its 1,000 top managers by having them attend an intensive, two-day management-training program, 100 at a time. Before each session, the participants went through a 360-degree nonevaluative review in which critical elements of their individual performance were ranked by ten of their subordinates. The company's

Succession planning	Have I identified potential successors?	It's important to nurture future leaders who can grow the business. If you haven't identified possible successors, you're probably not delegating as much as you should, and you may even be a decision-making bottleneck.
Evaluation and alignment	Am I attuned to business changes that may require shifts in how we run the company?	All businesses encounter challenges posed by changes; for example, in customers' needs or the business's stage of maturity. To determine how best to evolve your business, regularly scan for changes, seek fresh perspectives from talented subordinates, and envision new organizational designs.
Leading under pressure	How do I behave under pressure?	During crises, employees watch you with a microscope—and mimic your behavior. By identifying your unproductive behaviors under pressure (such as blaming others or losing your temper), you can better manage those behaviors and avoid sending unintended messages to employees about how *they* should behave.
Staying true to yourself	Does my leadership style reflect who I truly am?	A business career is a marathon, not a sprint. If you've adopted a leadership style that doesn't suit your skills, values, and personality, you'll wear down.

senior management looked at the results, focusing on the top five and bottom five traits for each group. Despite this being an extremely well-managed firm, the ability to articulate a vision ranked in the bottom five for almost every group. Managers at that company did articulate a vision, but the feedback from their subordinates strongly indicated that they were not communicating it frequently or clearly enough to meet their people's tremendous hunger for guidance.

Employees want to know where the business is going and what they need to focus on. As the world changes, they want to know how the business vision and priorities might change along with it. While managers are taught to actively communicate, many either unintentionally undercommunicate or fail to articulate specific priorities that would give meaning to their vision. However often you think you discuss vision and strategy, you may not be doing it frequently enough or in sufficient detail to suit the needs of your people. Look at the CEO of an emerging biotechnology company, who was quite frustrated with what he saw as a lack of alignment within his top management team. He strongly believed that the company needed to do a substantial equity financing within the next 18 months, but his senior managers wanted to wait a few years until two or three of the company's key drugs were further along in the FDA approval process. They preferred to tell their story to investors when the company was closer to generating revenue. When I asked him about the vision for the company, the CEO sheepishly realized that he had never actually written down a vision statement. He had a well-articulated tactical plan relating to each of the company's specific product efforts but no fully formed vision that would give further context to these efforts. He decided to organize an off-site meeting for his senior management team to discuss and specifically articulate a vision for the company.

After a vigorous debate, the group quickly agreed on a vision and strategic priorities. They realized that in order to achieve their shared goals, the business would in fact require substantial financing sooner rather than later—or they would need to scale back some of the initiatives that were central to their vision for the company. Once they fully appreciated this trade-off, they understood what the CEO was trying to accomplish and left the meeting united about their financing strategy. The CEO was quite surprised at how easy it had been to bring the members of his leadership team together. Because they agreed on where they were going as a company, specific issues were much easier to resolve.

A common pitfall in articulating a vision is a failure to boil it down to a manageable list of initiatives. Culling the list involves thinking through and then making difficult choices and trade-off decisions. These choices communicate volumes to your people about how they should be spending their time. I spoke with the manager of a national sales force who felt frustrated that his direct reports were not focusing on the tasks necessary to achieve their respective regional sales goals. As a result, sales were growing at a slower rate than budgeted at the beginning of the year. When I asked him to enumerate the three to five key priorities he expected his salespeople to focus on, he paused and then explained that there were 15 and it would be very difficult to narrow the list down to five.

Even as he spoke, a light went on in his head. He realized why there might be a disconnect between him and his people: They didn't know precisely what he wanted because he had not told them in a prioritized, and therefore actionable, manner. He reflected on this issue for the next two weeks, thinking at length about his own experience as a regional manager and consulting with various colleagues. He then picked three priorities that he felt were crucial to achieving sales growth. The most important of these involved a major new-business targeting exercise followed by a substantial new-prospect calling effort. The regional managers immediately understood and began focusing on these initiatives. The fact is that having 15 priorities is the same as having none at all. Managers have a responsibility to translate their vision into a manageable number of priorities that their subordinates can understand and act on.

Failing to communicate your vision and priorities has direct costs to you in terms of time and business effectiveness. It's hard to delegate if your people don't have a good sense of the big picture; hence you end up doing more work yourself. This issue can cascade through the organization if your direct reports are, in turn, unable to communicate a vision and effectively leverage their own subordinates.

Managing Time

The second area to question is painfully simple and closely relates to the first: *How am I spending my time?* Once you know your priorities, you need to determine whether you're spending your time—your most precious asset—in a way that will allow you to achieve them. For example, if your two major priorities are senior talent development and global expansion but you're spending the majority of your

Testing Yourself

To assess your performance and stay on track, you should step back and ask yourself certain key questions.

Vision and Priorities

In the press of day-to-day activities, leaders often fail to adequately communicate their vision to the organization, and in particular, they don't communicate it in a way that helps their subordinates determine where to focus their own efforts.

How often do I communicate a vision for my business?

Have I identified and communicated three to five key priorities to achieve that vision?

If asked, would my employees be able to articulate the vision and priorities?

Managing Time

Leaders need to know how they're spending their time. They also need to ensure that their time allocation (and that of their subordinates) matches their key priorities.

How am I spending my time? Does it match my key priorities?

How are my subordinates spending their time? Does that match the key priorities for the business?

Feedback

Leaders often fail to coach employees in a direct and timely fashion and, instead, wait until the year-end review. This approach may lead to unpleasant surprises and can undermine effective professional development. Just as important, leaders need to cultivate subordinates who can give them advice and feedback during the year.

Do I give people timely and direct feedback that they can act on?

Do I have five or six junior subordinates who will tell me things I may not want to hear but need to hear?

Succession Planning

When leaders fail to actively plan for succession, they do not delegate sufficiently and may become decision-making bottlenecks. Key employees may leave if they are not actively groomed and challenged.

Have I, at least in my own mind, picked one or more potential successors?

Am I coaching them and giving them challenging assignments?

Am I delegating sufficiently? Have I become a decision-making bottleneck?

Evaluation and Alignment

The world is constantly changing, and leaders need to be able to adapt their businesses accordingly.

Is the design of my company still aligned with the key success factors for the business?

If I had to design my business with a clean sheet of paper, how would I design it? How would it differ from the current design?

Should I create a task force of subordinates to answer these questions and make recommendations to me?

Leading Under Pressure

A leader's actions in times of stress are watched closely by subordinates and have a profound impact on the culture of the firm and employees' behavior. Successful leaders need to be aware of their own stress triggers and consciously modulate their behavior during these periods to make sure they are acting in ways that are consistent with their beliefs and core values.

What types of events create pressure for me?

How do I behave under pressure?

What signals am I sending my subordinates? Are these signals helpful, or are they undermining the success of my business?

Staying True to Yourself

Successful executives develop leadership styles that fit the needs of their business but also fit their own beliefs and personality.

Is my leadership style comfortable? Does it reflect who I truly am?

Do I assert myself sufficiently, or have I become tentative?

Am I too politically correct?

Does worry about my next promotion or bonus cause me to pull punches or hesitate to express my views?

time on domestic operational and administrative matters that could be delegated, then you need to recognize there is a disconnect and you'd better make some changes.

It's such a simple question, yet many leaders, myself included, just can't accurately answer at times. When leaders finally do track their time, they're often surprised by what they find. Most of us go through periods where unexpected events and day-to-day chaos cause us to be reactive rather than acting on a proscribed plan. Crises, surprises, personnel issues, and interruptions make the workweek seem like a blur. I have recommended to many leaders that they track how they spend each hour of each day for one week, then categorize the hours into types of activities: business development, people management, and strategic planning, for example. For most executives, the results of this exercise are startling—even horrifying—with obvious disconnects between what their top priorities are and how they are spending their time.

For example, the CEO of a midsize manufacturing company was frustrated because he was working 70 hours a week and never seemed to catch up. His family life suffered, and, at work, he was constantly unavailable for his people and major customers. I suggested he step back and review how he was managing his time hour-by-hour over the course of a week. We sat down to examine the results and noticed that he was spending a substantial amount of time approving company expenditures, some for as little as $500—this in a business with $500 million in sales. Sitting in my office, he struggled to explain why he had not delegated some portion of this responsibility; it turned out that the activity was a holdover from a time when the company was much smaller. By delegating authority to approve recurring operating expenses below $25,000, he realized he could save as much as 15 hours per week. He was amazed that he had not recognized this issue and made this simple change much earlier.

How you spend your time is an important question not only for you but for your team. People tend to take their cues from the leader when it comes to time management—therefore, you want to make sure there's a match between your actions, your business priorities, and your team's activities. The CEO of a rapidly growing, 300-person professional services firm felt that, to build the business, senior managers needed to develop stronger and more substantive relationships with clients. This meant that senior professionals would need to spend significantly more time out of their offices in meetings with clients. When asked how his own time was being spent, the CEO was unable to answer. After tracking it for a week, he was shocked to find that he was devoting a tremendous amount of his time to administrative activities related to managing the firm. He realized that the amount of attention he was paying to these matters did not reflect the business's priorities and was sending a confusing message to his people. He immediately began pushing himself to delegate a number of these administrative tasks and increase the amount of time he spent on the road with customers, setting a powerful example for his people. He directed each of his senior managers to do a similar time-allocation exercise to ensure they were dedicating sufficient time to clients.

Of course, the way a leader spends his or her time must be tailored to the needs of the business, which may vary depending on time of year, personnel changes, and external factors. The key here is, whatever you decide, time allocation needs to be a conscious decision that fits your vision and priorities for the business. Given the pressure of running a business, it is easy to lose focus, so it's important to ask yourself this question periodically. Just as you would step back and review a major investment decision, you need to dispassionately review the manner in which you invest your time.

Feedback

When you think about the ways you approach feedback, you should first ask: *Do I give people timely, direct, and constructive feedback?* And second: *Do I have five or six junior people who will tell me things I don't want to hear but need to hear?*

If they're like most ambitious employees, your subordinates want to be coached and developed in a truthful and direct manner. They want to get feedback while there's still an opportunity to act on it; if you've waited until the year-end review, it's often too late. In my experience, well-intentioned managers typically fail to give blunt, direct, and timely feedback to their subordinates.

One reason for this failure is that managers are often afraid that constructive feedback and criticism will demoralize their employees. In addition, critiquing a professional in a frank and timely manner may be perceived as overly confrontational. Lastly, many managers fear that this type of feedback will cause employees not to like them. Consequently, leaders often wait until year-end performance reviews. The year-end review is evaluative (that is, the verdict on the year) and therefore is not conducive to constructive coaching. The subordinate is typically on the defensive and not as open to criticism. This approach creates surprises, often unpleasant ones, which undermine trust and dramatically reduce the confidence of the subordinate in the manager.

The reality is that managers who don't give immediate and direct feedback often are "liked" until year-end—at which time they wind up being strongly disliked. If employees have fallen short of expectations, the failing is reflected in bonuses, raises, and promotions. The feeling of injustice can be enormous. What's worse is the knowledge that if an employee had received feedback earlier in the year, it is likely that he or she would have made meaningful efforts to improve and address the issues.

While people do like to hear positive feedback, ultimately, they desperately want to know the truth, and I have rarely seen someone quit over hearing the truth or being challenged to do better—unless it's too late. On the contrary, I would argue that people are more likely to stay if they understand what issues they need to address and they trust you to bring those issues to their attention in a straightforward and prompt fashion. They gain confidence that you will work with them to develop their skills and that they won't be blindsided at the end of the year. Employees who don't land a hoped-for promotion will be much more likely to forgive you if you've told them all along what they need to do better, even if they haven't gotten there yet. They may well redouble their efforts to prove to you that they can overcome these issues.

During my career at Goldman Sachs, I consistently found that professional development was far more effective when coaching and direct feedback were given to employees throughout the year—well in advance of the annual performance review process. Internal surveys of managing directors showed that, in cases where feedback was confined to the year-end review, satisfaction with career development was dramatically lower than when it was offered throughout the year.

As hard as it is to give effective and timely feedback, many leaders find it much more challenging to get feedback from their employees. Once you reach a certain stage of your career, junior people are in a much better position than your boss to tell you how you're doing. They see you in your day-to-day activities, and they experience your decisions directly. Your boss, at this stage, is much more removed and, as a result, typically needs to talk to your subordinates to assess your performance at the end of the year. In order to avoid your own year-end surprises, you need to develop a network of junior professionals who are willing to give you constructive feedback. The problem is that, while your direct reports know what you are doing wrong, most of them are not dying to tell you. With good reason—there's very little upside and a tremendous amount of downside. The more senior and the more important you become, the less your subordinates will tell you the "awful truth"—things that are difficult to hear but that you need to know.

It takes a concerted effort to cultivate subordinates who will advise and coach you. It also takes patience and some relentlessness. When I ask subordinates for constructive feedback, they will typically and predictably tell me that I'm doing "very well." When I follow up and ask "What should I do differently?" they respond, "Nothing that I can think of." If I challenge them by saying, "There must be something!" still they say, "Nothing comes to mind." I then ask them to sit back and think—we have plenty of time. By this time, beads of sweat begin to become visible on their foreheads. After an awkward silence, they will eventually come up with something— and it's often devastating to hear. It's devastating because it's a damning criticism and because you know it's true.

What you do with this feedback is critical. If you act on it, you will improve your performance. Equally important, you will take a big step in building trust and laying the groundwork for a channel of honest feedback. When subordinates see that you respond positively to suggestions, they will often feel more ownership in the business and in your success. They'll learn to give you criticisms on their own initiative because they know you will actually appreciate it and do something with it. Developing a network of "coaching" subordinates will help you take action to identify your own leadership issues and meaningfully improve your performance.

Succession Planning

Another question that managers know is important yet struggle to answer affirmatively is: *Have I, at least in my own mind, picked one or more potential successors?* This issue is critical because if you aren't identifying potential successors, you are probably not delegating as extensively as you should and you may well be a decision-making bottleneck. Being a bottleneck invariably means that you are not spending enough time on vital leadership priorities and are failing to develop your key subordinates. Ironically, when leaders believe they are so talented that they can perform tasks far better than any of their subordinates and therefore insist on doing the tasks themselves, they will typically cause their businesses to underperform, and, ultimately, their careers will suffer as well.

The succession question also has significant implications that cascade through an organization: If leaders do not develop successors, then the organization may lack a sufficient number of leaders to successfully grow the business. Worse, if junior employees are not developed, they may leave the firm for better opportunities elsewhere. For these reasons, many well-managed companies will hesitate to promote executives who have failed to develop successors.

It is sufficient to identify possible successors without actually telling them you've done so—as long as this identification causes you to manage them differently. In particular, you will want to delegate more of your major responsibilities to these professionals. This will speed their maturation and prepare them to step up to the next level. By giving demanding assignments to these subordinates, you strongly signal an interest in their development and career progression—which will encourage them to turn down offers from competitors. Leaders who do this are much better able to keep their teams together and avoid losing up-and-coming stars to competitors.

A loss of talent is highly damaging to a company. It is particularly painful if you could have retained key employees by simply challenging them more intensively. I spoke with a division head of a large company who was concerned about what he perceived to be a talent deficit in his organization. He felt that he could not use his time to the fullest because he viewed his direct reports as incapable of assuming some of his major responsibilities. He believed this talent deficit was keeping him from launching several new product and market initiatives. In the midst of all this, he lost two essential subordinates over six months—each had left to take on increased responsibilities at major competitors. He had tried to persuade them to stay, emphasizing that he was actively considering them for significant new leadership assignments. Because they had not seen evidence of this previously, they were skeptical and left anyway. I asked him whether, prior to the defections, he had identified them (or anyone else) as potential successors, put increased responsibilities in their hands, or actively ratcheted up his coaching of these professionals. He answered that, in the chaos of daily events and in the effort to keep up with the business, he had not done so. He also admitted that he had underestimated the potential of these two employees and realized he was probably underestimating the abilities of several others in the company. He immediately sat down and made a list of potential stars and next to each name wrote out a career and responsibility game plan. He immediately got to work on this formative succession plan, although he suspected that he had probably waited too long already.

When you're challenging and testing people, you delegate to them more often, which frees you to focus on the most critical strategic matters facing the business. This will make you more successful and a more attractive candidate for your own future promotion.

Evaluation and Alignment

The world is constantly changing. Your customers' needs change; your business evolves (going, for instance, from high growth to mature); new products and distribution methods emerge as threats. When these changes happen, if you don't change along with them, you can get seriously out of alignment. The types of people you hire, the way you organize them, the economic incentives you offer them, and even the nature of the tasks you delegate no longer create the culture and outcomes that are critical to the success of your business. It's your job to make sure that the design of your organization is aligned with the key success factors for the business. Ask yourself: *Am I attuned to changes in the business environment that would require a change in the way we organize and run our business?*

Such clear-sightedness is, of course, hard to achieve. As a leader, you may be too close to the business to see subtle changes that are continually occurring. Because you probably played a central role in building and designing the business, it may be emotionally very difficult to make meaningful changes. You may have to fire certain employees—people you recruited and hired. You may also have to acknowledge that you made some mistakes and be open to changing your own operating style in a way that is uncomfortable for some period of time.

Because of the difficulty in facing these issues, it's sometimes wise to call on high-potential subordinates to take a fresh look at the business. This approach can be quite effective because junior employees are often not as emotionally invested as you are and can see more objectively what needs to be done. This approach is also a good way to challenge your future leaders and give them a valuable development experience. You'll give them a chance to exercise their strategic skills; you'll get a glimpse of their potential (which relates to the earlier discussion of succession planning), and you might just get some terrific new ideas for how to run the business.

This approach worked for the CEO of a high technology business in northern California, whose company had been one of the early innovators in its product space but, in recent years, had begun to falter and lose market share. In its early days, the company's primary success factors had been product innovation and satisfying customer needs. It had aggressively hired innovative engineers and marketing personnel. As new competitors emerged, customers began to focus more on cost and service (in the form of more sophisticated applications development). Stepping back, the CEO sensed that he needed to redesign the company with a different mix of people, a new organization, and a revised incentive structure. Rather than try to come up with a new model himself, he asked a more junior group of executives to formulate a new company design as if they had a "clean sheet of paper." Their study took a number of weeks, but upon completion, it led to several recommendations that the CEO immediately began to implement. For example, they suggested colocating the engineering and sales departments and creating integrated account coverage teams. They also recommended that the company push more of its engineers to interact with customers and focus on this skill in recruiting. The CEO regretted that he had not asked the question—and conducted this assignment—12 months earlier.

Even the most successful business is susceptible to new challenges posed by a changing world. Effective executives regularly look at their businesses with a clean sheet of paper—seeking advice and other perspectives from people who are less emotionally invested in the business—in order to determine whether key aspects of the way they run their organizations are still appropriate.

Leading Under Pressure

Pressure is a part of business. Changes in business conditions create urgent problems. New entrants in the market demand a competitive response. Valued employees quit, often at the most inopportune times. Leaders and their teams, no matter how smart they are, make mistakes.

The interesting thing about stressful events is that they affect each person differently—what causes you anxiety may not bother someone else, and vice versa. For some, extreme anxiety may be triggered by the prospect of a promotion; for others, by making a serious mistake; still others, by losing a piece of business to a competitor. Regardless of the source of stress, every leader experiences it, so a good question to ask yourself is: *How do I behave under pressure, and what signals am I sending my employees?*

As a leader, you're watched closely. During a crisis, your people watch you with a microscope, noting every move you make. In such times, your subordinates learn a great deal about you and what you really believe, as opposed to what you say. Do you accept responsibility for mistakes, or do you look for someone to blame? Do you support your employees, or do you turn on them? Are you cool and calm, or do you lose your temper? Do you stand up for what you believe, or do you take the expedient route and advocate what you think your seniors want to hear? You need to be self-aware enough to recognize the situations that create severe anxiety for you and manage your behavior to avoid sending unproductive messages to your people.

I've met a number of leaders who behave in a very composed and thoughtful manner the great majority of the time. Unfortunately, when they're under severe stress, they react in ways that set a very negative tone. They inadvertently train their employees to mimic that behavior and behave in a similar fashion. If your instinct is to shield yourself from blame, to take credit rather than sharing it with your subordinates, or to avoid admitting when you have made a mistake, you will give your employees license to do the same.

The CEO of a large asset-management firm was frustrated that he was unable to build a culture of accountability and teamwork in his growing business. At his request, I spoke to a number of his team members. I asked in particular about the actions of the CEO when investments they recommended declined in value. They recounted his frequent temper tantrums and accusatory diatribes, which led to an overwhelming atmosphere of blame and finger-pointing. The investment decisions had, in fact, been made jointly through a carefully constructed process involving portfolio managers, industry analysts, and the CEO. As a result of these episodes, employees learned that when investments went wrong it would be good to try to find someone else to blame. Hearing these stories, the CEO realized his actions under pressure were far more persuasive to employees than his speeches about teamwork and culture. He understood that he would have to learn to moderate his behavior under stress and, subsequently, took steps to avoid reacting so angrily to negative investment results. He also became more aware that subordinates typically felt quite regretful and demoralized when their investments declined and were more likely to need a pat on the back and coaching than a kick in the pants.

It's extremely difficult to expect employees to alert you to looming problems when they fear your reaction—and even more so when they think it's better to distance themselves from potential problems. This can create an atmosphere where surprises are, in fact, more likely as the company's natural early-warning system has been inadvertently disarmed. If you have created this kind of culture, it is quite unlikely that you will learn about problems from subordinates spontaneously—unless they want to commit career suicide.

Part of the process of maturing as a leader is learning to step back and think about what creates pressure for you, being self-aware in these situations, and disciplining your behavior to ensure that you act in a manner consistent with your core values.

Staying True to Yourself

Most business leaders ask themselves whether their leadership style fits the needs of their business. Fewer managers ask whether their style also fits their own beliefs and personality. The question here is: *Does my leadership style reflect who I truly am?*

A business career is a marathon, not a sprint, and if you aren't true to yourself, eventually you're going to wear down. As you are developing in your career, it is advisable to observe various leadership styles, and pick and choose elements that feel comfortable to you. Bear in mind, though, that observing and adopting aspects of other styles does not mean you should try to be someone else. During my career, I was fortunate to have had several superb bosses and colleagues with distinctive and unique leadership skills. While I tried to adopt some of their techniques, I also learned that I needed to develop an overall style that fit my unique skills and personality. Your style needs to fit you; even an unorthodox style can be enormously effective if it reflects your skills, values, and personality.

As you become more senior, you'll need to ask yourself an additional set of questions relating to style: *Do I assert myself sufficiently, or have I become tentative? Am I too politically correct? Does worry about my next promotion or my year-end bonus cause me to pull punches or hesitate to clearly express my views?* In many companies, ambitious executives may try to avoid confronting sensitive issues or making waves. Worse than that, they may spend an inordinate amount of energy trying to ascertain what their boss thinks and then act like they think the same thing. If they're very skilled at this, they may even get a chance to make their comments before the boss has a chance to express his opinion—and feel the warm glow of approval from the boss.

The problem is that confrontation and disagreement are crucial to effective decision making. Some of the worst decisions I've been involved in were made after a group of intelligent people had unanimously agreed to the course of action—though, later, several participants admitted that they had misgivings but were hesitant to diverge from the apparent group consensus. Conversely, it's hard for me to recall a poor decision I was involved in that was made after a thorough debate in which opposing views were vigorously expressed (even if I disagreed with the ultimate decision). Companies need their leaders to express strongly held views rather than mimic what they believe to be the party line. As a leader, therefore, you must ask yourself whether you are expressing your views or holding back and being too politic. At the same time, leaders must encourage their own subordinates to express their unvarnished opinions, make waves as appropriate, and stop tiptoeing around significant issues.

Successful leaders periodically struggle during stretches of their careers. To get back on track, they must devise techniques for stepping back, getting perspective, and developing a new game plan. In this process, having the answers is often far less important than taking time to ask yourself the right questions and gain key insights. The questions posed in this article are intended to spark your thinking. Only a subset of these may resonate with you, and you may find it more useful to come up with your own list. In either event, a self-questioning process conducted on a periodic basis will help you work through leadership challenges and issues that you invariably must tackle over the course of your career.

Originally published in January 2007. Reprint R0701H

Primal Leadership

The Hidden Driver of Great Performance. *by Daniel Goleman, Richard Boyatzis, and Annie McKee*

WHEN THE THEORY OF EMOTIONAL intelligence at work began to receive widespread attention, we frequently heard executives say—in the same breath, mind you—"That's incredible," and, "Well, I've known that all along." They were responding to our research that showed an incontrovertible link between an executive's emotional maturity, exemplified by such capabilities as self-awareness and empathy, and his or her financial performance. Simply put, the research showed that "good guys"—that is, emotionally intelligent men and women—finish first.

We've recently compiled two years of new research that, we suspect, will elicit the same kind of reaction. People will first exclaim, "No way," then quickly add, "But of course." We found that of all the elements affecting bottom-line performance, the importance of the leader's mood and its attendant behaviors are most surprising. That powerful pair set off a chain reaction: The leader's mood and behaviors drive the moods and behaviors of everyone else. A cranky and ruthless boss creates a toxic organization filled with negative underachievers who ignore opportunities; an inspirational, inclusive leader spawns acolytes for whom any challenge is surmountable. The final link in the chain is performance: profit or loss.

Our observation about the overwhelming impact of the leader's "emotional style," as we call it, is not a wholesale departure from our research into emotional intelligence. It does, however, represent a deeper analysis of our earlier assertion that a leader's emotional intelligence creates a certain culture or work environment. High levels of emotional intelligence, our research showed, create climates in which information sharing, trust, healthy risk-taking, and learning flourish. Low levels of emotional intelligence create climates rife with fear and anxiety. Because tense or terrified employees can be very productive in the short term, their organizations may post good results, but they never last.

Our investigation was designed in part to look at how emotional intelligence drives performance—in particular, at how it travels from the leader through the organization to bottom-line results. "What mechanism," we asked, "binds the chain together?" To answer that question, we turned to the latest neurological and psychological research. We also drew on our work with business leaders, observations by our colleagues of hundreds of leaders, and Hay Group data on the leadership styles of thousands of executives. From this body of research, we discovered that emotional intelligence is carried through an organization like electricity through wires. To be more specific, the leader's mood is quite literally contagious, spreading quickly and inexorably throughout the business.

We'll discuss the science of mood contagion in more depth later, but first let's turn to the key implications of our finding. If a leader's mood and accompanying behaviors are indeed such potent drivers of business success, then a leader's premier task—we would even say his primal task—is emotional leadership. A leader needs to make sure that not only is he regularly in an optimistic, authentic, high-energy mood, but also that, through his chosen actions, his followers feel and act that way, too. Managing for financial results, then, begins with the leader managing his inner life so that the right emotional and behavioral chain reaction occurs.

Managing one's inner life is not easy, of course. For many of us, it's our most difficult challenge. And accurately gauging how one's emotions affect others can be just as difficult. We know of one CEO, for example, who was certain that everyone saw him as upbeat and reliable; his direct reports told us they found his cheerfulness strained, even fake, and his decisions erratic. (We call this common

Idea in Brief

What *most* influences your company's bottom-line performance? The answer will surprise you—*and* make perfect sense: It's a leader's own mood.

Executives' emotional intelligence—their self-awareness, empathy, rapport with others—has clear links to their own performance. But new research shows that a leader's emotional style also drives everyone *else*'s moods and behaviors—through a neurological process called **mood contagion**. It's akin to "Smile and the whole world smiles with you."

Emotional intelligence travels through an organization like

electricity over telephone wires. Depressed, ruthless bosses create toxic organizations filled with negative underachievers. But if you're an upbeat, inspirational leader, you cultivate positive employees who embrace and surmount even the toughest challenges.

Emotional leadership isn't just putting on a game face every day. It means understanding your impact on others—then adjusting your style accordingly. A difficult process of self-discovery—but essential *before* you can tackle your leadership responsibilities.

disconnect "CEO disease.") The implication is that primal leadership demands more than putting on a game face every day. It requires an executive to determine, through reflective analysis, how his emotional leadership drives the moods and actions of the organization, and then, with equal discipline, to adjust his behavior accordingly.

That's not to say that leaders can't have a bad day or week: Life happens. And our research doesn't suggest that good moods have to be high-pitched or nonstop—optimistic, sincere, and realistic will do. But there is no escaping the conclusion that a leader must first attend to the impact of his mood and behaviors before moving on to his wide panoply of other critical responsibilities. In this article, we introduce a process that executives can follow to assess how others experience their leadership, and we discuss ways to calibrate that impact. But first, we'll look at why moods aren't often discussed in the workplace, how the brain works to make moods contagious, and what you need to know about CEO disease.

Idea in Practice

Strengthening Your Emotional Leadership

Since few people have the guts to tell you the truth about your emotional impact, you must discover it on your own. The following process can help. It's based on brain science, as well as years of field research with executives. Use these steps to rewire your brain for greater emotional intelligence.

1. **Who do you want to be?** Imagine yourself as a highly effective leader. What do you see?

   Example: Sofia, a senior manager, often micromanaged others to ensure work was done "right." So she *imagined* herself in the future as an effective leader of her own company, enjoying trusting relationships with coworkers. She saw herself as relaxed, happy, and empowering. The exercise revealed gaps in her current emotional style.

2. **Who are you now?** To see your leadership style as others do, gather 360-degree feedback, especially from peers and subordinates. Identify your weaknesses *and* strengths.

3. **How do you get from here to there?** Devise a plan for closing the gap between who you are and who you want to be.

   Example: Juan, a marketing executive, was intimidating, impossible to please—a

No Way! Yes Way

When we said earlier that people will likely respond to our new finding by saying "No way," we weren't joking. The fact is, the emotional impact of a leader is almost never discussed in the workplace, let alone in the literature on leadership and performance. For most people, "mood" feels too personal. Even though Americans can be shockingly candid about personal matters—witness the *Jerry Springer Show* and its ilk—we are also the most legally bound. We can't even ask the age of a job applicant. Thus, a conversation about an executive's mood or the moods he creates in his employees might be construed as an invasion of privacy.

We also might avoid talking about a leader's emotional style and its impact because, frankly, the topic feels soft. When was the last time you evaluated a subordinate's mood as part of her performance

grouch. Charged with growing his company, he *needed* to be encouraging, optimistic—a coach with a vision. Setting out to understand others, he coached soccer, volunteered at a crisis center, and got to know subordinates by meeting outside of work. These new situations stimulated him to break old habits and try new responses.

4. **How do you make change stick?** Repeatedly rehearse new behaviors—physically *and* mentally—until they're automatic.

Example: Tom, an executive, wanted to learn how to coach rather than castigate struggling employees. Using his commut-

ing time to visualize a difficult meeting with one employee, he envisioned asking questions and listening, and mentally rehearsed how he'd handle feeling impatient. This exercise prepared him to adopt new behaviors at the actual meeting.

5. **Who can help you?** Don't try to build your emotional skills alone—identify others who can help you navigate this difficult process. Managers at Unilever formed learning groups that helped them strengthen their leadership abilities by exchanging frank feedback and developing strong mutual trust.

appraisal? You may have alluded to it—"Your work is hindered by an often negative perspective," or "Your enthusiasm is terrific"—but it is unlikely you mentioned mood outright, let alone discussed its impact on the organization's results.

And yet our research undoubtedly will elicit a "But of course" reaction, too. Everyone knows how much a leader's emotional state drives performance because everyone has had, at one time or another, the inspirational experience of working for an upbeat manager or the crushing experience of toiling for a sour-spirited boss. The former made everything feel possible, and as a result, stretch goals were achieved, competitors beaten, and new customers won. The latter made work grueling. In the shadow of the boss's dark mood, other parts of the organization became "the enemy," colleagues became suspicious of one another, and customers slipped away.

Our research, and research by other social scientists, confirms the verity of these experiences. (There are, of course, rare cases when a brutal boss produces terrific results. We explore that dynamic in the sidebar "Those Wicked Bosses Who Win.") The studies are too numerous to mention here but, in aggregate, they show that when the leader is in a happy mood, the people around him view everything in a more positive light. That, in turn, makes them optimistic about achieving their goals, enhances their creativity and the efficiency of their decision making, and predisposes them to be helpful. Research conducted by Alice Isen at Cornell in 1999, for example, found that an upbeat environment fosters mental efficiency, making people better at taking in and understanding information, at using decision rules in complex judgments, and at being flexible in their thinking. Other research directly links mood and financial performance. In 1986, for instance, Martin Seligman and Peter Schulman of the University of Pennsylvania demonstrated that insurance agents who had a "glass half-full" outlook were far more able than their more pessimistic peers to persist despite rejections, and thus, they closed more sales. (For more information on these studies and a list of our research base, visit www.eiconsortium.org.)

Many leaders whose emotional styles create a dysfunctional environment are eventually fired. (Of course, that's rarely the stated reason; poor results are.) But it doesn't have to end that way. Just as a bad mood can be turned around, so can the spread of toxic feelings from an emotionally inept leader. A look inside the brain explains both why and how.

The Science of Moods

A growing body of research on the human brain proves that, for better or worse, leaders' moods affect the emotions of the people around them. The reason for that lies in what scientists call the open-loop nature of the brain's limbic system, our emotional center. A closed-loop system is self-regulating, whereas an open-loop system depends on external sources to manage itself. In other words, we rely on connections with other people to determine our moods. The

Those Wicked Bosses Who Win

Everyone knows of a rude and coercive CEO who, by all appearances, epitomizes the antithesis of emotional intelligence yet seems to reap great business results. If a leader's mood matters so much, how can we explain those mean-spirited, successful SOBs?

First, let's take a closer look at them. Just because a particular executive is the most visible, he may not actually lead the company. A CEO who heads a conglomerate may have no followers to speak of; it's his division heads who actively lead people and affect profitability.

Second, sometimes an SOB leader has strengths that counterbalance his caustic behavior, but they don't attract as much attention in the business press. In his early days at GE, Jack Welch exhibited a strong hand at the helm as he undertook a radical company turnaround. At that time and in that situation, Welch's firm, top-down style was appropriate. What got less press was how Welch subsequently settled into a more emotionally intelligent leadership style, especially when he articulated a new vision for the company and mobilized people to follow it.

Those caveats aside, let's get back to those infamous corporate leaders who seem to have achieved sterling business results despite their brutish approaches to leadership. Skeptics cite Bill Gates, for example, as a leader who gets away with a harsh style that should theoretically damage his company.

But our leadership model, which shows the effectiveness of specific leadership styles in specific situations, puts Gates's supposedly negative behaviors in a different light. (Our model is explained in detail in the HBR article "Leadership That Gets Results," which appeared in the March–April 2000 issue.) Gates is the achievement-driven leader par excellence, in an organization that has cherry-picked highly talented and motivated people. His apparently harsh leadership style—baldly challenging employees to surpass their past performance—can be quite effective when employees are competent, motivated, and need little direction—all characteristics of Microsoft's engineers.

In short, it's all too easy for a skeptic to argue against the importance of leaders who manage their moods by citing a "rough and tough" leader who achieved good business results despite his bad behavior. We contend that there are, of course, exceptions to the rule, and that in some specific business cases, an SOB boss resonates just fine. But in general, leaders who are jerks must reform or else their moods and actions will eventually catch up with them.

open-loop limbic system was a winning design in evolution because it let people come to one another's emotional rescue—enabling a mother, for example, to soothe her crying infant.

The open-loop design serves the same purpose today as it did thousands of years ago. Research in intensive care units has shown, for example, that the comforting presence of another person not only lowers the patient's blood pressure but also slows the secretion of fatty acids that block arteries. Another study found that three or more incidents of intense stress within a year (for example, serious financial trouble, being fired, or a divorce) triples the death rate in socially isolated middle-aged men, but it has no impact on the death rate of men with many close relationships.

Scientists describe the open loop as "interpersonal limbic regulation"; one person transmits signals that can alter hormone levels, cardiovascular functions, sleep rhythms, even immune functions, inside the body of another. That's how couples are able to trigger surges of oxytocin in each other's brains, creating a pleasant, affectionate feeling. But in all aspects of social life, our physiologies intermingle. Our limbic system's open-loop design lets other people change our very physiology and hence, our emotions.

Even though the open loop is so much a part of our lives, we usually don't notice the process. Scientists have captured the attunement of emotions in the laboratory by measuring the physiology—such as heart rate—of two people sharing a good conversation. As the interaction begins, their bodies operate at different rhythms. But after 15 minutes, the physiological profiles of their bodies look remarkably similar.

Researchers have seen again and again how emotions spread irresistibly in this way whenever people are near one another. As far back as 1981, psychologists Howard Friedman and Ronald Riggio found that even completely nonverbal expressiveness can affect other people. For example, when three strangers sit facing one another in silence for a minute or two, the most emotionally expressive of the three transmits his or her mood to the other two—without a single word being spoken.

Smile and the World Smiles with You

Remember that old cliché? It's not too far from the truth. As we've shown, mood contagion is a real neurological phenomenon, but not all emotions spread with the same ease. A 1999 study conducted by Sigal Barsade at the Yale School of Management showed that, among working groups, cheerfulness and warmth spread easily, while irritability caught on less so, and depression least of all.

It should come as no surprise that laughter is the most contagious of all emotions. Hearing laughter, we find it almost impossible not to laugh or smile, too. That's because some of our brain's open-loop circuits are designed to detect smiles and laughter, making us respond in kind. Scientists theorize that this dynamic was hardwired into our brains ages ago because smiles and laughter had a way of cementing alliances, thus helping the species survive.

The main implication here for leaders undertaking the primal task of managing their moods and the moods of others is this: Humor hastens the spread of an upbeat climate. But like the leader's mood in general, humor must resonate with the organization's culture and its reality. Smiles and laughter, we would posit, are only contagious when they're genuine.

The same holds true in the office, boardroom, or shop floor; group members inevitably "catch" feelings from one another. In 2000, Caroline Bartel at New York University and Richard Saavedra at the University of Michigan found that in 70 work teams across diverse industries, people in meetings together ended up sharing moods—both good and bad—within two hours. One study asked teams of nurses and accountants to monitor their moods over weeks; researchers discovered that their emotions tracked together, and they were largely independent of each team's shared hassles. Groups, therefore, like individuals, ride emotional roller coasters, sharing everything from jealousy to angst to euphoria. (A good mood, incidentally, spreads most swiftly by the judicious use of humor. For more on this, see the sidebar "Smile and the World Smiles with You.")

Moods that start at the top tend to move the fastest because everyone watches the boss. They take their emotional cues from him. Even when the boss isn't highly visible—for example, the CEO

Get Happy, Carefully

Good moods galvanize good performance, but it doesn't make sense for a leader to be as chipper as a blue jay at dawn if sales are tanking or the business is going under. The most effective executives display moods and behaviors that match the situation at hand, with a healthy dose of optimism mixed in. They respect how other people are feeling—even if it is glum or defeated—but they also model what it looks like to move forward with hope and humor.

This kind of performance, which we call resonance, is for all intents and purposes the four components of emotional intelligence in action.

Self-awareness, perhaps the most essential of the emotional intelligence competencies, is the ability to read your own emotions. It allows people to know their strengths and limitations and feel confident about their self-worth. Resonant leaders use self-awareness to gauge their own moods accurately, and they intuitively know how they are affecting others.

Self-management is the ability to control your emotions and act with honesty and integrity in reliable and adaptable ways. Resonant leaders don't let their occasional bad moods seize the day; they use self-management to leave it outside the office or to explain its source to people in a reasonable manner, so they know where it's coming from and how long it might last.

Social awareness includes the key capabilities of empathy and organizational intuition. Socially aware executives do more than sense other people's emotions, they show that they care. Further, they are experts at reading the currents of office politics. Thus, resonant leaders often keenly understand how their words and actions make others feel, and they are sensitive enough to change them when that impact is negative.

Relationship management, the last of the emotional intelligence competencies, includes the abilities to communicate clearly and convincingly, disarm

who works behind closed doors on an upper floor—his attitude affects the moods of his direct reports, and a domino effect ripples throughout the company.

Call That CEO a Doctor

If the leader's mood is so important, then he or she had better get into a good one, right? Yes, but the full answer is more complicated than that. A leader's mood has the greatest impact on performance

conflicts, and build strong personal bonds. Resonant leaders use these skills to spread their enthusiasm and solve disagreements, often with humor and kindness.

As effective as resonant leadership is, it is just as rare. Most people suffer through dissonant leaders whose toxic moods and upsetting behaviors wreak havoc before a hopeful and realistic leader repairs the situation.

Consider what happened recently at an experimental division of the BBC, the British media giant. Even though the group's 200 or so journalists and editors had given their best effort, management decided to close the division.

The shutdown itself was bad enough, but the brusque, contentious mood and manner of the executive sent to deliver the news to the assembled staff incited something beyond the expected frustration. People became enraged—at both the decision and the bearer of the news. The executive's cranky mood and delivery created an atmosphere so threatening that he had to call security to be ushered from the room.

The next day, another executive visited the same staff. His mood was somber and respectful, as was his behavior. He spoke about the importance of journalism to the vibrancy of a society and of the calling that had drawn them all to the field in the first place. He reminded them that no one goes into journalism to get rich—as a profession its finances have always been marginal, job security ebbing and flowing with the larger economic tides. He recalled a time in his own career when he had been let go and how he had struggled to find a new position—but how he had stayed dedicated to the profession. Finally, he wished them well in getting on with their careers.

The reaction from what had been an angry mob the day before? When this resonant leader finished speaking, the staff cheered.

when it is upbeat. But it must also be in tune with those around him. We call this dynamic *resonance*. (For more on this, see the sidebar "Get Happy, Carefully.")

We found that an alarming number of leaders do not really know if they have resonance with their organizations. Rather, they suffer from CEO disease; its one unpleasant symptom is the sufferer's near-total ignorance about how his mood and actions appear to the organization. It's not that leaders don't care how they are perceived; most do. But they incorrectly assume that they can decipher this information themselves. Worse, they think that if they are having a negative effect, someone will tell them. They're wrong.

As one CEO in our research explains, "I so often feel I'm not getting the truth. I can never put my finger on it, because no one is actually lying to me. But I can sense that people are hiding information or camouflaging key facts. They aren't lying, but neither are they telling me everything I need to know. I'm always second-guessing."

People don't tell leaders the whole truth about their emotional impact for many reasons. Sometimes they are scared of being the bearer of bad news—and getting shot. Others feel it isn't their place to comment on such a personal topic. Still others don't realize that what they really want to talk about is the effects of the leader's emotional style—that feels too vague. Whatever the reason, the CEO can't rely on his followers to spontaneously give him the full picture.

Taking Stock

The process we recommend for self-discovery and personal reinvention is neither newfangled nor born of pop psychology, like so many self-help programs offered to executives today. Rather, it is based on three streams of research into how executives can improve the emotional intelligence capabilities most closely linked to effective leadership. (Information on these research streams can also be found at www.eiconsortium.org.). In 1989, one of us (Richard Boyatzis) began drawing on this body of research to design the five-step process itself, and since then, thousands of executives have used it successfully.

Unlike more traditional forms of coaching, our process is based on brain science. A person's emotional skills—the attitude and abilities with which someone approaches life and work—are not genetically hardwired, like eye color and skin tone. But in some ways they might as well be, because they are so deeply embedded in our neurology.

A person's emotional skills do, in fact, have a genetic component. Scientists have discovered, for instance, the gene for shyness—which is not a mood, per se, but it can certainly drive a person toward a persistently quiet demeanor, which may be read as a "down" mood. Other people are preternaturally jolly—that is, their relentless cheerfulness seems preternatural until you meet their peppy parents. As one executive explains, "All I know is that ever since I was a baby, I have always been happy. It drives some people crazy, but I couldn't get blue if I tried. And my brother is the exact same way; he saw the bright side of life, even during his divorce."

Even though emotional skills are partly inborn, experience plays a major role in how the genes are expressed. A happy baby whose parents die or who endures physical abuse may grow into a melancholy adult. A cranky toddler may turn into a cheerful adult after discovering a fulfilling avocation. Still, research suggests that our range of emotional skills is relatively set by our mid-20s and that our accompanying behaviors are, by that time, deep-seated habits. And therein lies the rub: The more we act a certain way—be it happy, depressed, or cranky—the more the behavior becomes ingrained in our brain circuitry, and the more we will continue to feel and act that way.

That's why emotional intelligence matters so much for a leader. An emotionally intelligent leader can monitor his or her moods through self-awareness, change them for the better through self-management, understand their impact through empathy, and act in ways that boost others' moods through relationship management.

The following five-part process is designed to rewire the brain toward more emotionally intelligent behaviors. The process begins with imagining your ideal self and then coming to terms with your real self, as others experience you. The next step is creating a tactical plan to bridge the gap between ideal and real, and after that, to practice those activities. It concludes with creating a community of colleagues and family—call them change enforcers—to keep the process alive. Let's look at the steps in more detail.

"Who do I want to be?"

Sofia, a senior manager at a northern European telecommunications company, knew she needed to understand how her emotional leadership affected others. Whenever she felt stressed, she tended to communicate poorly and take over subordinates' work so that the job would be done "right." Attending leadership seminars hadn't changed her habits, and neither had reading management books or working with mentors.

When Sofia came to us, we asked her to imagine herself eight years from now as an effective leader and to write a description of a typical day. "What would she be doing?" we asked. "Where would she live? Who would be there? How would it feel?" We urged her to consider her deepest values and loftiest dreams and to explain how those ideals had become a part of her everyday life.

Sofia pictured herself leading her own tight-knit company staffed by ten colleagues. She was enjoying an open relationship with her daughter and had trusting relationships with her friends and coworkers. She saw herself as a relaxed and happy leader and parent, and as loving and empowering to all those around her.

In general, Sofia had a low level of self-awareness: She was rarely able to pinpoint why she was struggling at work and at home. All she could say was, "Nothing is working right." This exercise, which prompted her to picture what life would look like if everything were going right, opened her eyes to the missing elements in her emotional style. She was able to see the impact she had on people in her life.

"Who am I now?"
In the next step of the discovery process, you come to see your leadership style as others do. This is both difficult and dangerous. Difficult, because few people have the guts to tell the boss or a colleague what he's really like. And dangerous, because such information can sting or even paralyze. A small bit of ignorance about yourself isn't always a bad thing: Ego-defense mechanisms have their advantages. Research by Martin Seligman shows that high-functioning people generally feel more optimistic about their prospects and possibilities than average performers. Their rose-colored lenses, in fact, fuel the enthusiasm and energy that make the unexpected and the extraordinary achievable. Playwright Henrik Ibsen called such self-delusions "vital lies," soothing mistruths we let ourselves believe in order to face a daunting world.

But self-delusion should come in very small doses. Executives should relentlessly seek the truth about themselves, especially since it is sure to be somewhat diluted when they hear it anyway. One way to get the truth is to keep an extremely open attitude toward critiques. Another is to seek out negative feedback, even cultivating a colleague or two to play devil's advocate.

We also highly recommend gathering feedback from as many people as possible—including bosses, peers, and subordinates. Feedback from subordinates and peers is especially helpful because it most accurately predicts a leader's effectiveness, two, four, and even seven years out, according to research by Glenn McEvoy at Utah State and Richard Beatty at Rutgers University.

Of course, 360-degree feedback doesn't specifically ask people to evaluate your moods, actions, and their impact. But it does reveal how people experience you. For instance, when people rate how well you listen, they are really reporting how well they think you hear them. Similarly, when 360-degree feedback elicits ratings about coaching effectiveness, the answers show whether or not people feel you understand and care about them. When the feedback uncovers low scores on, say, openness to new ideas, it means that people experience you as inaccessible or unapproachable or both. In sum, all you need to know about your emotional impact is in 360-degree feedback, if you look for it.

One last note on this second step. It is, of course, crucial to identify your areas of weakness. But focusing only on your weaknesses can be dispiriting. That's why it is just as important, maybe even more so, to understand your strengths. Knowing where your real self overlaps with your ideal self will give you the positive energy you need to move forward to the next step in the process—bridging the gaps.

"How do I get from here to there?"

Once you know who you want to be and have compared it with how people see you, you need to devise an action plan. For Sofia, this meant planning for a real improvement in her level of self-awareness. So she asked each member of her team at work to give her feedback—weekly, anonymously, and in written form—about her mood and performance and their affect on people. She also committed herself to three tough but achievable tasks: spending an hour each day reflecting on her behavior in a journal, taking a class on group dynamics at a local college, and enlisting the help of a trusted colleague as an informal coach.

Consider, too, how Juan, a marketing executive for the Latin American division of a major integrated energy company, completed this step. Juan was charged with growing the company in his home country of Venezuela as well as in the entire region—a job that would require him to be a coach and a visionary and to have an encouraging, optimistic outlook. Yet 360-degree feedback revealed that Juan was seen as intimidating and internally focused. Many of his direct reports saw him as a grouch—impossible to please at his worst, and emotionally draining at his best.

Identifying this gap allowed Juan to craft a plan with manageable steps toward improvement. He knew he needed to hone his powers of empathy if he wanted to develop a coaching style, so he committed to various activities that would let him practice that skill. For instance, Juan decided to get to know each of his subordinates better; if he understood more about who they were, he thought, he'd be more able to help them reach their goals. He made plans with each employee to meet outside of work, where they might be more comfortable revealing their feelings.

Juan also looked for areas outside of his job to forge his missing links—for example, coaching his daughter's soccer team and volunteering at a local crisis center. Both activities helped him to experiment with how well he understood others and to try out new behaviors.

Again, let's look at the brain science at work. Juan was trying to overcome ingrained behaviors—his approach to work had taken hold over time, without his realizing it. Bringing them into awareness was a crucial step toward changing them. As he paid more attention, the situations that arose—while listening to a colleague, coaching soccer, or talking on the phone to someone who was distraught—all became cues that stimulated him to break old habits and try new responses.

Resonance in Times of Crisis

When talking about leaders' moods, the importance of resonance cannot be overstated. While our research suggests that leaders should generally be upbeat, their behavior must be rooted in realism, especially when faced with a crisis.

Consider the response of Bob Mulholland, senior VP and head of the client relations group at Merrill Lynch, to the terrorist attacks in New York. On September 11, 2001, Mulholland and his staff in Two World Financial Center felt the building rock, then watched as smoke poured out of a gaping hole in the building directly across from theirs. People started panicking: Some ran frantically from window to window. Others were paralyzed with fear. Those with relatives working in the World Trade Center were terrified for their safety. Mulholland knew he had to act: "When there's a crisis, you've got to show people the way, step by step, and make sure you're taking care of their concerns."

He started by getting people the information they needed to "unfreeze." He found out, for instance, which floors employees' relatives worked on and assured them that they'd have enough time to escape. Then he calmed the panic-stricken, one at a time. "We're getting out of here now," he said quietly, "and you're coming with me. Not the elevator, take the stairs." He remained calm and decisive, yet he didn't minimize people's emotional responses. Thanks to him, everyone escaped before the towers collapsed.

Mulholland's leadership didn't end there. Recognizing that this event would touch each client personally, he and his team devised a way for financial consultants to connect with their clients on an emotional level. They called every client to ask, "How are you? Are your loved ones okay? How are you feeling?" As Mulholland explains, "There was no way to pick up and do business as usual. The first order of 'business' was letting our clients know we really do care."

Bob Mulholland courageously performed one of the most crucial emotional tasks of leadership: He helped himself and his people find meaning in the face of chaos and madness. To do so, he first attuned to and expressed the shared emotional reality. That's why the direction he eventually articulated resonated at the gut level. His words and his actions reflected what people were feeling in their hearts.

This cueing for habit change is neural as well as perceptual. Researchers at the University of Pittsburgh and Carnegie Mellon University have shown that as we mentally prepare for a task, we activate the prefrontal cortex—the part of the brain that moves us into action. The greater the prior activation, the better we do at the task.

Such mental preparation becomes particularly important when we're trying to replace an old habit with a better one. As neuroscientist Cameron Carter at the University of Pittsburgh found, the prefrontal cortex becomes particularly active when a person prepares to overcome a habitual response. The aroused prefrontal cortex marks the brain's focus on what's about to happen. Without that arousal, a person will reenact tried-and-true but undesirable routines: The executive who just doesn't listen will once again cut off his subordinate, a ruthless leader will launch into yet another critical attack, and so on. That's why a learning agenda is so important. Without one, we literally do not have the brainpower to change.

"How do I make change stick?"

In short, making change last requires practice. The reason, again, lies in the brain. It takes doing and redoing, over and over, to break old neural habits. A leader must rehearse a new behavior until it becomes automatic—that is, until he's mastered it at the level of implicit learning. Only then will the new wiring replace the old.

While it is best to practice new behaviors, as Juan did, sometimes just envisioning them will do. Take the case of Tom, an executive who wanted to close the gap between his real self (perceived by colleagues and subordinates to be cold and hard driving) and his ideal self (a visionary and a coach).

Tom's learning plan involved finding opportunities to step back and coach his employees rather than jumping down their throats when he sensed they were wrong. Tom also began to spend idle moments during his commute thinking through how to handle encounters he would have that day. One morning, while en route to a breakfast meeting with an employee who seemed to be bungling a project, Tom ran through a positive scenario in his mind. He asked questions and listened to be sure he fully understood the situation before trying to solve the problem. He anticipated feeling impatient, and he rehearsed how he would handle these feelings.

Studies on the brain affirm the benefits of Tom's visualization technique: Imagining something in vivid detail can fire the same brain cells actually involved in doing that activity. The new brain circuitry appears to go through its paces, strengthening connections, even when we merely repeat the sequence in our minds. So to alleviate the fears associated with trying out riskier ways of leading, we should first visualize some likely scenarios. Doing so will make us feel less awkward when we actually put the new skills into practice.

Experimenting with new behaviors and seizing opportunities inside and outside of work to practice them—as well as using such methods as mental rehearsal—eventually triggers in our brains the neural connections necessary for genuine change to occur. Even so, lasting change doesn't happen through experimentation and brainpower alone. We need, as the song goes, a little help from our friends.

"Who can help me?"

The fifth step in the self-discovery and reinvention process is creating a community of supporters. Take, for example, managers at Unilever who formed learning groups as part of their executive development process. At first, they gathered to discuss their careers and how to provide leadership. But because they were also charged with discussing their dreams and their learning goals, they soon realized that they were discussing both their work and their personal lives. They developed a strong mutual trust and began relying on one another for frank feedback as they worked on strengthening their leadership abilities. When this happens, the business benefits through stronger performance. Many professionals today have created similar groups, and for good reason. People we trust let us try out unfamiliar parts of our leadership repertoire without risk.

We cannot improve our emotional intelligence or change our leadership style without help from others. We not only practice with other people but also rely on them to create a safe environment in which to experiment. We need to get feedback about how our actions affect others and to assess our progress on our learning agenda.

In fact, perhaps paradoxically, in the self-directed learning process we draw on others every step of the way—from articulating and refining our ideal self and comparing it with the reality to the final assessment that affirms our progress. Our relationships offer us the very context in which we understand our progress and comprehend the usefulness of what we're learning.

Mood over Matter

When we say that managing your mood and the moods of your followers is the task of primal leadership, we certainly don't mean to suggest that mood is all that matters. As we've noted, your actions are critical, and mood and actions together must resonate with the organization and with reality. Similarly, we acknowledge all the other challenges leaders must conquer—from strategy to hiring to new product development. It's all in a long day's work.

But taken as a whole, the message sent by neurological, psychological, and organizational research is startling in its clarity. Emotional leadership is the spark that ignites a company's performance, creating a bonfire of success or a landscape of ashes. Moods matter that much.

Originally published in December 2001. Reprint R0111C

RICHARD BOYATZIS chairs the department of organizational behavior at the Weatherhead School of Management at Case Western Reserve University.

HEIKE BRUCH is a professor of leadership at the University of St. Gallen in Switzerland.

CLAYTON M. CHRISTENSEN is the Robert and Jane Cizik Professor of Business Administration at Harvard Business School.

DIANE L. COUTU is a former senior editor of *Harvard Business Review*.

STEPHEN R. COVEY is vice chairman of Franklin Covey, a global provider of leadership development and productivity services.

PETER F. DRUCKER was a professor of social science and management at Claremont Graduate University in California.

STEWART D. FRIEDMAN is the Practice Professor of Management at the University of Pennsylvania's Wharton School.

SUMANTRA GHOSHAL was a professor of strategy and international management at London Business School.

DANIEL GOLEMAN cochairs the Consortium for Research on Emotional Intelligence in Organizations at Rutgers University.

EDWARD M. HALLOWELL is a psychiatrist and the founder of the Hallowell Centers for Cognitive and Emotional Health.

ROBERT S. KAPLAN is a professor of management practice at Harvard Business School.

CATHERINE McCARTHY is a senior vice president at the Energy Project in New York.

ANNIE MCKEE is on the faculty of the University of Pennsylvania's Graduate School of Education.

WILLIAM ONCKEN, JR., was chairman of the William Oncken Corporation, a management consulting company.

ROBERT E. QUINN is the Margaret Elliott Tracy Collegiate Professor in Business Administration at the University of Michigan's Ross School of Business.

TONY SCHWARTZ is the president and founder of the Energy Project in New York.

DONALD L. WASS heads the Dallas–Fort Worth region of The Executive Committee (TEC), an international organization for presidents and CEOs.

CPSIA information can be obtained
at www.ICGtesting.com
Printed in the USA
BVHW031032160419
545656BV00005B/81/P

9 781633 694477

Date: 12/1/16

LP MYS JOHNSON
Johnson, Craig,
An obvious fact

AN OBVIOUS FACT

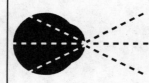

This Large Print Book carries the
Seal of Approval of N.A.V.H.

AN OBVIOUS FACT

CRAIG JOHNSON

THORNDIKE PRESS

A part of Gale, Cengage Learning

GALE
CENGAGE Learning®

Farmington Hills, Mich • San Francisco • New York • Waterville, Maine
Meriden, Conn • Mason, Ohio • Chicago

LIBRARY OF CONGRESS CATALOGING-IN-PUBLICATION DATA

Names: Johnson, Craig, 1961- author.
Title: An obvious fact / Craig Johnson.
Description: Large print edition. | Waterville, Maine : Thorndike Press, 2016. |
    Series: A Walt Longmire mystery | Series: Thorndike Press large print mystery
Identifiers: LCCN 2016036014 | ISBN 9781410486837 (hardback) | ISBN 1410486834
    (hardcover)
Subjects: LCSH: Longmire, Walt (Fictitious character)—Fiction. | Sheriffs—Fiction. |
    Wyoming—Fiction. | Large type books. | BISAC: FICTION / Mystery & Detective /
    General. | GSAFD: Mystery fiction.
Classification: LCC PS3610.O325 O27 2016 | DDC 813/.6—dc23
LC record available at https://lccn.loc.gov/2016036014

Published in 2016 by arrangement with Viking, an imprint of Penguin Publishing Group, a division of Penguin Random House LLC

Printed in the United States of America
1 2 3 4 5 6 7 20 19 18 17 16

For my brother, Greg,
who had his head run over once,
which explains a lot.

"There is nothing more deceptive than an obvious fact."

Arthur Conan Doyle,
The Bascombe Valley Mystery

ACKNOWLEDGMENTS

When I was very young, my father, who was always tinkering with something, brought home a model 841 Indian Scout motorcycle in a half dozen peach baskets and set about rebuilding it with my mother, brother, and me in attendance, none of us ever questioning how the thing had become unassembled in the first place.

The Scout had an intriguing past — the U.S. Army had commissioned it during World War II for desert fighting, and, in response, Indian designed and built the 841 — 8 standing for the new motor and 41 for the year. In fact, the parts that Dad labored over looked as if they might've been shipped from Cairo during the war, but with the ubiquitous red paint giving the impression that this Scout had been decommissioned and sold out of the surplus warehouse in Springfield, Massachusetts.

My mother said it was painted that color

to hide the blood.

For weeks my father assembled and re-assembled the parts, cleaning Linkert carburetors with toothbrushes, rewinding copper wire on the generator, and trying to find spokes that would fit the even then antique motorcycle. Finally, after hours and hours of intensive labor, the Scout was finished, and the three of us stood on the porch steps out of the way of trajectory as my father attempted to kick it into internally combusted life.

My father, a man of considerable strength and vocabulary, began stomping the starter lever on the Indian and when it proved to be uncooperative cut loose with a streaming commentary not fit for polite society.

Operating a motorcycle of this particular vintage was a tricky proposition with a shift lever that sat alongside the gas tank and a shift pedal that required a heel-toe pattern, and a kick-starter, all of which were familiar to my father.

Kicking the living daylights out of the old motorcycle again, my father swore some more and redoubled his efforts. A couple of the things he might not have been aware of were two of the primary reasons the 841 had been turned down by the army — a quixotic clutch and a faulty gearbox.

He kicked again and then paused in action but not in word.

The other thing he might not have known was that the 841 motor was built for the rugged conditions of the wartime desert, where fuel was not plentiful and so designed to run on a low compression ratio of 5.1:1, something he might've considered if he had been aware before adding a high-octane booster into the gas tank.

Mounting another Herculean effort, he tried again, and the twin-cylinder, side valve engine roared to life as he stood there holding on to the handlebars and revving the throttle, his grease-stained face grinning for all it was worth. It was at that instant that the 841 Scout decided it was off to war and took my father with it. Bursting into full, high-octane throttle, it managed to engage its faulty gearbox and shot away with my dad barely holding on with one hand.

We watched as he made the corner of the house and then turned in a sharp left angle up a hillside populated with pine trees with trunks of varying thicknesses. He bounced off a few before the rear tire caught traction and flipped him over backward, the two of them entangled and tumbling back down the hill.

My mother was horrified.

My brother and I couldn't wait to try it.

Thus began a lifelong preoccupation with things that are fast — horses, cars, trains, women, and, yep, motorcycles.

I'd like to throw a two-fingered salute out to my riding partners for all their help in getting *An Obvious Fact* up on two wheels starting with super agent Gail "Gear-Grindin' " Hochman and her henchwoman, Marianne "Smooth Rollin' " Merola. The sidecar over at Viking Penguin couldn't be fuller with Kathryn "Chrome Queen" Court, Lindsey "Wall of Death" Schwoeri, Victoria "Skid Mark" Savanh, Brian "Hold My Beer I Want to Try Something" Tart, Olivia "T-Bone" Taussig, and Ben "Pedal to the Metal" Petrone.

I know a little Arthur Conan Doyle but not as much as my friend Leslie Klinger and was glad to loan Henry a copy of Klinger's *The New Annotated Sherlock Holmes: The Complete Short Stories.* Thanks to Jamey Gilkey of Old Man G Performance and John Stainbrook for keeping me honest on the two-wheel thing. Thanks to my backup men, Michael Crutchley and Curt Wendelboe, for the motorcycle accident technology and the great K-9 stories. Thanks to Linda and Bob Prill and Dr.

Frank Carlton for the lowdown on skeet and trap shooting — those ashtrays are elusive and need to be put on the non-endangered list.

Hey, if you haven't ever visited Devils Tower you need to head over that way, and a great place to hang your hat or grab a meal is in Hulett, one of my favorite towns in Wyoming. Thanks to Chef "Jersey Boy" Dean and the Ponderosa Grill & Cafe, which serves one of the finest cheesesteaks west of the Schuykill River, just ask Vic. Thanks to The Golf Club at Devils Tower, which really isn't the den of iniquity that I make it out to be. . . . And in Rapid City, SD, a shout out to Piesano's Pacchia for the great pizza and Ron's Cafe for the marvelous pancakes, which kept me going on this marathon, iron-butt ride.

Music is really important to me when I'm writing, and I want to thank Rickey Medlocke for providing the soundtrack and the friendship — you know you've made it when you get an email from Lynyrd Skynyrd. And by the way, I don't think you guys sound like a garage band.

Finally, there's the only one whose arms I want wrapped around me as I take on the hairpins of life, my wife, Judy "Vincent Black Lightning" Johnson.

1

I tried to think how many times I'd kneeled down on asphalt to read the signs, but I knew this was the first time I'd done it in Hulett. Located in the northeast corner of the Wyoming Black Hills, the town is best known for being the home of Devils Tower.

I looked at the macadam blend, the stones shining in the mix that was still wet from the early morning rain, and sighed. With the advent of antilock brakes, it was hard enough to properly estimate the speed of a vehicle involved in a traffic accident, never mind in the rain.

"Do you see anything?"

I nudged my hat farther back on my head and turned to look at the large Indian leaning against the door of Lola, his Baltic blue '59 Thunderbird and my granddaughter's namesake. "How about you come over here and take a look for yourself."

Henry Standing Bear didn't move and

continued to study the large book in his hands. "I am on vacation."

I was kneeling at the apex of a sweeping curve on state route 24 where the road veered off toward Matho Tipila, the Cheyenne name for the first United States National Monument, so declared by Teddy Roosevelt in 1906.

"There is traffic coming."

I didn't hear anything, but that didn't mean he wasn't right, so I walked to the edge of the road and watched as a phalanx of motorcyclists came around the corner and descended toward us like a flock of disgruntled magpies.

They slowed — not for me, I wasn't in uniform — but because of the corpuscle-red Indian motorcycle with the modified KTM extended rear-axle dirt bike that roosted on the flatbed trailer behind the Thunderbird.

The leather-clad cyclists thumbed their horns and gave a collected thumbs-up to the Cheyenne Nation as he leaned there, looking as if he were negotiating a treaty, with his muscled arms folded over his chest, the first volume of Leslie S. Klinger's *The New Annotated Sherlock Holmes: The Complete Short Stories* in one hand.

"You could have waved back."

He shook his head. "That would not fit with the tourist's stereotypical vision of the stoic, yet noble, savage."

I glanced at the book. "Is that mine?"

"Yes, I took it from your shelves. I did not think you would mind if I borrowed it."

I glanced back at Devils Tower crowding the horizon. The geologic area around the megalith is not of the same composition as the tower itself, and the belief is that about fifty to sixty million years ago, during the Paleogene period, an igneous intrusion forced its way up through the local sedimentary stone, some saying it was an ancient volcano, some saying it was a laccolith, an uncovered bulge that never made it to the surface. "You know how it got its name, right?"

"Yours or ours?"

I ignored him and started back toward the T-bird. "When Colonel Richard Irving Dodge led an expedition back in 1875, his interpreter got it wrong and referred to it as Bad God's Tower, which then became Devils Tower, without the apostrophe as per the geographic standard." I opened Lola's passenger door and eased in.

The Bear climbed into the driver's seat and studied me.

I reached back and stroked Dog's head.

"You don't care."

"About what?"

"The apostrophe."

He hit the ignition on the big bird. "I care that a delegation of my people attempted to have the name restored to Bear Lodge National Historic Landmark, but your U.S. representative killed it. 'The name change will harm the tourist trade and bring economic hardship to area communities.' "

I knew the man he was talking about, and I had to admit that his nasal imitation was spot on. "But as an expert, what's your feeling on the apostrophe?"

He grunted and placed the book between us. " 'There is nothing more deceptive than an obvious fact.' " Pulling the vintage convertible into gear, he patted the book. "Sherlock Holmes."

"Did you borrow all three volumes?"

He pulled onto the vacant road. "Yes."

"Oh, brother."

It took a while to drive the nine miles into Hulett — eighteen minutes to be exact — because thirty miles an hour was as fast as Henry Standing Bear was willing to drive Lola (the car), especially while towing Lucie (the motorcycle), and Rosalie (the dirt bike).

18

The Bear liked giving vehicles women's names.

We skipped Hulett's main street to avoid the fifty thousand or so motorcycles parked on both sides of the road. The town's population of just around four hundred multiplies under the August sun as bikers from around the world arrive for the nearby Sturgis Motorcycle Rally, which pulls in close to a million bikers each year.

Held in the town of the same name just across the border in neighboring South Dakota, the rally lasts a week. On the Wednesday of that week, Hulett throws what they call the Ham 'N Jam, offering free music and a thousand pounds of pork, three hundred pounds of beans, and two hundred pounds of chips; they also celebrate something they call No Panties Wednesday, though nothing in the official literature mentions the missing undergarments.

Our destination was the Ponderosa Café and Bar and the Rally in the Alley, which was handy because the gravel back street was the only place where there was a parking spot large enough for the car and the trailer. Henry eased the Thunderbird through the crowd and parked behind a tent set up to sell T-shirts, patches, do-rags, and other souvenirs.

"Today's Monday, right?"

"All day."

I glanced around at the hundreds of people milling about. "And the actual Ham 'N Jam doesn't start until Wednesday?"

"My thought exactly."

"Do you think you should put the top up?"

He shut his door and looked at the very blue sky. "Why? I do not think it is going to rain again this morning."

I shrugged and glanced at Dog, the hundred-and-fifty-pound security system. "Stay. And don't bite anybody."

A woman in a provocative leather outfit, a lot of hair, and a multitude of rose tattoos paused as she passed us. "Is he mean?"

"Absolutely." As I said this, he reached his bucket head over the side door and licked her shoulder with his wide tongue. "Well, almost absolutely." She smiled a lopsided smile, which revealed a missing tooth, and continued on down the road. I looked at Dog. "Just so you know, you could get a disease."

He didn't seem to care and just sat there wagging at me.

Moving to the trailer, I watched as the Bear used a chamois cloth to remove what dust had collected on the Indian motorcycle.

"Why do people ride these contraptions, anyway?"

He checked the tie-down straps and stood. "Freedom."

"Freedom to be an organ donor." I glanced up and down the crowded alley. "T. E. Lawrence died on a motorcycle. You know what I make of that?"

"He should not have left Arabia?" Henry climbed over the railing and stood next to me. "Where are we supposed to meet him?"

"Here." I looked around. "But I don't see him."

The Cheyenne Nation took a step and glanced down the alley, choked with bikers of every stripe, and plucked the *Annotated Sherlock* from the fender rail where he had left it. "Maybe he was called away."

"The only police officer assigned to a fifty-thousand-biker rally?" I smiled. "Maybe."

He carefully placed the book under his arm. "There is always the Hulett Police Department." He glanced around. "If I were a police department, where would I be?"

"At 123 Hill Street, right off Main as 24 makes the turn going north."

"Far?"

"Almost a block."

He started off, intuitively in the correct direction. "The game is afoot."

I shook my head and followed as we made our way, taking in the sights, sounds, and smells that are Ham 'N Jam. "Doesn't smell too bad, but maybe it's because I'm hungry."

He nodded and smiled at two lithesome beauties in halter tops as they grinned at him.

"What happened to your Native stoicism?"

"Well, anything can be taken to excess."

The crowd in front of Capt'n Ron's Rodeo Bar on the corner was spilling onto the street in joyous celebration of the open container law, which allowed alcoholic beverages to be consumed in the open air during rally week. The party was in full swing, the sounds of the Allman Brothers' "Statesboro Blues" drifting through the swinging saloon doors.

I looked back at the Bear. "Two of the Allman Brothers died on motorcycles — what do you make of that?"

"That if you are an Allman Brother you should not ride a motorcycle."

I sidestepped a short, round individual who was wearing a Viking helmet and drinking from a red plastic cup, but Henry got cut off.

"How you doin', Chief?"

The Cheyenne Nation half smiled the paper-cut grin he reserved for just these situations. "I am not a chief. I am Henry Standing Bear, Heads Man of the Dog Soldier Society, Bear Clan." He leaned in over the man, the bulk of him filling the sidewalk. "And who are you?"

The Viking didn't move, probably because he couldn't. "Umm . . . Eddy."

The Bear extended his hand. "Good to meet you, Eddy. The next time we see each other, I hope you remember to address me in a proper fashion." They shook, and Henry left Eddy the Viking there, utterly dumbstruck — not that I think it took much.

"Oh, this is going to be an interesting two days."

We rounded the corner, the crowd thinned out, and we stood in front of the Hulett Police Department office, located next to what looked to be a fifteen-ton military vehicle.

The Cheyenne Nation rested a fist on his hip and stared at the white monstrosity. "What is that?"

I shook my head and pushed open the Hulett Police Department door. It was a small office as police offices go, with a counter and two desks on the other side. An older, smallish man sat at one of them with his hat over his face. He started when I closed the door, but the hat didn't move. "By God, before you say anything, whoever you are, there better be a bleedin' body lying in the street before you wake me all the way up."

"You haven't been all the way woke up since I met you."

He slipped the hat off and looked at me. "How the hell are you, Walt Long-Arm-of-the-Law?"

I spread my palms. "Vacationing."

He stood and placed the straw hat on his head. "In lovely Hulett, Wyoming?" He walked over and, making a face, shook my hand. "During Ham 'N Jam?" He glanced at the Cheyenne Nation and then extended the same hand to him. "Henry Standing Bear — you come over here to show all these lawyers, dentists, and accountants what a real outlaw looks like?"

Henry shook. "How are you, Nutter Butter?"

William Nutter had been the chief of police in Hulett for as far back as anyone could remember. A tough individual with a mind of his own, he kept the town running smoothly; if the man had an enemy in the world, I didn't have an idea who that might be.

"Ready to retire and even more so after this last weekend."

I nodded and threw a thumb over my shoulder. "What, in the name of all that's holy, is that behemoth sitting out there?"

He smiled. "An MRAP, stands for Mine-Resistant Ambush Protected. We got a bunch of that Patriot Act money that's still around and some funding from a local citizen, name of Bob Nance. He wrote up all the paperwork for us. Hell, the federal government's got twelve thousand of the things — we grabbed one before the ban."

"Your town has less than four hundred people in it."

He gestured toward the overcrowded street. "Not today, it doesn't."

Henry parted the venetian blinds and peered at the thing. "What are you going to do with it?"

Nutter shrugged. "I don't know — we've got to figure out how to start it first." His eyes played around the littered room. "I got the manual around here somewhere, if you guys want to give it a try."

"It's very white."

"It was used by the United Nations."

"What does it weigh?"

"About fifteen tons."

"And how many miles to the gallon does it get?"

"I don't know, maybe three." He leaned on the counter and tugged at his hat like he was saddling up. "We're not allowed to use any town or county money to maintenance the thing, so either Bob needs to come up with some more funding or what it's going to end up being is a big, white lawn ornament." He smiled as Henry continued to stare at the massive vehicle. "She's a beauty, though, isn't she?"

I scrubbed a hand over my face and changed the subject to the one at hand. "So, you want to tell us about the incident this last weekend?"

He shook his head. "No, I'd rather you talk to the investigating officer, who I assume is the one who called you?"

"He did." I studied Nutter, taking in the accumulation of lines on his face, more than I'd remembered from last time.

He moved toward a radio console and, holding up a finger toward us, picked up one of the old-style desk mics. "Woof, woof — hey, Deputy Dog, where are you?"

There was a pause, and then a voice I recognized came over the speaker. "Please don't call me that."

Nutter immediately barked into the mic again. "Woof, woof, woof! Where are you? The Lone Ranger and Tonto are here for a powwow."

There was another pause. "I'm down here in front of the Pondo doing a sobriety test on a guy who thinks riding drunk is the same as stumbling down the sidewalk." There was a voice in the background and more conversation before he came back on. "I'm right here on Main Street — how did I miss them?"

"We came in and parked in the alley."

Nutter relayed the message and then sent us on our way back to the Ponderosa Café and Bar. As we closed the door, he called out, "Don't forget to ask Deputy Dog how he got his name."

"It was stupid."

"It usually is." I leaned back in my chair, sipped my coffee, and studied the former Gillette patrolman and Campbell County deputy, Corbin Dougherty.

"Our K9 guy was a little weird."

"They usually are."

He sighed. "The dog companies were sending us all these samples — you know, shock collars and stuff? So the K9 guy gets to wondering how bad the shock is."

The Cheyenne Nation, who had been gazing out the window, turned back to look at the deputy. "What did he ever do to you?"

He shrugged. "His dog bit me. I mean, he's the K9 guy, so he should have control over his dog, right?" Corbin looked around the packed café and lowered his voice. "I told him he should try one on — you know, get a feeling for the things before he put them on his dog."

"No."

"Yes." He glanced around again. "So, we're in the day room, and this idiot puts the dog collar on. I don't mean just held it there; I mean he buckled the thing on around his neck. So, then he starts barking, real low, like 'woof.' "

I peered at him through the fingers covering my face. "Barking?"

"Honest to God — I guess he figured since it was a *dog* shock collar . . ."

"Let me guess what happened."

"Nothing at first, but he kept barking louder and finally it kicked in, and you've never seen anything like it. I mean, the things have these little prongs on the inside that are supposed to work through the insulation of the dog's fur, but this was bare skin on this idiot's neck."

I tried to keep from laughing, but it was

28

hard. "Then what?"

"It flipped him back over the table and put him on the floor. Honest, it was like he was struck by lightning — like a Taser, only way worse. Well, every time the thing shocks him he yells, so it shocks him again."

"What did you do?"

Corbin paused as a waitress arrived and set our breakfasts in front of us. He watched her go and then continued. "What do you mean what did we do? Nothing. Everybody hates the son of a bitch; that damn dog of his has bitten all of us. So, he's flopping around on the floor, screaming and getting lit up like a Christmas tree, and we've all got our cell phones out taking video."

Henry nodded. "The brotherhood of blue."

Corbin sipped his coffee. "Anyway, one of the other officers posted the thing on YouTube, and it went viral. The *Trib* did a story, and Sandy Sandberg needed a fall guy; I was the one with least seniority."

"So, here you are in Hulett."

"You weren't hiring."

I sipped my own coffee. "I'm always hiring."

The young deputy forked a strawberry. "Besides, it's nice over here, and I met a girl in Sundance."

The Bear and I looked at each other. "There is always a girl."

I remembered the pit bull we'd dropped on the young man last winter. "She like your dog, Deputy?"

He smiled. "More than me."

We started eating in earnest, and the conversation died down. Corbin, the healthiest of us, finished his oatmeal and fruit and straightened his paper placemat before introducing the subject of why we were there. "I hope you don't mind me calling, but I figured after you'd helped out with that mess in Campbell County . . ."

I leaned back in the booth. "This star for hire."

He looked up, a little panicked. "I can't pay you anything, Walt."

"That was a joke."

"Oh." He gathered his napkin from his lap. "Did you stop on your way in and look at the accident site?"

"We did, but it was wet and kind of hard to tell what had happened."

Dougherty glanced around at the crowded café again and whispered, "There was a lot of blood."

"Rain must've washed it away."

He nodded. "Yeah, I mean they had him stabilized down at County Memorial in

30

Sundance, but they moved him to Rapid City. Too small a hospital to keep him here."

"He?"

"The victim — last name Torres, twenty-two years of age, out of Tucson, Arizona. He's got a bunch of priors, mostly drugs along with a few domestics, and an aggravated assault and weapons charge."

"Had he been drinking?"

Corbin shrugged. "A little, according to the doctors, but nothing too bad."

"Current condition?"

"Assorted, along with a whopper of a traumatic brain injury. B-way —" He looked up at me. "That's what they call him, B-way — has got a diffuse axonal injury where the nerve cells are stretched and sheared inside the skull. He was out for six hours and then came to momentarily, but he was acting strange. He's pretty messed up."

"Anybody ask him about the accident when he regained consciousness?"

"I did. I tried to get a statement from him, but he wasn't capable of coherent thought, never mind speech."

"Think he will be?"

Dougherty shook his head. "I really don't know — neither do the doctors, I think. They put him back in an induced coma."

I nodded and then glanced at Henry, who

31

continued to gaze out the windows. "You file a report with DCI's Accident Investigation?"

"I did, and a guy named Novo is coming up tomorrow."

The Bear finally joined the conversation. "Mike Novo?"

"Yeah — you know him?"

Henry smiled. "He is the motorcycle expert in Cheyenne."

I watched Corbin for a moment. "So, what happened?"

"We got a call from Chloe, a local girl who was working one of the tents up here part time. She was headed home when she saw a guy and a motorcycle lying on the side of the road."

"I'm going to need to speak with her."

He nodded. "It was about one in the morning on Saturday night, and with the traffic we get around Sturgis, it must've just happened. I got there right as the EMTs did, and they scooped him up and took him to Sundance. Herb Robinson, who owns the wrecker service, came and got the bike but then hauled it over to the Rapid City Police Department impound yard. I guess Robinson had past problems with bikers who liberate their bikes without paying, and the

Rapid cops are the only ones with a fenced yard."

"What do you think happened?"

The patrolman pushed his empty oatmeal bowl away and rested his elbows on the table. "I think somebody hit him."

"Passing him? Rear-ended . . . ?"

"On purpose." He stared at me. "The bike was hit on the side, hard, and forced into the ditch. There's a culvert out there near the turnoff to the Tower —"

"Yep, we saw it when we stopped."

"Right." There was a pause. "What do you think?"

"I think you can jump to conclusions in these situations; there are just too many possibilities. Maybe it was a deer, the other driver was drunk, the kid was on his cell phone. . . ."

Corbin crossed his arms. "He did have a cell phone."

"Was it out?"

"His brains were out. . . . Everything was out."

I gave him another second. "I'll need to check the phone."

"Sure."

Leaning back in my chair, I listened to it squeal and finished my coffee. "So . . . why call us?"

"I guess this kid is a big deal with the Tre Tre Nomads, a motorcycle gang out of the Southwest, and things just got really weird really fast."

"How do you mean?"

"Members of the club were in Sundance already for the rally and strong-armed their way into seeing the kid at the Medical Center, but then he was transferred to Rapid City Regional and I guess they wouldn't let them in the intensive care unit. When I got back up here on Sunday, they were waiting for me at the police station."

"What'd they want?"

"They wanted to know who did it, who hit B-way." He shook his head and swirled the coffee left in his cup. "They said there was no way that he'd just had an accident, and they wanted a name." He leaned in. "I checked, and you know what? They're right. He's never had a traffic accident — everything else under the sun but not even a speeding ticket."

"Well, maybe they're just worried about the kid."

"No, it's more than that. I'm staying at one of the little cabins the city provides on the north end of town, and when I got through on patrol yesterday, one of them was waiting for me there."

"Okay."

"Big guy, kind of the enforcer, I guess."

"Alone?"

"Yeah."

"Okay."

"Wanted to know where we were on all this, what we were doing about it, and I told him that we were doing the best we could, but with the rally we didn't have the manpower to do a thorough investigation without help from DCI, but that they would be here pretty quick."

"And was he satisfied with that?"

"Not really." He studied me. "Can I ask you a question?"

"Shoot."

"What's the one percent mean?" He shoved his empty cup away. "When the enforcer, the strong-arm guy, said I better find out who did it, he said I better or I was going to meet the real one percent."

I nodded, allowing the information to surface in my memory. "The Hollister riot in '47. It was just a little after World War II, and they had this motorcycle rally in California in this little town. A lot more bikers showed up than they had anticipated."

"And there were riots?"

"Not really, but there were a lot of drunk bikers and racing in the streets. Things got out of hand. Hollister had only a nine-man police department, and they panicked and threatened to use tear gas and it got in all the newspapers." Somebody squeezed in near our table as I tried to remember the wording. "I think it was the American Motorcycle Association that came out and said the trouble was caused by the one percent deviants . . ."

". . . that tarnish the public image of both motorcycles and motorcyclists." I looked up to see a man in a leather vest, jeans, and motorcycle boots. "And that the other ninety-nine percent of motorcyclists are good, decent, law-abiding citizens." He slipped off his Oakley sunglasses, revealing what looked like a once-broken nose, and smiled down at Dougherty through a prodigious mustache and goatee. "The AMA came out later and said they never made the statement, but that's bullshit."

I picked up my coffee cup, studied the dregs, and then him, noting the do-rag under his reversed ball cap, his numerous earrings, and enough tattoos to print up a crew of merchant marines. "Hi."

He reluctantly averted his eyes from Corbin to me. "Hi."

"Were you there?"

He looked confused. "Huh?"

"Hollister."

He breathed a laugh. "No, bud, before my time. You?"

"Before mine, too."

He nodded. "Excuse me, but you mind if I continue my conversation with Officer Dougherty here?"

"Yep, I do. We're eating our breakfast, and we don't like being disturbed. Now, if you've got something you'd like to discuss, we'll be through with our meal here in a few minutes and will meet you out front."

He stared at me for a good long time, but I picked up my water glass and just kept drinking as he simmered. "Who the fuck are you?"

I finally set my glass down and stood, my size taking him a little by surprise. He was big — not quite as big as me — but he was younger, probably in his late thirties and built like a strong safety.

His hand dropped to the side toward the small of his back, at which point the Cheyenne Nation also stood, that move immediately getting his attention. As an aging offensive tackle, I was just as glad to have my running back with me.

I leaned in. "How 'bout we make our introductions outside?"

He hard-eyed Henry for a moment and

then, curving the corners of his mouth underneath his mustache, looked back at me. "I'll see you out front, bud."

I watched him leave, and we sat back down. I smiled at Corbin. "That him — the Enforcer?"

"Yeah, that's him."

We sat there for a while longer, but it seemed as if the conversation had fled the room, so I stood again. "What do you say we go out front?"

Corbin shook his head. "I think I'll change careers — fireman is looking good."

I grabbed his shoulder. "C'mon, Deputy Dog."

All eyes were on us as we exited the packed restaurant, and I noticed a few people were quickly vacating the area in front of the Ponderosa. I pushed the door open, and as we stepped onto the sidewalk, about a dozen bikers of all shapes and sizes immediately surrounded the three of us.

The Enforcer was seated on a chromed-out bike, a kind of turquoise in color, his legs crossed with a wrist hanging over one of the grips on his handlebars. "Welcome to my office."

"Nice view."

He shrugged as the others stepped back, letting him make his play. He was the alpha, and if he could handle us on his own, he would.

"Now, how can we help you?"

He pointed past me to Dougherty. "I need to talk to him."

"Why? Who are you?"

He stepped around the front of his motorcycle, came in close, and extended his hand. "Brady Post. I guess you could say I'm the spokesman for the Tre Tre Nomads." I took the hand; he tried the old trick of grabbing my fingers, but I slipped the meat of my palm in and gripped him back. My old boss, Lucian Connally, had the strongest grip I'd ever felt, but he'd never been able to break me, so I wasn't concerned as Post began applying pressure. I gave just enough back so that we stayed even. His eyes were a deep blue, almost cobalt, and as he brought himself up close to me, I was surprised that he smelled like Old Spice aftershave. "Who are you?"

"Walt Longmire."

From the flexing of his forearm, I could tell he was putting everything into it, and I had to admit that it was an impressive display. "And what are you, Walt Longmire?"

"Just an interested citizen."

"Yeah? Well, I'm interested in what Officer Dougherty and his department are doing about finding the guy who tried to kill our buddy."

"It's an ongoing investigation, and I'm sure you'll understand that Officer Dougherty cannot make statements that might undermine the department's work." My turn to put everything I had into it. "Anyway, we're not sure there was an attempt on anybody's life. It could've been a simple traffic accident."

He didn't wince but did glance at our hands, which were intertwined in a death match. "I wanna see a report."

"Mr. Post, I'm sure that, as the spokesperson for the Tre Tre Nomads, you've got a lot of responsibility, but in the eyes of the town, the county, and the Wyoming state government, you have no official standing. Any information Officer Dougherty has would be for family members only."

"We are family."

"Blood?"

"More than you want to know, bud."

I did my best to look unimpressed. "I'm sure, but until you can show Officer Dougherty here some ID that corroborates that fact, there really isn't anything we can tell you, either as an individual . . ." I glanced around for effect, "or as a group."

His face was turning red, but I didn't see any reason to tap the leader of the pack on the nose just yet, so I let off and was surprised when he did the same. He let his hand drop, but I noticed he flexed it to get the blood flowing. "We'll be waiting." I started to turn to the left, but the ring of men didn't make way, and it was about then that he called out again, this time to Henry, "Hey, Chief, I didn't get your name."

I turned to see he'd thrown out a hand and that it rested on the chest of the Cheyenne Nation, and all I could think was, Oh, boy, here we go.

The Bear's head turned like a tree swaying, and I tensed, knowing that what was about to happen was going to be scorched-earth massive.

"That's Henry Standing Bear, Heads Man of the Dog Soldier Society, Bear Clan."

I stood there for a second trying to identify where the statement had come from, and then, glancing to my left, I saw

Eddy the Viking, the guy who had spoken with Henry in front of Capt'n Ron's.

It was one of those weird little moments where nobody knew what to do, so we all just stood there like some contemporary Western tableau.

Eddy raised his red cup and saluted the

Bear. "I get that right?"

The Cheyenne Nation smiled. "Yes, you did."

I turned and walked between the two nearest bikers and continued on, with Dougherty and Henry following me like a funeral procession. After a few steps, I couldn't help but turn my head and ask, "Is the Viking one of the Tre Tre Nomads?"

Dougherty, happy to be out of the ring of fire, smiled an uneasy grin. "No, that's Crazy Eddy, one of the original Jackpine Gypsies; he lives over in Lead, been a fixture here at the rally for years, or so they tell me." Corbin glanced back at Henry, who was bringing up the rear of our little war party. "You know him?"

The Bear nodded. "It has been a short relationship."

There was a break in the crowd ahead of us that had allowed a real head turner to saunter up the sidewalk directly toward me. Lots of women perfect the sway at some point in their lives, but few get the rumble that this one had in spades. She was probably in her fifties, her dark hair with a sharp strand of silver in the middle swept back from her forehead. Very tall, and dressed in a simple black tank top and jeans, she split the crowd like an icebreaker, and both men and women watched her approach. Her sandals slapped the hot concrete on the sidewalk, as if teaching it a lesson.

I stepped to the side, but she countered, moved in front of me, and looked at me with frighteningly green eyes set in sun-kissed skin, her mouth wide and beautifully shaped, opened as if savoring the moment.

Corbin ran into my back, and Henry was turning to see what it was that might've stopped me dead. You would've had to measure the widening of his eyes with a micrometer, but it was there. He smiled broadly, and the woman did a hair flip that I would've given a 9.5, stepped in front of Henry, and then slapped the Bear's face with a tooth-shattering report.

The effect on the crowd was impressive, everyone freezing in place.

She stood there looking at him for a moment, then curtseyed in a quick dip of those magnificent hips and turned and walked away without a word.

Strangely, it was Dougherty who called out after her. "Lola?"

She kept walking, flailing a hand over a freckled shoulder in absolute dismissal.

I turned to Dougherty. "Lola?"

He cocked his head, watching her go. "Lola."

I turned back to the Cheyenne Nation. "*The* Lola?"

The side of his face still burned a burnished red as he rubbed it and watched her go with the slightest of head shakes and a knowing smile. "*The* Lola."

2

"Lola Wojciechowski?"

He shrugged. "I suppose. I never knew her last name."

I unloaded the trunk, shut the lid, and looked at the Thunderbird. "You named your car after her."

"It was only her first name; besides, it was not a verbal relationship."

The Bear unlocked the door to the cabin we had reserved and turned to me, his expression a little surprised. "It was a long time ago."

"Evidently it wasn't that long ago for her." Entering the doorway, I paused and looked at him. "Henry, you named your car after her, and you love that car." I brushed past him with our suitcases as Dog immediately jumped onto the nearest bed.

Setting a cooler by the door, the Bear stood, stretched, and then walked over to place two of the three volumes of the *An-*

notated Holmes on the nightstand. "She did seem upset."

"A little."

He glanced back through the open door with the first book in his hand. "What is our plan?"

"Maybe go back out and examine the accident site. Why?"

"I thought I would take the bikes over to Jamey Gilkey's shop in Sturgis and let him get Rosalie ready for the Jackpine Gypsies Hill Climb tomorrow."

I slipped off my clip holster and .45, placed it on the nightstand beside the books, and sat on the bed next to Dog. "Don't you think you're getting a little old for that stuff?"

"I have done the Climb every year since 1974, when I won."

"All the more reason to stop."

"Lightning could strike twice. It has been a new century, and my luck could change."

"You go ahead then, and I'll stay here. You okay without your phone? I was wondering if you could loan it to me so I can call Cady." I held my hand out.

He handed the device to me. "Did she find a place to live?"

"She got a little carriage house a couple of blocks from the capitol building — Joe

46

and Mary Meyer found it for her."

"It is good to have an in with the state attorney general."

I looked at the phone in my hands. "Yep."

"Emotional qualities are antagonistic to clear reasoning."

"Why don't you and Sherlock Holmes get the hell out of here?"

He shut the door, and I listened as he started up the Thunderbird and pulled away. Dialing the number and holding it to my ear, the phone rang a few times and then switched over to her message. "Hi, I'm not here — you know the drill."

"Hey, Henry."

"You're doing something."

"You've been kidnapped, right? There's no other way you'd be calling on a cell phone." She snorted. "Painting."

"What color?"

"Pistachio, with dark brown trim."

"Sounds interesting."

She huffed. "Don't start."

We had differing ideas about home décor, with my leaning toward off-white everything while she had more provocative tastes. "How's it coming?"

I could imagine her standing on the hardwood floor of the little carriage house, studying the green wall and wielding the roller like a weapon. "I'm not sure."

"Well, Punk, you can always repaint."

"Right, thanks."

"Lola helping?"

"No, thank God. She's asleep in her Pack 'n Play, under the watchful eye of her Nonnie Moretti."

Thankful that Vic's mother, Lena, was taking up the slack, I lay back on the bed and petted Dog. "How's things down at the attorney general's office?"

"Pretty general. Everybody here knows you from afar." Her voice relaxed a little, the tension fading so long as we weren't discussing paint. "They all think you're some kind of big deal."

"Have you been setting them straight?"

"A little — I told them about how you sometimes sleep with your mouth open."

Enjoying her voice, I closed my eyes. "That should do the trick."

"And that you never put the cap back on the toothpaste."

"I'm never going to be able to hold my head up again." There was silence for a while, so I figured it was okay to ask about the investigation into my son-in-law's death. "Any word from Philadelphia?"

"Still nothing."

"I haven't heard anything from Vic."

"From what Lena tells me, I think she's helping, on a purely unofficial basis, of course."

"Of course." I crossed my boots. "How are the rest of the Morettis?"

"Still stunned. An entire family of police officers for three generations, and Michael is the first to ever be killed in the line of duty." There was another pause, longer this time, and her voice lowered. "Lena is taking it hard. Michael was the baby, you know?"

"Yep, he was." There wasn't anything more to say, so I didn't. That's the thing about comforting — it's almost more important to know when not to talk.

"I'm lonely, Dad."

"I know you are." I breathed a deep breath. "I'm sorry."

"I mean, thank God I've got Lena or I sometimes think I'd go nuts."

There was a knock, and Dog barked, leaping off the bed and standing by the door. I figured it must've been the Bear, having forgotten something, because I couldn't think of anybody else who would know where we were.

I tucked the phone between my shoulder and chin and rolled off the bed. "Hold on, there's somebody here." Lodging my leg between Dog and the door, I opened it to find Lola Wojciechowski pointing a .38 Special, replete with a pink grip, at my face. "Howdy."

She poked the thing at me like it was a stick. "I've got a gun."

Dog barked again, and I thought she was going to drop the weapon. I nudged him back with my leg. "I can see that."

"Dad?" Cady's voice sounded in my ear.

I cocked my head and held the phone. "Hey, I've got to go —"

"Did I just hear somebody say something about a gun?"

"Yep."

"Call me back."

Her concern was touching. "Right." I pulled the thing from my ear, hit the button to end the call, and opened the door the rest of the way to allow her entrance. "C'mon in." Her arm wavered, and she pointed the weapon in the general direction of Dog as I turned back to her. "And don't shoot Dog; it just pisses him off."

She looked uncertain as to what to do with that information but came the rest of the way in as the beast sniffed at her leatherbound crotch. "Hey, you wanna call him off?"

"You want to put the gun away?"

"No."

"Looks like we're at a standoff." I sat back on the bed and gestured toward the chair by the door. "Have a seat."

She swung her purse around behind her. "Where's Bear?"

"Gone." I didn't feel any reason to give out more — I'm like that in armed conversations.

She moved over and sat, pushing Dog's head away with her free hand. "This is not going the way I planned."

"That's the problem with the gun thing — usually it doesn't."

She crossed her legs and leaned forward, resting her elbow on her thigh and keeping the barrel of the .38 on me. "You don't seem too concerned."

I plumped up some pillows and leaned back on the bed, patting it for Dog to join me, which he did; then he sat there, looking at her and panting. I could imagine she got that response all the time. I gestured toward the .45 on the nightstand that she hadn't noticed. "I get a lot of guns pointed at me in my line of work."

She redoubled her aiming effort. "And what do you do?"

Carefully unsnapping the pocket on my shirt, I pulled out my badge wallet and flipped it open for her to see. "Absaroka

County sheriff."

"Oh shit."

"Yep." I waited a moment more and then stuffed the hardware back in my shirt. "Now that we're getting to know each other a little better, do you want to put the gun away?"

She thought about it. "No."

I eased back on the bed, took off my hat, and placed it over my face. "Well, I'm taking a nap."

"What?"

I spoke into the crown of the palm leaf. "Sorry, I don't mean to be rude, but I haven't gotten a lot of sleep lately."

"Well, you're not going to get it now."

I tipped my hat up and looked at her. "Look, if you've got something to say, say it or get out of here. Henry's not going to show up any time soon, and I don't have the time to play twenty questions with you." I pulled my hat back down and sat there under it wondering what was going to happen next when I heard a snuffle. I propped my hat up again and could see she was crying. "Oh, please don't do that."

She smeared the tears away with the heel of her hand and looked at me. "I can't help it; I'm upset."

I turned toward her. "Look, Lola . . ."

She re-aimed the .38. "How do you know

my name?"

I sighed. "You wouldn't believe how familiar I am with your name — evidently, my granddaughter is named after you."

"Huh?"

"You don't know Henry named his car for you?"

"No."

"Well, he did, and then my daughter for some godforsaken reason named my granddaughter after the car, so we've got vehicles, children, and heaven knows what else running around with your name on them."

She sniffed. "He named the T-bird after me?"

I tried not to let my eyes roll back in my head on that one. "Yep, he's sentimental that way."

"Where is he?"

I pointed at the gun, and she pulled a small purse around, unsnapping it and dumping the revolver inside before closing the bag back up and hanging it on her chair. "There. Now, where is he?"

"Gone to Sturgis."

She started to stand. "Great."

I held out a hand to stop her. "Look, why don't you tell me what's going on? I'm not crazy about you and that .38 leaving here in pursuit of my best friend."

She settled and studied me. "How long have you known Henry?"

"My whole life."

"Can you be more specific?"

"Ever since a water fountain altercation in grade school."

She didn't look as if she believed it to be the truth. "You've known him longer than I have?"

"I guess, but he hasn't named any vehicles Walt."

I watched her weigh her options. "I need some help."

"With what?"

"My son's been hurt."

I had a sinking feeling. "How?"

"He was in a motorcycle accident. Why are you making that face?"

Resting said face in my hands, I asked, "Is your son Bodaway Torres?"

She fumbled with the purse, and I held out my hand to stay her. "Please don't get the gun out again; Corbin Dougherty called me and said that there had been an accident involving a young man and that he thought there might be more to it than just a routine traffic incident."

"They tried to kill him."

"Who did?"

She looked at her hands and then started

54

to get up again. "I need to talk to Henry."

"No, you need to talk to me. Corbin, a traffic analyst from the Division of Criminal Investigation by the name of Mike Novo, and I are going to be heading up the inquiry as to what happened to your son, but we could use your help."

She studied me. "I don't even know you."

"I'm a nice guy." She didn't seem convinced, so I added, "I grow on people."

She bobbed a sandal. "Like a fungus?"

I ignored the remark. "So, how did you and Henry meet?"

She studied me some more and turned to get her bag. "I should go."

I smiled. "Where?"

"To see my son."

I surprised her and stood. "How 'bout Dog and I go with you?"

Fortunately, Lola Wojciechowski drove a dilapidated, slightly dented, faded gold '66 Cadillac DeVille, so there was plenty of room for all of us. I shouted across the expanse as Lola careened through the sloping hills of the Devils Tower landscape, the monument peeking down at us every now and again. "I noticed the Arizona plates. You live down there?"

She shouted back after checking the

rearview mirror and the reflection of Dog, dead center. "For quite some time now. My ex has a custom bike shop in Maryvale — Crossbones Custom."

"That would be Mr. Torres?"

She leaned over and, pushing a button in the dash and gesturing toward the yawning glove compartment, handed me the pocketbook containing the .38. "Yeah, Delshay."

I placed the purse in there and carefully closed the compartment. "Motorcycles, I'm assuming?"

"No, Huffy and Schwinn. . . . Of course, motorcycles."

I smiled and looked through the windshield. "Ever heard of a motorcycle club by the name of the Tre Tre Nomads?"

She glanced at me. "No."

I watched the scenery some more as she put her foot into the Caddy, sending us down a straightaway toward Moorcroft at a good ninety miles an hour, passing motorcycles as we went. "You know, I know the HPs that prowl this part of Wyoming during the rallies, and they don't have much of a sense of humor this time of year."

She kept her foot in it a bit longer but then let off.

I placed an arm on the doorsill and adjusted the side mirror so that I could watch behind us. "And point of interest: when law enforcement asks you a question, we generally already know the answer."

She simmered a bit and then pushed a big wave of the black and silver hair from her face. "What do you want to know?"

"Is Bodaway a member of the Tre Tre Nomads?"

"I guess."

I adjusted my sunglasses and stared at her.

"Yes. Yes, he's a member."

"So what are the chances that his accident is gang related?"

"Everybody who knows him loves him."

"That doesn't answer my question. Does he have any known enemies?"

She gestured as another group of maybe thirty motorcycles passed us, headed for Hulett. "He's in a motorcycle gang — everybody is his enemy, including you." Driving the big car with one hand, she threaded her fingers through her hair. "You people . . ." I waited for the rest. "People don't understand these clubs; they think you join them to break heads, take drugs, and generally fuck up society — but the reason you join is because society fucks with you. Do you know what it's like out there on the streets? I'm not talking about Cornhole, Wyoming; I'm talking about a real city

57

with people in it."

I sighed. "I'm not completely unfamiliar with those environs."

"It's family, you know? A tribe — something to help keep the wolves at bay."

"So, why do you need Henry?"

She turned her head as if the answer were obvious. "He's the biggest, baddest wolf I know."

I smiled. "Okay, then who are the leaders of the other packs?"

"I'll have to think about it."

"You haven't already?"

She turned her head to look at me but then returned her attention to the road.

"If you think somebody's responsible for your son's accident, then it would make it a lot easier if you'd let us know of any suspicions you might have — could help us narrow the field."

"The Hells Angels, Mongols, Pagans, Sons of Silence, Outlaws, Bandidos, Warlocks, Vagos. Take your pick."

"Are all those groups represented here in Hulett?"

"Yeah, it's like an asshole convention."

"Weren't you just standing up for all these outlaw motorcycle clubs?"

"Only ours." She gave me a dazzling smile and passed another group of motorcyclists, barely getting back in our lane before scattering another cluster headed the other way. "The rest are pieces of shit."

"Right. Would you mind keeping it under the speed of sound? I'd like to visit your son, but I'd rather not share a ward with him." She let off the accelerator, but I could tell it wasn't something she was used to doing. "Well, it has to be someone with a car or truck."

"Why is that?"

"I'm no Evel Knievel, but it seems to me it would be hard to run a motorcycle off the road with another motorcycle without ending up in the ditch yourself."

She nodded in agreement. "Hey, you really are a sheriff, aren't you?"

"So, who would be here with a four-wheeled vehicle?"

"Tons of guys; a lot of them bring trucks and vans and tow their bikes."

I watched as a few more motorcyclists passed but then did notice a few vans and SUVs pulling covered trailers. "I thought the idea was to show how tough you are by riding distance."

"You ever ride a Harley a couple thousand miles?"

"Never ridden one a couple hundred feet."

She shook her head. "How does a guy

your age ever get to now with never having learned how to ride a motorcycle?"

I philosophized. "Common sense?" I turned to pet Dog. "So, are you a member of the Tre Tre Nomads?"

"No, they don't patch women." She saw the confusion on my face. "When you become a full member of a club, you get the patches to go on your leathers or your kuttes."

"What are kuttes?"

"Short for cut-offs — you know, denim vests or jackets where the sleeves have been cut off."

"Oh." I glanced at her leather ensemble but could see no patches. "So, no female members, huh?"

"No, but you can be somebody's old lady, and that carries a certain standing."

"And whose old lady are you?"

"Delshay Torres, my ex."

"The one that owns the Huffy/Schwinn shop."

"Right. We went our separate ways a few years ago, but I've still got status."

"Bodaway, Delshay . . . Those don't sound like Spanish names."

"Yavapai Apache."

Rapid City Regional Hospital is the largest

and most advanced facility in the four-state area, so it doesn't come as much of a surprise that they transferred Bodaway Torres there.

A large man, built like a sumo wrestler, was taking up an entire bench as we entered the waiting room outside the ICU. He stood when he saw Lola. He didn't say anything but gave me a hard look before sitting his prodigious, leather-clad rear back on the bench and folding his massive arms, which just barely reached across his chest.

We continued toward the viewing window down the hall. "One of yours?"

"Big Easy."

"He from New Orleans?"

"No, he's just big and easy — he'd drink my bathwater if I let him."

I made an attempt to change the subject. "You think your son needs a bodyguard?"

"Brady thought they might come back and try to finish the job."

"Brady Post, the guy that says *bud* a lot?"

"You've met."

I nodded. "Momentarily. He seemed like someone who would be hard to get along with."

She shrugged. "If you're not one of us, I'd say yes."

You couldn't see much of the kid behind

the glass, but from what you could, I'd have to say he was one of the handsomest young men I'd ever seen. His long black hair was splayed across the pillows, and his face was unmarked by the accident. Bodaway's features looked like they'd been cut with diamonds; he could've been a model for one of those bodice-ripper romance novel covers. "Handsome kid."

"Yes." She stood at the glass, her fingertips touching the cool, smooth surface. "Twenty-eight years old."

"What's the prognosis?"

"Traumatic brain injury, contusion type. We're lucky it wasn't a hematoma type because —"

"I know all about it — my daughter was assaulted in Philadelphia; she had the hematoma injury, and they had to cut part of her skull to allow for the swelling." I studied the young man. "She was out for the better part of a week."

She turned her face and looked up at me. "How is she now?"

"An assistant attorney general down in Cheyenne with an eight-month-old, who is named after you, well, in a way." She continued to stare at me. "Remember, she's the one who named my granddaughter after the car that is named after you?"

"I like her already." She smiled. "Anyway, that gives me hope." Her eyes were drawn back to the unmoving face and the array of EEG electrodes. "They had to shave some of his head; he's not going to like that."

I now noticed where they had removed the hair from his temples. "I don't suppose he was wearing a helmet?"

"No."

I struggled to think of something positive to say, knowing from experience how she was feeling. "It's good that it didn't mess up his face."

"And he's so totally unaware of how good-looking he is." Her hands came off the glass, and she stuffed them in her jeans. "You should see the girls hanging off of him; it's obscene."

"Like mother, like son?"

I wasn't sure, but I was willing to bet that she blushed just a bit. "More like father; he was really handsome — an asshole, but a handsome one." She studied her son a bit more and then, glancing at a fancy gold watch with a turquoise face, stepped away from the glass. "They're going to open the room up for an hour in about ten minutes and that's when I go in there and hold his hand and talk to him. I'd invite you, but they say that too much stimulation can agitate him and raise his blood pressure, so . . ." She reached into a pocket and handed me a set of keys. "I didn't mean to strand you, so just take the Caddy and do whatever you need to do. I'm staying at the Hulett Motel, too, so you can just leave the car there when you're done."

"What about you?"

She nodded toward the Buddha in the waiting room. "Big Easy or somebody can give me a ride. Just leave it at the motel with the keys in it."

"You're sure?"

She took my hand and forced the keys on me. "I like you, you seem like the real deal." Then she added. "Don't let me down."

When I got back to the hospital parking lot, there was a dog sitting in the driver's seat of the '66 DeVille, which was now parked next to a battered pickup. We'd put the top up before we had gone into the hospital, in an attempt to contain the were-creature I referred to as Dog, and, wagging and smiling, he looked at me through the glass. I was about to unlock the thing when a voice sounded from behind me.

"What do you think you're doing, bud?" I turned to see Brady Post walking across the parking lot toward me. "That's not your car."

I went ahead and unlocked the door of the Cadillac. "Yep, my highly developed powers of deduction tell me that."

He shoved my shoulder, hard, when he got there. "Do you know whose car this is, bud?"

I turned and squared off with him, both of us suddenly aware of the growing growl resounding like a speedboat at idle behind the window of the Caddy. "As a matter of fact, I do."

Post gave Dog a look and then turned his eyes back to me. "Then what the hell are you doing?"

I studied him, getting a read on the way he held himself. Better than the usual bar-room brawler, he was steady on both legs, with his weight evenly distributed and his arms hanging relaxed, but with his shoulders turned just a bit to give him the trajectory he'd need to take that first swing with the chrome-plated, three-link belt he held in one hand. I imagined that he wasn't likely to let me up after that if I went down and would use the steel-toed boots to finish the job. "That's really none of your business, Mr. Post."

Dog, a shrewd judge of character, lunged

at the glass and snapped his big alligator jaws, and I watched as the biker started. "Gimme the keys, bud."

"No, I don't think I will. Post. Is that your real name, or is it an honorary title they gave you because you're *dumb as a . . .* ?"

He wrapped the chain one more twist in his hand, and all I could think was that I was tired of being hit and tired of hitting. I went through the choreography of violence and saw myself raising an arm to effectively block the chain, then wrapping my hand around his head and bringing it forward to where I would introduce my right fist to his face. If he really was tough, it was possible it might take two shots, or I could just bounce his head off of the pickup in an attempt to save the quarter panel on the gold-toned Cadillac.

All of these things were running through my head when I hit upon a simpler response. Pushing the button on the handle of the Caddy, I swung the door wide.

You would think that, at over 150 pounds, Dog wouldn't be that fast, but I'm pretty sure that DNA strain of his used to run down buffalo and maybe even my ancestors a few thousand years ago.

Say what you want about the Enforcer's intellectual capacities, he knew a life-threatening situation when he encountered one and scrambled for his very existence. He got the lead on Dog, and I reached out to get hold of the beast, but the monster was too fast and was scrambling on his claws and sliding sideways to get around the back of the jacked-up pickup in order to lock his massive jaws into the biker.

Post, realizing that his lead wasn't going to last long, hurdled over the far side of the truck and fell into the bed as Dog leapt up after him, but it was just too high. The biker scrambled backward toward the cab and was getting ready to swing the chain at Dog when I walked over and motioned to get his attention. "You hit my dog with that chain and, in the words of my old boss and mentor, Lucian Connally, I will scatter your chickenshit brains all over this parking lot."

Dog was still throwing his bulk against the side of the truck, and I would've been worried that he might hurt himself, but the thing looked like it had been dragged from a salvage yard. The Enforcer stayed in the middle as Dog, trying to find a way up, circled the truck.

"Call off the fucking dog, bud!"

"Drop the chain."

He did, and I patted my leg. "Dog!"

In the great balancing equations of Dog's

mind, there are two things he cannot resist — ham, and me holding open a vehicle door. I'm pretty sure that ham is first and the only reason me holding open a vehicle door is in the running is because it might mean that we are going somewhere to get ham.

The beast looked a little disgruntled, but with one last glance at his prospective lunch, he hopped in the DeVille and sat in the passenger seat as though nothing had been amiss.

I glanced at Post and tipped my hat at the biker as I climbed in after Dog. "Happy motoring, bud."

The Rapid City Police Department's evidence impound lot happens to be wedged in between the city cop headquarters and the Pennington County Jail. Knowing on which side my bread was buttered, I entered the sheriff's office and asked for him.

They asked me who I was, and I told them that I was a sheriff too and that we needed to touch badges so we could recharge. The nice receptionist looked doubtful and then disappeared across the large room just as I heard Irl Engelhardt's voice. "Walt Longmire!"

Venturing across the room, I met the lean

man at his doorway, and he invited me in. I stood next to the guest chair in his immaculate office and glanced around at the startling order of the place. "You ever do any work around here?"

He sat on the corner of his desk and folded his arms, palming his chin. "As little as I can get away with. Have a seat, Walt. What are you doing on this side of the Black Hills?"

I continued standing. "Maybe I'm vacationing."

He shook his head. "Try again — I've known you for too many years to count, and I've never heard of you taking even a day off."

"Maybe I'm changing my ways."

"Uh huh." He looked down at the blotter on his desk. "Hey, I heard about your son-in-law."

"Yep."

"I'm sorry."

I nodded. "We all are."

"How's Cady holding up?"

"Surprisingly well — Joe Meyer gave her a job."

"Down in that nest of smiling vipers in Cheyenne?"

"Yep."

"Well, she should be able to fend for

herself; she comes from good stock."

"Thanks, Irl."

He laughed and stood. "It's funny, you know. . . . I guess if we didn't all think we were ten feet tall and bulletproof, we wouldn't do this job."

I sighed. "I'm beginning to think I'm about nine two and only bullet resistant."

"What can I do for you, Walt?"

"You've got a motorcycle in your evidence impound lot that has to do with a traffic incident up in Hulett, near Devils Tower."

He nodded and gestured toward the door. "Somebody have one too many and run off the road looking at the scenery?"

"Something like that."

We moved back through the bull pen, out another door, and down a stairwell. "I can't tell you how much of that we get this time of year, and it gets worse as the baby boomers get older. These guys finally get enough money to go out and buy the motor-cycle of their dreams — the one they wanted when they were eighteen — but they seem to forget that they're not eighteen anymore and that they haven't been on one of the things for thirty years."

He pushed a heavy door open, and we were back on the sidewalk where I'd parked. "You mind if I get my dog out of the car and let him have a little walk?"

"No problem."

Sheriff Engelhardt raised an eyebrow as I freed Dog from the Cadillac. "Is this what the stylish Wyoming sheriff is driving these days?"

"Not mine. It belongs to the mother of the accident victim."

Dog bounded up to Irl and nudged him with his muzzle as the sheriff rubbed his head. "A friend?"

"Of Henry's."

"Oh."

The sheriff disengaged himself from Dog and waved at a young deputy in a booth by the gate as we walked into the decidedly urban environment of the vehicle evidence lot. Surrounded by buildings on three sides, the fenced-in area had razor wire circling the top and myriad damaged vehicles lined up in the diagonal parking spots.

"Did you hear about Sturgis last year?"

"Can't say I did."

"Seventy-fifth anniversary. They had over a million bikers."

"Sounds like a good time to spray for them."

He shook his head. "What've you got against motorcycles, Walt?"

We walked past the cars, trucks, and SUVs

71

to a tarped area that held a half-dozen bikes, all of them statuary testaments to the fact that the two-wheeled conveyance wasn't such a great idea. "It's not so much the motorcycles themselves; it's this bogus, outlaw culture that goes along with them — the black leather, chrome death's head crap — that I find tiresome. It's all just fake. I've almost got more respect for the real outlaws than the corporate/consumerist/choreographed version, but not much."

The sheriff pointed toward the closest one. "Well, there's Bodaway's bike."

I studied it. "Doesn't look that bad."

"Glance over here at the other side."

I did, and you could see where something had slammed into the motorcycle, bending all the protruding metal inward. "Wow, somebody meant business."

Engelhardt stooped beside me. "It's an '09 Cross Bones, a model they made a few years, springer front with a softail rear; they bobbed the fenders and put those ape-hanger bars on it to give it a more custom look."

I glanced at him.

"Hey, I know bikes." He stood up. "Who you got coming from Cheyenne?"

"Mike Novo."

He nodded his head. "Well, Mike'll be

able to tell a lot more than you and I can." He stared at the bent handlebars, crushed saddlebag, and mashed up floorboard. "Looks like it was broadsided."

I picked at the tufts of grass and dirt lodged between the bent wheels and the deflated tires. "From what I understand he went into the barrow ditch just before a culvert."

He clapped his hands together with a loud smack that startled me. "Bike hit that and sent the kid over the handlebars?"

I reached a finger out and flicked at the crushed side of the motorcycle. "I'd imagine."

"They take him over to Rapid City Regional?"

"Yep."

"How's he look?"

"Not so good — brain trauma." I sighed. "I guess he woke up after six hours, but was incoherent and went unconscious again, maybe for good." I scratched my fingernail across one of the extruding pieces of metal, held the fingernail up to my face, and studied the paint underneath.

Looking back over my shoulder, I studied Lola's Cadillac parked at the curb, the gold reflecting in the broad daylight.

3

In 1938 Clarence "Pappy" Hoel, Sturgis Indian Motorcycle dealership owner, businessman, entrepreneur, and anything-two-wheeled enthusiast, founded the Jackpine Gypsies Motorcycle Club, one of the first sanctioned organizations of that nature in America, and began the Black Hills Classic. The Classic consisted of a single race of a half mile on a dirt track with only nine participants and an audience of about the same number. The vaunted prize: beer money.

Seeking a broader audience for the event, with the philosophy that if you wreck it they will come, the Gypsies elected to include intentional board wall crashes, ramp jumps, and head-on collisions with automobiles. The mayhem worked, and the crowds grew, with only a brief respite during World War II, when activities were curtailed by gas rationing.

In 1961, the craziness that is the rally was elevated to a whole new level of insanity with the addition of the Jackpine Gypsies Hill Climb, where racers from all over the world partake in just what it sounds like: a race to the top of an escarpment that you probably couldn't walk up. Over the years, the competition has escalated to the point where the bikes are modified with such things as extended travel arms and nitro-injected engines that shoot flames from their tailpipes like two-stroke blowtorches.

The first time Henry Standing Bear attempted the hill climb, he was a high school senior and rode on his newly acquired '63 Swedish-built Husqvarna 250 cc with the nifty red and chrome gas tank. The results were: three broken fingers, one shattered radius, a broken tooth, two broken ribs, a punctured lung, and a totaled bike.

He did not win, but that didn't keep him from continuing to try. He finally won in 1974, but one victory was not enough, and he had been trying to win it again ever since.

If I were to catalog the bizarre things my friend the Bear has done in his life, I'm pretty sure it would make the *Sears Wish Book* look like a pamphlet, but the Sturgis Jackpine Gypsies Hill Climb would be listed in the section *A Special Kind of Crazy*.

Henry has unique friends for his more eccentric activities, and I watched in the late afternoon's horizontal light as Jamey Gilkey adjusted the nitro injectors on the newest brand of idiocy, a KTM 450 SX-F named Rosalie that looked more like a four-stroke rocket ship than a motorcycle.

It was the time trials, a preliminary before the big race tomorrow. "Who was Rosalie?"

The Bear adjusted some elbow pads on the outside of his INDIAN DUNES MOTOCROSS, VALENCIA, CALIFORNIA 1975 jersey sporting, of all things, a war-bonnet-wearing, tomahawk-swinging motorcyclist. "A woman I used to date."

"A woman, huh? You usually say girl."

"Rosalie Little Thunder was, by all accounts, a woman."

I turned and watched as one of the riders came unglued, as they call it, and tumbled back down the hill with his bike cartwheeling on top of him. "What was Lola?"

Henry glanced up and watched as the combination rider/motorcycle crashed in a heap at the bottom of the hill. "That was a bad line." Then he glanced back at me. "When I met her, a girl."

"Well, she's all grown up now, with a son."

"Bodaway." He considered the name, tasting it. "Apache?"

"Yep."

He nodded. "The last I heard of her, she had moved to Arizona."

"Well, she's got a problem, and she thinks you're going to solve it."

"Why me?"

"Because you're some kind of bad motor scooter."

He put on his old open-face helmet and tightened the chin strap. "And what is the problem?"

"In case it slipped your mind, somebody tried to kill her son."

His eyes cut to mine. "You're sure of that?"

"Yep, but there's a twist."

Jamey stepped back as the Bear threw a leg over the motorcycle, straddling it for action. "With Lola, there always is."

I sidestepped around him and stood in front of the motorcycle so he'd have to run over me to escape. "I went to the impound lot in Rapid and took a look at the kid's bike, and it had gold paint on it where it had been broadsided."

His face was impassive as he adjusted his goggles. "So?"

I gestured toward the parking lot behind a chain-link fence, where the Caddy sat, quite prominently. "Lola's car is gold and has damage on the right front fender."

He shook his head. "Have you spoken to her about this?"

"No. When she had me at gunpoint we discussed other things — mostly you."

"Gunpoint?"

"Yep, she showed up at the cabin with a .38, but then things got more conversational and I joined her in going to the hospital, where she was kind enough to loan me her car."

"The one she ran over her son with?"

"Well, we're still not clear on that. I figured I'd ask her about it when I return the Cadillac to the Hulett Motel later this afternoon." I folded my arms and looked at him, still steadfastly in his way. "If you don't mind me saying so, you don't seem all that interested in the case."

"It is a case?"

I shrugged. "As a favor to Corbin, sure."

"In answer to your question, no."

"No, what?"

"No, I do not mind you saying I do not seem all that interested in the case."

A younger rider rapped the throttle on his bike and shouted through his face shield as he pulled up in front of Henry. "You gonna give it another shot, old man?"

The Bear showed his teeth. " 'My mind is

78

like a racing engine, tearing itself to pieces because it is not connected up with the work for which it was built.' "

The kid studied us questioningly and then sped away, throwing dirt and gravel.

Lowering the arm that had protected my face, I made a guess. "Obviously not an Arthur Conan Doyle fan."

The Bear watched him go. "Last year's winner." He gave the KTM a violent kick, racked the throttle a few times, and sat there, looking at me. I waited a moment, then stepped aside, gesturing toward the hill with a touch of dramatic flair and watched as, balancing on the pegs with his old Roger DeCoster boots, he sped off toward the starting gates.

I fanned away the dust and exhaust and turned to look at the bearded man who was standing next to me. "Was it something I said?"

He shook his head and walked back toward his truck with the tools he had gathered, throwing them in before sitting on the tailgate in preparation for the show. "It ain't you; it's Lola. She spins his crank whenever he gets around her." I joined him on the tailgate of the GMC. "I'm pretty sure that if you look up 'drama queen' in the dictionary, the illustration is Lola Wojciechowski."

"Were you around when they met?"

He laughed. "Oh, yeah."

We watched as the Bear spun up to the starting rack and waited for his chance to lodge his back wheel against the massive log they had chained there for a backstop.

"Well?"

"I'm not so sure it's a story I should be telling. Why don't you ask Henry?"

"I have, and he's not talking." I raised an eyebrow, applying pressure.

"You know she was a dancer, right?" He leaned back, his hands splayed on the metal. "I mean, not the Bolshoi Ballet kind."

"Right."

We watched the riders in the lineup perform as they rode their best for time, the queue slowly moving toward the end where Henry waited. One or two actually made it to the top, but most flipped out, did dramatic U-turns, or just dug into the reddish dirt, burying their bikes and themselves before casually stepping off their mounts, one even kicking his.

"You remember that itty-bitty-titty bar that used to be out on Tilford Road, about halfway between Sturgis and Rapid — the Cattle Kate?"

"The one they used to launder money for the mob?"

"Yeah, that one. Well, there were about a half dozen of these guidos who were giving one of the dancers a hard time — you know, trying to drag her into one of the back rooms. Henry happened to be there saying hey to this monster buddy of his who was a bouncer, Brandon White Buffalo."

The time-trial adjudicators with the clip-boards had finally gotten to Henry, and we watched as one of them at the top of the hill raised a green flag. "I know Brandon."

"Well, he had 'em stood off, but they had guns, so Henry backed Brandon's play. There was a lot of shouting and the usual stuff when Henry proposed that they pick out a couple of representatives, one from each group, and then let the two of 'em go out in the parking lot and settle things like real men."

The flagman dropped his arm, and the Bear was off.

"The guidos went along with it, but said it had to be Henry and not Brandon because Brandon is so big, you know?"

Henry sped across the short flat and dug in, the KTM bouncing from one berm to another, chewing up a few sparse patches of sagebrush.

"Big mistake."

"No shit. The mob guys selected this

81

weight lifter that they had with 'em. The guy swings this haymaker at the Bear, who does a double arm block, pivots his elbow into the guy's gut, and then brings the back of his fist up into the guy's face — three seconds, done."

Henry shot up the hill and bounced over the approach rollers that kept the rider from establishing too much speed too quickly. He flew a good twenty feet and then navigated to the side of the devilish curve to dig in and then caught traction, again shooting up the hill through the tufts of prairie grass.

"What did the mob guys do?"

"They didn't know whether to shit or go blind, so they just stood there and then carried the guy back to their car and went back to Jersey, I guess."

Henry was approaching the top but had lost some momentum as the front tire began slowly lifting from the turf.

"So, the dancer was Lola?"

"No, but Lola was there, and I guess she liked the cut of the Bear's jib or something like that."

Both Jamey and I slid off the tailgate, unconsciously drawn to the hill like spectators to a train wreck. The front wheel of the KTM kept rising, even with all of Henry's weight hanging over the handlebars, but he was so close to the precipice that I thought for sure he was going to make it.

"Anyway, they hooked up after that and were together off and on for a while."

The Bear held on till the last second and then flipped over backward.

"Uh oh."

We watched as Henry rolled to the side to get out of the way of the out-of-control motorcycle that missed him only by inches and then cartwheeled down the hill before slamming to the ground. He sat and watched it.

"More off than on."

When I got over to the Hulett Police Department, Chief Nutter was inside the MRAP, trying to figure out how to start it. "We're going to drive it through town."

I stood below, looking up into the cab at him. "Why on earth?"

"Gape and awe — we're going to show these bikers what they're up against if they start anything." He gave me a thumbs-up like a fighter pilot and held the tough-guy look for as long as he could but then broke up laughing. "Gas station is on the other side of town, and if we don't put fuel in the damn thing, it's going to be useless."

"Bill, you don't want my opinion on that."

I stepped on the running board and glanced around at all the hi-tech. "Why don't you bring the gas over here?"

"Do you know how much fuel this thing holds?" He glanced around the cab, looking for a gauge he could recognize. "Hell, I don't know how much fuel the thing holds. You think it's gas or diesel?"

"You better hope it's diesel, if you're aiming to get even a mile to the gallon." I took a look down the crowded street. "I'm trying to find Corbin."

"Last I heard he was settling a dispute at the campground, but he should be back any time." He gestured toward the dash. "Hey, you were in the military; you should know how to start this thing."

"Not really." I glanced around the interior at all the monitors and switches. "The stuff we had in Vietnam was decidedly less advanced, but I'll go hog wild and venture an opinion: Does it have a key?"

"No, just had a padlock and a chain holding the doors closed, which are hydraulic like in *Star Trek*. Took us forever to figure out how to open and close 'em."

"Then there's a switch."

"No, there's not."

"It probably doesn't look like any switch you've ever seen, and there's probably a coil preheating mechanism." I started climbing up. "Get over in the passenger seat and let me take a gander."

He did as I said and turned to look at me as I scanned the dash. "What do you need Deputy Dog for?"

Spotting the less-than-obvious switch, I glanced at it to see if, as in most diesels, you just turned it in the opposite direction to preheat, but there was nothing. Finally spotting a safety toggle to the left, I hit it and watched as a red light came on beside the ignition along with a spiral coil that lit, then flickered and went out. "He supposedly has the Torres kid's cell phone, and I'd like the name of the woman who found Bodaway after the accident."

"Bodaway?"

"The kid that was in the wreck. That's his name — Apache."

"Oh."

I hit the starter, and the gigantic engine in the MRAP rattled to a lopsided cant, sounding a lot like *Steamboat,* an old B-25 I'd flown in years ago. Reaching over and tapping the fuel gauge — a habit I'd picked up from my old Doolittle Raider boss who had piloted the vintage bomber — I glanced at Chief Nutter. "How far is it to the gas station?"

"About a mile."

"You might make it."

"Well, let's go then."

I laughed. "I'm not driving this thing."

"Then who is? You're the one who was a jarhead and all." He nodded toward the crowded street. "I'm likely to run over a building or something."

I sighed and hit the push button to engage the drive, assuming *R* was reverse. "All right then, let's bring the mountain to Moham-med."

He shook his head. "You sure do know a lot of biblical quotes for a fellow that doesn't go much for churchin'."

I started easing the fifteen-ton behemoth backward, attempting to see if there was anything behind me on the street. "That's not the Bible — it's Francis Bacon, from an old Turkish proverb."

He shook his head some more and looked at me. "Hey, you're good with names; what should we call it?"

"How about the Pequod?"

He thought about it but changed the subject. "I'm going to turn the red and blues on. You know, to let 'em know we're cops." He reached overhead and flipped another toggle. "I know where that is, because I was the one who had 'em installed." He held out a piece of paper with a diagram. "Shows the lights right here. There's also a PA system if you want to announce our presence with a sense of authority."

Having successfully backed the MRAP, I was looking point-blank at the quarter mile of Hulett's main and only thoroughfare, the direction we would be heading before taking a left and pulling into the Dakota Gas Company like happy motorists. "I don't suppose there's a siren, just to let people know that this thing actually moves, is there?"

"There could'a been, but I didn't order that."

I nodded, straightened my hat, and pressed the *D* button. Hitting the gas, I was appalled at how fast the gigantic vehicle moved and immediately adjusted the weight of my foot on the accelerator. "Wow."

"Dual turbos and an overdrive." He giggled. "I opted for those, too."

We went down the hill at a reasonable speed, and it was interesting to see the crowd's reaction to the bright white colossus, most just standing with their mouths agape, figuring they were being invaded.

I paused at the only intersection in town, but I needn't have bothered since the Gape and Awe portion of the exercise appeared to be holding sway. There were about eight bikers on one side and a pickup truck, sedan, and a few more bikes on the other, but they were all stopped, probably afraid that we were going to open fire. I glanced around, half expecting to see a turret and .50. "Is this thing armed?"

Bill had broken out what I assumed were the copious manuals for the vehicle and was now studying the door in search of a window crank. "How do you think the windows work?"

"They probably don't; that would compromise the Ambush Protected part of the MRAP title."

"How the hell are you supposed to yell at everybody?"

I pulled forward through the intersection. "That's what the PA system would be for."

"Oh, we gotta find that —"

"Oh, no we don't."

He studied the manual some more. "In answer to your question, no it doesn't have any guns on it. Hell, it's just a big truck that's hard to blow up, but you'd think we were trying to bring a tank in here when I was fighting with the county commissioners about the thing. There's this one old hippie on the board from Sundance, and she's sure we're trying to militarize the police department. Hell, there's only two of us, so I'm not so sure how much militarization we could summon up."

"What was the name of the guy that underwrote this thing for you?"

"Bob Nance — one of those computer whizzes from out of California — a specialist in acoustic something or other. He's got a place up at the golf course. Comes out here in the summers to play and pretend he's a cowboy. 'Course, I never met a cowboy with a log mansion on the ninth green."

Traveling at a majestic five miles an hour, we were approaching the Ponderosa Café at midtown, where I could see Corbin Dougherty leaning on his vehicle as he talked to a group of bikers, all of them pausing in their conversation to watch the rolling fortress pass by. "Hell, there's Deputy Dog. You wanna stop, and I'll figure out how to open the door?"

I kept moving. "Why don't we spare ourselves the embarrassment? I'll get the information I need from him on the walk back."

Bill looked a little unnerved. "You're not going to drive it back for me?"

"Wasn't planning on it. Anyway, you're

going to need the practice."

"What if I run over somebody?"

"You'll hardly feel it." I made the left, careful to avoid Lola's Cadillac parked next to the sidewalk adjacent to the motel, where I'd left it earlier, the keys in the ignition as she'd requested. We crossed the Belle Fourche bridge, and I was just glad the thing held. Amazingly enough, the MRAP had turn signals, and I clicked the stem down, indicating an impending left. The oncoming bikers had already stopped, never having encountered a great white whale like this one.

I spun the wheel, goosed the accelerator, and the big truck leapt across the lanes and roared into the Dakota Gas Company lot, where I figured out pretty quick that it wasn't going to fit under the awning. "Oh, ye whale, now what?"

"There's a big-rig island in the back; just circle around there."

I did as instructed and pulled up to the diesel pump with the green handle, then hit the *N* button and subsequently the *P*. "There you are, Captain my Captain — she's yours from here on out."

He reached around behind him, then began patting all his pockets with his hands. "Um, I appear to have left my wallet back at the office. You wouldn't happen to have some cash on you, would you?"

"How's the bike?" We were sitting in the Ponderosa Bar behind the Ponderosa Café. Actually, we were sitting at a picnic table in the alley behind the Ponderosa Bar behind the Ponderosa Café, because it was the only place where there were a couple of seats together, and we were soon to have guests. "Irreparable, I hope?"

The Bear rewrapped the gauze and Ace bandage around his hand after readjusting the nonstick pad that covered the burn he'd received from the KTM as it had attempted to squash him like a bug. "I bent a few things, but we'll be ready for tomorrow."

"Why?"

Exasperated, which I could tell only from a slight change in the angle of his head, he turned and looked at me. "You act as if I am the only one who does crazy things."

"Name one crazy thing I do."

"It is pinned to your shirt."

I sipped my Rainier. "Actually, it's in a natty leather wallet in my pocket."

"You know what I mean."

It was a velvety evening in the Black Hills, and the slight breeze carried the scent of the pines and the clear high-country air —

or maybe it was the lumberyard on the other side of the river. "That's different; it's my job."

He raised an eyebrow and savored his Snowden cabernet. "Why is that different? I am thinking it might actually be worse."

"Why?"

"Mine is driven by passion, yours by wages."

I gave him the eyebrow back. "Civic duty, if you please."

"Even worse — insanity as a duty?"

"The insane part of my work is accidental, an improvisational by-product, whereas you are actually courting crazy."

"Not true. I am, like you, participating in actions which may or may not lead to certain results which you deem as crazy."

"No, you choose to do these things."

He gestured with the wineglass. "And you did not choose to wear that badge in the natty leather wallet?"

I considered it and then raised my bottle in a toast as he joined me. "Touché."

"What are you guys toasting?"

I looked up at the smiling man with the blue sweatshirt and mop of silver hair. "Well, if it isn't No Go Novo." I scooted over and made room for the traffic expert for the Division of Criminal Investigation.

He sat, and I noticed that he'd already fortified himself with a beer from the bar, a
prudent action seeing as how we hadn't
spotted a waitress in twenty minutes.

The investigator glanced around, pushing
the hair from his face. "Kind of crowded
around here."

" 'Tis the season."

Mike nodded to Henry. "You make your
time trial over in Sturgis?"

The Bear smiled. "Nine-tenths of it."

"Uh oh."

I shrugged. "He's in the front third."

Mike seemed impressed. "Well, that means
they think you'll actually make it; the guys
they throw in the back third are doomed."

Henry nodded. "I know, I have been
there."

"What time is the race tomorrow?"

"Eight."

"In the morning?" He drank from his
beer. "I'm not through throwing up by
then."

Spotting a waitress rounding one of the
other tables, I flagged her down and turned
back to my comrades. "I'm getting another;
you guys want something?" Agreeing that
we might not have another opportunity, I
ordered a double round and then turned
back to Mike. "Did you have a look at Bod-

away's bike?"

"No, but I saw the incident location."

"And?"

He took a couple of sips of his beer, encouraged by the hope of another. "It rained, of course, and there's been no end of traffic on that road —"

"Yeah, yeah, yeah."

He smiled. "There are about three different types of gyroscopic instability on a motorcycle. The ones that happen at high speed are weave and wobble, both occurring at more than eighty miles per hour and on dry pavement. Weave is a snakelike oscillation of the motorcycle around its center of mass. Usually confined to the rear of the bike, it doesn't have much of an effect on the steering but does generally cause the bike to weave from side to side along the path of travel."

"And wobble?"

"Wobble is uncorrected weave, where it begins to affect the frame of the bike and then the steering axis. The transition from weave to wobble is about .02 seconds, and I don't even think the great Henry Standing Bear has reflexes that quick." He smiled at the Cheyenne Nation. "Once the wobble sets in, the motion becomes so severe that the rider loses control and the bike is slammed to the pavement, resulting in a totaled bike and a dead rider."

"Factors?"

He palmed a chin and looked at me through the silver curtain, partially hiding eyes that had seen more vehicular mayhem than I would ever want to. "Weight distribution, center of aerodynamic pressure, tire inflation, tire size, tread shape and wear, and rider weight."

"He's not a large man."

"And the bike?"

I paused for a second and then recited what Sheriff Engelhardt had said to me at the impound lot. " '09 Harley Cross Bones, springer front with a softail rear, and I have no idea what I just said."

"Big bike."

"It looked big to me, but that just makes it a larger death trap. Can't you just slow down?" I finished my beer as the other drinks arrived. "Um, does anybody have any money?"

They both looked at me. "The gas station over here doesn't take credit cards, and I had to use all my walking-around money to fill up Chief Nutter's MRAP."

Mike studied me, pretty sure this was the most elaborate way of getting out of paying a check he'd ever heard. "A what?"

The Cheyenne Nation handed me a fifty, which I transferred to the waitress. "Keep the tip."

Henry shook his head as I handed him his two glasses of wine and Mike his beer back-ups.

"So, can't you just slow down?"

"It happens too fast, and at that speed most riders make the mistake of slamming on their brakes instead of redistributing their weight by transferring it from the saddle to the pegs. And add-on accessory boxes can change both the weight distribution and the aerodynamics." Mike glanced at me. "You saw the bike?"

"I did, and I saw the kid, too."

Sticking to the subject at hand, he asked about the motorcycle. "Was it stock?"

"How the heck should I know?"

"You say it had the springer forks?" I looked at him blankly. "Did the front have a set of springs, kind of vintage looking?"

"Yep."

"Those models can get out of tune and cause problems."

"There's something else . . ."

"Were there any saddlebags on it, big ones?"

"Um, no — but there was gold paint."

He looked at me. "What color is the bike?"

"Black."

"You think somebody hit him?"

"I can't be sure, but I think you'd better take a look at the bike and then the car I've got on loan."

"Well, when I get down to Rapid, I'll . . ."

I pulled the phone from my pocket and handed it to him as he gave me a questioning look. "When did you start carrying a cell phone?"

I pointed at Henry. "It's his. I took pictures; well, Irl Engelhardt did." I gestured toward the device. "I barely know how to take a photo."

"It's pretty easy to operate; you just hit the little icon that looks like a camera. Here, see?" He showed me and began swiping through the photos, finally glancing at the Bear. "You mind if I send these to my email so I can look at them on my computer?"

The Cheyenne Nation tipped his wine. "Feel free. I just own the thing."

Mike smiled and began pushing buttons. "By the way, Walt, you described the bike magnificently — it almost sounded like you knew what you were talking about."

"Thanks." As the investigator worked, I glanced at the Bear. "Why would Lola hit her own kid?"

Henry shrugged. "You have a child; you

97

know how it is." His face tightened in a slight smile, and I looked past him where I could see a table of women who were openly staring at him. I sometimes forgot the effect that the Bear had on the opposite sex, but then, when I saw any of them around him, I remembered.

"Seriously."

"Walt, you have to remember that my interaction with this woman is almost thirty years old; I have no idea what her relationship with her son is like, and with someone like Lola, I am not remotely willing to guess."

Novo handed Henry his phone and then turned back to me as the Cheyenne Nation checked for messages.

"You said there were three specific types of gyroscopic instability on a motorcycle."

Mike smiled. "I did, and though the third usually doesn't leave marks on the pavement, we were lucky that the kid was riding in the emergency lane, and the pavement was remarkably fresh."

"Wait — he was riding on the edge of the road?"

He nodded. "Just on the other side of the rumble strip."

"Where he ran off the road."

"No, he was riding there for quite a ways,

and here's the thing: there was an instability, but it was a low-speed phenomenon called flutter, which is when the front tire and steering assembly experience rapid oscillation — think of an unsupported castor on a shopping cart. It happens only one way, when the rider's hands are not on the handlebars."

Henry and I looked at each other and then back to Mike. "So, you're saying that he was riding on the edge of the road with his hands doing something other than steering?"

Mike nodded again. "Yes, and if flutter is the case, then that means there must've been something on the rear of that bike."

"Like the heavy saddlebags you mentioned?"

"Or . . ."

"Or what?"

"From the photos you took, I could see that there was a seat pad on the Harley."

The Cheyenne Nation carefully set his wineglass on the uneven surface of the old picnic table, his voice rumbling in his chest. "Then someone was on the back of the motorcycle."

4

The Bear decided to stay at the Pondo, as the locals called the bar, and talk with Jamey and some of the other hill climbers who had arrived as our little party was breaking up, but I was worried about Dog back at the motel cabin. I thought the quiet by the river might be a chance for him to get out, and evidently he thought so, too.

I walked along after him in the thin fog that rolled off the water as he sniffed at the high stalks of grass and the cattails that had sprung up near the edge. "Don't get any wise ideas — I'm not sharing my bed with a wet dog."

He ignored me and trotted on along the bank to where I could see someone in the mist. I was about to call Dog off, but he seemed to know who it was. After another step, I recognized her profile, and I joined them. "Hello, Lola."

She didn't look at me but petted Dog's

wide head. "Hi, Sheriff."

"Did you get your keys?"

"No."

"I put them under the floor mat on the driver's side."

"You don't have to do that; nobody outside of the Tre Tre Nomads would touch that car."

I stopped and turned to look at the river, the fog rolling tendrils from the surface, the water reflecting the high clouds just starting to disappear in the dusk. "I guess it's the lawman in me, but I can't leave the keys in the ignition of a car, especially in a town with thousands of bikers in it."

She glanced at me.

"Although, I am sure ninety-nine percent of them are good, law-abiding citizens." I looked around. "I'm amazed you found a quiet spot."

She took out a cigarette and lit it, taking a deep drag. "Might be the only one."

"You mind if I ask you a question?"

Her voice took on an officious tone. "Where were you on the night of January sixteenth?"

"Something like that."

She stared at me. "You're serious?"

"I am. Where were you the night of your son's accident?"

101

She took another drag on her cigarette. "Who wants to know?"

"You wanted an investigator; this is called investigating."

"Me?"

"Everyone's a suspect until we find out who did it."

"So, you do think somebody did it?"

Dog was getting too close to the water, so I patted my leg. "You're not answering my question."

She studied me for a moment more. "The Dime Horseshoe Bar in Sundance for the Burnout."

"The what?"

"They put up a big platform on the street, and then guys ride their bikes up onto it and do these epic burnouts — you know, locking up the front brake and spinning the rear? Lots of smoke, lots of beer and leather — an All-American spectacle."

"Were you driving your car?"

It took her a few seconds to answer. "No."

"Then who was?"

"What are you saying?"

"Without laboratory analysis I can't be absolutely sure, but it looks to me as if somebody hit your son with your car. There was gold paint on the Harley and there appears to be damage to the right front fender of the Cadillac."

"There's damage all over my car; it's a beater."

"It's a flake gold beater, a pretty unusual paint job." I folded my arms and studied her. "I'll ask again: Who was driving your car?"

"And I'll say how the hell should I know? Everybody borrows it." She smoked some more. "The thing was sitting where it is now that day with the keys in it, so I literally have no idea."

"Who usually borrows it?"

"Everybody — everybody in the club anyway." She stopped talking and looked up at me.

"I think your exact words were, no one outside the Tre Tre Nomads would touch that car."

"It couldn't be someone from our club."

"You're sure of that?" She didn't seem so, all of a sudden. "How many club members are there here?"

"A couple dozen maybe?"

"Can you get me a list?"

"No, I can't do that." She took another drag on the cigarette. "It would be like dropping a dime on them — ratting them out, you know?"

I smiled my everybody's-an-outlaw-until-the-outlaws-show-up smile. "Well, I don't have the time to go around and ask fifty thousand bikers if they happen to be members of the Tre Tre Nomads."

"I can point them out to you."

"And then what? I ask them if they happened to borrow your car on the night your son was run over? No, I think it would be a lot easier if you just asked around among your friends."

"They're not my friends."

"No, the exact term you used was family."

She said nothing, and we both watched as a tandem of motorcycles thundered across the bridge above.

"Just tell them that somebody used the car and didn't fill it up and that you want some gas money, or tell them that somebody left something in the car and you want to give it back to them."

"Like what?"

"I don't know — money."

"They're not going to buy that."

"Well, then think of something. You're an enterprising woman."

Finishing her cigarette, she turned back toward the river and flicked it into the water, where it disappeared in the mist but for a brief sizzle. "Thanks for your help."

She turned to go, but I called out to her.

"Look, I'm willing to do this, but if you want to know what happened to your son, I'm going to need your assistance."

She lodged a hand on her hip. "Junior detective, huh?"

"Something like that."

"I'll think about it."

"Don't think too long; after Henry's race tomorrow, we're out of here."

She cocked her head. "Maybe I'll just ask Henry."

"You're welcome to, but I'd advise against it."

"And why's that?"

I gestured toward the river and, more important, the bridge. "Lot of water, huh?"

She studied me for a moment more and then swiveled on a heel and walked away.

When I got back to the cabin, I was surprised to see one of the two Hulett police cars preparing to back out from the spot in front of our door. Dog and I came around the left rear just as the reverse lights came on, so I tapped the quarter panel and Dougherty jerked to a stop.

I leaned on the sill. "How come you're not driving the new and improved MRAP?"

"He's calling it the Pequod; even ordered up decals to put the name on the side. Now where did he get that name from?"

"Heck if I know, troop. Better than the *Andrea Doria.*" I checked on Dog, who was sniffing the squad car's tires. "What's up?"

He handed me a bulky manila envelope through the window. "This is the cell phone that was on Bodaway, or, more exactly, lying in the grass where the incident took place. Sorry it's taken so long to get it to you, but I've been kind of busy."

I stuffed the envelope under my arm. "Anything else?"

"The preliminary accident report along with the testimony of the witness."

"Witness?"

"After the fact." He reached up and tapped the package. "Local girl by the name of Chloe Nance; she's the one that found him."

"Nance. Why does that name sound familiar?" The thought struck as the words left my lips. "Related to Bob Nance, the guy that underwrote the Pequod?"

"Yeah, that's him. He's underwritten about half the county." He gestured toward the manila bundle again. "Look, the phone is dead, and I haven't had time to find a charger to fit it."

I pulled the device out and studied it and was pretty sure it was similar to Henry's.

"I'll find a way to get it to talk, even if I have to use a rubber hose."

I started to back away so that he could get going when he called after me, "So, what the hell is a Pequod?"

"You mean other than the ship in *Moby Dick*?"

"Yeah."

"A Native tribe in Connecticut, although it's spelled differently now, with a *T* instead of a *D*. By the early twentieth century, there were only a little over fifty of them left."

"Are they still around?"

"One of the richest tribes in the country — casinos. Good night, troop."

"Good night, Sheriff." He backed the cruiser the rest of the way out and crunched gravel as he left.

Dog and I made our way to the cabin door, and I was surprised to find it ajar when I was pretty sure I'd closed it. Figuring it might've been Henry, I gave pause but then slipped my .45 from the small of my back just in case. Training it through the opening, I pushed the door wide.

"I thought for sure that cop was going to come in here, and that would've been bad." He was sitting on the guest chair, leaning backward against the wall with the television on mute. In one hand he had a beer and in the other a 9mm semi-automatic. "Hope you don't mind, but I made myself at home."

I kept the Colt on Brady Post, the Tre Tre Nomad enforcer, and stepped inside, sticking a leg out to restrain the growling beast behind me. "I don't mind, but I think he does."

"Keep a handle on that dog or I'll shoot him."

"You do, and he won't be the last one to get shot here tonight."

The biker lowered the Glock and stuffed it in the front of his pants. "I figured you and I ought to get introduced; besides, the ice machine is broken up at the Pioneer."

I waited a second and then lowered my weapon. "I thought we had been."

"Not formally." He reached into his pocket again and tossed something onto the bed near me.

It was a nifty leather wallet not unlike the one in my shirt pocket, but unlike mine, his read DEPARTMENT OF THE TREASURY.

"ATF?"

"Special Agent Post at your service. I don't usually break cover to the locals, or anybody for that matter, but you seem pretty capable and I could use some help — sure didn't throw any kind of scare into you at the hospital parking lot earlier today."

"Generally, I'm too stupid to be scared."

"Oh, I doubt that."

Holstering my Colt, I picked up his badge and ID card. "So, which one is it, alcohol, tobacco, or firearms?"

"Firearms — the Nomads are responsible for about thirty percent of the illegal guns showing up in the Southwest these days, mostly imported from their chapters in Mexico."

I sat on the bed and called Dog over. He still growled at Post but recognized that the dynamic had changed. "So, the enforcer for this particular chapter happens to be a federal agent?"

He set the beer bottle on the nightstand, crossed the room, and closed the door. "Sorry, can't be too careful these days." He crossed back and sat, reaching a hand out to Dog, who pulled back a lip, giving his interpretation of the night of the long knives. "Whoa . . . easy there."

"He'll warm up to you; just ignore him." I folded my fingers in my lap and looked at the man, younger than I'd thought underneath the Buffalo Bill facial hair. "So, what's the deal with the kid, Bodaway?"

"A major pain in my ass is what it is." He picked up his drink and took a long draw.

"Bodaway is involved in the gun trafficking — he's the conduit to all the other clubs."

"Gangs."

"Whatever. Anyway, all cats being gray in the dark, the kid is getting weapons to all the other gangs and I've been working on his source, but so far, nada."

"I thought you said it was the connections in Mexico that were coming up with the guns."

"Until recently. We were able to motivate the *Federales* with all the Fast and Furious fallout, and when that source dried up, we thought we had them, but now they seem to be getting them from here in the U.S."

"So you're just shadowing Bodaway to find the source?"

"That and some information on some other things — been deep undercover for more than nine months now."

"Like what information?"

"I'm not at liberty to say."

"Lola have anything to do with it?"

He shook his head. "I don't think so, but who the hell knows with her."

"Any sign that she's involved up to now?"

"No, but she loves the little asshole and would do anything for him — including getting you and your Indian buddy involved."

"Cheyenne." The three of us looked up to

110

see Henry standing in the doorway, leaning on the jamb with his arms folded, neither of us having heard the door itself open. "If you please."

"Henry Standing Bear, meet Special Agent Brady Post." I turned to look at him as Dog sidled over to the Cheyenne Nation. "Is that your real name?"

"No."

"Do you want to tell us what your real name is?"

"No."

I shrugged and turned back to the Bear, gesturing toward the tattooed man in the chair. "ATF."

Post interrupted. "Why don't you just tell everybody?"

"My bet is that he heard everything anyway."

Henry nodded and closed the door behind him. "I heard about the guns and the fact that you have been in deep cover for the last nine months. Amazing that you have risen as far as you have in that short amount of time."

Post gestured with a thumb toward the accessories on the back of his denim vest. "Fully patched."

"So, what is it you want from us?"

"Well, I thought it would be nice if we

111

weren't working at cross-purposes." He turned back to me, picked up his beer, and rolled it between his hands. "Look, I know you're investigating the accident at local request, and I'm assuming also because of Lola Wojciechowski?"

I shrugged again. "It's still debatable as to whether we're going to take the case."

Henry smiled. "We?"

Post sipped his beer and studied me for a while before slowly smiling. "That why you've got a manila envelope under your arm that says Bodaway Torres?"

Amazingly enough, Torres's phone fit the Bear's charger. Henry plugged it in and set it on the nightstand between the beds. I studied the small screen as he stripped off his motorcycle gear. "Isn't it supposed to do something?"

"It is probably so dead that there is no power to the screen yet."

"How long does that take?"

He climbed in his bed in his underwear and a T-shirt. "You know, I think I am going to buy you one of those things one of these days."

A dim red light appeared on the screen inside a graphic of a depleted battery. "It's charging."

He flipped off the reading light on his side. "It will take almost an hour to fully charge; are you going to watch it the entire time?"

"Technology fascinates me."

He grunted and rolled over, and I could see the road-rash scrapes on his back through the thin shirt. "You do not have to keep me informed as to the progress. Good night."

"Good night." Dog rested his head on the bed and looked at me. I patted the spread, and he was up in an instant, occupying a full half of the surface area. "Hey, Henry?"

"What?"

"Why don't you want to help this woman?"

"She is a manipulator, and I do not think she has done anything in the last thirty years besides sharpen her skills." He waited a moment before adding, "Not all fair maidens are worthy of rescue, Walt."

"Maybe she is this time."

He studied me over his shoulder and then, reaching out, turned off my light. "I never make exceptions. An exception disproves the rule."

I sighed, stood, and undressed, hanging my clothes on the chair by the desk. I went to the bathroom, brushed my teeth, and then stood there looking at myself, trying to figure out what to do next. Corbin Dougherty needed my help, Lola Wojciechowski needed my help, maybe even Bodaway Torres needed my help. On the other hand, Special Agent Brady Post didn't need my help, and Henry Standing Bear didn't appear to want to be involved with anything that included *the* Lola.

Sometimes it was like that, I suppose; some people become so important in your life that they're almost like a trademark, but then they're gone. Sometimes they might reappear, but they're nothing at all like what you've assembled in your mind since their departure; sometimes you can't even stand them anymore, because they break up the legend and nothing dies harder than a good, personal legend.

I looked at the crumbling giant in the mirror, nowhere near as young as he used to be. Maybe if I were thirty or even forty I might think about hanging around Hulett, but I'm not. Plus, it was the Bear's call since he knew Lola, and the Bear was softly snoring in the next room, blissfully unconcerned.

So tomorrow I'd watch him attempt another hill, and then we'd load up and go home. It was that simple — that, or I wanted it to be.

By the time I got back to the bed, Dog was taking up a full two-thirds, and I was relegated to the one-third left, clutching the mattress like a mountaineer in a hanging bivouac. I had just closed my eyes when I heard a buzz.

Flipping the light back on, I looked at Bodaway's phone, but it was dark. Then I noticed it was Henry's cell lying next to it that was making noise.

The Bear hadn't moved, so I picked it up and stared at the screen, confirming the fact that I was in deep trouble. I hit the button and took my medicine.

"So, you're not dead?"

I kept my voice low in an attempt to not wake the Cheyenne Nation. "Nope, I, uh . . . escaped with my life. Just now."

"You know, if you had called me back I would've been worried." Her voice took on a fake Western tone, emblematic of every bad cowboy movie made in the '40s. "The last time we encountered the good sheriff he was at gunpoint. . . ." Her voice slipped to serious. "So, who's pointing a gun at you this time?"

"People are always pointing guns at me."

"Daddy?"

"Lola."

There was a pause. "You don't mean *the* Lola."

"I do."

"Henry's Lola?"

"The one my granddaughter is named after."

"Don't start." Another pause. "I assume she's gorgeous?"

"In a rough, roadhouse kind of way."

"Oh, my."

"Yep, her son was hurt in a motorcycle accident over here."

Another pause. "Umm, so how are she and Henry?"

"They're not."

She laughed that lovely, melodious laugh that reminded me so much of her mother. "Then don't you get involved."

"I wasn't planning on it."

"Planning has nothing to do with it."

"Right." I smiled and held the phone close, knowing full well that part of it was that she was my daughter, but also just from the sheer joy of knowing her. "Did you call just to give advice to the lovelorn?"

"No, I called to make sure you didn't have any bullets in you."

"I'm bullet-free. So, how's *my* Lola?"

"Sleeping, finally. She's a night owl. Was I like that?"

I glanced at the time on the phone. "You still are."

"Yeah, I guess so. Hey, I thought I'd better give you a heads-up. Lena said that Vic is planning on flying into Rapid City tomorrow and surprising you guys."

I dropped my voice even lower. "I hope she gets in early. Henry's talking about skipping the Show and Shine and just heading home after the hill climb tomorrow."

"He's not going to show Lucie this year?"

"I guess not, so hopefully Vic will get here early." I smiled into the receiver. "Is my undersheriff's imminent arrival the reason you warned me about Lola?"

"No, I warned you because you're stupid when it comes to females of all shapes and sizes when they are in distress."

"That's the second time I've been cautioned about that tonight." I tried to touch on the next subject as lightly as possible. "So, there's still nothing going on with the investigation in Philadelphia?"

"No, and she says she misses Wyoming, but I think she misses you." I wasn't quite sure what to say to that, so I just remained quiet and listened as her tone changed yet again. "Hey, when are you coming down here to see the new digs?"

"Probably next week. I told Ruby that I

was taking a few days off to go spend time with my family."

She yawned. "Good. We miss you, too, you know?"

"I do. Get some sleep, Punk; that little one'll be up soon enough."

"Roger that. Love you."

"Love you, too. Over."

She giggled. "Over."

I turned the thing off and laid it on the nightstand just as the other phone there began vibrating. Evidently, it had summoned enough energy to work. Curious as to who was trying to contact the young man, I picked it up. It had buzzed twice, which I had learned means a text message, and I stared at it for a moment, checking the date and time to see if it was old, but the date was today and the time, two minutes ago.

MEET ME AT THE NINTH GREEN

The sender's name had not come up, but the number was a 310 area code. I just lay there looking at the message, making sure it said what I thought it said. I hesitated, looking at the time of morning and thinking about whether I really wanted to continue being involved with this case, but then went ahead and did what I knew I was going to do — and sent back two letters in return.

OK

I guess it all comes down to the fact that I hate mysteries, and I wanted to know who had attempted a vehicular homicide on Bodaway Torres. I quietly dressed, went to the door, and looked back at Dog. He raised his head and looked back at me, but then lowered it and didn't make another move.

So much for backup.

I closed the door behind me, fingered the Cheyenne Nation's keys that I'd taken from the nightstand, and walked around the cabin just in time to interrupt two scruffy-looking guys attempting to unlock Lucie, the Bear's Indian motorcycle, from the trailer.

The nearest one tilted his Viking helmet back, smiled, and waved as I approached. "How you doin'?"

"Good. You?"

"Oh, we're having trouble with these locks." He noted that I'd stopped and was watching him. "Um . . . this yours?"

"Might as well be."

The other scruff, who was holding a tire iron, stepped back. "Then you're saying we shouldn't be doing this?"

"If I were the real owner you never would've heard him, and they would've found your bodies in the Belle Fourche

River tomorrow morning."

The one with the tire iron palmed it a few times, attempting to send a message via Morse code. "He a tough guy, like you?"

"Tougher."

"Well, how 'bout we see how tough you are."

I sighed and looked down at the more reasonable of the two. "Look, Eddy, I'm old and tired and if you piss me off bad enough I'm going to have to pull this .45 I've got at the small of my back and shoot you just to show your friend how tough I am."

He studied me as his buddy started sidling to the left back of the trailer. "We know each other?"

"That Indian belongs to Henry Standing Bear, Heads Man of the Dog Soldier Society, Bear Clan."

"Oh, shit."

"Oh, shit is right."

"How come I'm the one that gets shot?"

I gestured toward his buddy, now coming around the back, supposedly out of my line of sight. "He looks too stupid to learn from it, but you know, I just might be changing my mind." I slipped the Colt from my back and turned to look at number two. He froze when he saw the semiautomatic hanging at my thigh. "Go home, or wherever it is you go; nothing good ever happens this late at night, and the two of you are liable to get killed."

Tire iron's mouth unfroze. "Is that a real Colt?"

"Yep, it is." I gestured with my sidearm. "Go. Home."

"I hear they jam a lot."

"Not this one." I raised the weapon. "I said, go home."

They left, mumbling to each other, something about life not being fair. Figuring I'd pushed my luck borrowing the real Lola's Cadillac all day the day before, I slipped behind the wheel of Henry's Lola and started her up. Dodging through the remaining motorcyclists who appeared to be impervious to both exhaustion and alcohol, I made my way across town toward the only golf course I knew existed in Hulett.

The Devils Tower Club sits on a private mesa above the town, which gave me the first indication as to who might be attempting to contact Bodaway. I turned the vintage bird and trailer in a broad arc, lined up in the diagonal parking at the center of the lot, and killed the engine. To my right was what I assumed to be the clubhouse, a beautiful if predictable structure of stone and massive logs.

There were no other vehicles, just a few carts parked near the building. I quietly got out of the T-bird and walked over to a large, hand-engraved map to look for the ninth green. It was a red moon that shone across the clipped fairway and I struck off, careful to stay on the cart path in the shade of the conifers.

I climbed a rise, and when I got to the top I could see someone standing under a tree by a water hazard, and I listened as the frogs croaked at each other. A trail cut through the trees so that I would come up behind whoever it was. I stopped about fifty yards away and studied the figure long enough to know that it was female.

I got a little closer and noticed she was wearing a set of earbuds, her head bobbing to the music — so much for stealth. I stepped to the side and raised a hand, trying not to scare her. "Howdy." I needn't have bothered with that, either — she screamed loud enough to be heard by Mount Rushmore. I held up my hands in surrender. "Hey, it's okay."

She had an arm in a sling but managed to yank the earbuds out to scream at me some more. "Who the hell are you?"

"Sorry — my name is Walt Longmire."

"You scared the shit out of me."

I folded my arms over my chest to show her I didn't mean any harm, meanwhile studying the extraordinarily beautiful young woman. "Sorry."

"Where's Bodaway?"

It seemed like an odd question. "As far as I know he's still in a hospital room at Rapid City Regional."

"He's still in the hospital?"

I stared at her. "Well, yes. I was under the impression that you were a witness to the accident."

"Who told you that?"

"Corbin Dougherty, the officer here in Hulett."

"And who are you again?"

"Absaroka County Sheriff Walt Longmire."

She didn't seem impressed and swiped a long lock of blonde from her face. "And where the hell is that?"

"About two hours from here."

"Wyoming?"

"Yep." I studied her in return. "You're not up too much on Wyoming geography, are you?"

"I'm from California, and I don't give a shit."

"Fair enough."

"Excuse me, but do you know who I am?"

"I was under the assumption that you are Chloe Nance."

"Yeah, but do you know who I *am*?"

One of the great trials in law enforcement is the "do you know who I am" question, which pops up every now and again. Usually it's a county or city councilman from somewhere else or a state representative, but I didn't think she fit the bill. "Um . . . Bob Nance's daughter?"

"Well, that's one thing, and do you know who he is?"

"Not really." I took a step past her and looked out at the picturesque scenery, only partially marred by little flags and golf-ball washers. "Look, Miss Nance, are you a witness to Bodaway Torres's accident?"

She tried to fold her own arms but then remembered the sling. "Why should I talk to you about it?"

"I'm assisting the investigating officer."

She sighed and looked away. "My father says I'm not supposed to say anything to anybody, that it'll just lead to trouble with those people."

"Well, seeing as how you're an eyewitness to what may or may not have been an attempted homicide, I can get a subpoena and we can have this conversation down at the Hulett police headquarters or the Crook

124

County sheriff's office."

"I found him, okay? I didn't witness anything."

"On the side of the road."

"Yeah."

"Was he alone?"

"Yeah."

I turned and looked at the young woman. "Can you give me an indication as to what kind of condition he was in?"

"What do you mean?"

"Was he conscious, unconscious?"

"He was unconscious."

"Did he have anything with him on the motorcycle that you saw lying around — saddlebags or anything like that?"

She took a long time to answer. "No."

I looked pointedly at her injured arm. "Was there anybody else on the motorcycle with him?"

"No."

I gave her the long pause I'd learned from Lucian — the one that crept like an epoch-eating glacier — just to let her know I had my suspicions. "Then I guess I've got only one more question."

"Yeah?"

"When did you get his cell phone number?"

A voice sounded from behind me. "I think

you've answered enough of the sheriff's questions, Chloe."

I turned to see a fireplug of a man with a shaved head standing behind us, aiming what looked to be a sporting-clay over-and-under shotgun mostly at me. "Mr. Nance?"

He strolled up a little closer, and I could see two men standing behind him in matching black polo shirts. "You're supposed to follow that with 'I presume.'"

I shrugged. "It's late, and the guy who does my Sherlock Holmes is asleep."

Next to big-game hunter Omar Rhoades's log palace back in the home county, and Versailles, Bob Nance's ranch house was just about the most extravagant place I'd ever visited.

"Will you still be needing us, Mr. Nance?" The muscle in the black shirts continued to glance at me. "We can stick around if you need us."

Nance, with his back to the three of us, was mixing two drinks. "That's fine, Mr. Frick. I think we'll be okay."

I watched as they left and turned back as Nance handed me one of the drinks. "Is the other one's name Frack?"

He ignored my joke. "Vintage '66, thirty years in cask 559, and bottled on June

126

eighteenth of 1996 at the Laphroaig distillery." He handed me a tumbler, neat, and then adjusted the flames on the river-rock fireplace with a remote. "I know it's summer, but I like the ambiance — a little like Dick Nixon in that regard." He lifted his glass. "I hope you enjoy it."

"I have to tell you this is the most civilized stickup in which I've ever taken part."

He sat in an overstuffed leather chair, throwing his polished boots onto a matching ottoman. "We strive to please."

I took a sip of the amber liquid and was pretty sure that it was the finest stuff my palate would ever touch, and that if I wasn't careful I'd be asleep by the time I finished it. The room was lined with bookshelves, and there was a gigantic burled-wood billiards table at the center, with red felt where he had laid the Krieghoff K-80 Pro Sporter. "Nice place — almost as nice as mine."

"Is yours log?"

I nodded. "Yep, and I believe my whole house would fit in this one room."

He smiled and glanced up at the timbers, a good forty feet in the air. "It's kind of over-the-top, but you know how it is when you think you're building your last one."

"I haven't even finished my first."

"Well, the ex got the other three — one in

Palo Alto, one in Grosse Pointe, and one in Paradise Valley — so I guess I felt entitled." He took another sip of his scotch and studied me. "So, how can I help you, Sheriff?"

"Your daughter is a pretty girl."

"Yes, she is, and you can see why I'm a little protective of her, especially since it's rally week." He put his scotch on a massive Indian drum, which had been turned into a coffee table. "I heard her try the old 'do you know who I am' on you."

"It was done pretty well."

"She's an actress."

"You don't say."

"Or was till she got into trouble." He gestured toward a few framed one sheets near the fireplace. "You mean to say you haven't seen *Barasharktapus* or *Pagan Women of Planet X*?"

I walked over to the posters, which were far worse than anything anybody could've imagined. "I've let my subscription to the Metropolitan Opera lapse, I'm afraid."

"Crap, all of 'em, and this is her father talking. . . . But she tries, you know?"

"Must be a difficult business."

"Four years at NYU and then two more at UCLA and a stint at the Guildhall School of Music & Drama. I tell you, I sat through

128

more crappy, esoteric one-act plays with people in black leotards than you can shake a stick at."

"I can shake a lot of sticks at crappy, esoteric one-acts."

"I wish I had. Anyway, what's going on, Sheriff, and why am I talking to you instead of the sheriff of Crook County or Chief Nutter?"

"I'm assisting the Hulett police with an investigation concerning a young man who we believe was forced off the road."

"And what does that have to do with my daughter?"

I walked toward the pool table and glanced at the stairwell where Chloe Nance had disappeared. "From what I am made to understand, your daughter was a possible witness to the incident."

"She wasn't a witness — she just found that young man on the side of the road, after the fact, and did what any decent human being would do and tried to help."

I pulled the mobile from my pocket and touched the screen, then turned it so that Nance could read it. "Is that your daughter's cell phone number?"

He got up and came over and stared at the screen for only an instant. "Yes."

"You're sure?"

"I pay for the damn thing once a month, so I know the number."

I placed it back in my shirt pocket. "How do you suppose your daughter has Bodaway Torres's number if they'd never met before the accident?"

Nance leaned against the pool table and fingered the adjustable comb on the Monte Carlo Turkish walnut stock of the shotgun that probably cost as much as my truck. "You shoot, Sheriff?"

"Trap?" I shook my head. "Not so much lately."

"It's a sport known for its congeniality, like golf." He set his glass on the bumper and picked up the 12 gauge, swinging the 30-inch barrels around toward the flying mounts of two pheasants above the fireplace. "I've learned that it's the relationships in life that really matter, Sheriff Longmire, whether it's with your family, your business associates, or your community."

"Like the MRAP?"

He nodded. "The MRAP for the local police and why I give so much to so many charities and organizations." He lowered the shotgun and looked out the windows. "I mentioned some trouble concerning my daughter."

I waited and said nothing.

"She had a little substance abuse problem in L.A." He handed me the Krieghoff. "We've got a little benefit shoot tomorrow evening, and I'd like you to come up and take part as my guest."

I held the expensive beauty and thumbed the top-tang push-button safety, locked in the off position. "So, you're thinking that she might've met Bodaway previously and was attempting to obtain drugs?"

"It wouldn't be the first time. I've been running interference for about eight months now."

"We're still going to need to have her come in and make an official statement."

He smiled and took the over-and-under back, throwing it over one shoulder like he knew what he was doing. "That's fine, Sheriff. I'd just rather she not make it on the ninth green after midnight."

5

I watched as the Cheyenne Nation held the bike steady while Jamey, who was whistling a Beatles tune, made the final adjustments on the KTM. We all turned at the sound of a racer's engine just in time to see another of the hill climbers flip over backward and have his motorcycle land on top of him, man and machine intertwined as they slammed back down the slope.

"This is a really dumb sport."

The Bear pulled on his helmet and tightened up the chin strap. "Well, not all of us are lucky enough to go shooting sporting clays with the millionaires up on snob knob."

We watched as the EMTs scraped the kid off the hill and loaded him into a van, another in a bunch that had gotten carted off to Rapid City Regional.

"Wasn't my idea."

He pulled on his gloves and took in a

crowd that was much larger than the previous day's seated on the makeshift bleachers. "Any idea where all his money comes from?"

"Nope, but I figure I'll ask Corbin and get the story."

As I finished speaking, the youngster who'd razzed the Bear just the previous day pulled up and rapped his throttle a few times, shouting to be heard over his own noise. "You up for it today, old man?"

Henry ignored him, so I answered. "Hey, Evel Knievel, why don't you go find a canyon to fall into?"

He smirked, and this time I was quick enough to get my arm up to protect my face as he spun out toward the starting gate and sprayed all three of us with a rich coating of South Dakota dirt.

The Bear dusted himself off. "Do you think he knows who Evel Knievel is?"

"I don't know." I watched as the kid took his place in line, waiting to back up against the buttress log and make his run. "But I really wouldn't mind seeing him bust his ass all the way down that hill."

"He had the fastest time trial yesterday."

I glanced at the Bear. "What, he got his training wheels off?"

He scanned the competitive field. "They

all look young, do they not?"

"To us? Yep, they do."

He twisted his head, stretching the muscles in his neck, and all I could think was that if he didn't climb the hill, he could always take a pickax and destroy it. "I am thinking this might be my last run."

"Well, think about staying for the Show and Shine. Vic may be flying into Rapid City."

He studied the hill, and I wasn't sure if he'd heard me.

He had been here at sunup, slowly climbing the course on foot, studying the terrain, and getting a read that you couldn't get even from the closeness of a motorcycle. He'd taken his time and stooped to look at the rocky knobs, the tufts of prairie grass, and, most important, the ruts and berms left by the other racers. There would be no surprises for Henry Standing Bear on the run this morning, and if he lost, he would be satisfied in the knowledge that he had done everything humanly possible to win and more. "Or not."

I sighed. "I'm headed over to the peanut gallery where I can join the throngs in safety." I could see the third-row spot that Corbin and Lola had saved for Jamey and me. "Looks like your old flame wants to see you in action."

"She would probably not mind seeing me bust my ass all the way down that hill."

"Or that." I patted him on the shoulder. "I'll see you in the winner's circle."

He gave a curt nod and then kicked the dirt bike to life, circling toward the starting line as Jamey ambled along with me.

"That kid posted a 14.01 — that's faster than Henry's ever been able to climb that hill and nobody's ever broke 14."

I noticed that the Bear had pulled up at a respectful distance to watch the other riders try their luck. "Why do you think he does it?"

The biker shrugged. "You'd know better than me, dude."

We went through the gate in the chain-link fence and moved over to our seats as the EMT van pulled away. "Not about this. I've never understood it."

"If it was anybody else, I'd say they were trying to recapture their youth, but not him. I think it's just the challenge." He looked back and smiled through his bushed-out beard. "I don't think he's used to partial success, Walt."

"You're probably right about that." The others made way, but Jamey motioned toward his truck in the pits. "My tools are all out over there, so I think I'll watch from the tailgate in the cheap seats."

Lola watched him go and then turned, studying me through a large pair of Italian movie-star sunglasses. "I don't think he likes me."

I turned back to the hill. "There seem to be an awful lot of people who don't particularly care for your company."

She adjusted the glasses and studied Henry. "And here I've always thought of myself as such a likable person."

I turned toward Corbin. "What are you doing out of uniform, troop?"

He shrugged. "I go on at noon, so I thought I'd get out of town for a few hours before the real rally starts."

We watched as the smart-aleck kid backed into the log and made ready to make his run. There was a lot of screaming and yelling as the crowd began cheering for the odds-on favorite. The flag on the hill dropped, and he rooster-tailed it, rocketing through the short straightaway and then timing the loop-de-loops. He got a little sideways but was able to pull it out just before the prairie grass got hold of him and bounced him like a pinball. He started to stall but then gassed it and flew over the top with a flourishing cross up. The kid was good, you have to admit.

"Hey, I met a patron of the Hulett Police Department last night."

"Who's that?"

"Bob Nance."

Dougherty looked genuinely surprised. "Where in the world did you see him?"

I leaned forward and looked toward the hill where the young rider had posted a 14 flat, and then glanced at Lola for her response, but there didn't seem to be one. "On the ninth green with a very expensive shotgun in his hands."

"You were at his house?"

"Eventually." I turned a little toward Lola. "Hey, do you know if your son was associated with a young woman by the name of Chloe Nance?"

The corner of her lip nearest me curled up just a bit. *"Associated?"*

"For lack of a better term."

"Chloe Nance?"

"Yep."

"Never heard of her." She turned toward me, but it was difficult to read her expression through the glasses. "But like I told you, he had lots of *associates.*"

Corbin interrupted the interrogation. "Wait, you met Bob and Chloe?"

"Yep. Last night after you dropped off

Bodaway's phone, I plugged it in and a text came from Chloe wanting him to meet her at the golf course. I got dressed and went up there and met her father, too."

We all watched as another rider made an emergency dismount and did a comic bow as his bike catapulted back down the hill. Corbin checked his wristwatch, probably estimating the time it would take to get back to Hulett and his shift. "She's a pain in the ass, but the old man's all right."

"Sure, he just bought you guys a million-dollar truck."

Lola broke in. "Hey, don't knock people that buy you things."

We watched as Henry got closer to the starting point. "How did he make all his money, anyway?"

"He worked for the automobile industry — developed some kind of ceramic stuff they use on exhaust manifolds and still holds the patent. He's rich about ten feet up a bull's ass."

"So it would appear." The Cheyenne Nation was having a brief conversation with the officials — it seemed as though there was a problem up top. "Any idea how Chloe could've been involved with Bodaway?"

"Nope."

I turned to Lola. "You?"

138

"Me what?"

"Any idea why this young woman might've gotten in touch with your son?"

I got the curve at the corner of the lips again. "I told you, he's popular."

"Your son wasn't dealing in anything illegal, was he?"

I got the full sunglasses this time, and it was like looking at two identical versions of myself. "Like what?"

"Drugs?"

"What makes you say that?"

"The young woman's father mentioned that his daughter had a substance abuse problem, and I was just wondering if that might've been a connection."

"There isn't."

"You seem pretty sure of that." I waited and then continued. "He's had a few run-ins with the law."

"Nothing involving drugs."

"No, but . . ."

"But what? He's an Indian kid, a biker with a few brushes with asshole cops and so he must be bad news, huh?"

"That's not what I said."

"But it's what you were thinking."

I smiled and started getting the feeling that Henry was right to keep Lola at arm's length. "You know, I can hardly do enough thinking for myself, so if you'd like to do some of mine for me, feel free."

She studied me for a good long time and then stood. "I'm taking a walk. I'll see you later." She sauntered away toward the pits.

"Do you think it was something I said?"

"Absolutely."

I nodded and watched as the Cheyenne Nation backed up against the starting log and looked at that hill the way I'm sure his ancestors had studied the Seventh Cavalry. There was a war about to happen, and I wasn't going to miss it because Lola Wojciechowski was having a fit of pique.

I've seen some pretty amazing feats of derring-do, but I could tell this was going to be special. We watched as the Bear leaned up over the handlebars and made ready, the official at the top raising the green flag.

It wasn't a complete hush, but there was a stillness in the crowd. All the old Jackpine Gypsies knew Henry and respected him for his one triumph and the years he'd spent attempting to replicate it. They knew he was a tough competitor, but there is a time when you stop doing certain things, and I think that the Bear was there and everybody knew it.

The flag fell, and the Cheyenne Nation was off.

The reason the loop-de-loops are there at the beginning of the course is to keep the riders from gaining too much momentum, allowing it to carry them halfway up the hill, but the Bear was having none of it and the KTM's motor screamed as he shot off the log like a clean-hit baseball from a gigantic wooden bat.

I'm pretty sure his front wheel never touched the ground till he hit that first hill, but I can guarantee nothing touched the second. He landed on the downslope at a much higher rate of speed than the other riders had, and the front wheel levitated again as his right hand peeled back the throttle and he blew up the hillside in a direct path, ignoring the routes that the others had taken.

There was a reason why no one else had tried the more direct route: there was a concave area dug into the hillside that, if you took it head-on, was likely to shoot you back out into open space where a fall the rest of the way down the hill was certain.

The Bear hit the indentation but then kicked to the right, taking a slight berm that shot him back toward the middle. I was wondering what the next part of his plan would be when he threw the handlebars to the side and leapt up the center third of the hill at a ferocious diagonal.

I wasn't even aware that I'd been drawn to my feet but then noticed that the hundreds around me were standing, too.

Henry couldn't keep going in that direction or he'd go out of bounds, so he slammed into another hillock, teetering for only a second, and used the force of impact to ricochet back up the hill with the same momentum he'd started with. Unlike all the other racers, he didn't pause at the sandy precipice but took another diagonal that flew both the KTM and him over the heads of the scrambling officials in one final blast, like a Saturn V rocket headed for the ghostly shape of the moon in the blue South Dakota sky.

13:59.

Henry and Jamey were seated on the tailgate of Jamey's truck and passed a bottle of champagne back and forth, each smoking a cigar as Lola and I approached through the crowd that surrounded them. KOTA Territory News was interviewing the Bear, and it looked like all of Sturgis was trying to have a word with him.

We waited at a respectful distance, and when the crowd began to thin, she sidled up to him and they looked at each other. I wasn't close enough to hear what she said, but I guess it was pretty important because he reached out a hand and stopped her when she started to walk away. He stood and said something to her, and she said something back. He stood there for a moment more and then let his arm drop.

Whatever it was she said, I'd never seen a look like that on the Bear's face.

She gave him one last hard stare and then turned and walked away.

I'd been in enough wars and a few relationships to realize when a bomb had been dropped, so in deference, I stood back a moment before leaning over the side of the pickup bed. "Pretty good trick for an old Indian."

He turned but didn't smile. "Not bad at all."

He handed me the trophy, and I looked for his name on the plaque, but it wasn't there. "When do they engrave it?"

"This afternoon." He thought about it, staring at the crinkled leather of his old motocross pants. "I suppose if we stay for the Show and Shine, I could go to the ceremony this evening and pick it up."

"If you win the Show and Shine, you might get two trophies out of it."

"And leave them in a dumpster here in

Sturgis."

I handed him back the trophy and studied him. "You okay?"

"Yes."

"You don't seem like it."

"I have some things on my mind."

"Has Lola finally leveraged you into this investigation?"

He barked a short laugh with no humor in it and then carried his gaze back toward the hill he'd finally conquered. "It is beginning to look like that might be the case."

"Well, congratulations."

"For what?"

"Winning."

"Is that what I'm doing?" He stood, still holding the half-full bottle of cheap champagne, and, puffing on his cigar, walked toward the hill.

I studied him for a good long time and then figured if he wanted to really talk he'd get around to it on his own. I glanced over at Jamey, who was quietly packing up his tools and trying his best to appear uninterested. "When is the Show and Shine?"

He stopped working and smiled. "Noon, over in Sturgis near the Bucket of Blood Saloon."

"Then I guess we'd better get going."

I helped Jamey load up the tools, paraphernalia, and the KTM, and we strapped it down on the trailer as Henry continued to study the hill.

Maybe it didn't have anything to do with Lola. Maybe it was just what happens when you finally get something you want and it turns out not to be what you wanted after all. You spend most of the time in life running after things that aren't that important, and the pursuit becomes more desirable than the prize.

I started out toward where the Bear stood but stopped. "I'm thinking he needs some time."

The biker joined me. "Maybe so. You got somewhere you have to be?"

"A friend of ours is flying into the Rapid City airport this morning, and I was thinking I should pick her up, but it's supposed to be a surprise, so maybe I'm not."

"Not what?"

"Supposed to pick her up."

"Oh." He glanced at Henry and then back at me. "You can borrow my truck, but is there anybody you can call to ask whether or not she's really coming?"

"Well, I could call the person in question, but that's going to blow the surprise, too."

He shrugged. "If it was me I'd call; life has enough surprises as it is."

145

I fished Bodaway Torres's cell phone from my pocket; it was evidence, but there was no reason why it couldn't be useful.

I punched in Vic's cell phone number and listened as it rang. After a moment she answered. "Who the fuck is this?"

"It's me."

"What's me doing with a strange cell phone?"

"It belongs to a young man named Bodaway Torres. He wasn't using it; he's in the hospital."

"You put him there?"

"No."

"You just stole his phone."

"I borrowed it — it's evidence."

She snorted a laugh. "This is getting better and better."

"Where are you?"

"I'm in Philadelphia." She sniffed. "Why?"

"A little bird told me you might be surprising us and flying into Rapid City."

There was a pause. "You know, that little bird has a problem keeping things to herself."

"Yep, it's not her strong suit." I smiled. "So, where are you?"

"About twenty feet behind you." I turned and looked. "I bet you turned and looked just now."

146

I turned back around. "I did not."

"I'm getting my bag at the luggage carousel at Rapid City Regional Airport, which looks remarkably like a Mayan shopping mall with nothing in it. I heard you rode with Henry, so I figured I'd rent a car."

"You don't have to — Jamey says I can borrow his truck."

"What is it?"

I studied the vehicle. "It looks to be a late seventies —"

"I'll rent a car."

"Right."

"Where do I meet you?"

"I think we're headed for the Bucket of Blood Saloon in Sturgis for the motorcycle show."

"Did Henry bring Lucie?"

"He did."

"Cool — he owes me a ride. I'll meet you there."

She hung up, and I shook my head; life as we know it was about to get interesting. I looked at the phone and then tapped Jamey on the shoulder. "Hey, do you know anything about these phones?"

He shrugged. "A little — why?"

"Can you track the previous calls on this thing?"

■ ■ ■ ■

The Bucket of Blood Saloon during Sturgis is a marvelous place to get puked on, but then, during the rally, pretty much all of the town met that qualification.

Jamey knew the owner of the Bucket and was able to get Henry the prime corner spot for Lucie. The 1940 Indian Four was designed when the Indian Motorcycle Company of Springfield, Massachusetts, absorbed the assets of the Ace Motorcycle Corporation. Into the thirties, even though there was low demand for luxury motorcycles, Indian continued to develop and refine the inline four cylinder until the thing was capable of more than a hundred miles an hour, an unheard-of speed at that time.

With its large, decorative fenders, it looked like a jukebox on wheels, but its pedigree was so great that in 2006 it graced the 39-cent stamp and was part of the Smithsonian Motorcycle Collection at the National Museum of American History.

The Bear's was nicer.

Adding to its worth was the matching factory sidecar, which I thought resembled a chrome-trimmed prow of a boat. "Who in the heck would ride in that thing?"

148

Jamey studied the vintage contraption. "I guess it's as safe as riding the motorcycle."

"My point exactly. You know, Pete Conrad died on a motorcycle."

"Who's Pete Conrad?"

"The third man to walk on the moon." I sipped my canned iced tea and looked up and down Sturgis's crowded Main Street for what might pass as a rental car. "Where's Henry?"

"Inside having a drink."

I pulled out my pocket watch and frowned, placing it back in my jeans. "A little early for that, isn't it?"

"He didn't look like it was open for discussion."

"Oh, boy."

About a half block down I could see a neon-orange coupe moseying its way through the throng. Every once in a while, when someone was a little slow getting out of the way, the driver revved the engine, causing the offender to hop a little quicker.

When she got closer, I could see she was holding her badge out the window. I walked over and leaned on the passenger-side door. "What is this?"

My undersheriff smiled her crocodile smile, the one that showed no innocence. "Hemi Challenger; it was the only thing the rental guy had left, so we made a deal."

"I bet you did." I glanced around. "Where are you going to park this thing?"

She raced the motor again. "Anywhere I want."

I gestured toward the beer garden outside the Bucket of Blood. "We're over there where the red umbrellas are."

Pulling out, she barely missed another mass of bikers. "See you in a few."

I hopped back up onto the curb to keep my boots from being run over.

Jamey was waiting as I slid between some of the other classic bikes. "Who's that?"

I watched as the Great Pumpkin made a right and then a U-turn to dodge into a parking spot across the street. "A force of nature." I glanced toward the bar and saw that Lola was headed inside. "When my undersheriff gets here, bring her over, will you?"

"You bet."

Fighting the current on the sidewalk, I tacked my way toward the corner entrance of the bar and finally pushed through the swinging saloon-style doors. The Cheyenne Nation was seated at the last stool of the bar, up against the wall with a motorcycle boot propped up on the adjacent seat. Throwing back a shot and looking over the crowd, he puffed his cigar.

We were in trouble.

We were all in trouble.

I hadn't seen that particular look in decades, and I had been hopeful that I'd never see it again. The Bear was looking for a fight, and odds were, he'd find one.

Lola was rounding the table beside the bar where the bikers were four deep and making a lot of noise. I thought I better get over there quick but was given pause by the fact that I might be interrupting a personal conversation.

There was a high-top table by the window that had just been vacated, so I grabbed it and waited for Vic and Jamey to arrive. As I sat, a dark-haired young woman in a skin-tight Sturgis tank top paused and asked if I wanted a drink other than the can of iced tea in my hands.

"No, thanks."

"You gotta have a drink if you're gonna sit."

I pulled out my pocket watch and acquiesced. "Give me a Rainier, a dirty martini, and a Jack and Coke."

"Bud, Bud Light, and Coors."

I sighed. "Coors."

Satisfied with that, she turned and walked away.

Lola had pulled up an arm's length from the Cheyenne Nation and stood there talking with him as he clinched the cigar in the corner of his mouth, both the cigar and the Indian smoldering.

I felt someone lift my hat and turned in time to see my undersheriff place it on her head. She surveyed the place, raising her voice to be heard above the raucous music that blared from everywhere. "Bucket of Blood, huh?"

I half-yelled back, "That's what they call it."

"Bucket of pig shit, looks like to me."

"Maybe." I kicked a stool out and Jamey ushered Vic onto her seat. The waitress arrived with the drinks, and I palmed her a twenty. "Keep the change."

Vic, looking adorable in jeans and a plaid shirt tied at the waist, tipped my hat back on her head. "You making friends already?"

"Trying."

"Looks like they've got hot and cold running venereal diseases in here. You didn't catch anything while I was gone, did you?" Jamey pushed the martini toward Vic, and she sipped it, watching Henry and Lola. "You go over there?"

"Not yet."

Vic studied the couple in question. "That's

152

her, huh?"

"Yep."

Her eyes narrowed like a gunfighter's. "Looks like ten miles of bad road, if you ask me."

"A bit bumpy, yes."

"So, what does she want from Henry?"

"To look into who might've hurt her son."

She took a swallow of the cloudy martini, rife with olive brine. "I thought she wanted you to do that."

"It would appear that she doesn't think I'm up to the job alone."

"Hmm . . . she doesn't know you very well, does she?" Vic watched as Lola continued to talk at Henry. "How's that conversation been going for her?"

"Not so well as near as I can tell, but she's upsetting him and I'm not sure what to do about it."

"Henry upset, huh?" She set the martini glass down and spread her hands across the lacquered surface of the table, and I noticed her fingernails matched the rental, casting further doubt on her having acquired the muscle car by accident. "I know this isn't my usual response in these types of situations." She smiled. "But stay the fuck out of it."

Jamey nodded, backing up Vic. "I was

153

thinking the same thing."

It was about then that one of the bikers at a table adjacent to the conversationalists said something to the Bear.

Vic turned her head, and we all watched as the Cheyenne Nation said something back. The bikers looked at each other, and the talker laughed and said something again.

Henry responded, but this time his answer was shorter.

The biker reached out and slapped the Bear's boot, indicating, I think, that he should move it and let Lola have a seat.

"Oh, no."

The Cheyenne Nation removed the cigar from his mouth and stubbed it out in the shot glass.

Both Jamey and Vic were already standing. "We'd better . . ."

Henry slowly rose from the stool like a bird of prey.

There were five of them, but it didn't matter.

6

Sturgis is in Meade County, South Dakota, and not so surprisingly, its jail was full. Pennington County, where I had been just the previous day, had not been and was receiving, so here I was once again in the sheriff's guest chair.

"Four of them are in the hospital."

"He's responsible for only three of the five. She's the one who hit the guy with the popcorn maker."

Vic turned toward me from the other chair. "Bad road — I told you."

Irl Engelhardt closed the file and smiled at the two of us. "That's four. What happened to number five?"

Vic smiled back at him. "He ran."

The sheriff studied us some more. "The brains of the outfit, huh?"

"So it would appear."

"They're pressing charges."

Vic laughed. "Five on one, and they're

155

pressing charges?"

"Four on one."

"Whatever."

He leaned back in his chair. "I might be able to talk them out of it, but somebody's going to have to pay the damages at the Bucket."

I interrupted before things got out of hand. "I'm sure Henry won't have a problem with that; he's a business owner and knows how these things work."

Engelhardt placed the file in his lap and rubbed his nose; finally letting his hand drop, he sat there looking very tired. I had a feeling that it was what I looked like most of the time from this side of the desk. "Walt —"

"I know what you're going to say, Irl, and I apologize. I know this is a busy week for you."

"The busiest."

"Yep, well, I promise it won't happen again. Things just got out of hand."

He was nodding his head. "All right, go get your friend, but tell him I told you that if we have any more shenanigans like this I'm going to have to lock him up for real."

"Thanks, Irl. Where is he?"

The Pennington County sheriff tapped a few keys on his desk phone. "Brenda?"

156

"Yes, Sheriff."

"Where have we got Defending Champion Henry Standing Bear?"

There was a rustling of papers from the desk outside Irl's office. "Medical. He was complaining of headaches, and the staff thought he might have a concussion, so they shipped him over to Rapid City Regional."

"Thanks, Brenda." He tapped the button again. "You know where that is?"

We stood. "Um, yep."

He reopened the file in his lap. "What do you want me to do with the woman?" He looked back up at us. "Wojciechowski?"

"Have you got anything like solitary confinement? It might be the only way to keep the world safe." Vic followed me toward the door and closed it behind us as we made a speedy retreat.

"I'm glad I made it back before all the excitement was over with." As we crossed the bull pen and made our way down the steps, she shook her head. "You've got to admit, as fights go it was pretty impressive."

"On one side it was."

We stepped through the glass doors onto the sidewalk as she raised the key fob and unlocked the Dodge. I opened the door and struggled to fit. "How do people get in these things, anyway?" I watched as she pulled a

157

parking ticket from under the windshield wiper and tossed it into the back. She climbed in and hit the ignition. "I'm guessing you're not going to pay that?"

Vic made a face, slammed the selector in gear, and, after laying a good twenty feet of rubber as we sped off toward the hospital, weaved through traffic like she was in a Friedkin film. "I'm on the fucking job."

I fastened my seat belt as quickly as I could. "Who did you say were your driving instructors — the Blue Angels?"

I pointed the way, she turned a corner, and I felt the car go slightly airborne as we went over some railroad tracks. "I like driving fast — I like doing things fast." She gave me a side-glance. "Most things, that is." I indicated a right-hand turn, and she flat tracked the Dodge around another corner, expertly correcting the drift. Rocketing into the hospital parking lot, she slipped into a diagonal spot and cut the engine. "So, you miss me?"

I still had both hands braced against the dash. "Can I open my eyes now?"

"Pussy."

I shook my head and got out of the car, happy to be on solid boot leather. "C'mon, the ER is this way."

She caught up as we weaved our way

through the parked cars, and I swallowed. "Where are we on Michael's case?"

She took a deep breath and then shot it out through her shapely nostrils. "Zip-nada. The woman who witnessed the incident from the building across the street couldn't identify her own husband in a lineup, and it looks like we've ground to a halt." She stepped in front of me and stopped me in my tracks. "I've got the files."

I chewed the skin on the inside of my cheek. "The originals?"

"Yes."

"Katz and Gowder gave them to you?"

At the mention of the Philadelphia police detectives, she stiffened a bit, and I had my answer before she spoke. "*Gave* is a relative term."

"Vic —"

"He's my little brother, Walt, and he's dead."

I stuffed my hands in my jeans and stared at the parking lot's painted lines. "I'm sure that they —"

"You're the best, and I need the best; this is personal."

"I know."

"It's what you do."

"I know."

She tilted her head back and squinted up

at me. "You'd do it for any citizen on the street, so why not for me?"

"You're right."

"What?"

Taking a deep breath, I repeated myself. "I said you're right." She looked as if she wasn't quite sure what to say next, so I helped. "Copy the files and give them to me, and I'll go through them." I waited a moment. "It's personal for me, too. He was my son-in-law."

Her eyes clouded, and she reached out and grabbed my shirtfront, pulling herself in and muffling her voice against my chest. "Thanks."

Just then, a sheriff's deputy hustled from the ER. Moving toward his unit at a clip, he was rapidly followed by another. They jumped in and backed out, barely missing us.

"What's up?"

The deputy looked a little anxious, but I think he recognized me from my visit to their headquarters the previous day. He called out as he slapped the car into drive. "Fugitive at large."

"Who?"

I barely caught his voice as they peeled away. "Some damn Indian."

Vic's face pulled back from my chest as

she watched them go. "Uh-oh."

Boy howdy.

"So, why are we searching in the one place he supposedly escaped from?"

The fact that I'd gotten lost twice in the labyrinth of Rapid City Regional did nothing to lessen the assurance of my next statement. "I've got a hunch."

"About?"

"Bodaway Torres is in the ICU here, and I think Henry might've decided to look in on him. Lola's been hitting him pretty hard, and I'm thinking it's had an effect."

I finally found the ICU at the end of yet another hall, and I could see the giant Lola had introduced me to still sitting in his chair. I waved at the man with the dark sunglasses, but he didn't move. "Hey, Big Easy."

Vic murmured. "What, he's from New Orleans?"

"Yep, um, I'm not sure. It's complicated." We stopped, and I looked past him toward the nurse's station, but the one woman there was ignoring us and I brought my eyes back to the large man. "Easy, I'm looking for . . ."

I leaned in closer and examined him, Vic joining me. "What the fuck, he's asleep?"

161

I took one of the giant's hands, lifting it and then letting it drop. "Out cold."

"He's a sound sleeper."

I examined a dent in the drywall behind him, about where the biker's head would've been if he'd been standing. "Might be more than that." I felt the man's pulse, just to be sure he was alive, and then glanced in his nostrils, where I could see blood, and at his face, where the beginnings of two black eyes were hidden beneath the sunglasses. "He's unconscious, but he's all right."

My undersheriff made a face. "Have I told you lately how scary your friends are?"

I moved past him toward the observation window around the corner. "You're one of my friends."

She followed after me. "Case in point."

The Cheyenne Nation was standing there with his arms folded, the torn motocross jersey still hanging from his shoulder with a few bloodstains here and there — fresh from the Indian Wars.

I stood beside him and looked in at Bod-away, nothing having changed. The Bear didn't say anything, but there was a look of sadness on his face.

Vic came up and stood with me. "Hand-some."

I nodded, glanced at Henry again, and

then looked back at the young man. There's something profoundly sad in the striking down of a young person in his prime, an injustice that offends beyond all others. I've had numerous engagements with the Reaper, but it's outside the lines when he takes the young — just plain cheating.

I studied Torres's profile, the strength of the jaw, the powerful nose, and the black, black hair. I stood there for a long while, not trusting what might come out of my mouth next.

My undersheriff turned, leaned her back against the glass, and looked at the two of us. "So, what happened?"

"Um . . . he was riding out near Devils Tower and somebody ran him off the road. Mike Novo did a preliminary and said it was possible that he wasn't going particularly fast but that he had some weight on the back, either saddlebags full of something heavy, or possibly a passenger."

Her eyes drifted over to the Bear and then back to me. "No witnesses?"

"No, but there was a young woman named Chloe Nance who found him, and I'm thinking there might be a connection there. According to her father, she has a substance abuse problem and Bodaway here might've been supplying."

"You think it was drugs on the back of the bike?"

I shook my head. "His mother says no, and besides, they wouldn't weigh enough to be a factor, but he is under investigation by the ATF for illegal gun sales."

"The Alcohol, Tobacco, and Firearms ATF?"

I glanced around to make sure that Big Easy was still out. "None other. I got a visit last night from Brady Post, one of the chief enforcers for the Tre Tre Nomads; he's fully patched and undercover with these guys." I paused. "And then there's the paint issue."

She folded her arms. "The paint issue?"

"Irl let me in to the impound lot at the sheriff's department, and I found gold paint on the side of the Harley Bodaway here was riding."

"Gold."

"Lola Wojciechowski drives a '66 Cadillac DeVille, gold in color."

There was a predictable pause. "You think she ran over her own son?"

I glanced at Henry. "The more you get to know her, the more it seems like a possibility, but then again it appears that the vehicle is something of a staff car for the entire Tre Tre Nomad gang."

"So, somebody in his own gang ran over him?"

"Possibly." I pulled out the cell phone, handed it to Vic, and gestured toward the young man in the bed. "This is Bodaway's phone. Can you pull up his previous calls?"

She took it and began pushing buttons at an alarming rate. "Made or received?"

"It can do both?"

She shook her head. "You are such a Neanderthal."

Henry cleared his throat, and I turned to look at him. "You okay?"

"Yes."

"You want to talk?"

"No."

"Okay."

I started to look at Vic but then turned back. "You ever going to want to talk?"

"No."

"Okay."

Vic showed me the phone and started counting. "Seventeen calls from the Nance household, a couple from the 310 area code, thirty-two from Lola Wojciechowski, nine from a number with a Phoenix area code but no ID, and twenty-one from a place called The Chop Shop, with a few from a pizza place, the last two both here in Rapid City." She looked at the phone screen. "I

165

say we start with the pizza place. I'm famished."

I looked back at the Bear. "You need a getaway car, and we've got one."

Studying the Cheyenne Nation just as I had, Vic pushed off the glass window. "And a driver, but you'll have to hunker down in the back, seeing as how you're on the lam and all."

Piesano's Pacchia is a joint up on Canyon Lake Drive, reputed to make the best pizza in the Hills, and when the Philadelphian concurred, I feigned a heart attack and slumped in my half of the booth.

"No, really, this is good pizza." She chewed and postulated. "Not as good as my uncle's, but it's good."

I sipped my iced tea and glanced outside where a large man with long, dark hair sat on the hood of an orange muscle car with his back to us.

The waitress, a cute little blonde, came over, refilled my tea, and offered Vic more wine, but my undersheriff showed restraint. Vic waited until the waitress departed and then set down the rules. "Okay, I'm going to ask a few questions, but I don't want you to do anything but answer the questions one at a time. No embellishments."

166

I turned back to her. "Okay."

"How old is Bodaway Torres?"

"Thirty-two."

She nodded. "How long ago did Henry know Lola?"

"A little over thirty years ago."

There was a pause as she thought about how to proceed, deciding on her usual course: straight forward and full speed ahead. "Asking the question as a crass white woman, would you say that Bodaway bears more than a passing resemblance to Henry fucking Standing Bear?"

I sighed. "The thought more than crossed my mind when I saw the two of them together."

She turned her head and watched him. "Have you ever seen him this upset about something before?"

"I've known him my whole life, so a few times, yes, but not many."

She turned the tarnished gold eyes back to me. "You are now free to embellish."

"I don't know."

"Walt . . ."

"I grant you, there is a resemblance."

"They look exactly alike." She shook her head. "If you were to go to the Henry Standing Bear Store and they were out of Henry Standing Bears, they would offer you

167

a slightly more diminutive Bodaway Torres."

"Why would she wait this long to tell him?"

She sipped her soda and postulated. "I don't know; she's nuts?"

"There's that." I slouched in the corner of the booth and poked my boots out the end. "Working on the supposition that you're right and there is a connection, maybe she didn't have any intention of telling him, but then this happened and she truly is desperate."

She shook her head at me.

"What?"

"You are such a goof ball for women." She set her glass down and leaned in across the table. "I know this is going to come as a surprise, but there are women out there who are capable of doing anything as horrible as a man can do and worse."

A large shadow suddenly darkened our table. "What are you two talking about?"

Vic scooted over so that Henry could have a seat, since there was more room on her side. "Um, nothing."

I gestured toward the half a pie. "Want some pizza?"

"I am not hungry."

"I would offer you something to drink,

168

but that led to your being a fugitive."

"But I like pizza." He picked up a slice and took a bite, grabbed Vic's wineglass to spite me, and took a sip.

Vic and I looked at each other. "So, what are the chances?"

He took another bite and chewed, obviously hungrier than he had thought. "I do not know."

Vic leaned forward, looking at him and maybe making an aesthetic analysis. "He looks like you."

"Yes."

"Has Lola ever said anything to you?"

"No, I have not heard from her in over thirty years."

Vic ventured a question. "Um, not to put too delicate a point on this, but can you remember the last time you and Lola . . ." He turned to look at her. "I mean a date, time of year?"

"No." He stared at her. "I did not keep a diary."

"Gimme my wine back."

He handed it to her. "I am saying it is improbable. I am not saying it is impossible."

She sipped. "I'd like to see a photo of the Delshay Torres of record."

I looked up at a clock on the wall and

noted the time. "If we get back to Hulett before Chief Nutter closes up shop, we can ask him to take a look on the National Crime Information Center database. They've probably got a photo of him."

Vic watched the Bear. "You really don't think he's yours?"

"I do not know." He pulled his own phone from his pocket. "I have received a text from Jamey saying he has Dog in his truck and is wondering where you would like him deposited."

"If he doesn't mind Dog-sitting, he can just hang onto him till we get back. Dog doesn't like being in the motel room alone."

"I will text him." He did and then returned the phone to his pocket. "What do we do now?"

"We were thinking that was your call."

He nodded and reached for Vic's wine again, and this time I could see where the skin had been stripped from his knuckles. "Why would the ATF be so interested in the distribution of guns?"

Vic barked a laugh. "Because it's illegal, and because their jurisdiction is alcohol, tobacco, and — let's see, what's the last one? Oh, yeah — firearms."

The Cheyenne Nation shook his head. "When we met Agent Post in the motel room, it seemed like more than that." He glanced at me. "Almost a year of undercover work to infiltrate one of the most violent biker gangs around just to locate some random hardware?"

"What are you thinking?"

He shrugged and then turned his head, watching the sun start to make its own escape behind the Black Hills. "Something that would fit on a motorcycle."

"So, smaller than a bread box?" They both looked at me. "It's a box you put bread in." They continued to look at me. "So, do you want to go get what may or may not be the mother of your child out of jail?"

"No."

"Okay." I pulled out Bodaway's phone and looked at it again. "You said seventeen calls from Chloe Nance, a couple from the 310 area code, thirty-two from Mom, nine from a number with a Phoenix area code but no ID, twenty-one from The Chop Shop, and three from this pizza place." I sipped my tea and glanced at the waitress behind the counter. "So, let's start with the easiest." I gestured to get her attention. "Miss, could I get some more iced tea?"

She hurried over. "Sorry, I was folding napkins."

I watched as she filled my glass and then

looked at Henry. "Would you like something?"

"No, I am fine."

She studied him, and I asked, "Miss, we're looking for my friend here's son and was wondering if you'd seen him. Bodaway Torres?" I quickly added. "B-way?"

She smiled a dazzling grin toward Henry. "I was just thinking he looked like you." She stuck out her hand. "I'm Tiffany. I'm sure he's told you about me?"

The Bear matched her grin for grin, enveloping her hand in his. "Tiffany, of course he has."

"You tell that dirty bird I'm mad at him; he hasn't called or anything for days."

I redirected the conversation. "He's been kind of tied up lately. As a matter of fact, we've been having trouble tracking him down ourselves. You wouldn't happen to know who he's been running with these days?"

She thought about it. "There's that guy with the do-rag and the tattoos."

"Tall with a goatee?"

She nodded. "And the broken nose, yeah."

I glanced at the others. "Brady Post."

"Yeah, that's him. I remember him saying his name."

"Anybody else?"

She stepped back, and the smile died; I guess I was pushing a little too hard. She looked at Henry. "You are his dad, right?"

The Bear broadened his grin, displaying stunning white ivories against his sun-bronzed skin. "Far as we know."

She relaxed and punched his shoulder, but withdrew her hand and wiped it on her jeans, just now realizing his jersey was torn and had blood on it. "Um, there's Billy ThE Kiddo. That's the only other person I ever saw him with."

"Billy the Kiddo?"

"No Billy ThE with a capital E. You've never heard of him? He's got his own TV show — *Billy ThE Kiddo's Chopper Off?* It was huge till he punched some producer and they canceled it. Word is he's in negotiation with another cable network, and they're gonna have another series based on him." She shrugged. "At least that's what they say. He's originally from here and has a custom motorcycle place just down the street called The Chop Shop."

"The Chop Shop." I shook my head. "Do you have an address?"

"Oh, you can't miss it." She glanced at Henry again. "You tell B-way to text me, okay?"

■ ■ ■ ■

We decided to call Sheriff Engelhardt to ask him to check on Torres Senior, and after the Cheyenne Nation apologized, Irl agreed to message a photo of the man as soon as they found one. As a precautionary measure, I had him look up Billy ThE Kiddo, just so we'd know what we were up against.

"Kiddo? That's his real last name? Shit, I'd get a nickname, too." Vic parked the Challenger across the street from The Chop Shop, which was housed in a remodeled corner gas station still replete with old-fashioned pumps albeit modern neon.

The Pennington County sheriff read to me over the speakerphone. "Oh, he is a real piece of work, Walt." I glanced at the face on the screen and then held the phone for the others to see. Irl continued, "Behold Billy ThE Kiddo, six foot two, two hundred and twenty-seven pounds. Over a dozen cases of aggravated assault, two domestic violence charges, one assault with a deadly weapon charge, and once even choked a K9 unit dog unconscious in Orange County, California."

Vic studied the mug shot. "He's got a mullet."

Irl laughed. "It's a nice one, isn't it? I doubt he hears much with that party going on in the back of his head. He can build bikes though. Started over in Sturgis at those build-offs and somebody from Hollywood saw him and figured he was a genuine American outlaw and gave him his own reality show. He was living out there in Los Angeles, but something happened and he's back here with a couple of those motorcycle places set up like franchises."

Henry turned the phone his way and looked at the photo, and at the multitude of tattoos and piercings. "I do not think he is the president of Rotary."

"Originally from Rapid City and a good family; it's undisclosed exactly where the poor little lamb went astray."

Vic opened the glove box, took out her Glock, checked the magazine, and slapped it back in the 9mm.

Irl interrupted. "Excuse me, but was that the sound of a semiautomatic pistol's magazine being expertly reintroduced between the weapon's grips?"

I made a face at my undersheriff. "Nope, just the glove box."

"Walt?"

"No trouble, I promise."

He continued, "We've had a number of

175

zoning problems with this jaybird and a few charges for dumping harmful chemicals into the local water system. You want me to send a few guys around to back you up?"

"No, we're just going to ask him a few questions about the kid that got hurt. I guess they knew each other."

"All right, but don't shoot anybody."

I assured him. "Right."

"Vic?" Evidently he was not assured.

"What?"

"What are we not doing today?"

She climbed out, flipping the seat forward and allowing me egress as she took the phone and began making squelch noises with her mouth. "Schweeesclerbleee, swurchscwerch, scweee . . . can't hear you, Irl, you're breaking up. Schweeesclerbleee, swurchscwerch, scweee scwch scwch." She made a few more noises into the phone, then hung up and handed it back to me.

"I just want you to know, I'm never falling for that one again."

She curtseyed as she stuffed the Glock in the back of her jeans. "Sure you will."

As we walked across the street toward The Chop Shop, the music of air wrenches drifted out to meet us, along with the sound of an acetylene torch turning metals into liquids.

It was one of those vintage gas stations with a rounded glass-block front and vaulted canopies that covered the old pumps and stretched out toward the street. The building was painted black, and there were a multitude of outrageous-looking motorcycles to match lined up everywhere, in different stages of disrepair and assembly. Through a door in the work area were a few young ladies in skimpy outfits and smoking cigarettes, loafing in what must've been the office.

One of them looked up as we walked into the bays. "Hi. Welcome to Billy ThE Kiddo's Chop Shop. Can I help you?"

I smiled. "Do you have to say that every time somebody comes in?"

"Pretty much."

"Is Henry McCarty, aka William H. Bonney, around?"

She pushed off the edge of the desk and abandoned her companion. "Huh?"

"Billy ThE Kiddo."

"You got a bike problem?"

She was talking to me, but she was looking at Henry, not that I blamed her.

Henry saved us by speaking up. "I have got a shovelhead rebuild that I am doing, and I am past the wrist-pin alignment and the pistons are ready to go in. Now I know

177

the ring gaps should never be in line with each other or placed on a thrust area of the bore. The major thrust area is the rear of the cylinder wall and the next minor thrust area is the front, but will the oil ring expander come in contact with the cylinder bore or the oil ring scraper rail gaps?"

You could see the struggle as she thought about bullshitting the Bear but then thought better of it. "Um . . . maybe you should talk to Billy."

The Cheyenne Nation showed some teeth. "That would be nice. Thank you."

The dishwater blonde threw a thumb over her shoulder toward the bay where all the noise was coming from. "He's welding, so shield your eyes."

She left us, and we ambled toward the back where a very lithe-looking individual was crouched down working on the gas tank of a bike that looked as though it had undergone a great deal of modification. It also looked like a death trap.

As we waited, I glanced around the shop and noticed a very heavy security door led to the back and had to admit that it was an impressive operation — a little grimy but impressive.

"What do you want?"

I turned around and discovered that The

178

Chop Shop's chief cook and bottle washer was holding the brass nozzle of the torch away from his work and had nudged the dark glasses up onto his rooster-like platinum hair.

"We're looking for Mr. Kiddo?"

"Billy — people call me Billy ThE." He stood, closed off the acetylene, and turned to face us, and I'm not sure if I'd ever seen that much defined muscle on one person before. He had the easy smile of someone who was used to getting what he wanted, and I was betting we were seeing a good seven thousand dollars' worth of dental work; then there were the diamond earrings, which probably cost a couple thousand more. He hung the nozzle on the rack with the tanks, pulled a red shop rag from his back pocket, and wiped off his long, tattooed fingers. "Well, you found him. Now what?"

"Do you happen to know a young man by the name of Bodaway Torres?"

"Yeah, I know B-way. What about him."

"Do you mind telling us what your dealings with him might've been?"

He studied the three of us. "You guys cops?"

I gestured toward Vic and myself. "Two out of three."

He tossed the rag onto a nearby tool rack and then turned back to scrutinize us. "Well, two out of three of you can go fuck yourselves."

The Bear glanced at us and then back to ThE. "Does that mean that I get to stay and ask questions?"

Kiddo smiled and even went so far as to crack his knuckles like some cartoon bad-ass. "It means you get to stay, and I can stick my boot so far up your ass I'll be using your mouth as an ankle bracelet."

The Bear smiled, and I watched as he seemed to grow and swell, or maybe the room was just becoming smaller. "Really."

Kiddo's grin grew wider as he reached over to the same bench and picked up a disc metal cutter. "You know, I hate it when people don't take my threats seriously."

"Maybe you should get better writers or work on some better threats."

ThE took a step forward with the cutter and punched the trigger so that he had to speak over the dangerous whine of the thing. "You ever try to pick up your teeth without fingers?"

The Bear looked at me. "That wasn't bad."

"I'd give it an eight."

Henry turned back to Kiddo. "No, but

when we were kids waiting on the bus in front of the Jimtown Bar in Lame Deer, we used to pass the time picking up teeth in the parking lot after the weekend fights."

I nodded toward the Cheyenne Nation and half-yelled over the whine. "That was better — it had a personal quality and didn't sound like a line from a crappy Chuck Norris movie."

Billy ThE stood there with the cutter, and I swear he was thinking of using it on us just as Vic pulled the 9mm from the back of her jeans, letting it rest alongside her thigh. "So, you're the kind of asshole that brings power tools to gunfights?"

7

"He says you threatened him."

I held the phone to my ear and tried to remember how I'd gotten involved in this mess but then recalled it was a damsel in distress who was more like a dame. "He started it with a metal cutter."

"He said Ms. Moretti was brandishing a gun."

I glanced at my impromptu posse leaning on the fender of the screaming-orange Dodge, one watching the horizon and the other checking her nails. "Define brandishing."

"Walt."

"Okay, she brandished it a little bit." I sighed. "Look, Irl, it isn't like we got anything out of him."

"You got a restraining order, harassment, and a charge of cease and desist. He learned a lot of litigious lessons out there in California, and, pending court action, you're not going to be able to go within a hundred feet of him."

"What's he hiding?"

"Heck if I have any idea, but he's all lawyered up now, so it's going to be a lot harder to find out."

I sighed and began pacing back and forth. "Anything interesting from his sordid past?"

"Other than the things I've already mentioned?" The sheriff sighed and then chuckled. "A couple of years ago, he was back on a visit and attempted to shoot his next-door neighbor with a .40 for mowing his lawn on a Sunday afternoon."

My response was slightly incredulous. "He's religious?"

"About football."

"Oh."

"Came charging out of the house but must not be much of a shot with that Glock 22, because he fired the thing twice before killing it."

"The lawn mower, I'm assuming we're talking about."

"Yes."

"Is lawn implement destruction a felony here in South Dakota?"

"Nothing runs like a Deere or smells like a John." Engelhardt laughed outright. "He bought the old guy another one, but Billy can be hell on wheels. He trashed a bar in Deadwood a few months back — stuck some guy's head in a toilet." I listened as he rustled some papers. "Don't be fooled; he can be charming as hell in court — shows up in a coat and tie, all Hollywood business-man, and makes jokes about not being able to grow up. You'd be amazed how many middle-aged jurors want to get free work on their bikes around here."

"So, no serious time inside, then?"

"No, he's pretty careful about that kind of thing. I mean, it's all just assault and bat-tery type stuff, like I told you." There was silence over the phone. "Why are you so interested?"

"Bodaway Torres called his shop twenty-one times in the last week."

"Maybe he was having bike problems."

"Maybe."

There was another pause. "All right, then, but would you keep me informed so I don't have to find these things out via APB?"

"Roger that." I hit the off button and walked back toward the Dodge. "We are free agents once again, but Irl says ThE is law-yered up and that we need to leave him alone."

"They say that genius is an infinite capac-ity for taking pains. It is a very bad definition, but it does apply to detective work." The Bear turned and looked at Vic. "Arthur Conan Doyle." He shrugged and looked back at me. "All we wanted to do was talk."

"I guess he's got nothing to say."

Vic stared at the Cheyenne Nation and then at me. "Neither of you want to hear what I have to say next."

The Bear scratched the side of his face. "Then do not say it."

She continued to thwart him by looking at me. "There was this guy I know who taught me that when an investigation grinds to a halt, you go back to the beginning and start over."

I thought about it. "You know, I hate that guy who taught you that." I leaned on the fender with her. "That was me, right?"

Henry interrupted. "And where, pray tell, is the beginning of this case?"

We both looked at her as she smiled.

Following the gold Caddy on the highway, Vic and I watched as the two heads turned toward each other, their hair whipping in the wind. "What do you suppose they're talking about?"

"Probably the two thousand dollars of bail money she owes him."

"I imagine she'll tell him to put it on her tab."

Vic wound her way through the Black Hills, her foot in the Challenger, causing it to bellow as we raced along behind the Cadillac. "That tab is getting to be pretty big." She glanced at me, sideways. "So, you think he's Henry's kid?"

"No."

"Why?"

"Because he says he isn't."

"Boy, I want you on my side in a paternity suit." She nodded toward the car ahead of us. "Of course, she says he is."

"Well, like I said, Lola Wojciechowski's turning out to be less and less a credible entity."

"Momma's baby, Poppa's maybe."

"I just don't think it would've taken her thirty years to get in touch with him about it."

My undersheriff cocked her head. "She's tough."

"She's had to be." I studied the car and could see Lola was putting a little distance between her and us. "I'm beginning not to trust her any farther than I can throw her."

"So, it's solely about justice for the kid?"

I took a deep breath. "As far as I'm concerned, but I'm not sure about Henry."

186

"Did you talk to the doctors?"

"No."

"I did."

I turned and looked at her again. "Oh, now why don't I like the sound of that?"

"That kid's never coming back, Walt."

I nodded my head and turned to watch the road being gobbled up by the muscle car. "Never?"

"Not one chance in a thousand."

"That's not what his mother thinks."

"Yeah, the doctors told me about that, too. The one I talked with said he explains the situation to her, but then she keeps coming back with all kinds of scenarios, not a one of them with any medical credibility." She watched me as I continued to study the rapidly passing outskirts of Rapid City. "I suppose you didn't want to hear that, huh?"

I settled into the bucket seat, evidently larger than a bucket. "Not really — makes me sad."

"I'm sorry, Walt. I just don't want you pinning your efforts on bringing that kid back."

I nodded, glancing at the speedometer and noticing we were approaching a hundred. "Um, you think we're going a little fast?"

She gestured with a hand toward the windshield. "You want me to keep up with Maria Andretti here or what?" We banked another turn and started climbing an extended hill just as a siren sounded from a long way behind us. I watched as Vic glanced up into the rearview mirror. "Company."

Swinging around, I could see the flashing lights of a black South Dakota Highway Patrol car gaining on us. "Well, hell." It was about then that I heard the bellow increase and the Challenger felt as if it were shooting out from under me. "What are you doing?"

She gestured through the windshield again. "She's out on bail; you think they're going to let her get away with doing a hundred on an interstate highway?"

"Probably not —"

"I'll bait and switch — give this highwayman a run for his money; besides, if he catches us, I'm sure you can talk our way out of it."

"I don't suppose we could just pull over and talk to him?"

She glanced at the speedometer. "Maybe before we went past a hundred and twenty."

I reached out and clamped a hand on the dash.

Lola and Henry's pace now seemed sedate as we blew past. Vic waved in the rearview and then checked on the HP's progress.

"He's still gaining on us." She glanced at me, smiling just enough to reveal the slightly oversized canine tooth, increasing her lupine features. "He's gamer."

Just before we topped the hill, I glanced back to see the trooper pass the Cadillac as if it were dragging an anchor. "Mission accomplished — we are now his sole and exclusive target."

The Challenger became very light in the tires as we weaved between the cars on the road and leveled off, starting down the hill. "What's the next town?"

"Sturgis."

"Is there a main artery leading out?"

"Alternate 14, which heads toward Deadwood and Boulder Canyon Road."

The speedometer was now tipping one hundred and sixty as she blithely steered the Dodge into the emergency lane to pass two semis running in tandem. "This first exit. Here?"

I swallowed and tried to work up enough spit to speak. "No, the second one."

Rocketing past the trucks and the startled driver of a minivan, she tipped the wheel, and the muscle car leapt back into the open lane like an animal on the hunt. "Cool, hodaddy."

I turned to see if the trooper was a member of the Joie Chitwood Danger Angels, but so far he hadn't caught up, possibly slowed down by the eighteen-wheelers. "Take the next exit and then left under the underpass and out of town, but there's going to be some traffic with it being rally week."

"I like traffic — it's cover." She spotted the exit up ahead and, predictably, there was a lineup of cars and trucks with trailers hauling motorcycles backed up almost onto the thoroughfare. "You said left, right?"

"Yep, left."

Slicing down the emergency lane, she decelerated and tipped the wheel just enough to get the rear end of the Challenger to break traction and begin a sickeningly slow slide to the right as the two back wheels attempted to catch up with the front.

I looked straight ahead at the intersection that was rapidly approaching, aware that the light was red and that traffic was streaming by in front of us.

Vic casually countered the drift just enough to keep the Dodge in play and, slowing her speed, continued turning to the right, glancing up at the overpass where the highway patrolman was sliding across the bridge with his antilock brakes fully locked. "Gotcha."

A truck driver, pulling across the intersection, suddenly looked up the ramp in time to see us rapidly approaching slideways. He slammed on his brakes as Vic threw the Dodge across the opposing lanes, beat out a sedan, and put her foot into the more than seven hundred horsepower, slinging us forward as she took the emergency lane again, shooting past more cars, then roaring back onto the road and weaving her way through the lanes of traffic.

I could still hear the whine of the HP's siren and turned to see that he had made a U-turn farther down the road in order to take the Boulder Canyon exit in the opposite direction. "He's still back there."

"Where does this road go?"

I glanced out the side window, the pines compressed by the speed like the opening credits of a movie not formatted to real life. "Deadwood."

"Anything between?"

"Some small secondary roads in Boulder Creek and Oak Ridge."

We leapt across a bridge and made a hard right, following the geometry of a curve not designed for almost ninety miles an hour. "Is that Boulder Creek we just went over?"

"I suppose — we were going too fast for me to read the sign."

She dipped her head forward, indicating the road beyond. "He's going to radio ahead, and they'll be waiting for us at the cutoff in Deadwood."

"I'd say that's probably true." A sign that read BOULDER CREEK COUNTRY CLUB flashed by. "Take the next road on the right."

"What?"

"Do it."

She pressured the brakes and broadsided through the turn onto the tiny road. "Apple Spring Boulevard — really?"

"It's not on the maps, but there's a dirt road that connects with Crook Mountain and leads back up to Whitewood and Route 34 that'll get us back to Hulett. Tim Berg told me about it a while ago."

She bellowed up the two-lane past the assorted houses, slowed at the end of the pavement, and stopped just before she cut the engine. "The human pencil holder?"

Vic referred to Tim's propensity of sticking pencils and pens in his prodigious beard and then losing them. "And the Butte County sheriff, yes."

She rolled down her window, and we listened to the highway patrolman's approach. There was only a small break in the pines, but after a moment the black sedan flashed by. She raised a fist and smiled at me. "Let's hear it for the Philadelphia Police Academy Tactical Driving School."

I cleared my throat and attempted to settle my stomach by stepping out of the car. "No offense, but I don't ever want to do that again."

Vic slipped out the other side and looked at me over the hood. "You getting sensitive in your old age?"

I ignored her and leaned on the grille, feeling the heat from the Hemi engine as it ticked and cooled.

She joined me, crossing her arms and bumping her shoulder into my side. "What's up?"

"I don't mean to sound like a child . . ." I shook my head, clearing it with the scent of ponderosa pines, Black Hill spruce, quaking aspens, paper birch, bur oak, and green ash in this island of trees surrounded by a sea of grass. "But I really don't want to be here."

"Then go home."

"I can't."

"Because of the kid?"

"Yep." I stubbed the toe of a boot in the pine needles on the ground. "It was all up for grabs until I saw him, and now it seems like it's something I have to do."

Vic laughed. "And this is a revelation?"

"Not exactly, but I'm fighting the feeling that I'm some kind of windup toy that, when faced with a criminal enigma, falls into a mechanical response in order to solve the mystery."

"You just answered your own question." She laughed. "Walt, however it is you look at what you do, whether it's a job, a duty, or — when I watch you do it — an art, you're very good at it, and for my money you're doing it for all the right reasons." She swung around and stood in front of me. "You're not doing it for that woman, you're not doing it out of some bullshit sense of duty or some philosophical construct called justice; you're doing it for that kid who can't speak for himself. I swear you're like this detective for the disenfranchised. Everybody that nobody gives a shit about, the people out there on the fringes — those are the people you speak for and that's why I love you."

I stared at her.

"That last part was just me."

I continued to stare at her.

"And if you don't say or do something right now, I'm going to kick you in the nuts."

I leaned forward and gently kissed her on the top of her head.

It might've gone further, but then two

more highway patrolmen howled by like internal combustion bandits on Boulder Canyon Highway, one after the other.

She looked at the pine needles I had disturbed, then turned back to me, and I could tell the spell was broken. "Speaking of cases that have ground to a stop . . ."

I nodded and thought about the man who might've been responsible for Michael's death. "I've got feelers with the FBI."

"McGroder?"

"Yep. He's got contacts over at State and the NSA, and they are looking for anything on Bidarte. Some of the leads say he's near the border in that Copper Canyon area, but others say he's in Mexico City."

"When do we leave?"

I took a deep breath. "It's not that easy."

"No? The asshole killed my little brother."

"We don't know that for sure."

She shrugged, unconsciously hugging her abdomen. "That's okay; there are plenty of other reasons to kill the son of a bitch."

I reached out, draped an arm over her shoulder, and pulled her in close. "Yep, I just want to make sure which one it is before we go hunting for him."

"You're so law abiding."

"I try." I looked up the dirt and gravel road leading to the top of a ridge and turning to the left. "So, you ready to go four-wheeling?"

She shrugged. "Fuck it — it's a rental."

The Challenger did pretty well, but there were a few spots where we could hear the low-slung undercarriage dragging on the rocks and catching on the sagebrush. "I don't think this is what this thing was made for."

We topped the ridge and barely missed the trunk of one of the aforementioned pine trees. "You could be right."

"I think it's only about a quarter mile or so to the paved road, so we might make it."

There was a small wallow and then a turn, and I could see the gravel lot and turn-around where the pavement started up again. I could also see the Pennington County sheriff sitting on the grille guard of his shiny black Tahoe, and replacing his worn-out chewing gum with another stick.

"Been chewing that gum long?"

"Three sticks. I figured you would've showed up by now."

I shut the door on the Dodge. "We were enjoying the environs."

"I bet." He pulled himself off the hood and stretched his back.

"Where's the Highway Patrol?"

"I don't know, probably out patrolling the highway." He smiled at Vic as she closed her door, and then walked around the front and extended his hand to her. "We meet again?"

"Always a pleasure."

He turned back to me. "Just because I know where you are doesn't mean they know where you are. We got to the road-block in Deadwood, and they said this pumpkin latte hadn't showed, so I started thinking."

"And here you are."

"And here I am." He waited a moment and then asked. "Explanation?"

I shrugged. "Which part?"

"What's so interesting about this kid over in my hospital?"

"I'm not sure, but I'm thinking it must have something to do with guns or drugs."

Engelhardt breathed a sigh. "Usually does."

"The problem is, how do you haul enough of something on a motorcycle to make it worth killing somebody for?"

"How do you know it was something on the bike and not just something personal?"

"Mike Novo ran the scene, and he says it was weight or possibly somebody else on the bike."

"Mike would know. Who found him, anyway?"

"A young woman by the name of Chloe Nance."

"Bob Nance's daughter?"

"Yep."

"He's kind of a big dog around these parts. Is that the only connection, the daughter finding the Torres kid?"

"Maybe not. I came into possession of Bodaway's phone, and she had called him a number of times before the incident."

"Chloe." He tilted his head. "She had a drug problem herself."

Vic sat on the front of the Challenger. "Hell, heroin is a hundred and ten dollars a gram, with crack cocaine at six hundred; methamphetamine is sixteen hundred dollars an ounce, and LSD three thousand a gram. In a single set of saddlebags the kid could've been carrying millions."

I shook my head. "Funny enough, he doesn't have any dealings with drugs on his rap sheet."

My undersheriff seemed incredulous. "Nothing?"

"Nope."

Irl listened as another siren rose in the distance and then quieted. "What was the other thing you mentioned?"

"Guns — he's got a record of gun running."

Engelhardt made a face. "I don't hardly think you could carry enough guns on a motorcycle to make it worth attempting to take somebody's life. Any history of dealings in antiquarian weapons? I mean, he wasn't carrying around Jesse James's pistols or something?"

"No, just street stuff."

"Then I think you're going to have to stick with drugs. Who knows, maybe he's broadening his horizons — Lord knows the money's better." He tipped his hat back and studied the two of us. "Now, maybe you can tell me why it is you were going a hundred and fifty miles an hour on my highway?"

Vic smiled, webbing her fingers together and cracking her knuckles. "One seventy."

Irl looked at the Challenger with renewed respect. "This big dude'll do that, huh?"

Vic ran her hand over the hood as if petting an oversized cat. "Advertised at just under two hundred."

I interrupted. "Lola was driving over the speed limit by a somewhat wide margin, and my undersheriff decided to provide a decoy to keep her from going back to slam."

"I see."

"You're not going to arrest us, are you?"

He sighed. "No, I'm just trying to think of how to get you out of here. I could call in the situation, but I'd just as soon not owe them a favor."

Vic pushed off the Dodge and stood. "Trade cars with us; then, if they pull you over, you can say you found the ditched car and are impounding it."

He shook his head at her. "Boy, if you want to know how to break a law, ask a cop." He laughed. "How do I get my car back?"

"We'll drive it to Rapid tomorrow and pick up the Dodge; by that time the heat will have simmered down."

"That's all fine and well for you, young lady, but what about me? I'm going to get pulled over by every highway patrolman between here and my impound."

"And then they'll owe you a favor for pulling you over and wasting your time."

He turned to me. "She's got an answer for everything, huh?"

"Welcome to my world."

"Well, speaking of favors." He hitched his thumbs into his duty belt. "Walt . . ."

"Yep, I know."

"Do you? Like I said before, this is the biggest week of my year, and instead of paying notice to the things that require my attention, I am continuing to babysit you and your staff. Now, I appreciate you taking care of the investigation for those fellows up in Hulett with this hit-and-run, but it's not in my county, not my state, and not my problem."

"I'm aware of that, Irl."

After a second, he smiled with one corner of his mouth. "You goin' all cowboy on us?"

I shook my head. "No. None of this was planned. We'll try and be a little more circumspect."

"I'd appreciate it, at least for the next week." He tossed the Tahoe keys to Vic and then pointed at her. "Not one scratch, young lady."

She crossed her heart. "Hope to die."

"Where are the keys to this ridiculous conveyance?"

"In it."

He paused. "You had this planned out all along?"

She smiled again. "You bet your ass."

He shook his head and walked around, calling out before climbing the rest of the way into the car, "I'll be heading south on Crook City Road, so you head north and in Whitewood you can jump on 34 to Belle Fourche; then it turns into 24 in your godforsaken state and takes you straight into

Hulett." He started to duck his head but came back up with one last warning. "Keep 'er under the speed of sound, would you?"

As we drove through the bucolic beauty of western South Dakota, Vic caught me glancing at the clock on the dash of the souped-up Tahoe. "What, you've got an appointment?"

"I was invited to a benefit trap shooting competition up at the Hulett golf course."

"By who?"

"None other than Bob Nance."

Vic navigated the sweeping turns of the Bear Lodge National Forest. "Oh, la de da."

I pulled my hat off, rested it on my lap, and leaned back in my seat. "I'm thinking it's something I should do."

"I assume you can bring a guest?" She glanced at me. "So, are we doing this because we're good citizens or because we want to give the daughter a look?"

"Well, there's something going on; I'm just not sure what. I mean, what was she doing out on the road at that time of night, and why was she calling him so many times?"

"Did you ask her?"

"Surprisingly, I did."

"And the answer?"

202

"Noncommittal, but her father mentioned that he'd been running interference on a potential relationship for almost a year now."

"A year?"

"Eight months."

"So, this isn't just some met-him-in-a-bar-and-took-him-home-and-clean-his-plugs-and-blow-out-his-lines kind of thing."

I turned my hat over and looked at the band with the letters of my name faded gray. "I guess not."

"You said this Bodaway character was from Arizona?"

"Tucson area."

"And she's from here?"

"Well, I guess lately Los Angeles — aspiring actress."

"And Daddy was here?"

"I suppose." I was starting to see what she was getting at. "So, how did California and Arizona hook up, and, more important, how did Big Dog break it up from Hulett?" She stepped on the accelerator. "And it's been going on for eight months? That's a lot of driving time in that three-way."

"Yep."

"Well then, let's go shooting."

A few minutes later she made the left heading up the plateau to the Golf Club at

Devils Tower clubhouse and the packed parking lot overshadowed by the massive MRAP, now fully decorated with the emblems of the Hulett Police Department and the name PEQUOD on the rear.

"What is that?"

"Oh, just a little gift from Bob Nance to the local constabulary."

"We need one of those."

"No, we don't."

The construction I'd seen the other night was now a series of platforms arranged at the edge of the cliffs looking back toward the snaking Belle Fourche River and the town. We got a few strange looks as Vic parked the Pennington County sheriff's vehicle in the NO PARKING area — the wrong county and the wrong state.

She shut the car door and came around to meet me in the front. "So, we're going to assume that Henry's all right?"

"He's a big boy and can take care of himself."

"Uh-huh." Vic scanned the assembled crowd and checked out the high and low towers on each end of the elaborate decking. "What the hell is all this, anyway?"

"The original discipline back in the 1900s was called 'trap' for the cages they used to hold the pigeons in before releasing them."

204

"And blowing them out of the sky."

"Um, yep. With fluctuating sensibilities, the sport switched over to clay pigeons."

"The ashtrays?"

I nodded. "They are even biodegradable these days. Anyway, the sport evolved further, taking the name 'skeet,' which, oddly enough, came from Gertrude Hurlbutt in Dayton, Montana, who won a hundred dollar magazine contest with the word that's derived from the Scandinavian for 'shoot.' "

She stopped and, shaking her head, studied me. "I am consistently stunned by the shit in your head."

I looked for a place to check in. "They used to do it in a circle, but that proved awkward for spectators."

"I bet."

"The typical course spans one hundred and eighty degrees and has ten to fifteen different shooting stations." I spotted an event table to the right and began angling that way like a pulling guard, with Vic following closely. "And now we have sporting clays, which started in England and spread here in the '70s. They are laid out to simulate the unpredictability of live-quarry shooting with different trajectories, angles,

205

elevations, speeds, and distances, usually on a trail."

We got to the table, and Vic studied the elaborate setup, which looked almost like a cliff dwelling. "So, golf with shotguns."

"I guess." I stood at the table and waited until the man I'd met the previous night finished up with the shooter in front of me. He shifted a piece of paper to his cohort, Frack, as I glanced around for Nance. "Mr. Frick."

"Sheriff."

"I was invited by Mr. Nance to participate in the tournament."

He sighed and ducked his suntanned face into the popped collar of his black polo shirt. "What's your name again?"

"Longmire, Walt Longmire."

He studied the sheet, flipped a few pages, and then looked back up at me again, this time with a smirk. "You're not on the list."

"Is Mr. Nance around?"

He looked over his shoulder. "He's probably at the shooter's table getting ready to compete."

"Well, is there any way to ask him?"

"Not me; he gets real serious when he's shooting." He glanced past me at my undersheriff as she watched the participants approaching the different stations. "All the shooters have registered, including the alternates — so there isn't any room anyway."

I nodded, just as happy not to compete. "Okay, but if you could let him know I'm here and that I tried, I'd appreciate it."

He nodded and glanced at his friend. "Frick and Frack, huh? I've heard that my whole life; do you know where it comes from?"

"They were a pair of Swiss skaters who came to the U.S. back in 1937; they were in the Ice Follies shows and became a household phrase."

He stared at me. "Before my time, pops." I nodded and we started to surge our way back through the crowd as he called after us, "Hey, I said there weren't any spots in the men's bracket, but we had somebody drop out in the women's, so do you think your friend would like to shoot?"

Vic looked at him and then tilted her head back — showing off the elongated canine tooth. "Fuck yeah."

8

Not for the first time in our collective lives, we needed a shotgun.

Lucky for us Chief Nutter was shooting in the second round, and even more fortunately, he was a small man and had extra equipment, including a lovely 332 Remington that had been cut down an inch, making it a perfect fit for the Terror. While the first-round shooters peppered the air with pellets and the hillside with broken pottery, Vic tried on Nutter Butter's old shooting vest, which, with a little adjustment, fit like a dream.

"I need my shooting gloves."

"Where are they?"

She looked at me as if I were the raw recruit who'd just been brought up from stupid. "They're on the seat of the Tahoe with my Flyers hat. Could you get that for me, too?"

"Anything else?"

She examined the beautiful over-and-under. "Lessons?"

When I got there, Dougherty was studying the SUV as if it had dropped out of the sky. "What are you doing with Irl Engelhardt's car?"

"It's a long story." I tossed the gloves in the orange and black hat. "You stuck doing crowd control or can you watch the competition?"

"I can't. I've got to move around and keep people from getting into trouble. Hey, I saw your dog down at the Ponderosa Café with Henry and Lola." He cocked his head. "The conversation seemed pretty intense."

"I bet." I started back. "Well, you might want to try to see some of the tournament — Vic's shooting." When I got back to the competition, there was a group around my undersheriff, all of them giving her advice.

Vic nodded and smiled the way she did when she wasn't listening. I arrived with her equipment, and she pulled her Broad Street Bullies hat down low, just above her space-age Oakley Radarlock sunglasses.

She thanked everybody for the pointers, hooked her arm in mine, and looked at the late afternoon sun. "Okay, what the hell am I supposed to do — hit the little ashtrays?"

"Yep, and make a visual connection with

the target — keep a good line with it, don't start low when you're shooting high. The better you get set up, the more efficient you become."

"Got it."

"Attack the target line but don't rush."

"Got it."

"Stay loose and lead fast. Those ashtrays are moving pretty quick."

"Got it."

"Have fun."

She nodded, pulling the gloves on and wrapping the Velcro around her wrists. "I always have fun with a gun in my hands."

I followed her back to where Chief Nutter was polishing the proffered weapon. "Where'd you get that antique, Bill?"

"Oh, my wife bought it for me before we got divorced — she got the house and I kept my guns. No harm no foul." He looked at the sheen sparkling off the stock. "It ain't nothin' too fancy, just a working man's gun, but she's true and shoots straight with no idiosyncrasies, which is more than I can say about my ex-wife." He handed the shotgun to Vic.

Vic held it like a baby, smiled at the old chief, and then turned toward the assembled competitors with a predator's eye. "Who am I up against?"

"Some of the best shooters in all of the upper Midwest." He pointed at a blonde woman with a straw cowboy hat. "Connie Evans, two-time national champion from Sioux Falls." He gestured to a dark-haired woman. "Patricia Frontain out of Chicago, teaches at the National Sporting Clay Association. And that cool drink of water on the end is Annemarie Potter, who can out-shoot most of the men here." He tiptoed to see the others. "Raye Lankford, all-Midwest, and Kelly McBride on the end down there won it all last year."

I nudged her shoulder. "Scared?"

She barked a laugh. "Hell with that; I'm used to targets that shoot back."

Carefully watching how and what the other women were doing, she joined them with the Remington's butt cupped in her hands, which were laced at her crotch.

There seemed to be an unstated pecking order, with Evans going first. She was good, very good, catching the targets on a perfect line, graceful and balanced. The Frontain woman was faster but clipped one of the clays in a double and you could feel the others sensing a weakness. The tall woman, Potter, was a natural but didn't keep a good line with the target, and I could see that she could be beaten — so did Vic. Lankford was a short blonde whose shooting was flawless, but she didn't seem as bloodthirsty as the rest, and that lack of competitiveness might be her downfall later in the shoot. McBride shot like Evans and was a problem.

Like a nervous groom, I watched as Vic stepped up to the station and carefully raised the over-and-under.

The puller lifted the remote that would signal the high and low houses and spoke in a loud voice: "Ready?"

All the other shooters had barked their command, almost as if the added impetus might help them in destroying their nemeses, but Vic was loose and draped around her weapon like a gunfighter. Although the place was almost silent, I had to listen carefully to hear the word drifting out like a sigh of foregone conclusion. "Pull."

Firing points at one and six launched the two targets like miniature flying saucers, and they'd no sooner gotten to their separate trajectories than they both disappeared in two sequential blasts that almost sounded as one.

The chief leaned over to me. "That was her taking her time?"

"I guess."

He whistled quietly. "Shee-it."

Evans, McBride, and Vic graduated to the

next level. The other shooters were talking, but Vic, with the Remington on her shoulders, stood looking into the distance like a major league pitcher throwing a shutout.

Bob Nance was in the finals of the men's competition but had made time to come over to where Chief Nutter and I were standing. Now leaning on the steel divider that separated the contestants from the hoi polloi, he squinted at me. "You bring a ringer to my tournament?"

"It's her first time."

"You're kidding."

"Nope, but she's got experience with shooting things. Four brothers who . . ." I paused and then started over. "Three brothers who are active-duty police officers, and a father who's the chief of detectives north back in Philadelphia."

He looked at me out of one eye. "What's she doing in Wyoming?"

"I ask myself that a lot of the time." I waited a moment and changed the subject. "Where's your daughter?"

He shook his head as he glanced around at the circumstance, if not the pomp. "She's bored silly by this stuff, but then she's bored silly by most of the things that I enjoy."

"I'm sorry to hear that." I waited again.

"Hey, how long has your daughter been in county?"

He thought about it. "It's August, so I guess it's been about two months."

"Before that she was in Los Angeles?"

"Yes." His eyes stayed with mine. "Why?"

"You mentioned the other night that you'd been running interference on this relationship between your daughter and Torres for eight months."

He continued to look at me. "So?"

"You said she's only been here for two months, so I guess they knew each other in L.A. or Tucson?"

He glanced at Chief Nutter and then back to me. "And why do you care, Sheriff?"

"I'm just trying to get a clearer picture of the relationship between Chloe and Bodaway in hopes that it might shine some light on the accident that may end up costing the young man his life."

He crossed his arms over the Krieghoff K-80. "Are you accusing Chloe?"

"Nope."

He glanced at Chief Nutter again to register his disapproval at being interrogated in this manner and then spoke slowly as if I might not understand English. "I have business dealings in Phoenix. I stay at the Biltmore, but my daughter, who used to stay

214

there with me, said it was too stodgy, so she set herself up at the W, which evidently doesn't monitor the individuals who frequent their poolside bar." He took a breath. "That's where they met and established a long-distance relationship, which I have been attempting to end for eight months."

"I see."

"Good, I'm glad you see."

"And where were you the night that Bodaway Torres was run off the road?"

His eyes clinched down like the bore on the gun he held. "You know, Sheriff, I invited you here because I thought it might be fun, but you're proving to be tiresome."

I smiled. "Oh, just give me a chance; I can get a lot more mundane."

He studied me for a long while and then moved back among the other shooters.

"I don't think he likes me."

Chief Nutter turned and rested the small of his back against the steel bar. "Is that your method, to go around pissing off all the people you're investigating?"

"Go with your strengths, I always say."

"I know he's a little on his high horse."

"And I know he bought you a truck."

The chief was silent for a moment and then leaned over into my line of sight. "You got something you want to say?"

"He hates that kid lying in a hospital bed in Rapid, and when I'm looking for somebody who might've done a victim harm, I generally look for a suspect who doesn't particularly care for that victim."

"And if I told you Bob Nance didn't have anything to do with injuring that boy, you'd believe me, right? Because the night Bodaway Torres was hurt, Nance was drinking with me at the clubhouse over there." I stared at him, and he looked at the power broker. "So, I guess that means I'm one of the bad guys now, huh?"

I watched as the other women in Vic's round began to shoot. "Not necessarily."

"Well, I'll tell you, I truly wish I had the finely tuned instrumentation that enables you to tell the difference between right and wrong, Sheriff."

"Speaking of high horses."

He smiled — it was slow, but he smiled. "He's divorced, too. Sometimes when I finish a shift, it's just easier to come up here than sit down in town with all the people I arrest for DUIs. Last week when that kid got tagged, Bob was here with a bunch of friends, playing cards into the wee hours."

"Good enough." I folded my arms over my chest. "Speaking of Bodaway, did I mention that both Mike Novo and I found gold

216

paint on the young man's bike — the same gold paint that's on his mother's convertible?"

He made a face. "Jeez, Lola ran over her own kid?"

"Think she's capable of it?"

"Yes. Well, no. Well, I'm not sure, to be absolutely honest. I don't know her that well."

The Evans woman stepped up, preparing for the targets that would be pitched from the opposite towers, both high and low. She shot, annihilating the first clay but barely clipping her second.

I tipped my hat a little forward so that I could see better. "The car was parked at the Hulett Motel that night with the keys in it, so I suppose anybody could've been driving it."

"You ask her?"

"I did."

"And?"

"She says it wasn't her."

"You believe her?"

I chuckled. "Well, I'm not sure, to be absolutely honest."

Vic stepped up to the fifth station, which was made out of redwood and dug into the hillside, the 12 gauge broken down and cradled in the crook of her arm. She tightened her gloves, adjusted her hat, and then loaded the Remington with the two rounds one of the pullers handed her.

The chief unconsciously straightened his own hat. "She gets two clean hits, and she'll advance." He turned and grinned at me. "And then she'll shoot against the men's finalists, who I'm pretty sure are going to end up being your buddy Bob Nance and that surgeon from Billings."

"Well, that should be interesting."

The puller looked at Vic. "Ready?"

Once again, you could barely hear her voice, and it was epic watching her raise the thirty-inch barrels like a cobra rising to strike. "Pull."

The target flew in a flat trajectory, different from the ones launched before, so Vic had to re-aim, but the result was devastating, the clay pigeon exploding. Something must've happened in the release of the second bird, though, and it was already speeding in the opposite direction when Vic sighted it. She waited just a split second.

Nutter was clutching the steel bar. "She's waiting too long, it's going to be too far for . . ."

At that second my undersheriff jerked back with the blast of the shotgun, and the clay target burst apart at the very edge of the Remington's range.

The crowd erupted, and she turned and bowed, slinging the shotgun on her shoulder, whereupon they roared some more. She popped the two empty shells and gave them to a puller and then walked straight toward us. Handing Nutter the 12 gauge, she smiled through the carnival-glass optics of her glasses with millions of tiny rainbows dancing. "I like this game."

He laughed. "It shows."

She pulled the earplugs. "I think I could get good at it."

I nodded toward the blonde woman. "Looks like you and Evans are going to be representing the gentler sex in the next round."

She turned her face, scanning the other shooters. "Who's next?"

"Bob Nance and Frank Carlton, that older hotshot over there with the khaki hat. The chief here says he's some kind of five-time national champion."

"They miss anything yet?"

"Nope."

"Well then, we're all even."

Nance sauntered over and, leaning on the railing, studied my undersheriff. "Bob Nance."

"Vic Moretti."

I thought he was attempting to get a little edge. "Hey, you're pretty good."

"Thanks."

He smirked. "You're pulling just a bit when you fire."

" 'There is no hunting like the hunting of man, and those who have hunted armed men long enough and liked it, never care for anything else thereafter.' "

Unsettled at being interrupted, he caught himself. "Excuse me?"

Vic's smile narrowed, and her jaw muscles bunched just a bit. "You come over here to mind-fuck me, Bob? Because if you did you're going to end up getting fucked yourself." She gestured toward the elaborate walkways and towers. "This golfing with guns is fun, but I've been trying to hit shit that was shooting at me since I was in my twenties, so if, indeed, you are trying to mind-fuck me — go fuck yourself, because I fuck back."

He stood there for a stunned moment and then, at a loss for anything else to do, turned and looked at me. I grinned. "She does and not gently."

He stood there for a moment more and then, without another word, turned and walked away.

"Hemingway — that's where the quote

came from."

Nutter laughed. "Bullshit that you know that."

I glanced at the chief. "She's got a T-shirt from the Philadelphia Warrants Department with that quote on it."

Vic grinned. "I love that shirt — it's one of my favorites."

My undersheriff's partner came over and extended a hand toward me, the late-in-the-sky sun playing off her curly blonde hair and Pacific-colored eyes. "Cornelia Evans."

"Nice to meet you." I turned toward Bill. "This is Chief Nutter, and I assume you've already met my undersheriff, Victoria Moretti?"

She leaned in closer to the Terror. "Hey, generally we split and do mixed doubles for the finals; is that okay? You know, Sadie Hawkins. You can pick first."

My undersheriff looked baffled. "Huh?"

I translated, gesturing toward Nance and Carlton. "Ladies' choice."

"Oh." She smiled and glanced at the two men. "I'll take the old guy, the surgeon."

"Carlton's good, but he's getting a little long in the tooth. Are you sure you don't want Bob?"

"No, he's a prick." She made the statement as if it were the time of day.

221

It took Evans a few seconds to regain her composure. "Okay then." She stuck her hand out. "Good luck."

"Thanks." They shook, and Evans continued on her way toward the two men to deliver the news.

After a brief conversation, the older gentleman came over to meet his new partner, and in a soft, Southern accent murmured, "Well, hello young lady; how should we go about vanquishing these upstarts?" Vic smiled as they shook hands, and he glanced at me. "Walt Longmire, the much-vaunted sheriff of Absaroka County, Wyoming."

"You and I have a connection, Dr. Carlton."

"And what might that be?"

"Back in the late eighties you had a patient in Billings, a young girl of Japanese descent, who was in an automobile accident and had to be helicoptered down to Children's Hospital in Denver."

He clutched his chin like it was a knuckleball and took a second to think. "*Amaterasu,* shining over heaven. As I recall it was a difficult case, and the helicopter didn't make it to Denver." He didn't say anything more, and I could see that he was unsure about asking.

"It didn't, but she did. Came into my office a while back at Christmas — she lives in San Francisco. Maybe we'll have a beer sometime, and I'll tell you the whole story."

"I would enjoy that." He turned back, smiled at Vic, and gestured toward the course. "In the meantime, young lady, we have work to do."

It was decided that the two teams would face off at station four and shoot with random pulls just to make things a little more interesting. If needed, the two teams would go into a second round or even a third if things stayed tight.

Nance and Evans were going to shoot first, and, evidently, Bob wasn't into the whole ladies-first thing since he strode up to the platform and lifted his shotgun into a median position.

He barked the call. "Pull!"

It was a tough one, the first target being the high house and coming from the left. He nailed it and then drew down on the one that had just taken flight from the low house and his right. The thunder of the 12 gauge echoed against the Black Hills, and the second clay exploded.

Chief Nutter nodded. "Bob's good — there's not too much doubt about that."

"Yep, but let's see if the surgeon can carve

him up."

Carlton looked every bit the national champion as he raised the barrels and focused in on the upcoming targets. If you were doing diagrams on how to shoot skeet, you could've done worse than the figure the older man presented — classic was the only word for it.

The first clay came out of the high house again, and Carlton smashed it. Then the next came from the same direction but at a lower trajectory; the surgeon quickly adjusted and shattered that one as well.

He cocked his head as he turned back toward the crowd, and I noted that there was more applause for him than there had been for Nance — evidently the doctor was a fan favorite.

Evans shot well but barely clipped her first clay with an overenthusiastic shot; she then tagged the second.

Vic carefully placed the plugs back in her ears and stepped up onto the station without a shred of self-consciousness. The trigger hand sat at her side like a coiled spring, her slender fingers flicking every so often, and she carefully loaded the Remington.

The puller regarded her. "Ready?"

My undersheriff's hand relaxed and came up in a graceful arc, snapping the shotgun together and in place, her soft voice once again like a pin dropping. "Pull."

The two clays came from the low tower to her right simultaneously, and Vic peppered them with 12-gauge shot.

Carlton shook his head as he stepped up; he hit his first target but cleanly missed his second shot. I could see him apologizing to Vic as he stepped from the stand.

I watched as Nance coached Evans, but the two-time national champion missed one and we were tied.

There was a brief conversation at the stand, and the pullers and judges got together with Nance and Evans as Vic and Carlton stepped over to where we were.

I smiled at her. "How you feel, deadeye?"

The Terror pushed her cap back and pulled her earplugs. "I'm cool, but I could use a drink."

Nance approached with a couple of judges; Evans was not with them. He leaned on the rail again. "Frank, Connie's graciously elected to step down, and if you're willing to do the same, Miss Moretti and I can go head-to-head Tour Pro style."

The older man stepped to the side. "I'm afraid all I'm doing is holding my partner back, so I'm happy to acquiesce."

Nance smiled and glanced at Vic. "Tour

Pro style then?"

"Fuck yeah." Vic bared her teeth, especially the extended canine. "What's that, anyway?"

Nance didn't say anything but turned away toward the range.

Carlton watched him go and then shook his head. "You shoot multiple times. They'll place a row of rounds in front of you and as you fire, you break the shotgun down and fire again, sometimes as many as a dozen rounds instead of the two."

She studied me. "Like tactical with pop-ups?"

"Pretty much."

She snapped a finger and pointed before walking away. "Hendrick's — stirred, not shaken."

Chief Nutter and Carlton both looked at me. "Dirty martini, her favorite. Olives with the juice and onions."

Carlton nodded. "Fighting scurvy, is she?"

Nutter watched Vic's nether parts as she stalked toward the shooting stand. "Somehow, I don't think scurvy would stand a chance."

Gentlemanliness be damned again, Nance strode to the platform and stood, blocking Vic's way as my undersheriff casually placed the butt of the Remington in her cupped hands again, the barrels lying easily against her shoulder.

It was easy to see why Nance chose this form of shooting for his finale. He handled the mechanics of reloading impressively and didn't miss a single shot until the last set, where he missed the lower clay completely but then caught it with the second shot — scoring an eleven and a half.

There were cheers from the crowd. Like him or not, it was damn fine shooting.

I didn't see how Vic was going to be able to do it.

The Terror ignored Nance's smirk, stepped to the station, and stretched her neck to one side and then the other as I'd seen her do at hundreds of weapons qualification shoots down at the academy in Douglas.

Nance moved to the far side of the narrow table but then stopped and stood there, just barely in Vic's line of sight. I waited for the attendants or judges to make him move, but they didn't.

Vic's hand dropped again and twitched once.

The puller seemed hesitant but then asked, "Ready?"

She gave the barely perceptible nod and then brought her hand up in the elegant arc again, slipping two of the shells from the table, loading the shotgun, and raising the barrels in one infinitely supple move. Her head dropped like a mongoose ready to strike, and her lips pursed. "Pull."

Like a machine-fed shotgun, she adjusted her aim, dropping the barrels and reloading after each twin pieces of destruction, moving down the course like a ballerina working the barre. The closer to her opponent she came, the wider his eyes grew. Science was meeting art, and art was kicking science's ass.

I've seen some shooting in my life, but I don't recall ever seeing an exhibition like the one Vic was giving just now. There was a rhythm to her that was otherworldly, a matching of flesh and metal resulting in a series of explosions that echoed off the hills like a paradiddle of percussive beats. You could feel the crowd leaning forward as her momentum grew until two of the next-to-last targets dove with the wind. There was the briefest of pauses as she dipped the barrel, but the Terror's aim was true and the clays exploded as if she'd reached out with a talon and crushed them one by one.

I'd like to think that Nance jarred the table by accident. Vic's last two shells fell over and, like a ship hitting an iceberg or a dirigible bursting into flames or two loco-motives slamming into each other on an elevated trestle, they rolled off the edge of the table in agonizingly slow motion.

The crowd buzzed, but without pause, Vic cracked open the Remington with one hand and stooped but could catch only one shell, which she slipped into the breech, slamming the 12 gauge erect. The first target sailed, having been caught by the wind again, but the other launched in a direct trajectory, and I'm sure the Terror was smiling that subtle little smile that made only one wrinkle at the corner of her perfect mouth as they crossed paths just above the bead sight on the Remington.

She blew both of them out of the sky with the single shot.

9

As I slipped the champion into the bed in our room at the Hulett Motel, she slurred her words just a touch, having succumbed to her fifth dirty martini. "Get in here wi'me."

I sat beside her. "I can't. I have to go find Dog."

She clutched my arm. "He can climb in'ere, too."

I glanced at the smallish bed. "I don't think there's room."

She stuck her tongue in my ear. "You can have som'ma my room."

"I just want to make sure he and Henry are all right, considering the company they're keeping."

Releasing me just a little, she turned her head and smiled at the monstrous loving cup on the nightstand that barely left room for the lamp. "You seen my trophy?"

I pulled away a little and nodded. "Yep, I have."

"I won that."

"I know you did."

" 'Ma helluva shot."

"Yep, you are."

"Get in'ere."

I stood, her hand still holding my wrist. "I'll be right back."

She ran her tongue along the web of my thumb and curled her legs. "Promise?"

"Yep."

Her eyes strayed to the nightstand again. "Y'see my trophy?"

"Yep."

"I won that."

I pulled my hand loose and retreated, not quite sure if I could turn my back on her just yet. "I'll be back."

"Promise?"

"Yep."

She slumped into her pillow with a smile, her eyes closing. " 'Kay."

Slipping the door shut behind me, I stepped out into the cool, clear air of night. It had been quite a party up at the Golf Club at Devils Tower clubhouse.

And as far as I knew, it was still going on.

Nance had taken the loss better than I'd thought him capable, and the bar had been open to all. I'd had a beer, but the Terror, flushed with victory, had imbibed like a sailor on shore leave; actually, she put them to epic shame.

I made the corner of the motel in time to see the two miscreants who'd attempted to steal Rosalie, Henry's motorcycle, now attempting to find the hood release on Lola, which was parked next to the Pennington County sheriff's Tahoe. "You know, you guys need to find another line of work. Honestly."

Eddy the Viking was the first to speak. "We were just wanting to look at the engine. It's got the 430 Interceptor motor in it, right?"

I shrugged. "I guess. I'm not much of a car guy, but the man who owns it is, and if he catches you monkeys fooling around with his vehicle, he's likely to kick your asses so long you'll be wearing them as hats."

They looked at me blankly.

"Your asses."

They still stared at me.

"As hats."

They didn't move.

"Never mind." I walked past them, deciding that I'd rather take in the air than drive the two blocks with the trailer in tow. I pointed at Irl Engelhardt's cruiser. "Get out of here before I lock the two of you in the back of that thing with the radio tuned to the rap station in Rapid at high volume."

I crossed the motorcycle-ridden street, passed the art gallery at the corner, and, cutting through a beer garden to the alley behind the Ponderosa, tried my best to get there without getting anything spilled on me.

I sidestepped around a row of bikes and could see a large crowd. There was a lot of yelling, which even conquered a really bad garage-band rendition of "What's Your Name." As I got closer and could see over the rabble, I caught a glimpse of a tattooed, platinum-haired man in one of those blue service-station jackets, who was pushing someone hard enough to collapse his rib cage.

Figuring there were enough people around so I really didn't have to get involved, I slid along the side in hopes of making it to the Ponderosa.

As I took another step, I could see between the two guys in front of me that the pugilist who was losing the battle was none other than Patrolman Corbin Dougherty. Frozen for a split second, I watched the rookie's eyes get wide as the biker kept after him.

It was pretty much every police officer's

nightmare — to be surrounded in unsure territory with no backup and facing a much greater physical opponent. There were two equalizers, however — that piece of metal on his shirt and the even bigger piece of metal in the holster at his side. The first one having failed, I watched as he began reaching for the second.

There was a crate of some kind behind me, so I stepped up and pushed off it between the two guys in front of me. I rolled my right fist like a cudgel and brought it down in a full swing with all my body weight into a blow that came from above, striking the antagonist in the side of the head like a falling tree limb.

The guy looked like he had a hard head, so I didn't figure it would kill him, but it might've come close. He dropped like a poleaxed steer, pausing for only a second at his knees and then falling the rest of the way onto the gravel surface of the alley, face first.

I landed somewhat clumsily but then righted and turned a full circle just to make sure that no one was going to rush me in retaliation, even going so far as to look for a little reinforcement from Brady Post, the ATF agent, but he wasn't there. Everybody looked a little stunned, but none of them appeared to be ready to make a move, so I turned and focused on the patrolman. Dougherty sat there with his opponent lying between his legs as I held my left hand out, quietly flexing the feeling back into my rapidly swelling right. "Fight's over."

He took my hand, and I pulled him up as he wiped some blood from the corner of his mouth with the back of a wrist. "I'd say."

Quickly dusting him off, I turned to look at the assembled pack of onlookers who were just now getting their bearings, their challenger still doing his best impression of a biker-skin rug. "Break it up and get out of here before we run all of you in."

One of the ones in the back shouted, "You some kind of cop or something?"

I zeroed him out as he tried to duck behind another guy, and I held up my badge wallet, letting it fall open to display my own piece of trusty metal. "Absaroka County sheriff. Beat it. Now."

There was more mumbling and a few veiled threats, but they moved off, leaving the tattooed man still lying facedown and showing no signs of getting up. So much for the camaraderie of the road. He was breathing, but I stooped anyway and felt the pulse at the flames inked at his neck, satisfied that he was still among us.

I looked back up at Dougherty. "What happened?"

He shook his head. "I was walking down the alley, and he ran his shoulder into me, so I turned around and said something. It just got stupid from there."

I nodded, thinking something about the cold-cocked fighter looked vaguely familiar; I pulled him over by the shoulder, revealing the somewhat warped head of Billy ThE Kiddo. "Oh, hell."

"You two know each other?"

"We met earlier today." I glanced around for some help as I checked him for any weapons. "I don't suppose you could call in some backup to help you get him to the jail?"

"Why can't you?"

I stood, convinced that Billy wasn't carrying. "Because he's got a restraining order against me."

The patrolman glanced at the man at our feet. "I can see why." He pulled the mic from his shoulder and called it in, then turned to look at me. "Get out of here."

I started off. "You bet."

He called out as I hurried away, "And thanks!"

The Pondo was crowded, but I saw two of

my favorite life-forms seated on a bench in the far right-hand corner. I threaded my way through the throng and was glad to see that Lola wasn't there.

Finally reaching the elevated cable spool that served as a table, I slid onto a stool opposite the Cheyenne Nation and my faithful companion, who smiled and wagged his massive tail. The Bear looked up from what I assumed was a sparkling water with a lime slice and then at the half-filled wineglass in front of Dog. "I am attempting to get your dog drunk, but he is not cooperating."

I caught the eye of a waitress, gestured toward a Rainier at an adjacent table, and then turned back to the two of them. I reached over and ruffled the hair behind Dog's ear. "He's generally smarter than we are."

"I heard Vic won the shooting competition."

"She did."

"Is that what took you so long?"

"Well, that and we were running interference with the highway patrol for you and Lola."

"So, that is what took so long."

"That . . . and a few other things." I glanced back toward the alley. "Do you think it's a hundred yards between here and that beer garden on the corner?"

He studied the swollen knuckles on my right hand. "Why?"

"Nothing." I turned back, tucked my fist under the table, and studied him, taking in his lackluster demeanor. "What's up?"

He brushed his hair away from his face and taking a piece of paper from his shirt pocket, tossed it on the table between us.

"What's this?"

He said nothing but sipped his sparkling water and eyed me as I picked it up and unfolded it.

At the top were the printed words DNA Genetic Ancestry, University of Arizona. I read down and could see that the registry listed Native American first, Plains Indian second, and Northern Cheyenne third, to be specific. "Yours?"

He set the glass back down. "Bodaway's."

I stared at him. "I thought you were sure."

"So did I."

"I thought he was Southwest — Apache."

"So did I."

Reading the rest of the sheet, I could see that the breakdown of the young man's heredity and genealogy matched Henry's very closely except for the part that was Polish or Mazovia by way of Kujawy. The date of the testing center's findings was less than a month earlier. "She did this in anticipation of meeting you here?"

"So it would appear."

I flipped the piece of paper back on the table as the waitress came over and set the Rainier down. "Buck fifty."

I handed her two and waved her away. "It's just a piece of paper that says you and he share a genetic ancestry, but it isn't absolute proof that he's yours."

"No, we would need a blood test for that."

I spun the paper around and looked at the registered blood type, O — the same as Henry but still a pretty common type. "Does she want you to take a test?"

"No."

"You should. Do it and then you'll know — till then she's messing with your head."

He sipped his water and, leaning over, nudged Dog with his shoulder, whereupon the beast reciprocated by licking the side of the Bear's head. "What if he is mine?"

"Then you have a son."

He smiled. "Is that the way it works, Grandpa?"

"No, well yep. . . . But it's worse than that, Henry. Vic talked to the doctors at Rapid and their considered opinion is that Bodaway's injuries are serious enough that they don't think he's coming back."

His big hand covered the bottom of his face, and he mumbled through his fingers, his eyes still on me. "No chance?"

"They seemed to indicate none."

He breathed a laugh that would've frozen sagebrush. "That would be about right. I would have had a son for thirty years, and the weekend I was to first meet him he would go into a coma with no hope of awakening."

"Do a blood test."

He let his hand fall to his lap. "I am not much of a test taker these days."

"So, what are you going to do?"

He looked away. "Go by my feelings."

"Just so you know, that's usually what you warn me not to do."

"Am I usually right?"

"Only ninety-nine percent of the time."

"So, we have an obvious fact."

We talked for another twenty minutes until I felt the pressure of a revolver muzzle pressed into my right ear and heard a very angry voice. "Did you hit me?"

Fortunately, Henry's first move was to grab Dog's collar or else the hundred-and-fifty-pound brute would've launched off the bench to sink his teeth into the arm of the individual I figured was holding the .38 in my ear. Instead, Dog pulled back his lips in a promise.

I raised the beer and took a sip, attempting my best Leo Gordon. "Have a seat, Kiddo, and I'll buy you a beer."

He nudged the two-inch barrel farther into my ear canal with his left hand and repeated the question. "Did you hit me, motherfucker?"

Setting the Rainier down, I slowly turned, and he traced the muzzle across my cheek until it now rested on the bridge of my nose. His face was red, and all I could think was how did he get away from Dougherty and where did he get the sidearm after I'd checked him. "Why, yes, I did."

If it was possible, his face grew even redder, and I was calculating what my next tactical move would be. The saloon was crowded, and I didn't want anyone else to be hurt, which meant I would have to kick him at the same time I grabbed the revolver, shoving it upward, flipping it, and pushing it into his body so that if he did pull the trigger, the only one who would be hit with a round would be himself.

"You sucker punched me, cocksucker?"

It was a risky business, but the alternatives weren't so great.

I was about to make my move when a hand shot out, bent Billy ThE's up and back, snatched the revolver out of his hand before either of us could breathe, then cried havoc and let slip the Dog of War.

When primates are properly motivated, we can move with the best of them, and Billy ThE Kiddo was highly motivated. Scrambling backward, he pulled a neighboring table down in front of him, which succeeded in deflecting Dog to the right just long enough for Kiddo to turn and lunge for the alley.

Most everybody in the bar, realizing that a were-monster had been loosed, vacated the immediate area in what I assumed would be an attempt to acquire torches and pitchforks.

Having the advantage of four legs, Dog caught his balance, turned to the left, and shot for the alley where ThE was desperately attempting to flee.

Me? I sipped my beer.

Henry examined the revolver. "Odd gun." He handed it to me. "Consider it a gift."

I took the thing without looking.

There was a great deal of noise from the passageway where the two antagonists had disappeared, and then one agonizing scream. "I guess I'd better go see about that."

Henry sipped his sparkling water and

studied the paper on the table. "I suppose you should."

It was about then that I looked down and saw the pink grip of the .38 revolver.

"Where did he get this gun?"

Dougherty looked at the colorful sidearm. "He had a gun?"

Holding the pistol out to him, I glanced around the Hulett Police Department's empty office. "When Kiddo stormed into the bar, he shoved the barrel of this in my ear."

"You searched him. I figured you would've found it if he'd been carrying."

"That's right, I would have. He must've gotten it after you got him up and loaded him into the car. Who else was there?"

"Nobody."

"Who helped you load him?"

"Nutter But— . . . Chief Nutter and a highway patrolman."

"You didn't cuff him?"

"I did, but when I got him back to the jail here, and was walking him in, he was suddenly loose and elbowed me in the face."

"You're lucky you're alive." I gestured toward the holding cell. "Nobody came near him, touched him? Anything?"

"No. Wait." He thought about it. "When I

got him over here there were a bunch of bikers out front."

"Men, women?"

"Both. They whooped and hollered and patted him on the back as I was bringing him in." He studied my face. "You're thinking . . ."

"Was Lola one of them?"

"I don't think so, but maybe. I'm not sure. Why?"

I twirled the revolver. "Because this is hers."

We walked to the back where an EMT was tending to Billy ThE Kiddo as he lay on his stomach on a bunk, his left wrist attached to a chain support with a pair of cuffs, and his pants pulled down, exposing his perforated posterior. "I'm gonna own this town when I'm through with you fuckers."

I knelt beside him. "Just a little more piercing done. What's the harm?"

"Fuck you. You aren't supposed to be anywhere near me. I've got a restraining order."

"I don't think that restraining order works when you push gun barrels in my ear."

He grimaced and cried out as the EMT continued to stitch him up. "You hit me!"

I ignored the outburst and held up the pink revolver. "This gun."

He stared at it and then at me. "I never seen that gun before."

"I've got a whole bar full of witnesses who saw you holding it in my ear before my friend Henry took it away from you."

"Yeah, and I've got an entire alley full of people who saw you punch me in the head."

I sounded bored, even to myself. "As you resisted arrest and attempted to visit grievous harm on Officer Dougherty here." I leaned in closer. "ThE, ol' buddy, where did you get the gun? You see, I know who owns it — and I'm betting you do, too. Now, if she gave it to you, that'll make it a lot easier in that I won't have to worry about where she might be if you took it away from her."

"Go fuck yourself."

I stood and gestured to get the EMT's attention. "When you get done, you can sew up this end, too."

Walking back into the bull pen, I turned to Corbin. "Put a general out for Lola and that gold Caddy; she doesn't strike me as the type to go around unarmed."

He sat in a dejected manner and pulled the old stand-up mic toward him. "I screwed up pretty bad, huh?"

"Not really. So far the only one who got hurt in all of this is the human Kong in there." I shrugged as another yelp emanated from the holding cell. "And I'd say he deserved it."

"What are you going to do?"

I spread my hands. "Where in the world is Lola Wojciechowski?"

The Bear and Dog were waiting for me outside, leaning on the MRAP as a group of bikers observed the two of them from a distance. "Are they going to have to put ThE down?"

"I wish."

"What is next?"

I held up the revolver. "Any ideas?"

He glanced down the hill at the throngs of black leather, his eyes narrowing. "Is there a pool table in this town?"

I stepped back toward the office door and yanked it open. "Corbin, is there a pool table around here somewhere?"

"Capt'n Ron's Rodeo Bar, in the back past the dance floor."

"Got it." I shut the door and gestured down the hill. "Conveniently located a hundred feet that way."

The Bear started off with Dog. "I wonder, in the course of recent developments, if they will allow pets?"

We stopped at a large barn door opening

into another outside beer garden. "I keep telling you, he's a service dog."

The bouncer at the door, an amiable-looking cowboy almost as wide as he was tall, asked, "And what service does he provide?"

"Bomb detection."

He shook his head. "Works for me — there are plenty of them going off in there."

Dodging inside with the beast, we angled to the right and could see Lola taking a shot and stretching across the far-side pocket, revealing more than a little décolletage to the admiring members of the sporting life.

"Lola."

Even I was taken aback by the thunder of the Cheyenne Nation's voice in the raucous noise and music of the filled-to-the-gills bar.

She took a second to steady herself and then took the shot with her custom cue, a banking roller that sunk the two ball in the farthest corner. She stood, cocked a leg, and rested her hip against the table as Big Easy, the guard-biker we had last met at the hospital, stepped into our line of sight, speaking in a slight Samoan accent: "Problem?"

I held the revolver up. "A pink one."

"Not your color, my man."

I nodded past him toward Lola. "No, but

it's hers. Tell her we'll meet her outside and not to make me come looking for her or I'll see she gets seven months of high-security, low-amenity lodging in Sundance."

As we started to turn and walk out, the big and easy Samoan reached over and touched Henry's shoulder, the arm attached having powered the biker's head into the drywall of the Rapid City Regional Hospital. "I know you?"

The Bear smiled the one-crease-at-the-corner-of-his-mouth smile. "Momentarily."

We waited by the door longer than I would've liked, but she finally came sauntering out and stood with her arms crossed. "I'd like my gun back."

I glanced at the revolver tucked in my belt. "You mind telling me how he got it?"

"How who got it?"

"Star of stage, screen, and reality TV, Billy ThE Kiddo."

"And who the hell is Billy ThE Kiddo?"

"A good friend of your son's."

She wrapped her arms around herself and came closer. "Define good."

"Bodaway called him about seventeen times before the accident — if indeed it was an accident."

She straightened up and dropped her arms. "Look, I honestly don't know what you're talking about, let alone *who* you're talking about. You put the gun inside my purse in my car's glove box the last time I saw it."

"Your car, this gun . . . you're kind of lax with your possessions."

She glanced at the Cheyenne Nation. "What can I say? I'm just a material girl in a material world."

The crypt voice returned beside me with enough timber to fill the Black Forest. "Lola, there are lives at stake."

She snorted. "That's funny, 'cause that's what I've been trying to convince you of for days." She hooked her thumbs into the belt loops of her jeans and turned coquettishly to me. "Imagine my surprise: I came here looking for a red knight in shining armor and all I find is a Watson to your Sherlock Holmes. Feel free to put my gun back where you found it." With this final pronounce-ment she turned and rejoined the swarm in the bar with her hands raised above her head, snapping her fingers, swaying and singing to Jerry Lee Lewis's "C.C. Rider."

We stood there for a while before he handed me the leash.

"I'm starting to see how this relationship didn't work out."

"Yes."

"I'm sorry."

He glanced at me. "For what?"

"Trying to get you involved in this. It was stupid, and I didn't really know what I was getting you into."

"She is something of a contagion."

I nodded and rubbed Dog's head. "Let's go get you a blood test at the Rapid hospital tomorrow and put this all to rest — then we can head home."

"Deal." We turned and began walking the rest of the way down the hill, stopping at the corner and waiting for another assemblage of motorcycles to go by. "It is funny, but I was just getting used to the idea of being a father, even if it was with Lola." I studied him, and he began talking again. "I watch you with Cady."

"Well, she's yours, too." I sighed. "Sometimes I think she's more yours than mine."

"But she is not."

We crossed the street, and I thought I'd better lighten the subject matter. "Starting to have regrets concerning your ill-spent youth?"

He smiled. "No, no. I just sometimes wonder."

"What your life could've been like?"

"Yes."

"Take my advice — don't do that." Pull-

250

ing up Dog in front of the Ponderosa Café, I turned and looked at him. "Regret is my turf, buddy."

He smiled a little more broadly. "Sorry."

"You were right about steering clear of her, and I drove us right back in there."

We began walking again. "It's your maiden-in-distress syndrome; you have a difficult time resisting."

I laughed. "Yep, but I'm starting to get the idea that Lola is the kind that ties people to the railroad tracks."

"One of the disadvantages of operating in the contemporary American West is that not all the bad guys have handlebar mustaches."

We crossed the last street toward the motel and walked across the parking lot toward the cabins on the end near the river, where we saw Lola's gold '66 Caddy parked on the grass. The mist from the Belle Fourche almost hid the thing, but the moonlight glistened off the chrome and quarter panels like jewelry.

"Evidently, she also has unique ideas on parking." I pulled the pink-gripped revolver from my belt and handed it to him. "Here, you can put it in her glove box."

"You are giving it back to her?"

I jiggled my jacket where the five rounds rattled in my pocket. "Empty."

He palmed the thing and started off toward the car, only to stop.

I stood there looking after him in the half-mist. "Something?"

He gestured with an open hand, bidding me to follow. "Someone. In the car."

We both walked over to the convertible. ATF field agent Brady Post was sitting in the passenger seat, his head turned to the side with his eyes closed and his mouth gaping open, looking like he was snoring and dead asleep. On closer inspection, however, he was simply dead, a hole in his chest.

10

We couldn't decide what we were going to do with the Caddy, so we leaned against it.

"Need I remind you that what we have here is a dead federal agent?"

"I'm aware of that, but I'm also aware that if this goes public, whoever did it is going to go to ground and we'll never find out what was happening here, let alone who's responsible."

"What do you suggest?"

"They have a vehicle shop at the Hulett Police Department."

"The tin shed?" He studied me. "You want to move both the body and the car as well?"

I glanced over my shoulder toward the bridge, where traffic had appeared to have disappeared, it being the wee hours. "We drive him up there, and then I'll contact McGroder, the AIC in Denver."

Henry looked back at the dead agent and

shrugged.

"We'll say we were trying to maintain the integrity of the crime scene."

"By driving it across town."

I held a palm up, feeling for imaginary drops. "It might rain."

He shook his head and reached for Dog's leash. "Do you have gloves?"

I pulled a well-worn pair that I used to shoot with from my jacket. "If you would, put Dog in the room and try and not wake up Vic. I'll meet you at the cop shop."

He inclined his head. "You are not going to give me a ride?"

I skimmed off my jacket as I walked toward Post and carefully placed it over the agent's head. "You were the one getting squeamish."

"I'm over that now; pick me up in the motel lot." And off he went with Dog.

I watched the two of them walk away and then turned back to Brady Post, kneeled down, and looked at him. "What did you get into?" I rested my chin on my arm and studied the dead man, a dull ache starting to form behind my eyes. "And what was it that was important enough to kill you for?" I leaned in close and did something I rarely did. "I'm sorry, but if I'm going to get whoever did this, I'm not going to be able to follow protocol." I patted his arm and gave it a squeeze. "But then, you didn't strike me as a by-the-book kind of guy."

I climbed in the car, started her up, and gently spun the wheels. Easing the accelerator, I backed onto the parking lot and headed for the area between the two buildings. When I pulled on the headlights, the two car thieves were standing in my way.

The shady one who was with the Viking was the first to speak. "Where are you going with Lola's car?"

"I'm parking it in a safe place, as opposed to down by the river."

He continued to talk as Eddy fidgeted. "Does she know that?"

"Everyone in the Western Hemisphere's been driving this car this week, and you guys are going to question me?" I rubbed my hand across my face. "Who are you, anyway?"

"A friend of Lola's."

"Really?" The thick-timbered voice came from behind them, low but loud enough to straighten their backs. The Cheyenne Nation draped an arm over each man. "Because I am a friend of Lola, too, and I do not remember seeing either of your names on the guest list."

They were silent, staring at the asphalt as

the weight of his arms curved their spines.

"I will tell you what — when we see Lola next we will tell her you said hello. Eddy the Viking and . . . ?" He hugged the other man, but he didn't appear to want to speak. "And?" I watched as Henry's forearm muscles bunched and the man's face was drawn in close to the Bear's.

"Phil Vesco."

Henry loosened his grip. "Eddy and Phil went up the hill. . . . I will be sure to recommend you to Lola for your sterling service."

I watched as he undraped himself and walked around the car. After slowly getting into the backseat behind the cloaked man in the front, he waved good-bye to the two road agents.

"He's what?"

"He's dead."

Corbin Dougherty's voice rose as he unlocked the steel doors leading to the maintenance shed behind the department's main structure. "Who killed him?"

"We're not clear on that, at least not yet."

He pulled the doors back and flipped the lights on inside. "He's a federal agent?"

"Yep."

"How do you know?"

I turned my head, and Henry and I looked

at each other for that briefest of moments as I pulled the Cadillac into the two-bay garage. "He introduced himself to us."

Corbin rapidly closed the doors. "Do they normally do that?"

"Not generally." I climbed out, and Henry flipped the seat and followed. "But the other night at the motel he badged us; he's ATF and working on some kind of gun-running scheme that Bodaway Torres might've been involved with in Arizona."

"Our Bodaway Torres?"

"Yep."

His face was the picture of bewilderment. "Smuggling guns into Wyoming?"

Henry and I looked at each other again. "Kind of sounds like coal to Newcastle, doesn't it? Look, maybe it's not that particularly, but something is going on and the only way we'll find out what it is is by keeping agent Post's death under wraps."

He looked at the enormous car and the dead man. "For how long?"

"I'll ask Mike Novo to get a cashier and some bag boys up from DCI in Cheyenne and have them begin a preliminary while I get ahold of the agency in Denver. Maybe my friends in the FBI can get some information from the ATF and we can get a little more to go on."

"I could see them having that response to me personally, but what in the world could they possibly have against the horse I rode in on?"

"Was that an official response from the ATF?"

Agent-in-Charge Mike McGroder laughed on the phone from Denver. "Pretty much. It would be different if we were all on the same team, but you know, Walt — the federal government is more like a loose coalition of warring tribes."

"Did they even admit that he was theirs?"

"No, and with the number of CIs surrounding them, it's going to be like a minefield as to who knew what he was and who didn't."

"CIs?"

"Confidential Informants. That's the way these guys get in and it's how they get their information."

"What are the chances that he's not ATF at all?"

"Difficult to say, but if he's out of the Phoenix area, I can make some calls to the RAC and the ASAC. I know the guy in charge down there and he might be a little more motivated, especially if I tell him one of his agents is dead."

I continued to advance my education. "RAC?"

"Resident Agent-in-Charge."

"ASAC?"

"Assistant Special Agent-in-Charge."

"Is that what you guys do in your spare time — sit around and make up acronyms?" I sighed. "I'm trying to keep this from becoming a circus."

"I understand you don't want this to turn into a know-and-go, but the ATF's Special Response Team is going to want its pound of flesh on this, Walt." There was a pause. "With a vengeance."

I looked out the Hulett Police Department's windows, the outside as black as a mine except for the ghostly white fender of the Pequod. "That's fine, but you know as well as I do that if the feds come in here in force, then whoever did it is going to fold up the tents."

There was a pause. "That puts a lot of pressure on you to find out who did it before that happens."

"Yep, it does." I hung up the phone and turned to look at Henry.

"The game is afoot?"

I sighed. "I wish you'd stop doing that."

259

Dougherty sat in another chair and looked at us. "What now?"

I glanced at the clock on the wall. "The DCI crew should be here in a few hours."

"Before eight?"

"I doubt it. Why?"

Incredulous, he looked at me. "Because then my chief shows up, and I have to explain what a Cadillac and a dead ATF agent are doing in our maintenance shed."

"Blame it on me."

He nodded his head emphatically. "I intend to."

"Well, in answer to your question, I think one of the key elements in the investigation is back in your holding cell." I glanced at Corbin. "He is still back in your holding cell, right?"

"Who?"

"Kiddo."

"Oh, him. Yeah, he's back there." My thought began dawning on him. "Why, are you thinking he's part of this?"

"I don't know, but there's a connection between him and Bodaway and a connection between Bodaway and a dead ATF agent. I'm thinking we take advantage of having the owner-proprietor of The Chop Shop in the holding cell and snoop around and see what he and Bodaway might've had

260

going on over there." I shrugged. "And we can take the Pennington County sheriff's unit back to him; as far as I know, Vic's race car is still in their impound lot."

Henry and I gathered up as Corbin threw me the keys to the Tahoe. "What do I tell the chief, other than it's all your fault?"

"That should do it for now." I paused at the door. "If we don't make it back before the DCI guys get here, just park their vehicle in front of the shed door and try and get them in there as quietly as possible." I reached out and handed him the pink-gripped revolver. "The first thing I want to know is the caliber of the weapon that did the deed."

He stared at the S&W. "You think it was this?"

"If it is, your friend in the back better get used to eating off trays."

The Bear was already in Engelhardt's Tahoe, and I fired the thing up, drifted out of town, and then, gaining speed, turned on the emergency lights.

He buckled his seat belt and settled in. "We are official now?"

"For better or worse."

"Are we going to return the sheriff's car or break and enter first?"

I accelerated toward Moorcroft, figuring

the more highway we had, the faster we could go. "In my experience, when you are committing a misdemeanor it's better not to do it in a purloined police car." I left the sirens off so that we could talk. "Why kill Post?"

He answered with the obvious response. "They found out he was ATF."

"We could find out where he was staying and see if he left any notes on what he was working on." I took the on-ramp and headed east. "Corbin had a point, though. Why would he reveal himself to us? In my experience, those guys are loath to do anything like that with anybody."

"Perhaps he was worried."

"Turns out he was right to be."

"Whatever he was looking for he discovered it in Hulett."

I thought about it. "Billy ThE Kiddo is involved in this. I'm not sure how, but he's involved."

"How long can you hold him?"

"As long as Nutter Butter is with us. I can press charges myself, if need be, and we can get the court to set bail so high that he has to mortgage his motorcycle shop to walk."

"Well, we know he will not be *sitting* comfortably for some time."

When we got to the Pennington County

Jail, it was still dark, and my eyes were feeling like a sand pit. I pulled the sheriff's car into the entryway of the impound lot as a young deputy, assuming his boss was arriving, snapped to attention in the booth at the gate.

I rolled down the window as he approached. "Hey, troop, we need to make a trade."

He stared at the sheriff's unit. "For what?"

I nodded toward the muscle car nearest his booth. "The Duke of Hazzard in there."

He looked dejected as he went back and retrieved a clipboard from his tiny lodgings. "Bummer. I was kind of hoping that one would go to auction."

There were three streetlights in the parking lot of The Chop Shop, making it impossible to get anywhere near the front of the place without appearing center stage.

"Remind me again why we are doing this?"

"It's the only outstanding lead we've got."

He studied the building in front of us. "Name the un-outstanding ones."

"Lola, which seems to be a dead end other than the fact that we are in possession of her vehicle."

"Along with a dead agent."

263

I ignored him. "Then we have Bodaway himself, who is in the hospital in a coma."

"There is the rich guy who lives on the golf course."

I nodded. "Yep, but I'm thinking that's just a personal thing between Bodaway and the daughter." I stared at the building across the lighted expanse of parking lot. "And the establishment in front of us."

"I think we should go around back."

"Agreed." I fired up the Challenger and listened as its exhaust trumpeted, heralding our every move. "I hate this car."

Taking the long way, we put in an extra block with the lights off and came up on a chain-link fence in the back enclosing what looked to be a salvage yard with a fair amount of rusting American chrome.

"I do not see a gate."

I looked up at the spiraling razor wire that looped its way around the perimeter. "I'm not climbing that thing."

He gestured toward a parking spot next to the building. "Slip in there."

I did as he said and watched as he whirred the window down and shimmied out, first standing on the sill and then the top. There was a brief thump as the sheet metal bent, and then he disappeared.

I turned off the obnoxious engine and sat

there thinking about how we were supposed to be heading back home today, but that the death of Brady Post had changed all of that. We were now committed in numerous ways, and if I didn't play this correctly, I was placing my friend, my brothers in blue, and myself in a prickly situation with the feds. I hoped that while we were involved in our covert operations, Mike McGroder was getting information that might make the nature of Post's investigation more clear.

I heard more noise as the Bear walked on the roof of the cycle shop; then the chain-link rattled, and I turned to see Henry standing on the other side of the fence. I slipped out of the Dodge and joined him, still looking for a gate and still not seeing one.

"There is an electronic security system."

"You're kidding. In this dump?"

"There is a seven-space keypad for an entry code at the back door."

"We're never going to be able to guess the code."

"In my experience you get three tries within a one minute period before the alarms go off and alert the authorities."

"So, our odds are three in, say, a million?" He shrugged.

"I hate to sound old-school, but what

about just breaking a window?"

He turned and walked toward the back door. "If they went to the trouble of installing a keypad, they probably included the windows in said system."

Feeling in my jacket for Bodaway's cell phone, I whispered after him, "You want me to call Corbin and see if we can get Kiddo's birth date or phone number?"

He didn't answer but studied the keypad and then punched in some numbers; evidently, we were now on the clock. He stood there for a moment, and then there was a soft buzz and the sound of a latch being thrown. He pushed open the door and walked in.

Unprepared for this development, I skittered around the exterior of the building, looking all the world like a felon, and soon found him holding open the front door to allow me entry. "What the heck?"

"The Harley-Davidson Motorcycle Company was incorporated on September 17, 1907."

I slid in, and he closed the door behind me. "Hmm . . . 9171907. I'll be damned."

"What one man can invent, another can discover."

"Oh, shut up." I followed as we moved through the office back into the bays of the

266

old service station.

"I wish we had a flashlight."

I pulled a mini Maglite from my hunting jacket.

"What else do you have in there?"

I held up three fingers. "Be prepared."

He took the flashlight and directed it toward the bike that Kiddo had been working on, focusing on what looked like modifications around the gas tank. "What do you think he was doing?"

The Cheyenne Nation stooped, carefully reached under a lip near the back of the tank, and, pulling it up, revealed a hidden compartment about half the size of a small shoe box. "The seams would be covered by a leather strap that goes across the tank."

"Drugs?"

"I do not know. Leaping to conclusions before one has the facts is the mark of a true amateur."

"I warned you about that Sherlock Holmes stuff." We studied the tiny space. "It has to be drugs."

"Need I remind you, Agent Post was investigating guns."

"What gun could be so important that you couldn't just carry it in a saddlebag or on your person?"

He straightened and sighed, as perplexed

as I was. "I do not know that, either."

We moved past the vehicle bay where there was a newer addition and a door that read PRIVATE that was padlocked. I studied the thing. "Too bad we don't have a key."

Henry pulled down a pair of bolt cutters with three-foot-long handles from a tool rack on the wall and stepped past me. He placed the clasp of the lock between the jaw-like blades. "This should do the trick."

Before I could say anything, he bit the thing in two, and we both watched as the lock fell on the floor.

I picked it up and stared at him. "How do we explain this?"

He shrugged and pushed open the door. "We do not; we simply take the lock with us and let them think somebody either lost it or did not secure it."

Shaking my head, I stuffed the padlock in my pocket, walked inside, and scanned the walls as we went deeper into a world I'd hoped didn't exist.

The extension that had been added on to the back was poured concrete with re-inforced metal beams above — a bunker, in more ways than one. The walls were fes-tooned with Nazi memorabilia and black-and-white photos of Hitler, Goebbels, Goering, Himmler, and Franz Stangl, Paul

Blobel, Josef Kramer, and Reinhard Heydrich, to name a few of the other maniacs. There were propaganda posters for the Third Reich with blond-haired, blue-eyed Nazis extolling the virtues of the party, and more cartoon ones expressing the distrust and loathing of Jews and other so-called mongrel races.

There was a large stage at one end draped with assorted Nazi flags and a podium with a swastika.

Along one wall were event tables stacked high with printouts, paper cutters, and pamphlets supporting the KKK, Aryan Brotherhood, and National Alliance. There were books like *The Turner Diaries,* the self-published, apocalyptic, white-supremacist novel that had been found on Timothy McVeigh, and *The Coming War,* a graphic novel of the same ilk, which came with an accompanying DVD. "Looks like we've stumbled into George Lincoln Rockwell's man cave."

The Bear picked up a copy of *The Coming War* and leafed through it, pausing at a point where the white protagonists were hunting Indians with rifles from open Jeeps. "My oh my."

"I guess they've decided to use comics to speak to their intellectual demographic."

"Hmm." He grunted and stuck the graphic novel and DVD under his arm.

"Think we should take a few samples for the FBI?"

He gathered some more. "I do not think they will be missed."

I glanced around the room, unafraid that my flashlight would be seen since there were no windows. "You know what I don't see?"

"Weapons."

"Yep."

He looked at the tables of propaganda. "I do not know if this is not more dangerous."

"The way a lot of these organizations get operating capital is from drugs."

"And gun sales."

"I've said it before and I'll say it again — you can't carry enough guns on a motorcycle to make it profitable."

I looked around some more but couldn't see any trapdoors in the concrete floor or hidden doors in the walls. "But we'd better get out of here."

The Cheyenne Nation followed, giving the room one more look-over before closing the door behind us. "Why would a Native like Bodaway be trafficking with these people?"

"Maybe he didn't know."

"My experiences lead me to believe that this sort are not very secretive in their political beliefs." He let me out the front and handed me the Nazi propaganda. "I will return the way I came and reset the alarm system."

"See you out back." Skirting around the building, I glanced across the parking lot and didn't see any lights on in the adjacent buildings. Feeling relatively assured, I made the corner at the alley and walked directly into the extended barrel of an S&W .357 Magnum.

"I just wanted you to see how bad planning feels." Engelhardt holstered his revolver. "Got a call about a half hour ago from Mrs. Hirsch, who lives across the way here. She's got an irritable bladder condition and happened to see a large man walking on the roof of this building and another large man entering through the front door."

"Here I thought we were being real stealthy."

"Hard to sneak by an irritable bladder."

"I'm going to have that needlepointed and put on my office wall."

We turned, and I followed him to the alley, where his Tahoe had us boxed in. He watched as Henry set the alarm on the back door, climbed up on the roof, stepped over the razor wire, and lowered himself to the top of the Challenger to join us.

271

"If you don't mind me asking . . ." Irl's voice stayed low but grew harsh. "What the hell do you guys think you're doing?"

The Bear shrugged. "I needed some parts."

I handed the sheriff a few of the pamphlets. "Looks like Kiddo's got his own little cottage industry."

Irl thumbed through the evidence. "Well, shit."

"Our thoughts exactly."

He gestured with the stack of propaganda. "You mind if I keep these?"

"Seeing as it's inadmissible evidence, sure."

The Bear plucked the DVD from the pile. "I would like to take a look at this."

Engelhardt nodded and then opened the driver's-side door of his unit and tossed the stuff onto the passenger seat as I explained what we'd found. He stroked his chin and listened. "So, we've got a guy who's acting as a mule for some neo-Nazis, but we haven't got any idea what it was he was carrying?"

Henry told him about Brady Post.

"Holy shit." He rubbed his chin some more. "ATF, huh?"

"Yes."

"Well then, it's one of three things." He

made a face. "No firearms inside?"

"Nope."

"Then they must have a place somewhere else." He glanced around, taking in the dawn-lit horizon. "Like anywhere in western South Dakota, huh? Well, I've got a file."

"I was hoping you'd say that."

"It sure would be easier if these feds would share their information with us."

"They seem to take that undercover thing pretty seriously."

He shook his head. "But this Brady Post just introduced himself to you guys?"

"To me, but then Henry opened the door and entered the conversation."

Irl shrugged as he slid into his unit. "Let me dig out my files on these shitbirds, and I'll give you a call." He paused. "You know, my uncle was one of the first guys into Buchenwald. He never talked about it except to say one of the buildings they liberated was a stables that was built to hold eighty horses and that they'd had over twelve hundred men in there, five to a bunk. He said the smell was horrific." He sighed. "I'll tell you, if he was still around and knew these turds were in South Dakota, he'd get out his deer rifle and finish the job." My fellow sheriff closed the door behind him and pulled the shiny black Tahoe into the empty streets.

We slid into the Dodge, and I fired up the twin trumpet exhausts, slipping the muscle car into gear and pulling back out onto the main drag. "I'm hungry."

Henry nodded. "I am sleepy."

"We sound like the two dwarfs." Looking for a place to eat, I drove toward Rapid City. "I'll make you a deal: we'll get something and then head back to the motel. I'll wake Vic up and you can have the room."

"When are you going to sleep?"

"When I'm dead."

The food at Ron's, not to be confused with Capt'n Ron's Rodeo Bar, and specifically their world-famous pancakes, was just the thing, but I might've overdone it, ordering a stack as big as dinner plates. "You want some pancakes?"

The Cheyenne Nation was doing his best with an order of biscuits and gravy that looked like it might feed two men and a hungry boy. "You ordered them, you eat them."

I cleaved off another chunk, dipping it in the syrup and forking it into my mouth. "Do you think we should bring something back for Vic?"

"I do not think her stomach will be ready for solid food."

Sipping my coffee, I thought about a more pressing matter. "What do you want to do about Lola?"

He stared at his plate and continued eating. "Meaning?"

"How hard do you want to lean on her?"

He still didn't look up at me. "She has earned as hard as it takes."

"Have you considered that she might just be concerned for the welfare of her son?" His eyes came up and weighed on me. "Just wondering if you've considered it."

"I have and then immediately dismissed it."

"I know she's manipulative."

"You do not know."

We stared at each other. "Look, I know she hurt your feelings, but do you really think she's involved in the criminal element of this investigation?"

His dark eyes went back to the table. "Why not? What, other than her gender, leads you to believe that she is in any way innocent?"

I thought about it. "Umm, not much."

"Thank you." He went back to his meal. "Still . . ."

He carefully put his fork on his plate,

placed his elbows on the edge of the table, and laced his fingers into a single fist. "When I strike you, I would like you to know why."

"I'm just saying —"

"Yes, and you have said it enough." He leaned back in his chair, the picture of restraint, his eyes closed. "You care."

"Yep, I do."

"It is one of your most annoying traits." He opened his eyes, and the weight of them lay upon me like darkness. "Please do not ever lose it."

There was suddenly a strange noise, and I glanced around, his eyes still on me. "It is Bodaway's cell phone in your shirt pocket."

"Oh." I fumbled with the thing and looked at it, a trick I'd picked up from every other person on the planet. "It's the Hulett Police Department. The guys from DCI must've arrived." He picked up his fork and, instead of stabbing me with it, went back to eating.

I hit the button and held the device to my ear. "Howdy."

"Walt, it's Corbin."

"Hey, Deputy Dawg, what's up?"

"He was wired."

"Excuse me?"

"Brady Post, the ATF agent? He was wearing a wire."

11

"Why didn't they find it?"

"Who?"

DCI combed the interior of the Cadillac, the halogen work lights that they had brought with them augmenting those in the Hulett Police annex building. Mike Novo and I were standing in an area draped with plastic sheets where the agent's body now lay.

"The person who killed him."

Mike pushed some hair from his eyes and stared at the dead man. "They didn't look. Whoever shot him just shot him; there's no evidence that he was searched or tampered with after the murder."

I held the device, about half the size of a pack of matches. "This thing actually records?"

He nodded, handing me the thin wire and the mic bud. "Yeah, much smaller now that they're digital, but you still have to have an exterior mic for sound quality. He wasn't recording at the time of his demise, and it was in the inside pocket of his vest with the mic and cord under his shirt and around his neck."

I held the thing up between us. "I don't have to tell you that this is Christmas, right?"

"No, but you do have to tell the ATF."

I turned to look at the woman with the familiar voice. "Hey, T. J."

T. J. Sherwin, the head of DCI's lab unit, trailed numerous nicknames in her wake. I called her the Little Lady, but there were others who referred to her as the Bitch on Wheels, the Wicked Witch of the West, and the Bag Lady, a sobriquet that referred to the defunct supermarket that served as the Wyoming Division of Criminal Investigation's headquarters in Cheyenne — i.e., cashiers and bag boys and bag girls.

"They're going to want these files before anybody else, and in my experience they don't play well and share, at least not without a federal court order."

"Files?"

"Still a dinosaur, I see." She took the recorder from my hand and held it up to a light. "There's a plug-in that transfers the information to a zip drive and then you download it onto a computer in an audio file. You can actually hear it, just like a real phonograph."

I stared at her. "C'mon, Little Lady, help a cowboy out?"

Sherwin glanced at Novo. "Go away."

He stood there smiling.

"Now."

"Oh. Right." He disappeared, and T.J. indicated that I should follow her toward the back of the shop where they had set up an event table with computers and lab equipment.

"Anything on the weapon?"

She handed me back Lola's .38 in a zip-lock bag. "Not this."

"Then what?"

She sat and began attaching cables to the tiny recorder and another thingamajig that attached to a laptop and a small black box, which swallowed a recordable CD. "Forty-gauge semi, probably a Glock, possibly a model 22."

She sat back in the folding chair and studied the freshly bagged gun. "Girlfriend of yours?"

"Henry's."

T. J. glanced past me to where the Bear was leaning against the fender of the De-Ville. "Well, that doesn't narrow the field."

279

"It's Lola's."

Her eyes widened just a bit. "*The* Lola, the one the T-bird is named for?"

"*The* Lola."

"Oh, my."

I took the empty revolver from the bag and stuffed it in my jacket pocket. "It's her son who is in Rapid City Regional Hospital."

"The donor cycle rider?"

I handed her the bag. "Yep."

She tossed it on the table and sighed. "I was wondering what you were doing over here in Crook County."

"Me, too."

She pulled a CD from one of the devices, placed it in a paper cover, and handed it to me. "Just so you know, I have broken numerous state and federal laws by giving you this, so whatever you find, I'd just as soon you listen to it and then destroy it. The ATF will have a copy that's permissible in court as federal evidence, so you've got that to fall back on, but as far as you and I are concerned this CD doesn't exist."

"What CD?" I stuffed it in my jacket. "Anything else I need to know as I attempt to break the big case?"

"He had sex."

"Excuse me?"

280

"The deceased engaged in copulation with a female no more than an hour before his death."

"That's unfortunate."

"For him or her?"

I glanced at the Cheyenne Nation, who was still leaning on the Caddy but now was looking at us. "Both."

"So, who else could he have fucked?"

I made a gesture for her to lower her voice as the waitress at the Ponderosa Café brought her another medicinal Bloody Mary. "Oh, how about any of the thousands of biker bunnies bouncing around here this week?"

My undersheriff sipped the drink from a straw, the liquid perfectly matching her fingernails. "The fuckee was Lola."

"Boy, both you and Henry have it out for her, huh?"

She raised an eyebrow. "I know women, he knows her, and you don't know shit."

"I'm beginning to think you both might be right."

"So, it was a .40 that killed the agent?"

"Yep."

"Well, that lets her off the hook for this one." She studied me as I stared at the table. "What?"

"Somebody mentioned a model 22 Glock."

"Recently?"

"Yep."

"Well, it would be important to know who that was." She leaned back in her chair and massaged her temples. "So, how come nobody mentioned that I shot myself in the head at the competition last night?"

"You don't think the half-dozen double dirty martinis had something to do with it?"

She yawned. "Your dog takes up the whole bed."

"Yep."

I waited, and she began studying the surface of the table as I had. "Just because it wasn't a .38 doesn't mean she didn't do it."

"No, but —"

"What the hell — did you decide to adopt her while I was knocked out?"

"Gimme a motive. I just don't see what she would've gained by killing Post."

She belched loudly. "Something she couldn't get by fucking him."

I leaned in. "Are there such things?"

"Not with me." She cocked her head coquettishly. "Her son."

"Excuse me?"

She repeated in a remedial fashion, "If the

G-man was after her son —"

I had to concede the point but then brought up my own. "Look, as far as we know she's never killed anybody before."

"As far as we know." She studied me now. "More important question: Who else have you got?"

"Billy ThE Kiddo."

"The South Dakota Nazi?"

It took me a long time to respond because suddenly the spokes in my wheel of thought began spinning. "Yep."

"Something?"

"When I was talking to Irl, he mentioned a Glock 22 in Kiddo's past, something about a lawn mower."

"You're kidding."

"Nope; as I recall, he shot his neighbor's lawn mower with a .40 Glock."

She finished off the rest of her Bloody Mary with a strong pull and then set the glass down between us. "Are we really going to go dig up some guy's lawn?"

I gathered my jacket from the back of my chair and looked down at her. "After I take a nap, we go have a chat with Billy ThE himself."

"Where are you taking your nap? Henry has one bed and Dog has the other."

"Probably in Lola."

She shrugged, getting up after me. "Why not? It appears to be where everyone else is sleeping these days."

There wasn't much human traffic, so we made quick time to the Hulett Motel's parking lot. I opened the door to the vintage convertible and looked at the center console in the front and then at the backseat, which didn't look nearly as big as I'd remembered.

"I don't think I'm going to fit."

She glanced in the back, spotting the Cheyenne Nation's blanket, and then, in the passenger seat, she saw the *Annotated Sherlock Holmes.* "Grab the blanket and book and we'll go down by the river and have a picnic."

I retrieved the supplies and shut the door. "We don't have any food."

"No, but I can read and you can put your head in my lap."

"Sold."

"Did you know that Doyle almost named Holmes Sherrinford?"

"In some of the early drafts, but he settled on Sherlock because of a cricket player he remembered." I kept my eyes closed, knowing full well that opening them would only encourage her.

"Did you know the first novel, *A Study in*

Scarlet, was a flop?"

"Yep, but the second was a hit after Joseph Stoddart convinced both Doyle and Oscar Wilde to serialize stories for his *Lippincott's Monthly Magazine. The Picture of Dorian Gray* was the only novel Wilde ever wrote."

"Does the name Sherlock mean anything?"

"Fair-haired."

I listened as she flipped a page. "Second most-filmed fictional character?"

"Sherlock Holmes."

There was a long pause as she puzzled on something that wasn't annotated in the book suspended above my head. "Who the hell is first?"

"Dracula." I opened my eyes and looked up at her. "Hey, I thought I was supposed to be taking a nap."

"Who's stopping you?"

"You."

"Yeah, I guess I am." She closed the book and set it aside. "An arrogant, drug-addicted sociopath — why do you suppose the character has been so popular through the years?"

"His perfect humanity."

Her face dropped to look at me. "Explain?"

285

"He's flawed, but he has an encyclopedic mind and relies on the human element of uncanny intuition, so when scientific method runs amok, he uses his brain. Contrary to popular belief, the method Holmes uses is abduction, not deduction. Abductive reasoning is based on conclusions drawn from observation, whereas deduction is a conclusion drawn from available data and is always true."

"I thought Sherlock Holmes was never wrong?"

"That would be a dreadful disadvantage to a true detective; you have to always be ready to rethink your abductions in the face of the evolving information in any case."

"Elementary, my dear Longmire?"

"He never said that in a single story or novel." I rose up and supported myself with a stiff arm. "How long was I asleep?"

"Less than you want to know."

"I guess I'm done." We stood, and I shook off the blanket, folded it, and placed it under my arm. "Any sign of Henry?"

She closed the book and glanced around. "Nope — must still be asleep in the room."

"I guess we'll leave Dog with him, then, and head over to the police station to have a chat with Billy."

"Sounds like a charmer."

We started toward the T-bird. "Oh, he is."

"What do you mean, he's gone?"

"Made bail, so he's scot-free."

"How?"

"Somebody moved up the bail schedule, and the judge ruled him a low flight risk in that he's a business owner and a celebrity."

"What about the fact that that business is in another state, as well as the assault with a deadly weapon on a peace officer?"

"The judge let that one slide because of the previous cease and desist that said you weren't supposed to be within a hundred feet of him. Not sure about the rest."

Vic sat on the edge of Corbin's desk. "What was bail?"

The patrolman smiled. "Two hundred and fifty thousand."

"Wowza."

"I guess the judge decided that even though he might be a low flight risk, he was going to make it tough on him by hitting him in the wallet, but Kiddo called the bluff."

"Where did he get a quarter of a million dollars?"

"It was a blanket bond from one of that bunch down in Cheyenne — Liberty Bail Bonds."

287

"Libby Troon? Hard to believe she'd pop for that without a percentage as collateral."

He picked up a square card and tried to hand it to me. "I've got her number here. You could call her up and ask her who's fronting for Billy?"

"No, she doesn't care for me very much. She's contacted me and Henry about free-lancing as bounty hunters for a few of her skip jobs and we've never bit."

"You could tell her it involves a murder case."

"That is the last piece of information I'd want Libby Troon to have." I looked out front and could see Chief Nutter herding some bikers away from the annex building. "Who picked him up?"

"Nobody. He just walked out and disappeared down the street."

"So, you think he's still around?"

"No, he said he was done with the rally and heading home. He also mentioned a lot of stuff about suing you, your dog, me, the city, the county, and all the fish in the Belle Fourche River."

"So, do you really think he went home?"

"It's likely."

"What's the address?" He stared at me. "I'm not hunting him; I just might be able to get a piece of evidence from his next-

288

door neighbor whose lawn mower he may have shot."

He stared at me some more. "You're kidding."

"I wish I were. Address, please?"

He clicked on the computer and wrote it down on a Post-it, and handed it to Vic, who was closer. "It's actually a nice part of town. From what I could tell it was his mother's."

Vic stuffed the piece of paper in her shirt pocket. "I'm sure she'd be proud."

We walked out just as Nutter Butter shooed away the bikers and turned to look at us. "As one professional to another, have you lost your mind?"

"I'm not so sure I had one to begin with, but thanks for adding me to your professional circle."

He lowered his voice. "A dead federal agent in my annex building?"

"We weren't sure where else to put him — or the car."

"You know, this shit seems to follow you wherever you go."

"It's an interesting life." Vic and I leaned against the front grille of the monstrous MRAP. "If you're not nice to me, I won't tell you how to start your truck."

He ignored me and continued. "Plus the

entirety of the Division of Criminal Investigation are back there."

"I didn't think you wanted to handle that part."

"I don't want to handle any of it."

I nodded toward the annex. "One of ours is dead." The chief calmed down and took a deep breath as I continued. "Somebody in your town killed him, and I think it has to do with Bodaway Torres. Now, you know as well as I do that if we keep this quiet, whoever did it is going to start worrying, and then they're likely to do something stupid as opposed to doing the smart thing, which is loading up and getting the hell out of here. So, you tell me what you would've done differently."

"It's a hell of a mess."

"And our job."

He sighed. "You think that turd Kiddo had something to do with this, then."

"Yep, but I'm still trying to figure out where he came up with the bail money."

"TV, I guess. You think he's got ties in Cheyenne, too?"

"No, it's just that Liberty Bail Bonds is the only one with pockets deep enough for a surety bond like this, and it just happens to be located in Cheyenne."

He shook his head, and we all sat on the

bumper of the military vehicle in a dejected fashion. "Must be a lot of money in fixin' up motorcycles on TV."

"He does have some other rather odd preoccupations."

He turned to look at me. "Like what?"

"The back room of his cycle shop looks like a bunker for the Nazi Rotary League."

He absorbed that one for a while, started to say something, then stopped and started again. "How the hell did you find that out?"

"Broke in last night and had a look-see."

He stood, took two paces, and turned to look at me. "You really have lost your mind, haven't you?" He glanced at Vic. "You wanna talk to your boss here?"

She shrugged. "I'm usually not a calming effect."

"What if they had caught you in there?"

I made a noise between my compressed lips. "They did."

"What?"

"Well, Irl Engelhardt did."

"Is there anybody else that doesn't know what's going on here besides me?"

"No, I think you're about it."

He closed his eyes. "Hey, do me a favor?"

"Sure."

"Let's pretend like this little conversation didn't happen so that I can go back to be-

291

ing as dumb as I have pretended to be."

I laughed, unable to help it. "You're going to pretend that you're oblivious enough to not know that a dead federal agent and an entire field laboratory from DCI have set up shop next door to your office?"

He took a deep breath and hooked his thumbs into his Sam Browne. "I'm about a year and a half from retirement, Sheriff Longmire, and you'd be amazed at the lengths I'm willing to go to to secure the stupidity I have acquired."

I stood up. "Consider yourself untold, then."

"Good." He nodded down the street. "I am now on my way to the Pondo for lunch if you two would like to join me."

"Thanks, but I think we're going to go listen to a new CD I've got."

"Who's on it?"

"You don't want to know."

"Roger that." He started to walk off but then paused. "Just so we're clear: if this turns out to be the case of the century, I'm going to want back in and with full credit for how magnificently I coordinated the whole thing."

"Of course."

He waved and turned his back on us in more ways than one, disappearing into the crowded street.

I turned to Vic. "The brotherhood of blue."

"No shit." She glanced behind her. "What the hell is this thing I'm sitting on?"

"It's an MRAP, or mine-resistant ambush protected vehicle, the centerpiece of the Hulett Police Department's motor pool."

"You're shitting me."

"Nope." I pulled the DCI envelope from my jacket pocket. "And believe it or not, it has a CD player."

Fortunately, Chief Nutter hadn't seen fit to remove the keys from the Pequod, probably because even with the keys most people wouldn't know how to start the damned thing.

The CD player was proving to be almost as difficult. "Where do you suppose the volume is?"

She studied the dash along with me. "Maybe the key needs to be turned to accessory?"

"I thought it was."

She glanced around the cab of the oversized military vehicle. "Why in the world would this thing have a sound system?"

"Nutter ordered it with all the bells and whistles."

She reached overhead to a console and a button that read AUDIO and flipped the switch. "Wonder what this does?" Her voice echoed off the building in front of us as the PA system projected her words over the valley. "Oh shit. . . ." Which also carried through town.

I reached up and flipped the toggle switch. "I don't think that's it." I looked at the dash again. "How about I just stick the thing in and see what lights up?"

"Always been my method of operation."

I ignored the remark and looked for the slot where the disc might be inserted, finally seeing what could've easily been mistaken for a design element. The slot accepted the CD, and it slowly disappeared.

She lodged her feet up on the dash, her Doc Martins in their usual position. "That it?"

"That, or I just lost the only copy we've got."

There was a popping noise and then someone counting. "One, two, three . . . testing one, two, three."

I listened to make sure the PA system was off.

"This is agent Brady Post of the ATF recording a meeting with CI Apelu concerning the activities of the Tre Tre Nomads and specifically Bodaway Torres and Operation Bad God." There was some scrambling and then the mic switched off.

"Who the fuck is Apelu?"

"More important, what's Operation Bad God?"

The mic came back on, and this time there were voices in the background along with some music and ambient noises, probably a bar from the sound of it. Brady's voice was low, as if speaking to someone confidentially. "So, I need a meet."

The next man also spoke quietly, but his voice was powerful, with just a touch of an unidentifiable accent. "No way."

"Hey, I don't work for anybody I never met, man."

"He don't meet people."

"What, he's a fucking hermit?"

"Yeah."

There was a pause. "Look, B-way wants me in on this, but without knowing where the juice is coming from . . ."

"Don't do it, then."

Another pause. "Look, I want in, but I just want to know who I'm in with, you know?"

"I read you, brother, but it ain't gonna happen." There were more noises, and I assumed the other man was adjusting himself

295

in his chair or in the booth, or whatever it was. "This is on a need to know basis — and you don't need to know."

Post mumbled something indiscernible.

"Hey, there's no need to disrespect me, motherfucker."

"Fuck you, asshole!" There was more fumbling around and then the unmistakable sound of the slide mechanism on a semi-auto being pulled back. "Hey, man . . ."

The voice became louder, and I was pretty sure the man was leaning in very close. "Let me explain the situation. B-way works for us, and he says you're the real deal, but we don't know that now, do we?"

"B-way and me go back long before Bird City."

"Dude, I don't care." There was another pause, and then the noise of the safety being engaged and the gun being put away. "You don't get to meet the man, and that's it."

There was some more noise, and then the mic cut out.

"Okay, we need to know what Operation Bad God is and who Apelu is, for starters."

"Well, the original name for Devils Tower was Bad God Tower, so it might just be a geographic reference to this area." There were more noises from the sound system, so I hurried the rest. "Torres is supposedly Apache, so this Apelu might've been one of his buddies."

The noise on the CD subsided, and there were mumblings but not much else when suddenly we could hear Post's voice. "Well, I gotta go to the can." We could hear him walking before closing what I assumed was a bathroom door. "Shit, shit, shit." There was more fumbling and then a sudden noise that sounded like a window opening. "Shit, shit, shit."

Vic glanced at me. "What the hell?" More undefinable noise and then nothing. After a moment there was a rhythmical sound. "What is that?"

It took me a moment to place it, but then I laughed. "Frogs."

We sat there listening to the croaking.

"He ripped off the mic?"

"And dropped it out the window, near the river I'd say."

We sat there as the frogs croaked, and I could feel a little ennui overtaking me.

"How long does this shit go on?"

I adjusted my seat back and pulled my hat over my face. "Let me know."

"More than an hour I listened to croaking frogs."

I yawned. "Nothing else?"

"No, just the sounds of the recently departed coming back to fetch his wire."

"Well, whoever it was, he must've made him plenty nervous." I flipped off the accessory switch, checking the battery levels first to make sure I hadn't killed the Hulett Police Department's apocalyptic auto. "There wasn't a lot on that recording."

"No." She studied me. "Now that you're rested, what's next?"

"We need to go see if we can find anything about where Post was staying — he mentioned the Pioneer Motel to the north of town."

She pulled the handle and began the long climb down. "Did he mention a room number?"

Hopping out myself, I reached up, shut the door, and met her at the front of the Pequod. "No, but I'm betting DCI has already found a key on his person."

Her eyes came back to me as she shook her head. "*Pequod* — really?"

"It's big, it's white, and it seemed appropriate."

After retrieving the motel's magnetic keycard, we borrowed Chief Nutter's vehicle and drove south a quarter mile to the Pioneer Motel. "Couldn't we have walked?"

I shut the door and headed toward the pleasant-looking strip of rooms only slightly blighted by the bikes and bikers littering the parking lot. "I didn't think you liked walking."

"I don't, but jeez, this seems a little like overkill." She stopped by the office and turned to look at me. "How are we playing this? I mean if we just go over and walk in, isn't anybody involved going to be suspicious?"

"We'll just flip the place and look around and maybe there'll be something else we might find along the way."

"There's this thing called a warrant? And inadmissable evidence?" She sighed and followed me into the office, the doorbell tinkling from the facing.

"Howdy."

A middle-aged woman looked up from reading the *Rapid City Journal.* "Sorry, we're full up through the rally."

"We're not looking for a room to stay in; we were just wondering if you might know which room this key goes to?"

She took it from me and examined it. "No way to tell; we just punch in the room number and then slide it through and encode it magnetically."

"Hmm." I took the key back. "You

wouldn't happen to have a room registered to a gentleman by the name of Brady Post?"

She opened an honest to goodness file box and pulled a card out. "Room number twelve, on the end out there."

"Do you mind if we take a look?"

She stared at her paper again and then at me. "Well, I don't know who he is, but it can't be good if Sheriff Walt Longmire is looking for him." She turned the Rapid City paper around and held it up for me so that I could read the feature article about the progress of the Save Jen campaign and the High Plains Dinosaur Museum — along with an enormous photo of me.

12

"That case was a good two and a half months ago; what the heck are they doing running an article on it now?"

Vic continued to read the borrowed paper. "It's more about the addition to the museum than the case. More to the point, where did they get this really hideous photo of you?"

I ignored her and slipped the card into the electronic mechanism, watched as it blinked from red to green, and pushed the door open. I have, in my time as the father of a teenage daughter, seen scenes of chaos and anarchy that no man should ever witness, and this was another of those. The furniture was turned over with the bed pushed against the wall, clothes and personal effects everywhere. Pictures had been thrown on the floor, and the closet doors had been pulled from the sliders.

Vic peered in after me. "So, you think they

were looking for something?"

I tipped the mattress from the wall for a look behind it, just making sure there weren't any bodies lying about, and then leaned it back. "Where do you want to start?"

She stepped over a pile of clothes and put the newspaper on a windowsill. "Can we rent a backhoe?"

Carrying the larger pieces of furniture outside onto the sidewalk under the curious eyes of the bikers coming and going from the parking lot, we finally got to where we could move around in the place without tripping.

Vic started by going through the clothes that were scattered all over the room, making a pile in the corner with the ones that she had examined, as I went through the drawers and the closet. "This was a real toss. If they found what they were looking for, it wasn't till the end of the search."

I felt along the top shelf of the closet under a blanket. "Whatever it was, they were looking hard."

There was a noise at the door, and we turned to find a drunk biker in a leather jacket and do-rag standing in the doorway with a bottle of beer in one hand and a cigarette in the other. "Hey, what are you guys doing in Brady's room?"

"Straightening up a little." I glanced around and then studied him. "Somebody trashed the place."

He nodded. "Yeah. Why did they do that?"

"Probably looking to see if the tags were still on the mattress."

"Do they still check those?"

I ignored the question. "Were you here when the place got torn up?"

He threw a thumb. "Two doors down."

"What time?"

"Late — after midnight."

"What'd they look like?"

"I don't know, a couple of guys in black polo shirts. One of 'em was really big."

"Bigger than me?"

"Yeah. Hey, are you guys cops?"

I ignored this question, too. "What about the other one?"

He leaned against the doorjamb. "He was smaller, but still a big fucker."

"What did they look like, other than their size?"

"I don't know."

"I thought you said you saw them?"

"Well, for a minute. I mean, I wasn't wearing any clothes, and there was all this noise, so I stuck my head out the door and yelled, but they told me to shut the hell up and disappear or they were gonna stuff me in a trash can." He thought about it. "And it was dark."

"How do you know Brady?"

He shrugged. "We had a beer out here at the picnic table a couple of nights back."

I nodded, figuring I'd gotten as much out of him as I was going to get. "What's your name?"

He deposited the cigarette into his beer bottle and stuck out his free hand. "Gogo."

"Gogo?"

"George, George Lance, but everybody just calls me Gogo."

I shook the hand and gave him one of my cards. "Nice to meet you, Gogo. Walt Longmire, sheriff of Absaroka County."

He studied the card. "Cool."

"If you think of anything else, you might let us know?"

"Sure." He pushed off the door facing and disappeared.

"You want to know what's amazing about that exchange?"

I turned to look at her. "What's that?"

"That you actually had cards." She went back to sorting through Brady's personal effects. "What phone number have you got on there, anyway?"

"The office number." She mumbled some-

304

thing — I wasn't sure what it was, but I figured that it wasn't complimentary — and went back to searching. "I'm checking the bathroom."

"I'll alert the press. You want some reading material? There's a lovely article in the paper on the sill you can wipe with."

"Thanks. I don't plan on being that long." Thinking it was a heck of a lot easier to search for something when you knew what it was you were searching for, I went into the bathroom. Knowing that the space for contraband on motorcycles was relatively small helped but not much.

I opened and closed the medicine cabinet and tried not to look into my tired eyes in the mirror. The shower curtain had been torn off the rings, and the towels were on the floor. After checking the back of the toilet, I piled the stuff on the seat and looked in the shower stall, the trash can, and on the windowsill.

Nothing.

I was about to turn and walk out when one of those old-fashioned ceiling fixtures with a rectangular glass shade caught my eye. I had had one just like it when I was a kid, with cowboys roping from horses painted on the inside of the surface, but there was a small shaded square in one corner on this one that didn't match.

I carefully stepped up on the toilet in the hopes that I wouldn't rip it from the floor and unthreaded the nut on the bottom of the shade, palming it so that I could pluck out the strange item.

I put the shade back on, and looked at the small object. It was a plastic cube of some sort, khaki in color, and about two inches square. If it was a box, I had no idea how you would open it since there were no ridges, creases, or cracks. "Hey, Vic?" I came out and offered the thing to her. "Any idea what this is?"

"A ring box?"

I handed it to her. "Open it."

She turned it in her fingers just as I had and then weighed it in her palm. "It's plastic but heavy." She examined it closer. "Where did you find it?"

"In the light fixture."

"No way it's part of the thing?"

"No, and it's a strange color if it's for any kind of construction."

She handed it back to me. "A Rubik's Cube for morons?"

"I have no idea."

"Well, this pisses me off. We go through the place with a fine-tooth comb and all we find is something that we have no idea what it is?"

"It's a plastic cube." Mike Novo turned the thing in his hand. "Solid, by all accounts."

Vic was annoyed. "So, what's it for?"

"Hell if I know. I mean it's not styrene or anything — it's hard." He handed it back to me. "Maybe it's a spacer of some kind."

I handed it back to him. "I need to know."

"You want me to send it to Cheyenne?"

"Yep."

"And then what?"

"X-ray it, test it. A federal agent possibly lost his life because of it, Mike. Do whatever it is you people do and find out what the heck it is."

"Okay." He stood and pulled out a FedEx box.

"T.J. get anything more from the body?"

He nodded toward the back. "You can ask her — she's finishing up the autopsy in the pop-up lab." He snapped his fingers and pointed at me. "Henry was by here looking for you. He had your dog with him."

"He say where he was going?"

"The Ponderosa Café. He said Dog was hungry, and they were going for a late lunch/early dinner."

I turned to look at Vic. "Hungry?"

"Starved."

"Let's go talk to T. J., and then we'll grab something to eat."

She followed me as I led the way. "Dead people and dinner, my favorite night out."

The Little Lady was pulling off her latex gloves when we shoved the plastic aside and stepped in. "No other traces. The killer placed the muzzle of the .40 against his chest and pulled the trigger." She threw the gloves in a nearby trash can. "From the angle of the shot, I'd say your friend here was asleep."

"Nothing else?"

She picked up a clipboard and began writing. "As noted, the decedent had sex before being shot; he'd eaten a little before that, and he also ingested a schedule IV controlled substance, probably Lorazepam, a high-potency, intermediate-duration, 3-hydroxy benzodiazepine drug, often used to treat anxiety disorders."

"Like being worried that somebody might shoot you in the chest?"

T.J. glanced at Vic, noting the fact that she had on her sunglasses in the gloom of the annex. "Exactly like that." Sherwin extended a hand. "How do you feel, Vic?"

My undersheriff looked dubiously at the hand for a moment and then shook. "Still hung over; how 'bout you?"

"Just tired. At least hung over means you *had* fun."

She glanced at me.

"You ordered without us?"

The Bear chewed a bite of his cheese-burger. "Dog was hungry." He fed him another fry. "He is always hungry."

Vic and I pulled out chairs and sat. "We found a plastic cube in Brady's motel room."

Henry wiped his hands on his napkin. "A what?"

"Plastic cube, about two inches by two inches by two inches — perfectly square and khaki in color. Any ideas?"

He puzzled. "Hard plastic?"

"Very."

He shrugged. "Let me see it."

"DCI's job. I gave it to Mike Novo to ship off just now."

Dragging another fry through the ketchup, he fed it to Dog. "Nothing else?"

"Nope, no more wire equipment, computer, nothing." The waitress arrived, and we ordered up. "Somebody destroyed the place, and I'm assuming they got everything."

"Except the cube. Whatever that is."

I glanced out the window at the comings

and goings of a couple thousand motorcycles in the early evening. "He hid it in the light fixture, so he knew it was a possibility that someone was going to be looking for it."

The Bear nodded and split the last fry with Dog. "It would be nice if we had access to the ATF agent's control officer. It is possible that he might know what Post was working on."

I leaned back in my seat. "I'm still waiting on McGroder to get back to me."

Vic rested an elbow on the table, pushing a wave of blue-black hair from her face and supporting her chin with a palm. "How?"

"Excuse me?"

"How is he supposed to get in touch with you?"

Satisfied with myself, I smiled and patted my jacket pocket. "I've got Bodaway Torres's cell phone."

"Have you checked it?" I suddenly felt a little less sure of myself as she reached over and pulled the phone from my pocket, thumbed a few buttons, and studied the screen as the waitress came back with our drinks and I sipped my iced tea.

The Cheyenne Nation studied Vic, still wearing her sunglasses. "How is your head?"

"Shitty. How's yours?"

"Fine, but I did not drink a vat of dirty martinis last night."

She turned the screen toward me. "Eight phone messages and three texts from the regional office in Denver, Colorado, of the FB of I."

"Oh."

"You hit the button that silenced it."

"Oh."

The phone suddenly spoke. "Hello?"

Vic gestured with the device. "Take it; it's McGroder."

I took the thing and held it to my ear. "Hey, Mike."

"Where the hell have you been? I've been trying to get you for what seems like days."

"This cell phone thing is kind of new to me. Have you got something?"

"This is a shit storm of incomparable magnitude, and none of us have an umbrella. This Post guy was a real deal, and an undercover operative for the last thirteen years with all the biker gangs. He was involved in a major bust on weapons in the Southwest, but evidently he had gotten into something even bigger."

"Like what?"

"The control officer wouldn't say."

"So big the ATF won't tell the FBI?"

"Apparently."

I thought about it. "What's he want done with Post?"

"Amazingly enough, he went along with your assessment of the know-and-go, but get ready because he's on his way there."

"Coming to Hulett?"

"Left today from Phoenix."

"Okay."

"His name is John Stainbrook." There was a long pause, and I listened as the FBI man shuffled papers on his desk. "Walt, don't jerk this guy around; he's the real juice, and unless you and your pals up there in the Wild West want to end up in an undisclosed facility in the Arizona desert, just tell him everything you know."

"Well, that won't take long, considering we don't know a lot." I reached down to pet Dog. "Hey, Mike, we found something in Post's motel room —"

"You searched his room?"

"Don't worry about it; we weren't the first. Anyway, we found a plastic cube, khaki in color, about two inches square — any idea what that might be?"

He sighed. "Walt, are you on drugs?"

"That's the only thing of interest we found."

He sighed. "I have no idea."

"Oh, well. Maybe the Stainbrook guy can

help us out."

"There's one more thing."

"I'm listening."

"Post wasn't alone."

"What's that supposed to mean?"

"The ATF has two undercover agents there in Hulett."

I watched as Henry continued to tinker with the metal detector we'd purchased at High Plains Pawn, in an attempt to get the thing to light up or do something that might indicate it was operable.

Vic looked out the window of the Dodge at the gathering gloom of one of suburban Rapid City's nicer neighborhoods, her eyes rising to the gigantic cottonwoods that wreathed the street. "I figure if I lived in a place like this I'd shoot myself."

"Why?"

"The incredible normalcy of it." She turned to look at me. "So, two ATF birds in one bush? Any guesses?"

"Not a one."

"So, this is not an informant or someone but an actual secret agent?"

"I don't think they call them secret agents."

"I know, but I like the sound of it — makes it sound espionage-y and shit."

I let that one settle. "According to Mc-Groder and this John Stainbrook character, there are two undercover operatives."

"Undercover operatives — I like that, too." She went back to watching a particular house down the street. "Well, be careful what you wish for; an hour ago you were wishing you could talk to these ATF guys about what Post was working on, and now you've got his boss hotfooting it up here."

"It must be important." I turned and looked at the Cheyenne Nation. "How's it going?"

"I do not know." He put the top back on the plastic case and pushed a button, which resulted in a high-pitched squeal from the thing. "I think it is working." He extended the wand with a disc on it toward the dash, and the thing started screaming again.

"Can you turn the volume down?"

Vic peered at the instrumentation on the Dodge. "Wow, who would've figured there was real metal in the dash."

The Bear adjusted the knob and fiddled some more. "It is set on the highest level of sensitivity, but I will adjust it when we get on the lawn."

Vic glanced at the sky. "Dark enough?"

I pulled the door handle and climbed out. "Unless we're going to hang around here all night." I met the two of them at the back of the pumpkin chiffon muscle car, the perfect vehicle for undercover work. "It must be the Tudor-looking one three houses up — the one next to the house with the cars parked on the lawn."

Vic shook her head as Henry continued to calibrate the metal detector. "So, tell me again what the hell we're doing out here?"

I opened the trunk and pulled out the new shovel I'd purchased at Shipton's Ranch Supply. "When I was talking to Engelhardt, he said that one of the run-ins he had had with Billy ThE Kiddo was when he shot his neighbor's lawn mower with a .40 Glock. Post was shot with a .40, so I thought we'd get the slug and hand it over to DCI and see if they could get a match — case solved."

She looked at the oversized lawns. "You're kidding."

I closed the trunk and balanced the shovel on my shoulder. "Got a better idea?"

She studied the house next to the Tudor. "Yeah, we get a warrant, go into the jackass's house, find the gun, and hand it over to DCI for testing."

"You think he's stupid enough to still have it?"

"I think he's stupid enough to open a wholesale stupid store and sell franchises."

Following the Bear, I started off down the street. "Well, if this doesn't work —"

She sighed and brought up the rear.

Staying to the far side of Kiddo's house, Henry dropped the wand and started detecting, moving it across the newly mown grass, whereupon it squealed softly and the yellow light on the instrument panel lit up. "A little too sensitive." He recalibrated it again, but this time the thing did nothing at all. "Hmm, a little too desensitized perhaps."

While he fiddled with the adjustments, Vic and I looked around. There were no lights on in either of the two houses, and it looked as though there was no one home in either one.

She leaned against a large cottonwood and studied the Kiddo abode. "So, in a nice neighborhood, this asshole parks his cars and motorcycles in the yard."

There was a noise behind us, and I turned to see Henry waving the metal detector over a small patch of God's little acre. I walked over. "Something?"

"Possibly."

Looking around one last time, I placed the edge of the blade into the turf and dug in. I lifted a chunk of sod, tipped it to the side, and then stomped another shovel full from the ground, carefully placing it beside the hole for reinterment. "How far down does that thing read?"

He shrugged. "I have no idea."

I shoveled again and this time felt something scrape. I handed the spade to Henry, took out my Maglite, shined it in the hole, and poked around, finally recovering an old railroad spike. "Hmm."

"Not what we are looking for?"

"No." I returned the dirt to the hole and then replaced the sod, stomping on it, as the Bear continued working the massive lawn. "This is going to take all night." I glanced around for Vic, but she'd obviously gotten bored and wandered off.

The machine made another noise, and I followed Henry to a spot about twenty feet away and repeated the procedure, which resulted in another spike. "What'd we find, the transcontinental railroad here?"

He shrugged again and moved on, but after another five railroad spikes, I was losing my enthusiasm. "I don't suppose you could dial that thing down again?"

"I could, but the difference between a railroad spike and a slug might be beyond this particular model's abilities." He adjusted the thing again. "It would be helpful if we had an approximate area where the shooting took place."

"Yep, I know."

I looked up and could see Vic standing just a little ways away.

"How's it going?" She stepped closer and raised a glass to her lips, sipped some wine, and glanced around in the darkness. "Don't quit your day job."

It took me a moment to ask. "I'm almost afraid to know, but where'd you get the wine?"

"Earl Heiple, who owns the yard we're digging in."

"Did you go introduce yourself to Mr. Heiple?"

"I did. He was reading in his den, so I knocked on his back door."

"And he gave you a glass of wine?"

"He's ready to give you one, too. He says he hates that riotous prick next door." She paused. "He's like a hundred years old, but called Kiddo a riotous prick — used those exact words." She took another sip. "I like him."

"He didn't happen to tell you where Billy ThE shot the lawn mower, did he?"

She gestured with the wineglass. "Yeah, out there in the middle someplace; he said he'd show us."

■ ■ ■ ■

"They used railroad ties near the sidewalk. They backfilled the front lawn in '27, but I guess the spikes are still there."

"Has your family always lived here?"

He nodded his gray head and pushed his glasses farther up on his nose. "Fourth generation South Dakota."

He noticed Henry's glass was a little low and reached an unsteady hand out to pour the Bear a little more cabernet. "This is the 2012 — it's very good."

"Thank you."

He gestured toward my glass, but I waved him off and he smiled. "I would've thought all that digging would've given you a thirst."

I returned the smile. "So, you didn't know we were out there?"

"Not until this beautiful young lady appeared at my door."

I picked up my glass and took a sip. "I'm thinking I should be apologizing."

He set the bottle back on the counter. "No need."

The house was massive and well furnished, the kitchen a wooden structure that had been added on to the backside of the stone house, a precaution that had been

made in the days when such rooms periodically burnt down. His den looked to be an
old porch that had been converted, and I
couldn't help but wonder why he appeared
to live the majority of his life in the more
modest portions of the huge house.

I glanced around the kitchen — homey,
but a little run down. "You live here alone?"

He nodded and sat on a stool opposite
the three of us. "Ever since Evelyn died
seventeen years ago."

"Children?"

"A son in Florida and a daughter in
Alabama; I think the Midwest winters took
a toll on them." He sighed and looked
around. "It's a museum, I know. They keep
trying to get me to move, but so far I've
resisted. I've lived here my whole life, and
I'm not sure I'd know myself anywhere
else."

The Cheyenne Nation warmed to the old
man. "What did you do? For a living."

He gestured toward the book lying on the
counter to our left, Herodotus's *The Histo-
ries*. "I taught world history at Black Hills
State."

" 'Men trust their ears less than their
eyes.' "

He nodded and looked sad. "He is rather
one-sided, but he's still the most reliable

historian of the ancient world." The old scholar considered me. "I find it hard to believe that a Wyoming sheriff quotes Herodotus."

"It's a magnificent book."

He placed a wrinkled hand lovingly on the tome. "I read it periodically to convince myself that we live in more civilized times."

"Where people shoot each other's lawn mowers?"

" 'From great wrongdoing there are great punishments from the gods.' " He glanced at me through the tops of his bifocals. "Are you here to punish wrongdoers?"

"Yep."

He stood and moved toward the door, and we followed. "The Kiddos were marvelous people, but their son's actions have always been questionable, to say the least."

We gathered our primitive equipment from the back stoop, and I watched as Vic surreptitiously slipped an arm through one of his, carefully steering him along the sidewalk toward the front lawn.

The old fellow was spry enough and led us to a spot near the property line but thankfully with an obstructed view of Billy's house next door. "I was mowing the grass myself when he came out of his house shooting like a madman. I think the first shot landed somewhere out near the middle of the lawn, but the second I'm sure of since it missed my foot by only a yard or so." He tapped a house shoe on a spot in the grass. "I would say here."

The three of us stepped back, and Henry ran the wand over the patch; the device immediately squealed and lit up.

I stepped forward with the shovel and repeated the procedure. I was starting to feel like a grave digger.

He watched me. "How far will a bullet go into the ground?"

I looked up at him. "Usually about a foot, depending on the weapon and the composition of the soil." I shoveled out another scoop. "Rocks can deflect a bullet quite a ways, so you can never be completely sure where they might go. How far away was he when he fired?"

He thought about it. "Twenty yards. He was truly crazed."

I scooped out another. "He still is."

Henry moved in and passed the wand over the hole, but the detector didn't respond. We looked at each other, and then he waved the thing over the pile of dirt I'd shoveled to the side; suddenly, it lit up and squealed.

"Bingo." I kneeled down and began sifting through the dirt with my fingers, feeling for the slug. "I'd say your powers of recollection are pretty amazing, Mr. Heiple."

He stood there, arm in arm with my undersheriff. "Perhaps, but if you've ever been shot at, and I'm sure you have, you tend to remember it." He paused for a moment and then continued, almost apologetically. "I was with Company One, Thirty-third Armored Regiment, Third Armored Division, First U.S. Army in the Battle of the Bulge. We were raw recruits brought in to replace the men who had been killed in the initial German offensive. On my first night, there we were deployed in the third Sherman tank that my crew had been given, the first two having been destroyed. We were guarding the fuel dump at Francorchamps above Stavelot late one night. I was smoking a cigarette and listening to the bats flying around my head outside my assistant-driver hole. After a moment the older and much more experienced driver poked his head out of his hatch, looked at me, and said, "You do know you're being shot at with that damned cigarette, don't you?" So I threw it over the side and scrambled in; then he told me that I'd just flicked a lit cigarette into a field of cans containing 124,000 gallons of gasoline."

I breathed a laugh and thought about the

neo-Nazi reality star living next door as I carefully plucked the bullet from the dirt. I brushed it off and held it up into the moonlight — a perfectly mushroomed .40 slug. "You never forget your first time."

13

"What good is it having a daughter who works for the attorney general if I can't get a confidential piece of information every once in a while?" I could feel her fuming three hundred miles to the south as I sat there watching the sun come up, thankful that I'd finally gotten some sleep. "That information is with the courts, and I don't have any pull over there." She paused and then growled, "I just started last week — I don't have any pull over here, either. If it's a blanket bail, then they don't have to disclose who supplied the money, Dad."

"Could you make a few phone calls for me?"

"I can't believe you're asking me to compromise my position."

"Heck, if you weren't there, I'd be calling the attorney general himself and hitting him up." I waited a moment before changing the subject. "How's the painting going?"

Her tone brightened a little but not much. "It looks really great, and Lola seems to like it. Speaking of, how's her namesake?"

I yawned. "Probably going to the women's prison in Lusk before this is all over with."

"Really?"

"I don't know. I'm concerned about her son being hurt, but with the death of a federal agent, that's kind of taken a backseat. Every time I think I've got something nailed down in this case, something worse happens that just complicates it."

"You'll figure it out; you always do."

"Right."

"There was a big article in the Cheyenne paper that they got from the AP wire about the Save Jen campaign and the High Plains Dinosaur Museum. Wasn't a very good photo of you, though."

"Yep, I saw it in the Rapid City paper."

She laughed. "You're a big deal."

"Right."

"Stop saying 'right.' "

I held my tongue.

"I found a nice lady who's been doing day care for *our* Lola. Her name is Alexia Mendez; they've got an extended family here in Cheyenne."

"She's nice?"

"Yes, and she's over six feet tall and probably three hundred pounds."

"Does Lola like her?"

"Crazy about her."

"Well then, she's okay by me."

"When are you and Henry coming down here for a visit?"

I sighed and leaned back in the folding chair on the old flagstone patio near our room at the motel and watched Dog as he watered the vicinity. "What about Dog?"

"Dog is always welcome, even when you're not."

The phone went dead in my hand. I deposited it in my jacket pocket as the aforementioned beast came over and set his hundred and fifty pounds on my foot. "How you doin', buddy?"

He wagged and lolled his head back to look at me.

"I gave up breakfast so we could have quality time, so have some time of quality, will you?"

I scratched the fur under his chin just as a man in full motorcycle regalia — boots, torn jeans, black T-shirt, well-worn leather jacket, hair tied back under an American flag do-rag, Ray-Ban sunglasses over his eyes — made the corner at the other end of the motel. I watched him approach the door to our room.

I cleared my throat loudly. "Can I help you?"

He looked at me and walked over the rest of the way but slowed a little when Dog stood. "Is he friendly?"

I got up and extended a hand. "Unless you're a honey-baked ham."

He patted Dog's head, and we shook. "Sheriff Longmire, I presume?" His voice was soft with a bit of California in it.

"Yep. You John Stainbrook?"

He pulled out a badge wallet hanging on a chain under his T-shirt and showed me his credentials, then dropped the badge back in its hiding place and gestured with a hand that had a lot of rings and tattoos on it. "If you could gimme some ID."

I pulled my badge wallet from my pocket and handed it to him.

"Sorry. Saw that photo of you in the paper yesterday, but you can't be too careful in my line of business." He took his time looking at it and then handed it back. "What have you got for me?"

"Other than the slug we dropped off last night with DCI?"

His face stiffened under what looked like a beard on a Persian statue, ringlets and all. "I'd just like to hear your version before we go any further."

I gestured toward the other chair, and he sat. "Not much I can tell you other than what you already know, but I was hoping that if we shared our collective info we could make some headway on this."

He nodded. "I'm hoping as well, but to do that I need to know what you know. This is a federal investigation, and even though I appreciate your intimacy with the situation, I'm going to need to see your cards first."

"Okay." I leaned back in my chair and told him about the first meeting with Post and, more important, about the second, when he had told Henry and me who he was.

"He told you who and what he was?"

"Yep."

Stainbrook, looking all the world like some ancient philosopher, shook his head and pulled at the beard. "Then he must've been under a lot of pressure. Brady never did that anywhere with anybody."

"I've got a trustworthy face."

He stood and walked a little away, finally standing at the edge of the patio and looking at the river. "Tell me about the hit."

"Textbook. Somebody, and we think we know who, placed the barrel of a .40 at his chest while he was either sleeping or resting in the Cadillac. No prints, nothing."

"Lola Wojciechowski's Caddy?"

"Yep." I stood up. "Hey, do you want to tell me what her connection to all of this might be?"

He turned and looked at me, even going to the trouble of taking off his sunglasses. "Her son, Bodaway, was moving guns for the Tre Tre Nomads, but then he got into business with some folks up this way and things got a lot heavier."

"In what way?"

"Know anything about ASPs?"

I shook my head and thought about it, finally throwing out a feeble bone. "Alleged Sensory Perception?"

"Advanced synthetic polymers."

"Well, look what the cat dragged in!"

We both turned to see Lola standing on the ramp of the parking lot that led to the cabins, hands on her hips.

Stainbrook was faster than I was. "Lola, baby! I was just askin' this cowboy where I could find you." He walked over to her, and they shared an embrace before turning back to me, arm in arm.

She gave me a hard look, flipping the black and silver hair from her face. "Where the hell is my car?"

"Excuse me?" I had to think fast and come up with a story so that she didn't just stroll into the Hulett Police Department

330

looking for it.

"My Caddy, where the hell is it?"

I struck on a scenario. "Impound in Rapid City — evidently there was a speeding violation and a number of parking tickets."

She stared at me. "You've got to be joking."

"Wish I were."

She turned back to Stainbrook. "Have you two met formally?"

He immediately stuck the same hand out I'd shook before, but this time he had a newfound name. "Ray Swift. Good to meet you. Any friend of Lola's is a friend of mine."

I shook the hand now turned covert. "Well, I don't know if I'd call us friends — maybe just acquaintances."

"Oh, Sheriff, now you've hurt my feelings."

He made a show of double-taking me. "Sheriff?"

"Yep."

He glanced at her again. "You hangin' with law-dawgs now?"

"Friend of a friend." She hugged him closer. "Buy me breakfast and gimme a ride over to Rapid City so I can get my car?"

"Well, there's a problem with that." He turned her, and they started to head back toward the center of town. "Let's go have breakfast, Lola, and I'll explain." He looked over his shoulder at me and winked. "I'll catch you later, Sheriff . . . ?"

"Longmire. Walt Longmire."

"Right." He made a gun with a forefinger and cocked it at me, firing wide.

"I'm sure we'll be seeing each other." I patted my leg and Dog came over, sitting on my foot again as we watched them jangle up the hill and across the parking lot, leaving me to thank the heavens that my facet of law enforcement was a little more straightforward. I'd briefly dipped into undercover work, but I always had trouble remembering who I was — and that stuff wore me out.

I scratched behind Dog's ears again and thought about the two-inch cube of plastic I'd found in Post's motel room. "Advanced synthetic polymers — that ring any bells with you?"

He wagged, and I took it as a yes.

"Well, it sure doesn't with me."

"Advanced synthetic polymers."

"That's what he said, but then Lola showed up, as she is wont to do, and we had to change gears. Evidently she knows him as Ray Swift."

Vic shook her head. "I need a player card."

"I know." We leaned on the trunk of the Orange Blossom Special as the Bear finished up an interview with *Iron Horse,* a biker/girlie magazine. "So, the cube we found in Post's room takes on a new importance. I'm not sure what it is exactly, but at least we know it's part of the equation." I looked at Vic. "I'll just have to get Stainbrook/Swift alone so that we can acquire more information."

She studied Henry as he talked to the reporter. "Well, we know the one thing that'll distract her more than anything else."

"True."

She reached in the window and petted Dog, who was commanding the driver's seat. "You think they're going to make him take his clothes off?"

"I think it's only naked women in that magazine, but times change."

"You're just jealous, because he's getting as much print as you are." She studied me for a moment and then took my arm and led me around to the other side of the vehicle, where we were relatively shaded from public view. Once there, she reached underneath her leather jacket, pulled her signature Glock 19, and handed it to me.

"What's this?" I glanced at the Bear and

the interviewer, who were paying us no mind. "You want me to speed up the interview?"

"You know, I'm glad that you came to me with this, because if you had gone to Stainbrook or DCI, they would've said, 'You know, we gotta get rid of this dumb-ass Longmire, because he's so amazingly stupid.' " She pointed at the wicked-looking semi-automatic in my hands. "Advanced synthetic polymer."

"Plastic guns?"

"Partially." She shook her head at me. "Realizing your technical advancement pretty much stops at muzzle loaders, I thought I'd save you some embarrassment." She pointed at the plastic portions of her sidearm. "ASPs."

"Oh." I handled the Glock, feeling again how lightweight it was compared to my Colt 1911. "So, how long have they been doing these things again?"

"There were earlier versions, but the ones that are popular now stemmed from the Austrian military and police service in the early '80s."

"Gaston Glock, right?"

"The Safe Action pistol, polymer-framed, short-recoil-operated, locked-breech semi-automatic." She leaned against the car's shiny flanks. "There was a bunch of shit about the reliability of a *plastic* gun, but that little baby right there holds the lion's share of sales to American law enforcement agencies, at, like, sixty-five percent."

"So what's the big deal about advanced synthetic polymers if they've been around for thirty-five years?"

"I don't know." She took her sidearm and stuffed it back in her pancake holster. "Even the tan color of the cube is no big deal — they've been making that color for years. Hell, three-quarters of the guys in Afghanistan and Iraq are carrying them." She stretched, raising her arms, which drew her shirt from her jeans, revealing her midriff. "And we still don't know who the second ATF agent happens to be?"

"Nope."

"I don't think it's Lola."

I couldn't help but chuckle. "I don't think so, either."

The Cheyenne Nation finished up with the fourth estate and came over, resting his back on the Tangerine Dream along with us.

"You make the centerfold?"

"I refused to be airbrushed." He raised an eyebrow and shook his head at her. "I feel like such a piece of meat."

"We have a job for you. Your ex has at-tached herself to the ATF CO, and I need to talk to him about this ASP thing."

We loaded into the General Lee and drove toward the center of all things Hulett. Vic shut the growling engine off and glanced around at the milling motorcyclists, just now dragging themselves out of bed after their previous night's revelries. "When are all these people going to go home and return to being a problem for their local law enforcement agencies?"

I pulled the handle, stepped into the alley, and caught a chorus of a garage-band ver-sion of Lynyrd Skynyrd's "Simple Man." "It'll start winding down the day after to-morrow."

"So, the clock is ticking?"

"In more ways than one." I turned to Henry. "How do you want to play this?"

He clasped the bridge of his nose with a thumb and forefinger. "It will not be hard; as soon as she figures out that he does not have a car, she will attempt to employ her namesake."

"You think you can get word to Stain-brook that we're out back?"

"I think so. What do you want me to tell Lola when we get to Rapid and her car is not there?"

"Knowing her, she's not going to go into the sheriff's office voluntarily, so you can just come back out and tell her that it was returned to Hulett, compliments of the South Dakota taxpayers."

"You are sure that DCI will be through with it later today?"

"One can hope, but if not, we'll deal with that burning bridge when we get to it." Without another word, we watched as he disappeared through the beer garden into the restaurant proper.

I turned to Vic. "I guess when Stainbrook comes out we'll pretend that we're taking him into custody and walk him up to the HPD and talk."

"I don't think it's Eddy the Viking, either."

"What?"

"The second ATF agent."

"You keep narrowing the field." I shook my head. "Let me know when you get it down to one."

Agent Stainbrook was impressed with the interior of the USS Pequod, even if Vic, sitting in the back with Dog, wasn't. "I think we should hang a shingle on this thing and let everybody know that we're establishing squatter rights in it and opening up an office."

Stainbrook glanced around the interior of the behemoth. "What are they intending to do with this thing, anyway?"

"I don't honestly know — go fishing, I guess." I turned in the seat and looked at his profile. "So, what's the big deal about ASPs?"

"All right, first off, I want you to know that it is against agency policy to give you this information in any form, and I'm placing myself and my people in a precarious position by telling you any of this."

I nodded, and then he looked back at Vic, who made the motion of locking her mouth and throwing away the key. I assumed Dog was exempt.

He took a deep breath and started in. "In 1986 the Congressional Office of Technology Assessment reported that a ninety-nine percent metal-less gun could feasibly be made of advanced synthetic polymers, with metal used just for springs, but that it was only a possibility." He pulled out his own sidearm, which looked remarkably like Vic's only slightly larger. "This is a Gen4 Glock G22, and it's got ASP parts like the grip and trigger guard. Now, it's difficult to recognize one of these on an X-ray scanner when it's disassembled, but it can be done." He handed it to me. "This weapon is eighty-three percent metal by weight."

I held the lightweight .40. "So?"

"In '88 there was a company based in Scottsdale, Arizona, called Dust Devil Development that claimed it was going to have a prototype of a completely ASP weapon in less than a year. Well, a lot of agencies figured it was just hot air to get investors interested in the company, but Congress lost their minds over the fact that these weapons could be impossible to detect. They ordered an investigation, and suddenly Dust Devil Development ceased to exist. Shortly after that, Congress passed laws that banned the production of any kind of fully ASP weapons."

"Scottsdale, huh?"

He nodded. "You see, the difficulty had been in the parts of the mechanism that would wear out. Those had to be made with metal; there just wasn't any ASP that was able to stand up to that kind of punishment."

"Till now?"

"You got it. Enter Bill Tichenor, a polymer technician out of Silicon Valley's Special Materials Division. Tichenor develops a ceramic material that's supposed to replace the metal exhaust valves in automobile engines, and this stuff is supposed to be as strong as steel. Well, this does not go unnoticed by the FBI, and they clamp down on the Special Materials Division and classify the formula for the stuff."

Vic leaned forward. "If they were so spooked by this, then why didn't they shut down production completely?"

"They did that for the car exhaust valves, but when they went through Tichenor's files they found designs for all kinds of applications, especially worrisome being the concept drawings for a small automatic pistol."

"Uh-oh."

"Wait, it gets worse. The CIA, seeing an opportunity, tried to argue with Congress about the viability of continued development."

Vic pulled herself up between us. "The CIA?"

"The agency's position was that the weapon would be used for antiterrorism purposes, and in situations where foreign powers had magnetometer security, they could still get weapons into hostage situations."

Vic laughed. "And vice versa."

"It all got shut down eventually, but here's an interesting tidbit: six weeks after the Department of Justice shuts Special Materials Division down for good in 1996, Bill

Tichenor is found without a head or hands in a dumpster behind 4014 North Gold-water Avenue in Scottsdale, Arizona."

"That's where Dust Devil Development was working on the plastic gun?"

"Precisely. There was communication between Tichenor and Dust Devil, a go-between." He paused. "That turned out to be Delshay Torres."

I thought about the conversation I'd had with Lola the first time we'd met: "Chief cook and bottle washer of the Crossbones Custom bike shop somewhere in the Phoe-nix area."

Stainbrook nodded again. "Maryvale, yeah."

"So, I'm assuming that Delshay got in-volved, and therefore Bodaway, because he was familiar with the fabrication of different materials and not likely to notify the Con-gress of his advancements?"

The ATF man leaned back in his seat. "Not likely then or now — suspicious hit and run in Nogales, just this side of the Mexican border, last year."

"So, what are the chances they've actually developed a fully ASP weapon?"

He laughed, but it wasn't funny. "Since my man Post got his hands on that sample you found in his motel room? I'd say pretty good."

"So that's what the cube was, a sample of metal-tensile-strength advanced synthetic polymer?"

He nodded. "We've already got people in Cheyenne with your DCI, and they've confirmed that that's what it is."

Vic looked at the two of us. "So, how does a shitbird like Billy ThE Kiddo get involved in something like this?"

Stainbrook sighed. "Material fabrication at his shop."

"We've been there."

"Where?"

"The Chop Shop — Kiddo's place in Rapid City." I was aware that he was staring at me. "It was after hours. Not that I'd know the difference, but it didn't look like they were up to anything that complicated, just the usual bodywork and paint." I took a breath. "And there's something more I should let you in on. Kiddo's got an entire shrine in his back room that looks like the beginning of the Fourth Reich."

He waved a hand at me. "I'm not surprised, and I don't give a shit. I don't want to appear callous, but when you've been doing this job as long as I have, you get used to seeing all kinds of bizarre stuff. I really don't care what their screwed-up belief system is; I just want to keep dangerous weapons out of their hands."

"And make sure that they pay their taxes."

"Yeah, that, too." He thought about it. "Billy ThE doesn't strike me as being all that smart."

"Well, he doesn't know the meaning of the word 'fear,' but then he doesn't know the meaning of a lot of words."

The ATF agent cocked his head and looked at both of us. "But he does know material fabrication."

"Yep."

Vic smiled. "Kind of a chopper savant?" She shrugged. "And muscle?"

He turned to look at her. "For who?"

She looked out the side window at the throngs of bikers down the street. "Good question."

We parted company with Agent Stainbrook at the Hulett Police Department annex and were assured by DCI that Lola's Cadillac would be released and sitting outside by the time she and the Cheyenne Nation returned from their round-trip.

DCI's mobile lab unit was preparing to return to Cheyenne, and T. J. was helping pack up the equipment. "We don't have the ability up here to match the slugs, but I already shipped the one you gave us ahead, so as soon as I hear anything I'll let you know."

"Sounds good." I glanced around. "Speaking of, has anybody seen or heard of the whereabouts of the presumed shooter, Billy ThE Kiddo?"

"You'd have to ask the locals about that."

I nodded, and we shook. "Thanks, T. J."

She held my hand. "You look like hell. I don't suppose it would do any good to tell you to head home and go to bed?"

"You know, women are always trying to get me to go to bed."

The chief of the Wyoming Division of Criminal Investigation's Lab Unit shook her head and glanced at Vic. "Take care of him, will you?"

She went out the door, and Vic stepped into my line of sight. "You know, if I wasn't in the picture, I've got a feeling you could have a pretty active social life."

I turned her by the shoulder, and we started toward the police department's office. "I don't think I'd have the energy for it."

Pushing open the door of the HPD, we found Chief Nutter in a heated conversation with a couple of bikers. "Look, it's not our responsibility to make sure your bike is safe if it's parked in a questionable area."

The leather-clad dudester howled, "It was parked on Main Street!"

Nutter shrugged. "What can I tell you? It's a tough town this week." He showed the disgruntled bikers the door and turned to us as they made their way out. "What do you want?"

"In the interest of interdepartmental co-operation, I was wondering if there had been any sightings of Billy ThE?"

"Probably back beneath the rhinestone-encrusted rock he crawled out from under."

"So, that would be a no."

Nutter glanced around. "Hell, find Deputy Dog; he's making arrests at a banner rate around here. As of last night, I don't have any more room in my holding cells. What'd you do to him, anyway?"

"Oh, just gave him a little confidence."

The phone rang, and the chief answered. "Hulett Police Department." There was a pause, and then he continued, "Well, when was the last time you saw your boyfriend? Really, that hardly ever happens during rally week. . . ."

I waved good-bye, and we made a hasty retreat outside, Vic looking past me and then down Main. "I don't think Nutter is

ATF, either."

"Agreed."

The streets were a little subdued, but it was still early as we made our way downtown, a half block away. Vic checked across the street for the possibility of a Kiddo sighting, and I kept an eye to the right, peering behind the tents that sold T-shirts, hats, jewelry, and biker paraphernalia. "How come you didn't ask Stainbrook who his number two was?"

"It didn't seem appropriate."

"Not Billy ThE."

"Probably not." I shook my head. "Maybe rather than trying to figure out who's undercover, we should be focusing on the case?"

She smiled. "My, aren't we testy this morning."

"I'm beginning to think that I can't operate without sleep as well as I used to." There was some noise coming from the area behind one of the tents on Vic's side, and I could just make out the back of Dougherty's head.

Vic was already on the move, and I did my best to keep up.

I figured we were going to have to do another intervention, but we were mildly surprised to find Corbin with a forefinger bouncing off the chest of a tall, skinny biker. "And if you don't get your act together, you're going to have to call your accountant boss on Monday and explain to him why you're spending the workweek in the Crook County jail in Sundance, Wyoming." The biker looked a little shell-shocked and started to say something, but Dougherty cut him off. "Not another word." He pointed down the dirt alleyway. "Go."

He gestured in the other direction at another man, and I had to cover a smile while the entire crowd drifted away, having been denied the drama. He was turning to go himself when he saw Vic and me standing there. "Hey."

"Hey, yourself." I nodded toward the dissipating crowd. "Looks like you've got things under control."

He rested a hand on his sidearm and nodded. "I think I'm starting to get the hang of this."

Vic put her hands on her hips and couldn't help but smile along with me as we followed him back onto Main Street. He held a hand up and paused traffic as we crossed.

"Hey, troop, you haven't seen Kiddo around, have you?"

"No." He slowed and glanced at me. "I'd imagine as much trouble as he's in, he's probably going to lie low until his court date. Why?"

"Just curious as to where he's hanging out and with whom."

"Probably back in Rapid, don't you think?"

"Maybe."

He stepped up his pace, yelling at a guy down the block who had just shoved another. "Hey, knock it off over there!" He turned to look at us as he sprinted away. "If you find out anything, let me know."

Vic stepped up beside me, and we watched him separate the two individuals. I glanced at her from the corner of one eye. "What do you think?"

"I think you've created a monster."

"Hmm . . ." There was a buzzing in my jacket that I'd slowly come to realize meant either Bodaway Torres or I was receiving a phone call. "I've been meaning to hand it over, but I keep forgetting that I have it." With Vic looking at me questioningly, I pulled the cell phone out, studied the screen, and hit the button. "Hello, Punk."

"You owe me."

"I always owe you."

"Yeah, but you owe me big-time now."

"Did you find out who sprung Kiddo?"

She readjusted her phone. "You don't

really owe me, Dad. I just went over to courts and mentioned your name and they made me a copy of the blanket bail receipt. If I'd known how much of an effect your name had, I'd have been throwing it around a lot sooner."

"It's only effective in certain circles."

"The other thing I've discovered is that helping you with cases is a great way of getting and holding your attention."

"So, who fronted the bail for Billy ThE?"

"I bought a new couch at Sofa Mart in Fort Collins — it's called the Homerun Sofa. It's a recliner in red leather with white stitching, and they don't deliver."

"Cady."

"I need you and the Bear to go down and get it and bring it up the fire escape in the back. It's kind of tight around the corners, but I think you can make it."

"Cady, please?"

I could hear her rustling a piece of paper. "Does the name Robert J. Nance mean anything to you?"

14

"Why would Bob Nance put up Kiddo's bail if he wasn't involved?"

"I don't know."

"He's smart and at the same time dumb enough, with plenty of cash, to front an operation like the one that Stainbrook described." She sippezd her lemonade and watched the traffic two-wheeling by as we sat on the running board of the Pequod again. "So, why don't we go in there and get the chief to look up his buddy Nance and see what he's been up to?"

"Because he's Nance's buddy; so, I'd just as soon Dougherty assisted us with this."

"You think Nutter is somehow in on it?"

"No, I just think it's an uncomfortable situation with the two of them being so cozy." I patted the fender of the military vehicle. "Nance bought him this battleship, among other things. I think if we're going to make a run at Nance, then we'd better make sure we've got our ducks in a row."

"Really."

"He's just the type to be able to buy or arrange a way to get out of this, and I'm not here just to get the outlaw bikers. If Nance is the money behind this operation, he's not going to just let it go. If he's using these fabricators to get a prototype together, then he's likely to take it to the next level and become an arms dealer."

"Internationally?"

"Just because the mainstream government doesn't want the things made doesn't mean there isn't somebody else who wouldn't."

"Like the CIA?"

"Exactly."

"So, we need a rundown on Bob Nance to see if there's anything in his background that might connect him to all this before we do anything?"

"Yep."

"You don't think he's crossed his t's and dotted his i's?"

"I'm beginning to wonder if anybody's ever given him a good, hard look."

"But this crap's been going on since when, '88 or '89?"

"Yep, with Tichenor killed in '96 and Torres Senior just last year."

"That's some pretty slow development."

"Hard to get it done when no reputable manufacturer will touch it with a ten-foot advanced synthetic polymer stick."

"And your technicians keep ending up dead." She sighed. "When does the blue knight get off?"

I pulled out my pocket watch. "About five minutes ago." Almost on cue, the young patrolman crossed the street toward us with a familiar man, his hands cuffed behind his back. "Speak of the devil and associate."

Dougherty slowed as we stood, bringing Eddy the Viking to a stop with him. "Hey, any news?"

"Some, but we'd rather speak confidentially, if possible." I glanced at the biker, who was, as usual, pretty well inebriated. "What'd Eddy do now?"

"Tried to get a random woman to show him some body parts, and when she wouldn't, he showed her some of his in hopes of some sort of trade-off."

I looked down at the man, who continued staring at the sidewalk, giving us the impression that he might charge us with his plastic horns. "Really, Eddy?"

He muttered. "I was set up."

"How?"

"You should've seen those tits."

I shook my head and turned to Corbin.

"Hey, can we use one of your computers to hook into the National Crime Information Center and do a little research?"

"Sure."

He disappeared inside, and we waited a few moments before Chief Nutter appeared and started toward Main Street without looking at us.

"Let's go."

The office reception area was overrun with the hired guns from other counties, towns, and the Highway Patrol. The only quiet place with a computer was Chief Nutter's office to the left. "You mind if we use Nutter Butter's office?"

He glanced up from fingerprinting the Viking. "Go right ahead."

Once inside, I pulled the chair out and indicated to Vic that she should sit in it. "You're a lot faster on these things than I am."

"You got that right." She eased herself into the rolling chair and began working her magic. "This is going to take a while with just his name. I wonder how many Robert Nances there are in the U.S.?"

I pulled out the borrowed phone. "Cady took a photo of the copy of the bail application, and I think that might have a lot of Nance's pertinent info on it." I handed her the phone. "I just don't know how to get at it."

She shook her head and brought the photo onto the screen. "You are so helpless." She stared at it and began reading the information. "Oh, we can find him with all of this."

As she worked, I glanced around Nutter's office, taking in the photos and plaques that you accumulate over decades in law enforcement, and thought about how the stuff on his walls looked a lot like the stuff on mine, although a lot of mine was left over from Lucian Connally.

"Okay, nothing till '97 when he was charged by a federal grand jury in California for conspiring to defraud the IRS and tax evasion that had to do with money owed for the two previous years. His wife was also charged."

"He said they were divorced, and she'd gotten three houses out of him."

Vic continued reading from the computer screen. "I can see how there was trouble in paradise. He sold a business in California, then didn't report it, and then tried to conceal the two years of monetary installments by filing false tax returns." She looked up at me. "It looks like he might have gotten his daughter to do it, too."

"Uh-oh."

"And then the whole happy family concealed the assets by opening a foreign bank account in a Caribbean island, using purported trusts. Over the next year or so he deposited more than six million into the account, but then they got divorced and I'm betting she dropped a dime on his ass."

I rested my face in my hands. "Then what?"

"He sold his business, probably in an attempt to pay off some of the taxes and accrued penalties." She looked up. "I mean, this guy was going to the big stony lonesome — Club Fed."

Leaving my face in my hands, I spoke through my fingers. "What was the name of his business?"

She scanned the screen. "Doesn't say."

"Which California grand jury address?"

"Oakland."

"Near Silicon Valley."

She nodded and took in a deep breath. "Home of Special Materials, who first came up with the formula for this particular ASP."

"Then what?"

Her tarnished gold eyes went back to the screen. "The next mention is when he wired the remainder of the proceeds to a law firm in Dearborn Heights, Michigan, but then he instructed them to wire 3.7 million to an account in, of all places . . ." She looked at me. "Scottsdale, Arizona."

"Home of Dust Devil Development and the dumpster where Tichenor was found the year before."

"Holy shit."

"It's all circumstantial."

"Are you fucking kidding?"

"Do me a favor? I'm curious about the Detroit connection, so type his name in along with Detroit and see what comes up."

"Nothing — no . . . wait. There's a picture of him, much younger, winning some kind of prize or award as an alumnus of the University of Michigan back in the seventies." She turned the screen so that I could see. "Isn't that him?"

"Yep. Put in automobile industry."

She tapped a few more keys. "Here he is again. He worked for GM for most of his early career."

"And was involved in engine and acoustical tile development?"

She nodded. "Yeah. And exhaust systems."

"Stainbrook mentioned that the first time they stumbled across this stuff was when they were developing polymer exhaust valves that were supposed to be as strong as steel."

"Shit. I'm betting he was in on developing it first."

"Yep, or at least got it started."

She slumped back in Nutter's chair. "Why wouldn't you just patent this stuff and sell it to the government for bags of money. I mean, the CIA wanted it."

"Just from the small amount we've gleaned from this, I don't think Nance has a very good opinion of the federal government, especially as a business partner."

"So, he gets Tichenor to advance the polymer further and then gets rid of him when he hands it over to research and development."

"Torres."

"And then when he's got a workable material, he gets rid of him."

"Or somebody does."

"C'mon, Walt, the guy is Professor Moriarty — he's leaving bodies around like the Black Plague."

"Well, by getting in bed with the Tre Tre Nomads via Delshay and Bodaway, he's certainly been introduced to the criminal element."

"Introduced?" She touched up the lipstick at the corner of her perfect mouth with the tip of a pinkie and stared at the computer screen. "Hell, they're fucking engaged."

■ ■ ■ ■

"So, what have we got?"

My undersheriff leaned against the front counter of the office, the three of us enjoying the brief lull. "Well, it's complex."

Corbin nodded and chewed his sandwich. "I figured."

I leaned on the other side of the patrolman and came clean. "It's looking more and more like Nutter's friend Bob Nance may be involved in all of this."

"Nance involved with Kiddo?"

"I think it's all connected to the investigation the ATF has been working on and why Agent Post was murdered."

"What's the deal?"

"Plastic guns." Vic went on to explain, adding Nance's industrial background as the last piece of the puzzle.

"But now we have to come up with some kind of concrete evidence that connects Kiddo to Nance. Henry and I did a little snooping in Billy ThE's shop, but there was nothing advanced enough to indicate that he was doing anything out of the ordinary, other than modifying bikes to carry either samples of the plastic or prototypes of the guns themselves." I stepped away from the counter and turned to look at Corbin. "Does Nance have any other properties around here where they might have a facility large enough to produce the ASPs?"

Having lost his appetite, he set his sandwich down. "I have no idea."

"I assume we'd have to go down to Sundance to go through the records and find out where all his real estate holdings are."

"Yeah, I guess." He thought about it. "Wait, you're looking for some sort of connection between Kiddo and Nance, right?"

"Yep."

"Well, Eddy worked for Kiddo for about two years before Billy ThE fired him this last winter."

Vic was incredulous. "Our Eddy — the drunk Viking?"

"Yeah."

"Go get him."

We could hear Dougherty's keys jangling as he disappeared into the back holding cells where the lawless awaited transport to the Crook County jail in Sundance.

Vic walked over with her head down, speaking softly as she chewed a nail. "I am having trouble thinking of a less reliable informant."

"Me, too."

Dougherty returned with Eddy and sat

him on a chair, his Viking helmet a little askew. It looked like Corbin had woken him up. A little goggle-eyed, he glanced at my undersheriff. "Is she going to show me her tits?"

"Probably not." I placed my hands on my knees and bent down to look him in the eyes. "Hey, Eddy?"

"Yeah?"

"You worked for Billy ThE Kiddo for a few years, right?"

"Yeah." He belched. "He's a prick."

I glanced at the others. "Yep, we kind of got that."

Still quite drunk, his eyes wobbled around the room. "Fired me. Said I didn't know shit. I told him —"

"Eddy." I reached out and took his chin to try to hold his attention. "Do you remember if Kiddo had another shop that he worked in?"

"Prick."

"The Chop Shop, Billy's place; was there another one?"

"No."

"You're sure?"

"Yeah."

"What about a guy by the name of Bob Nance — did Billy ThE ever have any dealings with Nance?"

"The rich prick?"

I tried to keep from laughing. "Could be."

"Asshole lives on a golf course. Has a jet that we went for a ride in. Went all the way to Daytona. . . . Fast, man."

"So, what did Kiddo do with Nance?"

"Stuff, man. He did stuff."

I grabbed his chin again. "Did Billy ThE work for Nance, and if he did, where? Did you ever go to his house?"

He pulled loose and flapped his hands in an attempt to keep mine away. "Yeah, man. I did a couple of times, and then we went to that bunker thing of his."

I stood, glancing at the others and then back down at him. "What bunker thing?"

"The hut, man. That half-round thing that sticks up out of the ground."

"A Quonset hut?"

"Yeah — I mean, that's what it started as."

"Where?"

He threw a thumb over his shoulder, gesturing toward who knows where. "On that road."

"What road?"

He gestured in another direction this time. "To the airport — the airport road."

"In Rapid City?"

"No, man. Here."

361

I turned to look at Dougherty. "Hulett, with a population of under four hundred people, has an airport?"

"It's the only airport in Crook County — took ten years to get it built."

Driving past the clubhouse, we headed south along the ridge where Vic had won the skeet event. "The only way to get to the airport is this road through the golf course?"

"Yeah."

"Convenient for Nance."

Vic slowed the Challenger and stopped at the precipice where we could see the 5,500-foot runway angling southwest to our right about a mile.

Corbin pointed toward a branch road that led north around a ridge. "That's the only other road, so it must be up there."

"Vic, park at that pull-off and we'll hike. I don't see any reason to advertise." She did as I said, and as we all piled out, I glanced at Dougherty. "Do you have any binoculars with you?"

He reached into a shooting bag and produced a pair in a plastic case. "Believe it or not, I use them for bird-watching."

Vic struck out in front. "I believe you."

We weaved our way through the pines that gave the Black Hills their name and up a

362

wash where the hillside must've collapsed after the road had been put in. There was some brush at the top and a lot more trees, so we could move without being seen toward the southern point of the high ground.

When we got there, I kneeled down and studied the small box canyon below. It was a relatively impossible site to sneak up on, with rock walls on three sides, and if I were a betting man, I would've guessed that the canyon had started out shallow but had at one point been excavated and used as a quarry, the walls now creeping up quickly around the structure.

If Nance was looking to build an impregnable fortress, he could've done worse. The bunker that Eddy the Viking had made reference to was about halfway up, and if it had started as a Quonset hut, it had evolved from there. The building was a concrete fortress with no windows and a razor-wire perimeter, and there were concrete vehicle blockades leading toward the entrance down by the main road.

"Hell."

Dougherty handed me the binoculars, and I lay down on the edge to take a closer look. There were security guards in black polo shirts near the entrance and down by the gate, including Frick and Frack, the same men I'd seen at Nance's house and the shooting event.

There were a couple of black Jeeps parked close to the building, black being the new black, but nothing else out in the open. "So, what could Nance be doing down there that's so important that he has to have armed guards around the place?"

Corbin was the first to respond. "Something worth a lot of money."

Vic was more succinct. "Something illegal."

Tired of resting my weight on my elbows, I rolled over onto my back and handed the binoculars to my undersheriff. "It's the Alamo."

She held the glasses up to her eyes and kept them there for a long look. "Then let's go get a couple hundred thousand Mexicans and take 'em."

"No, this is where we hand the stick off to Stainbrook and the ATF — they're set up for this kind of foolishness. We'll head back into town and tell them to get a task force out here to shut down Nance and Kiddo's operation."

Vic continued to focus the binoculars on the compound below. "I'd say just Nance's operation, 'cause it sure looks to me like they're taking Billy ThE Kiddo for a proverbial ride."

I rolled back over. "What?"

She handed the binoculars back to me. "Isn't that shit-for-brains getting loaded into one of the Jeeps?"

I focused in and sure enough, Frick was stuffing the Hollywood biker into the passenger seat of one of the Wranglers as Frack climbed in the back. "Could you see if Kiddo was handcuffed?"

"Yeah, he was."

I watched as they pulled out, were let through the gate, and then headed toward the main road. I turned to Dougherty. "Where do you think they're going?"

"This way, I'd imagine; the only thing in the other direction is the airport." We stood and hustled back toward the Dodge. "You think they're going to fly him out of here?"

"If he's lucky."

When we got back to Vic's rental, you could clearly see down the hill and there was no Jeep Wrangler coming our way.

"They must be going to the airport." Corbin opened the door and tossed his bag in the back. "Nance has a jet, one of those twin-engine Cessnas, so we'd better hustle if we're going to catch them."

Vic was already in the driver's seat, and I threw myself in in the nick of time, the

Dodge roaring sideways as we shot by the precipice and down the long slope. "Slow down when you go past the cutoff; we don't want to draw their attention when we go by."

Dougherty hung between the bucket seats. "The cutoff to the bunker is past the airport road, so just slow down when you get there. You can't see the hangars from the bunker, either — it's too far up the canyon."

We slowly turned at the airport and drove down into the parking lot. I drew my .45 as we did a quick circle around the half-dozen buildings, still seeing no Jeep.

"You think they're inside one of the hangars?"

"Not with the kind of aircraft you described. They would have to have that thing out here and warming up with a crew." I glanced at the gravel road that ran alongside the runway. "Where does that road go?"

He looked through the windshield past us. "There are a few hay fields down that way and some dirt roads that peter out into the forest before you get over to 24 or 183."

Vic turned to look at him. "So, there's nothing down there?"

"Not really."

She gunned the Challenger and laid a twenty-foot black strip on the tarmac.

"They're going to kill him."

We swung around another corner as Vic leveled out the Dodge and lit up all the cylinders, bringing the Hemi on line like an orange javelin. Dougherty flew across the backseat and crashed into the other side.

"I'd put my seat belt on if I were you, troop."

The big straightaway along the airport gave us the advantage by allowing the muscle car to flex and catch up with the cloud of dust roiling from behind what we assumed was the Jeep. "I sure am going to be disappointed if we're following some rancher on his tractor."

She put her foot even farther into the Dodge's accelerator. "I'll tell you here in a second." There was another turn, and I had to admire the way she flat-tracked the Challenger, throwing it into the gravel curve and keeping her foot in it the whole way as she focused on her prey. "Oh, you are mine, chicken-shit."

The vehicle ahead had followed the road to the left and quickly passed over an elevated bridge, where I could see that it was, indeed, the Wrangler. "It's them."

Vic sawed the wheel, and we shot off the road into the hay pasture, taking a more direct route to the bridge. "Got it."

Even though we were pounding the undercarriage of the low-slung muscle car, we made time, but I wasn't sure what was going to happen when we attempted to get back on the elevated gravel road or, worse yet, the bridge.

We screamed along, the bridge appearing to be approaching at an alarming rate; if we missed it, we would most certainly end up crashing into the guardrail buttresses or flying into the creek.

I braced a hand against the dash. ". . . Vic."

"Got it."

The Dodge flew up the embankment, skipped the edge, and, slamming onto the road's uneven surface, slid completely sideways, the buttress of the bridge looking more and more like a gigantic, swinging cudgel. ". . . Vic."

"Got it."

From the back, Corbin's voice sounded surprisingly conversational. "We are all going to die."

Whipping the wheel to the right, she nosed the hood of the car forward into the narrow aperture. We all held our breath as the tires pulled free, but the car met the road and blistered the wood planks, soared over the downgrade, and blew into the

368

hundred feet of remaining gravel road before thundering over a cattle guard into an expansive hay field still scattered with the thousand-pound square bales.

The Wrangler, traveling at a slightly more sedate pace, was running along to our right. Frick turned and looked at us as if we were crazy.

"I think we've caught up to them."

The Jeep swerved, and one of the hay bales, very green with alfalfa, shot between us. On the other side, we regained sight of each other, and I could see Frick had his window down and was giving us a questioning look.

Hoping to avoid anything dramatic, I pulled my badge wallet from my pocket and flashed it at him about the time that Vic swerved to miss another bale.

My hopes of keeping things civil were dashed as the back window on the Jeep began rolling down, and I could see Frack brandishing some sort of automatic machine pistol.

I gave it one last try, yelling over the noise of the two engines. "Absaroka Sheriff's Department — pull over!"

Frick ignored me, and Frack pointed the pistol at us.

"Vic."

"Got it." She locked up the brakes on the car and then swung hard, careening behind the Wrangler and then gunning it and coming up on the other side.

Corbin's voice rose from the back. "Won't the doors stop bullets?"

"No, they won't; even a .22 will go through most modern car doors, and maybe through the other side as well. Roll your window down — it'll give you another layer of insulation, if it makes you feel better."

"The window will stop a bullet?"

"Can't hurt."

Thank goodness the hay field was relatively smooth from years of plowing, and thank more goodness it had just been swathed, so that Vic could at least see where the really rough patches were. She swerved around another bale and angled toward the Jeep as he attempted to steer clear of her.

I could see that Billy ThE was handcuffed to the dash and didn't look too comfortable with the situation. It was about then that the rear window on the other side of the Jeep began rolling down and the automatic pistol made another appearance.

"I don't think they want to talk." She sliced around another bale and came in hard this time, clipping the back quarter of the Jeep, but Frick corrected and continued on.

Dougherty swung up between the seats again. "Do you want me to shoot?"

Vic and I both answered as one: "Just put your seat belt on!"

Pulling to one side, I slid my Colt from the holster just as Vic handed me her Glock. "Shoot 'em."

"I'm going to give them one more opportunity to stop."

"You're going to get us killed." She slid in behind the Jeep as Frick began a slow turn to the left in an attempt to stay in the field. "Hopefully Frack won't shoot out of the back." Watching Frick slalom through the bales, Vic stayed close but then swung out again, positioning us on the left as I hung my badge out for them to see.

"Absaroka County Sheriff. Stop the vehicle. Now!"

We hit some bumps, and there was some noise, but it was only when I saw the barrel of the automatic smoking that I realized that Frack had fired.

I glanced into the rear and could see that Corbin's eyes were wide as he looked at the holes punched in the interior panels of the car. "Are you hit?"

"No, and I'd just as soon not be."

371

Vic swerved around another bale, and I turned to see that Frack was aiming at us again. I extended both of my arms, a weapon in each hand, aiming low at the Jeep's tires, and began pulling the triggers until there was nothing left.

In a second I had blown out both tires, but the Wrangler was veering toward us now, and I could see Frick lowering his window, both men attempting to take careful aim at me.

Grabbing the extra magazines from my belt, I dropped the empty and jammed the fresh rounds into my Colt as Vic locked up the brakes, using another bale for cover and swinging behind the still speeding Jeep. "Okay, I'm ready to shoot them now."

"About time!" She turned the leather-clad wheel, and we feinted to the right — getting the backseat gunner to move to the other side — but then swung the Dodge's seven hundred horses back up on the driver's side. We overshot a bit, but by the time we drew even, I had the .45 fully extended and aimed directly at the driver's head, just hoping I didn't miss and hit Billy ThE.

As is usually the case, that split-second hesitation cost me.

There was a swale in the field, and both vehicles were thrown to the right, causing me to lose my position in the seat and hit my face on the door. I could feel the blood spilling from my nose as I clambered back up and swiped at my face in an attempt to clear my eyes; once I did, I could see both Frick and Frack extending their pistols and smiling.

It was about then that they ran head-on into one of the thousand-pound bales.

15

"That's something you don't see every day."

We'd pulled up beside the Jeep; the driver had buried its front into the bale, and its rear end was now sticking up off the ground at about a thirty-degree angle.

Keeping my sidearm on the door, I tossed Vic hers, and she went around to the other side with Corbin following her with his own drawn. "You two get Frick and Frack, and I'll get Kiddo."

The body of the Wrangler was crumpled and had impinged the door, but I pulled the handle and bent the door back on its hinges as the airbags deflated. Kiddo was slumped in his seat, handcuffed to it with the chain running through the chicken bar. I felt for a pulse and it was strong, so he wasn't dead. "He's out cold."

Vic had opened the other side and unceremoniously pulled the driver out, allowing him to sag onto the ground. "This one's alive — barely, but alive."

Reaching up, I pried open the rear door and stepped aside as Frack tumbled out. I went through the motions — flipped him over and took the machine gun — but could plainly see that he'd shot himself a number of times on impact. "This one's dead, a bunch of times over."

I went back to the front, adjusted Billy ThE's seat, slipped off the safety belt, and pushed him back. "Check the driver for cuff keys, would you?"

Corbin was already on it and patted the now-moaning Frick as Vic collected weapons. Dougherty brought the keys around, and I uncuffed Kiddo, pulled him from the vehicle, and placed him on my shoulder. I carried him around and laid him on the trunk lid of the Dodge, where I noticed he'd pissed himself.

Corbin looked around my shoulder. "Are you sure he's alive?"

"He's breathing." I glanced over at Vic, who was kneeling by Frick. "Can he talk?"

She reached down and none too gently smacked his face. "Hey, asshole, can you talk?" His face rolled a little to the side, and then he sputtered and raised a hand, which Vic immediately grabbed and placed under her knee. "I said talk, not move." He cried out, and she shook her head. "Stop being a pussy."

He gargled something about his knee killing him, and it was possible that he had a point, in that it was bleeding and had already swollen to the size of a cantaloupe even with the constriction of his BDU pants.

My undersheriff kneeled a little more pointedly on his arm. "Talk, asshole. My experience with types like you is that your mouths always work."

I moved in, getting the wayward attention of the driver. His eyes steadied on mine. "How are you doing, Mr. Frick?"

He gasped. "How the hell do you think I'm doing?"

I studied his knee, broken nose, sloped collarbone, and what looked to be a couple of broken fingers on his other hand. "Well, you look like shit."

"We need medical attention."

I glanced through the open doors of the Jeep at the body on the other side. "We? Nope, I don't think so. Your buddy's dead as Kelsey's nuts — must've shot himself about nine times — and I think your prisoner just has a case of the vapors." I studied him. "Where were you headed?"

"Lawyer."

I glanced around. "I don't think you're

going to find one out here."

He yelled it this time. "I want a lawyer!"

"And I want answers — maybe we can work out a trade."

Spitting the words, he repeated himself. "Lawyer."

Vic picked up the bloody machine pistol from the ground — where I had put it down in order to get Kiddo out of the vehicle — and sprayed the fender of the Wrangler with a frightening series of shots, then carefully placed the muzzle close to the guy's eye. "You feel the heat from that, shithead? Try and imagine how hot it'll be at over fifteen hundred feet per second when I pull the trigger again."

Frick still said nothing, choosing instead to exhale, blowing the coagulated blood from his nose.

Vic obliged him by closing up one of the nostrils with the automatic, the heat of the muzzle sizzling the blood before he could turn his head away. "I'm betting there's another twenty rounds in this thing that I can use to fill up that empty head of yours if you don't start talking."

"I'm not incriminating myself." He closed his eyes and swallowed. "But . . . um, whatta you want to know? I mean, off the record."

I glanced back toward the municipal

airport. "Somebody taking an early flight?"

"Yeah."

"Were you guys supposed to join the bunker bunch on board?"

He said nothing until Vic tapped his temple with the Sig Sauer. "Maybe, all right?"

"How long before they start figuring out something went wrong?"

He thought about it. "The head guy, he's making financial arrangements, so they can't get out of here till he gets that stuff done, but it won't be long." He winced. "Look, my fucking knee is killing me. . . ."

Vic moved and again reminded him about the 9mm.

"How fortified is the bunker?"

He snorted. "Forget it, Andy Griffith; you'll never get in there."

I nodded. "These guys, do they have a stake or are they just hired?"

"Hired, but they're good."

I looked down at him and smiled. "As good as you?"

I made Frick ride in the trunk with the dead Frack, mostly because there wasn't a lot of room but also because I thought he needed a lesson in humility.

We followed another series of hay fields,

reconnected with the gravel road that led around the airport, and swung back north to where we joined route 209 and finally 24, thereby getting back into Hulett without having to go near the bunker and raising suspicions. Vic parked the Dodge at the police station, and we tried not to draw too much attention to ourselves as we carried the bodies into the office, putting Frick in the holding cell.

"What in the hell?"

Chief Nutter held the door as we returned with Billy ThE draped between Corbin and me, finally placing him in the office chair. "Call in the EMTs down the street for the one in the cell and they can take the dead one, too." I turned to Vic. "Grab one of those handheld radios, get back on that ridge, and keep an eye on them. Give us a call if anybody moves, okay?"

She grabbed a radio and, with an extended burnout from the parking lot, was gone.

Nutter placed his hands on his knees and studied Kiddo's still unconscious face. "This one alive?"

"Enough to piss himself." I tapped the face of the star of *Chopper Off* with the back of my hand. "I would've figured he'd have been awake by now, but I guess not."

Nutter disappeared into the back and

came out with a couple of paper tabs in one hand.

"Ammonium carbonate?"

He nodded. "Smelling salts. Leftovers from my boxing days — they smell too bad to expire."

He snapped one of the tiny envelopes under Billy ThE's nose and his head jerked back, his instinct to avoid the burning sensation in his mucous membranes foremost.

Catching his shoulder, I held Billy upright as he glanced around, stretched his jaw, and then began retching. I grabbed the trash can from under the desk and set it in his lap as he accommodated me by vehemently throwing up into it.

I held the can as I pointed for Corbin to get some towels from the bathroom. After a few moments Kiddo's stomach settled, or he ran out of things to throw up, and I handed him one of the towels Dougherty had brought back, trading the patrolman the trash can. "You might want to take that outside."

I watched as he exited with the wastebasket and gave Kiddo a moment. "You know they were going to kill you, right?"

He took a breath, dry retching this time, and then fell back into the chair.

"They didn't need you anymore after you did all the polymer fabrication for Nance, and you'd become a liability, which is actually something you're probably used to being."

He stared at me.

"So, Nance and his friends are going to try and fly the coop?"

He finally nodded. "He's got connections in Mexico. . . . Oh man, this whole situation has turned to shit."

"I'd say that's the understatement of the year."

The front door opened, and Henry entered with Agent Stainbrook, both of them wearing quizzical looks.

Corbin closed the door behind them. "It's Nance, and he's got his private army bunkered up over near the airport where they've got a jet warming up for a clean getaway."

Stainbrook approached and shook his head at the biker. "You know, I had my doubts about you, but I didn't think you were this stupid."

Kiddo shook his head. "You're one of them?"

The ATF agent slipped his badge from under his shirt and held it out to Billy ThE so that he could get a better than good look. "Yeah, and so was my buddy, Brady Post."

Kiddo raised his hands. "I had nothing to do with that."

Stainbrook's face stiffened. "To do with what?"

"I overheard some of them talking while I was hiding out about somebody shooting the main enforcer on the Tre Tre Nomads, but it wasn't me that did it."

"Then who did?"

"I don't know — I don't kill people."

"Your gun did."

He made a face and appeared a little paler through the stylish facial hair and tattoos. "What are you talking about?"

"That .40 of yours was the weapon that did the deed, and we got an absolute ballistic match with the slug the sheriff here was able to dig out of your neighbor's yard from the time you attempted to shoot his lawn mower."

He glanced at me. "You have got to be fucking kidding."

I stuffed my hands in my pockets. "Nope."

"I haven't had that gun in forever — I think Nance had it when we were working on the design for . . ." He wiped the tears from his face. "It was just for show."

Stainbrook pulled out another chair and slid in close to the former TV star. "Then you put on quite a show, my friend."

Kiddo hung his head. "Look, this guy comes to me and says he's got this new space-age shit that's stronger than steel, says he's got it patented and everything, but that he's got to keep it under wraps to maintain his competitive edge. He had a shit-load of money, and I had debts — with the production companies and ex-wives and shit. . . . Then my show gets cancelled. When I started helping him, it was all about bikes, but then he started talking about the government and how that's where the real money was — you know, in guns."

I sat on the edge of the desk. "Did he also mention it was highly illegal?"

"Oh, man, it was a business deal." He sobbed. "I even came up with the idea of moving the samples in the hidden containers of the gas tanks. I was trying so hard to get him back on track and out of the gun thing."

"I don't suppose you're aware of what happened to his previous business associate who ended up in a dumpster in Scottsdale with no hands and no head."

He stared at me.

"I'm just trying to get a read on where your allegiances lie in all of this. Now, you can partner up with the ATF and me, or you can continue to play ball with the guys who were on their way to shooting you in the back of the head and burying you in a ditch beside a hay field — choice is yours."

His eyes flicked among all of us like a raccoon fresh out of trees. "What do you want to know?"

"How many men does he have in there?"

"I really don't know; they kept me in the front with a blanket over my head."

"What would you guess?"

"A half dozen, maybe."

"Are they armed?"

"I don't think so. I mean, they're just going to Mexico."

I let the absurdity of that statement pass. "Do they have supplies?"

"Like what?"

I fought the urge to pick him up by his Adam's apple. "Food, water?"

"I don't think so."

Stainbrook's eyes met with mine. "You thinking what I'm thinking?"

I stood, not liking the option, but knowing it was the most prudent. "Bottle 'em up and just hold 'em there till the cavalry gets here?"

He nodded. "They'll destroy the evidence, or as much of it as they can, but I don't want this asshole getting away."

"I think we're all in agreement on that."

There was a disruption at the door as somebody made to come in, but with the Cheyenne Nation blocking it, the chances of that were just about nil. But then the Bear stepped to the side and swept the door wide, reached out and grabbed whoever it was, and pulled him into the room one-handed.

After landing, Eddy the Viking stood there trying to look as if entering this way had been his idea. "Hey."

Corbin, the one who knew him best, seemed to be the person he was talking to. "Can I help you, Eddy? We're, um, kind of busy here."

"There's a gang of guys out front and they saw you carrying Billy in here and they say they're going to stir some shit up if you don't turn him loose or something." The Viking shrugged. "I guess they're big fans of the show."

Nutter shook his head and followed him toward the door. "Good grief."

I pointed to the patrolman. "Corbin, go with them."

"Right."

He followed, and Henry let them pass but then held the door open after them just to give the troublemakers a look at the re-inforcements. You could hear voices outside, but after a moment they died down, the Bear keeping his eye on them as he closed the door.

"There's probably something else you should know." We all turned at Kiddo's voice as his head dropped to his chest. "I mean, something kinda important?"

"What?"

His head came up slowly. "They've got a hostage."

"Who?"

Kiddo looked toward Stainbrook. "I want immunity. I want total immunity, or I stop talking right now."

Stainbrook stood, spun the chair, and then sat again, laying his thick arms on the back and scooting in close. "Let me explain something to you. One of my best men is dead. A guy who has two kids and a loving wife in San Diego is never going to get to see his family again, because you or one of your scumbag friends shot him in the chest. Now, if you don't tell us everything you know right now, I'm going to find one of those really hideous federal prisons and drop you in gen-pop and let them see how they like that tough-guy, movie-star ass of yours."

We all sat there staring at him as the front door opened again, and we watched as Corbin and Nutter strong-armed a handcuffed biker through the bull pen toward the holding cells. "We got your back, Billy ThE!"

Kiddo's head sagged. "Jesus." The Hollywood biker took a few breaths, stoking his courage, and finally spoke. "Lola."

I glanced at Henry, who was back to leaning against the front door like a sphinx, and it was as if Billy had commented on the weather.

He shifted in his seat. "And I guess that's partially my fault."

Henry's voice echoed against the concrete walls like a jackhammer. "Do tell."

Kiddo turned and looked at him but then evidently felt safer looking at me. "She wanted to meet Nance, and I didn't see any reason why not."

The Bear pushed off the wall. "You are sure she is in there?"

The reality star nodded. "Yeah, I heard her voice."

The Cheyenne Nation studied him for a moment, then turned to walk back and look out the window.

I ventured an opinion. "If we get them trapped, there's no way they'll hurt her."

The Bear glanced at me over his shoulder. "You are sure of that?"

I shrugged. "Of course not."

It was then that the radio console on the desk chattered.

Static. "Walt, are you there?"

Pushing Kiddo aside, I grabbed the desk mic and answered, "Yep, what's up?"

Static. "They're loading a cargo container onto a flatbed."

Stainbrook's hand came into view. "We need that stuff."

I spoke into the mic again. "Anything else? I mean are they loading people, or just the samples and equipment?"

Static. "Just stuff for now, but it's not going to be too much longer and they're gonna be headed for the friendly skies."

I leaned in again. "All right, keep me posted. And Vic?"

Static. "Yeah?"

"Keep a lookout for Lola."

There was a pause.

Static. "You're shitting me."

"Nope. Over." I stood and looked around the room for an answer, and, not finding one, asked in general, "Anybody got any ideas?"

Nutter volunteered from the doorway. "Call Ellsworth Air Force Base and have them shoot the sons-a-bitches out of the air."

"Anybody have anything a little less drastic?"

"Yes, but just barely."

I turned and could see that Henry was still looking out the window but was now pointing outside. " 'I think that there are certain crimes which the law cannot touch, and which therefore, to some extent, justify private revenge.' "

Ignoring the Sherlock quote, I walked over to where my best friend was standing, peering through the dusty slats of the venetian blinds in the late-afternoon sun at what filled the parking lot: the fifteen tons of white, mine-resistant ambush protected military juggernaut — the mighty Pequod.

16

"You have to admit that there's a certain dramatic irony in driving this thing up Nance's rear end, seeing as how he bought it and all." Rumbling through the cutoff to the golf course, I revved the monstrous thing into second gear as it effortlessly climbed the hill.

Henry was silent as I made small talk with Stainbrook. "So, tell me Eddy the Viking isn't your second agent on scene."

"Eddy the Viking is not my second agent on scene."

"Do you mean that?"

"Yes."

"I'm relieved. I thought we were in real trouble there for a minute." I rounded the turns that flattened into the parking lot beside the clubhouse where the skeet shoot competition had been what seemed a long time ago. "So, Apelu, aka Big Easy, was Post's confidential informant within the Tre

Tre Nomads?"

The ATF agent hung on to two of the straps, trying to keep himself centered in the backseat so that he could see through the windshield. "Big Easy was the primary, but there are others. We thought of approaching Kiddo, but he seemed like such a loose cannon we figured a week later he'd be attempting to negotiate another cable reality show." His voice assumed a fake TV announcer tone: "Billy ThE Kiddo, ATF!"

"It could still happen." I spun the wheel starboard and sent the Pequod down the road past the utility buildings toward the airport. "So, Nance tags the original scientist who came up with the polymer, then works with Torres, Bodaway's father, then gets rid of him, and partners up with Kiddo?"

"That's the way it looks."

"How did he ever think he could get rid of a celebrity like Billy ThE and get away with it?"

"I'd say he's desperate."

"Why try and kill Bodaway?"

"I have no idea. Maybe it just had to do with the daughter, but you can see from the score card that when these guys go to kill you they generally don't miss, especially on a lonesome road at night." There was a pause. "You really give a shit about this kid?"

I glanced at Henry and sighed. "I do. That's the case that I'm working on."

"Is that why you're driving an armored military vehicle through a golf course right now?"

"Ancillary; Nance and his plastic guns are your problem, but if I can work my case by helping you with yours, so be it."

"The daughter."

"Chloe."

"She says she found him on the side of the road?"

I shrugged. "Maybe she did."

"Do we have any idea where she is?"

I glanced back at him. "I was hoping you did."

He shook his head. "Not on our radar, but I'm sure we can find out."

"There were a lot of cell phone calls going back and forth between her and Bodaway."

"Maybe she was in on it."

"A beautiful girl, a handsome boy. Maybe they're just a thing."

The ATF agent paused. "I never thought of that."

I pulled the MRAP around the corner and parked beside the Oriental poppy colored

Challenger. "Agent, you've got to get out more."

Vic was standing on the hillside at the top of the berm, pretty much eye level with us as I opened the door of the Pequod and gestured like the lovely Carol Merrill.

She put her hands on both sides of her face in mock enthusiasm and spoke in a voice loud enough to be heard over the diesel engine. "Oh my, the fleet's in."

I smiled at our conveyance. "I think we've got enough fuel to get the job done and make it back to a gas station — maybe."

She dropped her hands and looked at me. "Where's Nutter and Dougherty?"

"Babysitting Dog and waiting for the squad of highway patrolmen that are on their way."

"So, our job is to . . . ?"

"Bottle them up till reinforcements arrive." I climbed out and watched as she negotiated her way down the embankment. "Have they finished loading the stuff?"

She swung the binoculars on her neck. "They're finishing up now, but I'm thinking that they'll likely go back to the bunker before finally heading out."

"I don't think the air crew are armed, but we've got to keep that thing on the ground."

"Split up?"

"Yep. You can take Stainbrook, and Henry and I will park the Pequod and blockade the bunker gate. We'll see what their plastic guns can do against it."

"What are you going to do about Lola?"

"What would they gain by hurting her?"

"A threat — she's the only ticket they've got to get out of here."

"They kill her, and they go nowhere."

She punched my arm and moved toward the Dodge as the ATF agent joined her on the other side. "That's your negotiation stance?"

I threw a thumb back at Henry, still seated in the passenger seat of the Pequod. "Got it from the Cheyenne."

She rolled her eyes and slipped inside, starting the Challenger with a subdued rumble.

Stainbrook looked back at me with the door handle in his hand, more than a little concerned. "Does she know how to drive this thing?"

The flatbed was making the return trip to the bunker, and fortunately the occupants weren't paying any attention to the road on the hill leading back into town. I'd let Vic advance a hundred yards ahead of me. I figured when she made her move I'd make mine, only slower, much slower.

I glanced at Henry, who sat there studying the road ahead and bouncing in his palm the foregrip of the Sig Sauer machine pistol we'd confiscated from Nance's dead gunman. "How are you doing?"

"I am not sure."

Nodding my head, my eyes followed his to where Vic had inched forward a few feet, probably for a better vantage point. "I can tell. Mixed feelings?"

"You could call it that."

"It's not important what I call it." I leaned back in my seat. "You're sure you still don't have any feeling for Lola?"

He turned and looked at me.

"Bodaway?"

His eyes went back to the windshield, and I watched as his breathing slowed. "He has not had many advantages in this life."

"No, he hasn't, and unfortunately I don't think he's going to be getting any anytime soon." I waited before saying the rest. "I know this is a case of the pot calling the kettle black, but you can't do everything for everybody, Henry."

"No, but the least I can do is keep his mother from dying."

I glanced around at the plethora of military overkill. "Hey, it was your idea to bring this behemoth to the party; you got something else in mind now?"

He leaned forward, trying to get a better look at the bunker. "If you roll up to the front with this, that should provide enough of a distraction to allow me to come in from the back."

"If there is a back. There aren't any windows, so I'm not so sure there's a door other than the one in front."

"What have we got to lose? You are going to need someone outside the vehicle, short of driving through the structure, which you cannot do without imperiling Lola."

"Shock and awe, huh?"

He finally smiled. "You be the awe, and I will provide the shock." He pulled the handle and climbed out, slinging the machine pistol over his shoulder and looking all the world like some high plains merc. "I will need ten minutes."

I pointed toward the muscle car. "Tell Bo and Luke Duke up ahead of us there." As he started to close the door, I asked, "How long were you going to sit there before telling me what you were thinking?"

The smile lingered, and he quoted me some more Arthur Conan Doyle: " 'When I glanced again his face had resumed that red-Indian composure which had made so many regard him as a machine rather than a man.' "

I took out my Colt and lodged it in the seat he'd been occupying up to now. "Get out of here before I shoot you myself."

The door closed, and he was gone into the twilight of early evening like an afterthought.

Ten minutes can be a long time, and this was one of those instances.

I stuffed my pocket watch back into my jeans and cracked the door open, the windows being inoperable, as Vic walked up alongside, stepping onto the running board of the Pequod. "It's been nine and a half minutes."

She glanced down the road. "They're loading up smaller items for the final run, so I think it's now or never."

"Okay. You guys head over to the airport and shut it down; I don't even want that thing capable of flight."

"Take the keys?"

"I don't know if jets have keys."

"We'll steal the distributor cap."

"I don't know if they have those, either."

"Fuckin' whatever, we'll stop it, okay?"

"If it seems secure, you can come over and help me."

"Deal."

"Don't shoot anybody unless you have to."

She made a face, looking at my ride. "And don't you run over anybody unless you have to." She then bit my arm and was gone, more like a forethought.

As I'd anticipated, she blasted the Dodge down the hill like an internally combusted luge sled, sliding through the s-curve and skidding onto the municipal airport tarmac next to the Citation jet.

My approach was a bit slower but carried a great deal more majesty, kind of like a house on wheels. Approaching an astonishing twenty miles an hour, I wheeled the MRAP into the cutoff leading up the box canyon to the bunker.

There were five men standing by the flatbed and a Suburban near the entrance, and they all turned to watch as I approached. I was wishing that Nutter had sprung for the sirens but figured the PA system would have to suffice.

Lodging the oversize vehicle in the fourteen-foot opening of the closed gate, I parked in close enough so that the only thing that could possibly pass on either side would be a man on foot.

I plucked the mic from the dash, flipped the toggle switch overhead, and heard my

398

voice echo off the surrounding rock walls. "Howdy."

They didn't move.

So far, the awe thing was working pretty well.

"This is Sheriff Walt Longmire, and I hate to ruin your day, but you're all under arrest."

They still didn't move, and I started thinking it was maybe too much shock. This particular thought was belayed by their next action, which was to draw their collective weapons and begin pointing them at me. My next thought was to wonder whether Chief Nutter had opted for the bulletproof glass option.

I decided to bluff my way in and keyed the mic. "I wouldn't make a bad situation worse by doing that. We've shut down your escape plane over at the airport, and there are about a hundred Wyoming peace officers converging on this area as we speak." I watched as they glanced around, but they didn't seem awed or shocked anymore. "Honest."

I'm not sure who fired first, or if it was even one of them, but at the report of the gunshot they jumped and one of them fired a round into the windshield of the MRAP, spidering the bulletproof glass.

As a reflex, I shied against the door as another volley cracked the rest of the screen, but it held. "Oh, Nutter . . . you magnificent bastard."

Figuring there wasn't much else for it, I slipped my foot from the brake and stomped on the gas. Until the thing came to a stop, I would just duck between the seats, along for the ride.

There was a burst of noise as the giant wheels of the Pequod rammed into the closest truck and began climbing up its rear. There was more noise and a lot of yelling, which I hoped meant that the shooters were running for their lives, which is what I would've been doing. The Pequod kind of settled out as it ran over the pickup, but then I felt another lurch as it slammed into the flatbed that had ferried the supplies to the airport.

I felt its tires give way and could hear the entire body being crushed under the weight of the fifteen ton military vehicle; at least Nutter hadn't put the Pequod on a diet.

The big truck lurched and grunted and, using the two civilian vehicles as traction, began grinding into the reinforced Quonset hut, taking the buttressed concrete front with it. The thing kept going, and I started getting the feeling that I should let up or I would be likely to run right over the building and flatten whoever might happen to be inside, including Henry, most likely Lola, and Nance.

Letting up on the accelerator, I felt the Pequod reluctantly lose speed, and it felt like it might have grounded its front suspension into the collapsed wall. It settled like a whale in a deep surf. Carefully lifting my head, I glanced around but couldn't see much on account of the amazing amount of dust in the air. As it abated in the slight breeze, I could see that my surmise had been pretty much on target.

The gunmen were on the surrounding hillsides running for the tree line, and I didn't blame them.

The radio rattled on the dash of the big truck. Static. "Stainbrook and I heard shots; are you all right?"

I gripped and keyed the mic. "Couldn't be better."

Static. "What happened?"

"They threw a few shots at me, so I ran over two of their trucks and into their building."

Static. "Where are the shooters?"

"Scattered hither and yon."

Static. "Did you get Nance?"

"Not yet, but I'm working on it. So is

Henry."

No one seemed to be interested in turning and throwing a potshot at me, so I pulled the handle and opened the MRAP's unencumbered driver's door. Stepping out onto the concrete rubble that had been the front wall of the bunker, I still held the mic. "What's the status on the plane?"

Static. "Grounded. There was one tough guy, but I popped him in the nose with the butt of my Glock and things calmed down."

I keyed the mic again. "Well, keep them there, and I'll ring in when we get the rest." I let go of the mic and watched as it launched back into the cab and ricocheted off the steering wheel.

I glanced back at the two flattened vehicles behind me. "Wow, that worked."

Slipping my Colt from my holster, I carefully picked my way down the rubble and, peering under the lip of the Quonset hut into the darkness of the very long building, tried to figure out how I was going to get in. Whatever door had been at the front of the structure was now buried, so, crabbing along the side and using the running boards as a railing, I went around the back of the Pequod and spotted a portion of the concrete wall that had collapsed to the inside.

Giving one more glance to the surrounding area, I could see that Nance's rental army had gotten to the rock walls, but I was pretty sure they wouldn't get much farther with the noose tightening.

Scrambling down the rubble, I raised a hand to steady myself on the Quonset's arced metal ridge and swung into what must've been a waiting room or reception area. Fortunately, there were no bodies, and I was feeling relatively sure that my impromptu frontal assault hadn't cost any lives.

I listened, but there didn't appear to be any noise coming from within. Stepping down onto the concrete floor, I could see a doorway to my left that must've led further inside, but with the interior wall having shifted, the jamb looked a little crooked, and when I tried the knob, it wouldn't budge.

Stepping back, I put a size 13 warrant into use, and the cheap, hollow-core door split in two. Leading with the Colt, I stepped inside.

There were a few sparks from the fractured overhead lighting, but other than that, not much illumination. It was definitely a manufacturing setup, and a lot of the equipment was still here, obviously too heavy to be loaded on the jet.

Working my way down the single aisle into the darkness, I thought about what a great target I must be presenting, backlit from behind. I figured that Henry must've found them and either had the situation in hand or was involved in some sort of standoff. Either way, I figured it was okay to yell. "Henry!"

There was some movement in the shadows about thirty yards away, and I raised the barrel of the .45, taking aim. "Henry?"

"Stop yelling; it is undignified."

I made out his familiar shape as he approached with the machine pistol at his shoulder. "Where were you?"

He glanced past me at the wreckage. "Running in the other direction because a madman drove a truck into the building."

"See anybody?"

He turned and started back. "Only a lowly gunsel whom I have tied to a chair."

"You only got one?"

"Where are yours?"

"Running for the Black Hills." I caught up with him. "Does he know where Nance and Lola are?"

"I was about to ask him when you attempted your drive-through."

True to the Bear's word, there was a

middle-aged individual sitting in an office chair, tied with what looked to be an extension cord. I gestured toward him. "Hey, Phil."

He was sweating profusely. "Would you please tell him to let me go?"

"And that would be because you are the number two agent on scene from the ATF?"

He glanced at Henry and then back at me. "I have no idea what you're talking about."

"Look, Post is dead and your AIC, John Stainbrook or Ray Swift, whichever one he's going by today, is also on scene, so if you want to spend the rest of the afternoon tied to a chair . . ."

"How did you know it was me?"

"You were always around, and I don't think anybody in their right mind would voluntarily spend time with Eddy the Viking." I looked toward the back door. "Where's Nance?"

"Not here."

"Yep, we got that much. Does he have Lola with him?"

"The biker chick, yeah." He shifted in the seat but then remembered that he was tied. "He said something about taking her to his house for something special."

I glanced at the Cheyenne Nation, but his face remained neutral. "Special, huh?"

405

"That's what he said." His eyes darted between us. "Look, I don't think he has any idea you people are here. He was going to take her to his place and be back in an hour."

"Was he armed?"

"He's always armed."

"Right." I stood and started back toward the MRAP. "Well, let's go to the golf course."

"Aren't you going to untie me?"

I paused, holstered my Colt, and threw a thumb at the Bear. "Ask him, Agent Vesco; he's the one who tied you up."

Getting the Pequod disentangled from the bunker wreckage and backed over the two vehicles I'd crushed was surprisingly easy, and I smiled at Henry as the giant, run-flat tires thumped back onto solid ground. "You know, I'm starting to think I do need one of these."

Henry rose up and peered through the cracks in the bulletproof glass. "It would take up your entire parking lot."

I wheeled the Pequod around to the lee side and started back for the gate. "It'd be great for rodeo parades."

I drove through, turned right, and headed up the hill. "So, why take Lola to his house?

To kill her?"

Henry shrugged, placing the MPX in his lap. "Probably."

"You don't seem too upset."

"What good would it do?"

"So, you really don't care about her anymore."

"I care about her enough to keep her alive for the sake of her son, but beyond that, no."

The radio rattled on the dash, and Henry fished the mic from the floor.

Static. "Hey, did you assholes just turn and drive up the road?"

Wisely, he handed the mic to me.

I took it and answered. "We found the other ATF agent on scene."

Static. "Who was it?"

"The little guy, Phil Vesco, Eddy the Viking's running buddy."

Static. "Him? I never would've figured it."

"I think that's what they count on. Anyway, tell Stainbrook he's walking down from the bunker, so don't shoot him. Nance took Lola up to his house, so we're on the way up there."

Static. "I wanna go."

"No, he's up there alone. Stay with the plane, just in case he gets by us or isn't there. The only way out is that jet, so keep

407

it bottled up."

Static. "You suck."

"Roger that."

It only took a few minutes to get to Nance's house, and I was tempted to run into it — a thought the Bear must've read. "It is a nice house, and he is going to lose it by going to prison, so why not do the future owners a favor and spare it?"

Pulling in behind the Range Rover in the driveway, I bumped it and parked. "Just a love tap." We climbed out and looked around but didn't see anybody peeking from the windows, or any rifle barrels, for that matter. "How could they not hear us?"

The Cheyenne Nation ignored me and went for the door, which was unlocked. I watched as he used the barrel of the Sig Sauer to swing it open silently; then he looked one way and the other. "Clear."

Following him in, I slid the 1911 from my holster and trained it on the balcony above, then dropped it back toward the entryway that led toward the kitchen. Indicating that Henry should go one way and I would go the other, I moved through the kitchen and trained the .45 on the great room where Nance and I had had our discussion just a few days before.

The Bear moved silently across that room

toward the other end, which must've led to the garage, as I went the opposite way toward a split staircase in the living room.

When I looked back, I could see Henry shaking his head no. I nodded and gestured for him to take the upstairs and began my descent.

It was a wide stairway with custom-made treads that looked like ironwood. There was a security door at the bottom of a landing, heavy with small windows that I could tell were two-way mirrors.

I stepped to the side and turned the gold handle, quietly pushing the door open and waiting a moment before stepping into the empty, carpeted hallway.

There were photographs on the walls, lots of them, with Nance and celebrities on boats, in planes, and in race cars. I started down the hall, only to have Lola open the door on the end and move toward me with her head down, wearing nothing but a large white towel.

I waited till she was easily in reach and then stepped forward, placing my hand over her mouth and gently pushing her to the wall and holding her there.

"Mphhhlph." Her eyes were wide as I held the barrel of the .45 to my lips to shush her.

She tried to speak, but I held my hand

firmly over her mouth. "From this point on, you don't make a sound; you simply nod your head yes or shake your head no. Got it?"

She did.

"He in there?"

She nodded.

"Is he alone?"

She nodded again.

"Is he armed?"

She nodded once more.

"Does he know we're here?"

This time she shook her head.

"Good." I loosened my grip. "Whisper. Where were you going?"

I could barely hear her when she finally spoke. "Bathroom."

"Go there and lock the door behind you. Henry's here, too." I glanced at the towel. "And he might just shoot you himself."

I watched as she slid back to the wall and disappeared behind me, quietly closing and locking the door. I waited a moment and then turned back toward the end of the hallway.

Another set of mirrors looked blankly at me, and I could only hope that Nance wasn't standing on the other side with one of his nifty little plastic guns pointed at me.

Considering the thought, I stepped for-

410

ward and pushed open one of the mirrored doors. I moved to the side, slipped in, and stood there in the half-light. There was a series of weapon lockers to my left and a gun safe beyond that, leading to a firing range about twenty-five yards in length with a standard man-shaped silhouette target hanging from a motorized track at the far end. The walls and ceiling were covered in cone-shaped, noise-absorbing foam, and there was a shooter's station with a number of what I assumed were Nance's polymer pistols in different states of disassembly lying on the counter.

There was a small observation area to the right behind a bulletproof glass wall and door, where a naked Bob Nance had his back to me and was evidently pouring himself a drink. "You okay, baby?"

I waited a moment before answering. "Yeah, I'm good."

His head turned slightly, but his hands stayed where I couldn't see them, his voice slightly muffled by the heavy glass. "Sheriff?"

"Yep." I trained the barrel of my Colt on his midsection. "You want to put those hands where I can see them?"

He didn't move. "Would you like a drink?"

"I want to see your hands."

He lifted a tumbler holding a few cubes of ice and probably a healthy dollop of scotch up past his shoulder. "Highland Park, twenty-five-year-old. As I recall, you enjoyed it."

"The other hand."

"C'mon, let's have a drink and discuss this like gentlemen." He turned a little but still kept the other hand hidden. "You've kind of caught me at an awkward time. I'm assuming you saw Lola?"

"The hand."

He sighed. "Um, actually, I've got one of my guns — would you like to see it?"

"Yep, I would."

He turned slowly, holding the tumbler in one hand and in the other, one of the completely assembled polymer weapons, but this was a strange one, a blocky, desert-tan revolver, which he had pointed toward the ceiling. "Are you sure you won't have a drink?"

"Put the weapon on the counter."

He didn't move the gun hand but did bring the glass up and sip his scotch. "Do you have any idea how much this thing cost?"

"In lives?"

He smiled. "In dollars."

"I don't care."

"It's a prototype. I wanted to see just how much power the new stuff could handle, so we made this all-polymer revolver in a .454 Casull model, the line of thought being that if the new plastic could hold up to this round, it could hold up to anything."

"Put it on the counter."

"You know one of the great things about the .454? It can deliver a 250-grain bullet with a muzzle velocity of over 1,900 feet per second and about 2,000 foot-pounds of energy, meaning it'll shoot through bulletproof glass like this one between us like a hot knife through butter." He sipped his scotch some more and lowered the barrel of the revolver on me. "And you know what the worst caliber to shoot through bulletproof glass is?" He continued to point the revolver at me. "That .45 ACP you're carrying. It'll make a dent, but it won't go through — muzzle velocity is just too slow." He gestured with the plastic gun. "Not like this."

I glanced at the closed glass door to my right.

"Don't do it; I'll shoot you before you make it."

I sighed. "Then what?"

"What do you mean?"

"I've got backup."

He smiled some more, and I really wanted to shoot at him, bulletproof glass be damned. "So do I."

"No, you don't. They're all running for the hills." He looked a little unsure now. "We've grounded your plane, and I ran over two of your trucks and crashed into your bunker with that MRAP you bought the police department." His eyes widened a little. "I guess you're not enjoying the irony in that, huh?" I pulled out my pocket watch and looked at it. "And in less than an hour every cop in Wyoming is going to be all over this place, not to mention the federal government and a really pissed-off Indian who is roaming your house with some kind of 9mm machine pistol which probably won't go through this glass either, but you're going to have to come out of that fishbowl sometime, Nance."

I glanced around at the acoustical foam walls of the million-dollar basement. Even when you talked, you could hear your voice sticking there, which made the delivery of the next words that much more enjoyable. "And when you do, nobody's going to hear you die."

EPILOGUE

I sipped my beer at the Ponderosa Café and watched Henry and Vic talking with another long-haired individual I didn't know. This guy looked a little different from the rest in that he was carrying a guitar case.

Things had settled back down into a regular August high plains summer day: the streets were pretty much cleared of tourist biker traffic, the vendors were striking their tents, and the whole town of Hulett had that after-the-carnival feel to it, as if the world had packed up and left the place behind.

Melancholy.

Or maybe it was just me.

I'd wanted to head home, but Stainbrook and the feds had asked us to stick around for the depositions that would assure Nance spent the rest of his life in rooms without light switches. Heck, I would've stayed in hell for that. Truth to be told, Hulett was a beautiful little town when not in biker

415

season, and I was attempting to enjoy the down time, aside from being on the phone in negotiation with the Greatest Legal Mind of Our Time about moving sofas and helping to paint ceilings.

"You're tall, and you don't have to use a ladder."

"I could bring Henry; he doesn't have to use a ladder and he actually knows how to paint."

"One of you can sleep on the new sofa after you go pick it up."

"Right." I held Bodaway's phone against my ear and reached over and petted Dog. "I've got a weapons recertification in Douglas and a parole hearing to sit through down there in Cheyenne, so we'll be heading that way soon."

"That Western Star thing?"

"Yep."

"Oh, Daddy, isn't it time to let that go?" It was silent on the line for a few moments. "So, have you seen Lola?"

"Other than when we passed her on our way in to make our statements to the feds, no."

"Do you suppose she's in Rapid City at the hospital?"

"It's where I'd be."

"It's where you've been." There was another pause. "So, everybody goes to jail?"

"Prison." I sighed, wishing I were in another line of work so that my daughter and I would have nicer things to chat about on the phone. "Nance is lawyered up, but he's never going to see the light of day. And they picked up his daughter in Rapid City for tax evasion, but it's looking more and more like she didn't have anything to do with all this; she and Bodaway were just in love. . . . Go figure."

"What about Billy ThE Kiddo?"

"Conspiracy and a number of other charges, but he's singing like Janice Joplin and he'll probably get away with suspended sentences and have another outlaw pelt for his resume. By the time he's done spinning it, he'll probably have saved all of the ATF and us single-handedly. There were some producers here already, looking to develop a new reality show with the inked idiot."

"You're kidding."

"I wish I were."

"What about the Nazi thing?"

"Not for public consumption and probably not good for ratings — part of the deal he made with the ATF; besides, it would all be inadmissible. I'm not worried about it, though, his type always ends up getting what they deserve eventually."

"Who killed the ATF agent Post?"

I sighed and continued on, figuring lawyering wasn't that much more pleasant than sheriffing after all. "Nance. They found Kiddo's pistol in Bob's collection in his private little shooting gallery downstairs, along with a bunch of others, like trophies — blowback on the barrels and still carrying his fingerprints. I wouldn't be surprised if they didn't connect him to a whole slew of other homicides before it was all over."

"But it is all over."

"Yep."

"So, when are you heading home?"

"Henry and Vic just got back from returning her rental car in Rapid City. They seem to be talking to a couple of guys from the garage band that's been playing here all week. We still have to hook up the motorcycle trailer, but then we'll be heading home."

"Be careful and don't get any more guns pointed at you, 'kay?"

"Sure thing, Punk."

"I love you."

"Love you, too." I pressed the button and disconnected — whatever happened to hanging up the phone? — and placed the mobile on the table as the two came ambling over; I noticed Vic holding a CD, still in the cellophane. "I can't believe that guy talked you into buying his music." I glanced past them and could see roadies still packing up the band's equipment. "I hope you told them to broaden their musical horizons; you can't get far in life just doing covers of Lynyrd Skynyrd."

Henry nodded. "Unless you are Lynyrd Skynyrd."

"What?"

Vic held out the *Best of* CD. "They *are* Lynyrd Skynyrd." She glanced behind, but the band members were gone. "At least they were."

I finished my beer, smiled, and quickly backtracked. "I thought they sounded awfully good for a garage band."

The Cheyenne Nation decided that in celebration of winning the Jackpine Gypsies Hill Climb, he would ride Lucie home with his trophy tied to the headlight a la Marlon Brando in *The Wild One.* We were to follow in the T-bird with Rosalie and Bodaway's Harley in tow on the trailer.

We watched as he checked the tie-down straps on them and then put on a pair of goggles and a Bell Boss helmet and straddled the four-cylinder Indian. "Are you sure you want to ride that thing all the way back to Absaroka County?"

"That is what it is for."

I glanced at Vic and gestured toward the sidecar. "Would you like to join him?"

She walked back and cracked the door of the Baltic blue convertible and ushered Dog into the back before flipping the seat and climbing in. "Thanks, but no thanks."

The Bear shrugged, kicked the vintage Indian to life, and throttled away as I walked back and climbed in the Thunderbird, pulling out from the Hulett Motel and circling the parking lot in a wide arc after him.

It was late in the afternoon, and the sun had already reached its zenith, slanting its rays in a golden horizontal that highlighted the landscape to its fullest effect. We rolled out of town, following the Indian on the Indian, and I couldn't help but feel a certain anticipation for the geologic wonder just ahead.

"What the hell is that?"

Bad God Tower must've had a peek at her as we topped one of the tiny hillocks and drifted south. I didn't say anything but just eased the big Thunderbird through the curves until we topped the last hill and swept down an easy slope on route 24 that opened into the wide straightaway where Henry and I had stopped on the way into town.

"Holy shit."

It was the effect that Devils Tower had on folks the first time they actually saw it. Photographs don't really prepare you for just how impressive the first United States monument is. I slowed the convertible, allowing Vic the full impact of the Matho Tipila as the Cheyenne referred to it. "It's something, huh?"

As we drifted slowly along, I saw that the Cheyenne Nation had pulled onto the turnoff to Devils Tower, possibly to idle a little in the majesty of the natural wonder; I then saw that it was an unnatural wonder that had caught his attention.

Slowing down still more, I stopped the convertible alongside the road at a little distance, allowing them some privacy.

Vic was paying no attention, her focus still on the tower as she unbuckled and kneeled in the passenger seat, her hands on the doorsill, to study the geologic wonder. "Wow."

Even Dog moved over to the right side of the backseat for a gander, but my attention was drawn ahead, where a red 1948 Indian sat in a wide pullover parked opposite a gold '66 Cadillac.

"Can we go see it?"

My attention was drawn back to Vic. "Um,

probably not now."

"C'mon. . . ." She turned in the seat toward me but stopped when she saw the tableau up ahead. "Hmm."

The Bear was still seated on the motorcycle now with his helmet off, but Lola Wojciechowski had pushed off the grille of the Caddy and was standing in a provocative manner with hands on swiveling hips.

"Boy, I wish I was a fly in a sidecar right now."

"Not me."

Vic turned and slid back in her seat, and Dog, recognizing the emotionally charged situation even from afar, registered a low whine. My undersheriff reached back and ran her hand across his muzzle. "Easy, boy."

"Are you talking to him or me?"

"Both." We sat there in the silence with a light breeze drifting from Devils Tower, the smell of the juniper and jack pines better than incense. "I wonder what they're talking about?"

"I think it's more of a 'who.' "

Lola moved closer, even going so far as to drape a wrist over the handlebars of the big Indian motorcycle. Henry didn't move, and she upped the ante by arching her back, her black leather jacket and cropped white T-shirt riding up, displaying the ring in her belly button. "Boy, she's playing it for all it's worth, huh?"

"Maybe, but I don't think he's in the game."

There was a little more conversation, but you could tell that Lola wasn't getting what she wanted.

After a few more exchanges, the Bear placed his helmet back on his head, pulled the goggles down, and slipped on his gloves. He cocked his head at something she said and then stood, kicking the Indian to life. He gave her a jaunty salute as she hugged herself with one arm, and then he throttled up and pulled out.

I fired up the Thunderbird and slipped it in gear, easing the convertible and trailer onto the state route. As we approached Lola, she stepped onto the road and held up a hand like a traffic cop.

"Just keep going."

As much as I wanted to heed Vic's advice, the gentleman in me slowed and stopped as the dark-haired woman with the silver shot through it rounded the front of the T-bird, laid an arm across the top of the windshield, and smiled down exclusively at me. "Hi."

"Hello, Lola."

She finally glanced at Vic, extending the other hand across me and bringing the scent of perfume, leather, and utter abandonment into my nostrils as they politely shook. "Lola Wojciechowski."

Vic batted her eyelashes, and her tone was buttery strychnine. "I've heard so much about you." She glanced back and then cracked open the passenger side door, stepping out and allowing Dog to follow. "We're taking a short walk." She glanced at me. "A short walk, and then we'll be right back." My undersheriff and my Dog strolled into the high grass, both of them gazing at the monolith in the distance.

"Kind of got you on a short leash, doesn't she?"

Tipping my hat to provide a little personal shade, I glanced up at her. "What do you want, Lola? I've got to catch up with Henry."

She grinned the killer smile and studied me. "I just wanted to say thanks."

"For what?"

"For everything — you were very nice to me, and I don't get that a lot."

I didn't say anything.

"See, still nice." Her eyes played over to Devils Tower, and I was beginning to lose my patience. "You probably think I need to be in jail, huh?"

"Not my problem."

She studied the landscape some more and then nodded. "I play the percentages, Sheriff — it's how I survive."

"And what were the percentages on having sex with Brady Post just before he died?" Her turn to say nothing, but she did swivel her head back to study me. "I'm fighting the thought that Nance put you up to it so that he could kill Post, postcoitus. What's it like to have sex with a man knowing he's going to die?"

She smiled and shook her head in a dismissive fashion, the silver streak falling over her forehead like a lightning bolt as her scary green eyes focused on me through the tangle of lush hair. "You're all dying, whether I decide to screw you or not."

I hit the starter on the Thunderbird and, ready to go, leaned back in my seat.

She grinned the wicked grin again and cocked her head, giving the impression that she was willing to hop in and give me one of her free samples, samples being all that Lola ever gave for free. "I'm not sure why it is that I'm thanking you, though." Her expression became a little graver. "You never did find out who ran my son off the road."

Hearing the motor on the big bird idling, Vic returned with Dog and let him climb in the back before taking her seat and closing the door after her.

I shrugged. "I would've thought it was an obvious fact, Lola — you did."

Delivering a pitch-perfect performance, she laughed and shook her head. "You're crazy."

I pulled the young man's phone from my pocket and handed it to her. "Either because he had Chloe Nance on the back of the bike or because you wanted him out of Bob Nance's gun business, you and that Cadillac of yours were what sent Bodaway off the road that night. I'll give you the benefit of the doubt and think you didn't know about the culvert that did the majority of the damage, but those are the facts, for what it's worth."

Her expression remained the same as she palmed her son's phone, staring at it.

"Now, if you don't mind, and even if you do, we'd like to go home."

She smirked a little and still held on to her vehicular namesake as if it were a life preserver. "If you believed that, Sheriff, you'd have me in jail."

I took a deep breath in an attempt not to be cruel, but some situations are deserving of it and some people, too. "Not really, because when I think about your son lying down there in the Rapid City Regional ICU, I figure there's nothing that the ATF, I, or the law could do to you that could possibly compare to the punishment you've constructed for yourself."

I slipped the lever into gear, but she still didn't move, maybe because she couldn't.

"Good-bye, Lola."

She had no resort but to let the shiny chrome molding of the windshield slip from her grasp as we pulled away, and I wasn't tempted to look into the rearview mirror, not even once.

ABOUT THE AUTHOR

Craig Johnson is the author of the Walt Longmire series. He has a background in law enforcement and education. He lives in Ucross, Wyoming, population twenty-five.